AUSTRALIA'S ASIAN POLICIES:
THE HISTORY OF A DEBATE

P.105

AUSTRALIA'S ASIAN POLICIES

The History of a Debate 1839-1972

A.W. STARGARDT

THE INSTITUTE OF ASIAN AFFAIRS IN HAMBURG

OTTO HARRASSOWITZ · WIESBADEN

Published by the Institute of Asian Affairs in Hamburg

VERBUND STIFTUNG DEUTSCHES ÜBERSEE-INSTITUT
(FOUNDATION GERMAN OVERSEAS INSTITUTE)

The Institute of Asian Affairs pursues and promotes research
on contemporary Asian Affairs. It co-operates with other
Institutes of regional studies in Hamburg which together
form the Foundation German Overseas Institute.
Opinions expressed in the publications of the Institute of
Asian Affairs are the authors'; they do not necessarily reflect
those of the Institute.

ISBN 3 447 01869 0

The order of ideas must proceed according to the order of things.

Giambattista Vico

Contents

PART FOUR: 1942–1949
AUSTRALIA IN SOUTH EAST ASIA

PART FIVE: 1950–1972
THE SEARCH FOR A NEW DEPENDENCE

APPENDIX OF DOCUMENTS

Contents

Preface

A DECADE has gone by since the first draft of this study; a decade full of change and of suffering in Asia. The war in Vietnam was extended to Cambodia, ending in a settlement no better for anyone than one obtainable during the preceding twenty years. In India, the National Congress disintegrated, but Indian democracy survived. A further Indo-Pakistani war resulted in an independent Bangladesh, whose first government was subsequently assassinated. A democratic revolution in Thailand was followed by counter-revolution. Everywhere in South East Asia, human liberty was diminished. When the decade began, China was in the midst of the cultural revolution, which ceased after the Soviet occupation of Czecho-Slovakia. That event opened the way for Chou En-lai's greatest achievement, the end of China's isolation and the assumption of her place in the United Nations. Before the decade was over, both he and Mao Tse-tung were dead.

In Australia, it was a decade of acrid political debate which, in 1972, led to the end of a long period of conservative rule. The international and domestic initiatives of the Labour government put new life into the debate which, however, turned into political warfare, touching the outer perimeter of the constitutional system with the overthrow of the Labour government in 1975.

The advent of that government and, in particular, Whitlam's foreign policy, had revived my interest in this manuscript and between my studies on the rise of the Asian system of powers and the Cambridge Neutrality Project, I began to revise and enlarge it, and to include a great deal more hitherto unused documentary material. The external events that caused me to complete this work bear only a very indirect relation to its subject matter, the history of the Australian debate about Asia. It ends with the conservative defeat in 1972 - the end of the last dynasty but one - which is as close to the time of writing as the historiography of imperial China might have proceeded and as any historical study ought to go.

I have sought to set the Australian debate in the context of international history in order to show how it stood in relation to the activities of the major powers. It seemed especially desirable to do this for the period of imperialist rivalries until and including the first world war. Before the point of entry of the newly-independent Asian states, in the 1940's, a similar sketch of Asian affairs seeks to relate the debate to the realities of Asia. Beyond this time, questions of proximity have prevented me from pursuing that dimension. I have further sought to illuminate the history of this debate by means of an appendix, comprising a series of important and little-known documents. Though too long for inclusion in the text, they throw light upon the stages of the debate with the directness peculiar to the contemporary source. Indeed, wherever possible, I have employed original documents. I have attempted to trace them even if an official printed version was more readily available. That labour has not been pointless, since the originals are frequently more vigorous than prints which are rarely complete. Where the debate was an open, public debate, the main sources have been *Hansard* or its equivalent, party documents and, to a limited extent, the press. I have selected on grounds of historical relevance and contemporary importance. Where an official report of a transaction - a debate, an expressed view or conference resolution - was available, I have preferred it to a newspaper account. Where a journal expressed a view, however, that is significant because of the interest it represented, then its intrinsic documentary value is treated as such. This applies in particular to journals specifically representing a class interest, whether of sugar planters or of trade unionists.

As far as possible, the inclusion of material made accessible hither-to by other scholars has been avoided. The first two volumes of the new series of Australian Diplomatic Documents became available in the closing stages of this work. I have checked all the British originals referred to. On one occasion - at the beginning of Part

III - I have quoted despatches from a British Minister in Tokyo, as they appeared in a Foreign Office Confidential Print, their point being the use to which they were put.

Little need be said on terminology. *Victorian* refers to the Australian colony and state, rather than to the historical period. *Communist* and *Communism* are used in the sense which has become established since the Bolshevik revolution. They refer to political parties, states ruled by them, and their practices, however diverse or contradictory they may have become. Their intellectual origin or their relationship to the ideas of Karl Marx or other socialist thinkers are separate issues of little concern to this study; their existence and its consequences, especially for the later debate, are another matter. *Commonwealth* tends to refer to the Commonwealth of Australia. Where it refers to the British Commonwealth or Commonwealth of Nations, that usage will be clear from the context.

The Australian Labor Party spells it name without the *u* in Labor, and where the full name or related official terms occur, that spelling is followed. In the nineteenth century *labor* and *labour* were interchangeable and they are found side by side in the papers of very literate people. No geographical or political significance attached to the spelling, before the retention of the *u* became a British rather than an American habit. *Pearl Harbor* is also spelt that way. Otherwise, the *Concise Oxford Dictionary, Hart's Rules* and Judith Butcher's *Copy Editing: the Cambridge handbook* have been followed. The latter and the *Cambridge Authors' and Printers' Guides* were very useful in the preparation of the book for publication. The system of indented sub-headings was adopted to make the Index more helpful to users. The Sources have been placed at the end of the book. They include, beyond simple references to quotations, bibliographic material as well as several longer quotations and occasional comments which, however relevant, would be distracting in the text.

I have benefitted from and enjoyed an exchange of ideas with a large number of scholars, politicians and diplomats. In Japan, I have enjoyed the friendship of many people, most especially of Professors Yoichi Itagaki, then at Hitotsubashi University and Noboru Yamamoto at Keio. In South East Asia, Soedjatmoko, the late Tun Dr Ismail and Dr Puey Ungpakorn have shared generously of their

the late

friendship and knowledge, giving me many valuable insights. In Australia, choice is even more inviduous, though I wish to mention A. T. Brodney, Don Dunstan and S. W. Nowak, with whom many a long evening was spent, discussing intractable problems. Bruce Grant was kind enough to look through the proof sheets in Cambridge and to make some valuable suggestions. Professor F. H. Hinsley's invitation to the Centre of International Studies and subsequent valuable discussions deserve my special thanks. I am very grateful to Professor Keith Robbins of the University of Wales for his help with a passage by Sir Edward Grey, to Dr Ian Nish of the London School of Economics and to Dr Ruth McVey of the School of Oriental and African Studies, University of London. Professor Martin Bernal of Cornell University and King's College, Cambridge, has helped with diverse sinic problems, and so did Dr Cheng Te-k'un. Professor Herbert Lüthy of the University of Basel is another friend whose thoughtful concepts continue to bear fruit long after one has enjoyed his company. I deeply miss the intellectual stimulus and the delightful company of the late Professor K. William Kapp, also of Basel.

then

In the institutions whose collections I have been allowed to use I owe thanks to the Controller of Her Majesty's Stationery Office for permission to use the Public Records and, in the Public Record Office, to the Keeper, Mr J. R. Ede, and to Mr N. E. Evans and Mr J. L. Walford who have been of great help in solving many a difficult problem. The same is true of Miss Illa Sarvia, Miss E. Johansson and Mr G. Colbran, in the Official Publications Department (the former State Paper Room) of the British Library in the British Museum. Likewise, I thank Mr Maurice Bond, the Clerk of the House of Lords Record Office for permission to use its holdings. Mrs Pauline Fanning, Director of the Australian National Humanities Library and Mr G. T. Powell, Principal Librarian, Australian Reference, at the National Library of Australia, have done a good deal more for me than even spoilt scholars would hope for and I thank them very warmly. The Mitchell Library in Sydney and the Archives Authority of New South Wales have likewise been most useful and pleasant institutions to work in as well as with and I thank in particular the Senior Archivist, Mr D. J. Cross. The same is true of the following institutions: The Keio University Library at Mita, the Library of the Faculty of Letters of the University of Tokyo, the Library of Hitotsubashi University at Kunitachi, the Tōyō Bunko and the National Diet Library in Tokyo, the Southeast Asia Center of the University of Kyoto and, especially Professor Y. Ishii, the State Library of Victoria, the British Library Newspaper Library at Colindale, the Library of the London School of Oriental and African Studies, the Far East Centre at St. Anthony's College, Oxford, and its hospitable and learned Director, Richard Storry and, of course, the Cambridge University Librarian, Mr E. B. Ceadel and his staff.

I am most grateful to Professor Wolfgang Franke at Hamburg who took the trouble to read the manuscript and to Dr Werner Draguhn, Director of the Institute of Asian Affairs at Hamburg, for his part in ensuring its publication. I wish to thank Dr Brunhild Staiger of that Institute and Nicholas Stargardt for their very painstaking and efficient proof-reading. Nicholas Stargardt also helped with making the Index and in other ways. Julian Stargardt assisted in the preparation of the copy for the printer.

Thanks are also due to the Editor of the *Bulletin* in Sydney for making a photograph of the cartoon reproduced on page 72 available; and to the Australian Government Publishing Service and the National Library of Australia for providing a photograph of the *Commonwealth of Australia Gazette*, No. 63 of 1939.

My wife Janice, who urged me to write this book, has helped me through all its stages in many ways, most of all with wise counsel, giving me her time when her own research demanded it. She is living proof of her father's *dictum:* 'If you need help, ask a busy person.'

Cambridge and Ernen, Switzerland, 1977.

ABBREVIATIONS

A.F.P.F.L.	Anti-Fascist People's Freedom League [of Burma]
A. I. F.	Australian Imperial Force (Volunteer forces in the 1914-18 and 1939-45 wars)
A. L. P.	Australian Labor Party
A. M. F.	Australian Military Forces (Militia)
ANZUS	Australia, New Zealand, United States [Security Treaty]
D. L. P.	Australian Democratic Labor Party
ECAFE	[United Nations] Economic Commission of Asia and the Far East [now _ . .
GATT	General Agreement on Tariffs and Trade
Gaimusho	[Japanese] Foreign Office
Gestapu	The September 30 *coup* [of 1965] *(gerakan september tiga pulu)*
H. M.	His *or* Her Majesty's
H. M. A. S.	H. M. Australian [war] ship
H. M. G.	H. M. Government
H. M. S.	H. M. [war] ship
I. L. O.	International Labour Office *or* Organization
LBJ	Lyndon B. Johnson, President of the United States
NATO	North Atlantic Treaty Organization
N. S. W.	New South Wales
O. E. C. D.	Organization of Economic Co-operation and Development
P. K. I.`	*Partai Kommunis Indonesia* (Indonesian Communist Party)
P. S. I.	Partai Sosialis Indonesia (Indonesian Socialist Party)
RAAF	Royal Australian Air Force
SEATO	South East Asia Treaty Organization

S. P. D.	*Sozialdemokratische Partei Deutschlands* (Social Democratic Party of Germany)
U. A. P.	United Australia Party
U. N. O.	United Nations Organization
UNRRA	U. N. Relief and Rehabilitation Administration
U. S. A.	United States of America
U. S. S. R.	Union of Soviet Socialist Republics
Zaibatsu	Financial Establishment of Japan

Prolegomena

I

NO COUNTRY had more pitiful beginnings. In none could men be less hopeful. Conceived in the interval between the American and the French revolutions, as a prison farm for the excess convict population produced by great economic upheavals, such was the origin of the British colony of New South Wales.

The misery and degradation of convict workers was matched by the brutality of their masters. This situation was tempered to some extent by the humanity and vision which most of the British Governors' and some of those with lesser authority displayed. The Governors' powers were limited only by instructions from Whitehall - many months away by sailing ship.

Social strife was intense, its forms brutal, its major fruits of lasting consequence. The convicts were ruled by the fear of hunger, the lash and the gallows - and by the hope of release: the ticket of leave or emancipation. The inhospitality of land and sea made escape a perilous if not a hopeless undertaking. The penalties on recapture were atrocious. The yearning for far-off release gave rise to a chimaera: 'Beyond the hills lies China'.

The original conception of the colony as a depository of convicts may have been a simple one. Yet, it did produce a society, and societies are not static. The earliest changes developed when numbers of convicts were emancipated, or paroled and allowed to remain in the colony; when, similarly, numbers of officers and men of the N.S.W. Corps elected and were permitted to stay upon expiration of their contracts; and, then, by the immigration of free settlers on a larger scale.

The introduction of sheep-breeding for wool provided the first as well as the major economic basis for development in Australia. It retained this position for nearly 150 years.

Emancipists and free settlers may have detested each other but they joined in the exploitation of convict labour, supplied by a government which they might oppose but still could not control. All of this fierce striving took place on the eastern rim of an island continent, equalling Europe only in size. In 1828, Australia's total European population stood at 36,598. Aboriginal Australians were not counted.

Outside communications depended on the sailing ship. Even in 1840, ships carrying government despatches took five to six months for a single journey between London and Sydney. Small wonder that all who had more than their chains to lose were subject to fear of foreign powers, bred of insecurity and loneliness. Small wonder that in this news-starved outpost, where even the most prominent citizens felt their collective insignificance, reports about any foreign vessel were the subject of alarm.

II

Fears about the intentions and activities of foreign powers had existed from the beginning of settlement, as they did in other colonies and outposts. They turned colonial thoughts towards the problems of local defence and those of Imperial officers in the field, and of some politicians at home, towards the desirability of forward actions and further annexations. They were among the reasons advanced in 1802, for the settlement of Van Diemen's Land.

In 1826, Lord Bathurst reacted to reports about French naval activities by instructing Governor Darling to form settlements at Westernport - now in Victoria - and in Western Australia, then known as New Holland. Darling acted accordingly. Yet, he was sceptical: 'The present settlement being retained', he wrote to Viscount Goderich on 13 October 1827, 'it is not likely that any foreign power would attempt to establish itself in New Holland. The Western coast, I apprehend, holds no inducement.'

Fear of other powers' intentions, supported by glowing descriptions of its potentialities, nevertheless led to the British annexation of New Holland in 1828. Stirling's memorial, requesting a land grant and a governorship, combined both factors nicely:

The above recommendations point it out as a spot so eligible for settlement, that it cannot long remain unoccupied. It is not inferior in any . . . quality to the plain of Lombardy, and, as by its position it commands facilities for carrying on trade with India and the Malay archipelago, as well as with China, and as it is moreover favourably circumstanced for the equipment of cruisers for the annoyance of trade in those seas, some foreign power may see the advantage in taking possession, should His Majesty's government leave it unappropriated.

Stirling has thus left us a paradigm of the arguments for annexation. He also set out Australia's concerns in the essential Asian conspectus and, in doing so, he stated, what was for long to remain, in the Australian debate, the classical conservative view: that Asia was an arena for action.

Though the original purpose in forming British colonies in New South Wales and Van Diemen's Land had been the disposition of convicts, within fifty years, free settlers predominated in continental Australia. These colonies were becoming colonies of settlement, and British colonists were clamouring with some success for an end to the great powers exercised by governors and lieutenant-governors. The future of the colonies for settlement, safe investment outlets in pastoral and agricultural industries, seemed bright enough and, by degrees, the powers exercised by British governors were whittled down. After 1842, two-thirds of the New South Wales Legislative Council consisted of elected members; it could initiate legislation and, on certain matters, overrule the Governor. At the same time, outer areas of settlement, then part of New South Wales, clamoured for separation as well as for self-government - from Sydney as well as from London. These two issues became linked and were seen as a measure of colonial maturity.

III

The separatist agitations were successful and colonial political development in the course of the nineteenth century was, therefore, divisive. In 1829, the whole of Australia having become British, there were three colonies: New South Wales and Western Australia, sharing the continent, and the island colony of Van Diemen's Land - renamed Tasmania in 1856. The present State boundaries were fixed by 1862: South Australia had become a colony of free settlers in

1836: Victoria was separated from New South Wales in 1851; and Queensland became a self-governing colony in 1859, when it was separated from the senior colony. Western Australia alone remained non-self-governing until 1891.

Whitehall seemed to have learnt the lessons of the Boston tea-party. But, in fact, the great transformation that had made Great Britain economically pre-eminent in the world, that had led to the victory of free-trade policies and legislation - not to say ideology - also led to a preference for informal empire over the old closed Imperial system. The separation of the colonies of settlement ceased to be unthinkable. Their continued Imperial connection may be summed up in the oft-repeated phrase about sentiment and interest, the former being fostered by those with the greatest interest. The interest was a direct result of the British origin and continued connection. It was primarily economic, by consequence political and, partly from fear, military. Far from existing separately or in isolation, these aspects affected each other in many ways. The political uses of arguments about insecurity were soon discovered and have never ceased to affect this debate. The consequences of acute imperialist competition in the latter part of the nineteenth century, helped to enrich its flavour.

Colonial separatism was at least partly due to poor communications over great distances of sparsely settled land. The fact that each colony was centred around a port which became its capital city, resulted in competitive concentrations of economic strength and political power. Once the colonies were self-governing, they extended their separatism into antagonistic trade policies with disparate tariffs, separate postal systems and worst of all, because of their long-term implications, differential railway gauges: the very costliness of rail standardization has acted as a bulwark for separatist interests. Nevertheless, there were striking similarities between the colonies. Allowing for some small groups of foreign origin, like Germans in South Australia and Queensland and, also in Queensland, groups of Russians, the population in the colonies was overwhelmingly British in origin. However, the non-English component was much larger than its proportion in Great Britain. Though mainly Irish, it contained a considerable proportion of Scots and Welsh. These were demographic consequences of nineteenth-century British economic and political history.

The parliamentary evolution of the colonies was based on the

Westminster model, with popular lower houses and upper houses that
were either appointed or elected on an exclusive property franchise.
At the pinnacle of the system the governors remained, representing
the Crown. In contrast with the safeguards for property and privilege
in the upper houses of the colonies, the lower houses quickly evolved
egalitarian institutions such as universal manhood suffrage and secret
ballot, in 1856, and votes for women, in 1894. Together with major
gains in working conditions such as the eight-hour day, in 1856,
these, for long gave Australia an international reputation as a
laboratory of social change and political progress.

IV

Although self-governing, the Australian colonies had, before their
federation in 1901, neither power nor responsibility for foreign
affairs which remained in the hands of the British government well
into the twentieth century.

In these conditions, the colonial pre-occupation with defence is
one of the most striking aspects of nineteenth-century political
thought in Australia. The highly developed sense of vulnerability
played a part in this, as did the strong identification with Great
Britain, through which Britain's potential enemies seemed equally
to pose a threat to Australia. It was in this last connection that
Asia first entered Australian calculations of security, since the nature
of the threats posed by Britain's potential European enemies was
envisaged as being directed against Australia through Asian and
Pacific territories held or threatened by those powers.

Powerlessness and isolation, as well as the fear of rebellion,
inspired a close link between thoughts about the outside world and
defence - especially that of major ports. The Royal Navy may have
ruled the waves, but the spectre of a sudden invasion, or of crippling
raids on those ports, haunted colonial thinking for most of the
nineteenth century. It has not ceased to affect the debate.

Any power that might disturb pax Britannica, that might intrude
between other British possessions and Australia, appeared in this
view as a potential threat. As the century went on, the number of
candidates for this role was enlarged by fine feats of imagination. At

one time or another, France, the Netherlands, the United States, Russia and later Germany appeared in the role of potential enemy. Had the colonists learnt of the British ideas in the 1860's, to offer Fiji or islands in Malay waters to Prussia, what an uproar there would have been. Even the prostrate Chinese Empire was at times confused with the export trade in coolies and China appears in this list.

The fear of invasion - however imaginary or far-fetched - was similar to that felt in other British colonies, whether in Ceylon, the Straits Settlements, Hong Kong or the Cape. Colonial governors - that is, British officers - were among the most consistent proponents of such views.

There are, however, two distinctions setting Australia apart from other colonies. The first is geographic. Australia's position made the translation of fears into further forward movements rather difficult. It is only in connection with the endeavour to create a plantation society in Queensland, late in the century, that the attempt was made, and it failed. This brings us to the second distinction. The class character of the people involved came into play far more clearly in Australia than in other colonies where class distinctions were covered by a veneer of ethnic or 'racial' issues. The very homogeneity of the population coming from the British Isles and the absence of an economically, socially or politically effective indigenous people, acted to make class a more readily obvious form of distinction in Australia than in other British colonies.

The fears and interests were mainly those of men of property who had much to lose as well as to gain. They were not only linked with British enterprise in economic terms as well as in social life; they felt part of it. The desire for social acceptance by the British establishment ran very deep among the Australian middle classes. It has not entirely disappeared. These links were re-inforced by those of the administrators, the military and the intellectuals - and by the honours the Empire could bestow. The economic interests and social concepts that arose in the nineteenth century, had a deep and lasting political influence on the later debate.

V

Once a colonial military establishment, however small, came into existence, the desire to use it in support of the mother country became first a policy and then a subject of debate. Support for wars like the Sudanese campaign and the Boer War was seen as support for the Empire. It was also seen as an assurance of future British help, should it be needed; and it involved a new element which satisfied the old sense of insignificance: the desire to play a part on the world stage. These considerations emerged with an artless and disarming frankness from the despatches about the disposition of the New South Wales forces, unwanted by the British government in the Sudan.

As a policy, reliance on a major power arose historically from the very character of the British settlements in Australia. It did not begin as a policy but as a state of affairs. It became a policy through growth, through self-government, through the rise of an articulate opposition questioning this state of affairs. It then became one set of ideas in the Australian debate. It has been fairly described by Menzies as the conservative view.

Conservative ideas in this debate appear more uniform because of their wonderful simplicity: remain close to the great protecting power, please its government and, *beyond this*, do as little as possible. Radicals have often questioned its wisdom.

Radical views were slower to arise and they are more diverse. They have found expression in the policies of the Labour Party although they are older, and not exclusive to it. If these ideas are described in general terms as radical, it is because anything more exact or more specific would be misleading.

It is much easier to say what these radical ideas are not, than to define them. The Australian radical tradition, like the English, includes many strains. But the similarities are limited by specifically Australian historical conditions. There was transportation and all that a part-free, part-convict society implied. There was the immigration of Irish labourers due to the great famines. There was the almost chronic shortage of manpower, especially of skilled workers which, in spite of privations, struggle and periods of heavy unemployment, militated against a large, permanent pool of unemployed, and favoured early trade union success. Then there were factors which, if difficult to pin down, were, nonetheless, important.

The reasons for which people of few means or none would undertake the long and perilous sea voyage to Australia, in order to live in a land of natural severity, must have included very strongly-held views about the economic, social and political conditions at home. However inadequate the individual migrant's ability to formulate these ideas, they did, without doubt, find political expression in a variety of ways, including the ballot box. They also helped to form the idealized, utopian concepts about Australia's future which many of these men battled to fulfill.

Radical ideas in Australia encompassed strong elements of democratic nationalism. Concepts of socialist internationalism also played their part: as early as 1872, a Melbourne group published a paper, "The Internationalist", which was in touch with the First International. Irish rebels, English, Welsh and Scottish radicals of all sorts had been among the earliest convicts transported to Botany Bay, as well as among the later transports. After '48, Chartists, Carbonari and a sprinkling of other revolutionaries found their way to Australia. They were partly submerged by the wave of seekers after treasure that flowed into the continent, once the discovery of gold had become widely known, causing a social fever of epidemic proportions. Our knowledge of individual immigrants, especially of political refugees from continental Europe, is scant, but that their political and other ideas helped to fertilize Australian radical thought is hard to dispute.

Considering the absorption with domestic problems, the international awareness of Australian radicals was remarkable. One need only to think of the response of the Sydney workers to the French prison ships, carrying the defeated Communards of 1871, or of the £31,000 which the Melbourne Trades Hall Council sent to the striking London dockers in 1889. These spontaneous expressions of solidarity then came to be reflected in views on policy, including foreign policy. There was opposition to military support of Imperial ventures of the mother country and, after federation, scepticism about accepting control over New Guinea from Great Britain.

The twenty-five years preceding the first world war, saw a great flowering of socialist ideas, as well as the rapid growth of the Labour Party - all of which fell victim to the great war: the conscription crisis, the new political repression, the great and crippling strikes, and then, in 1919, the establishment of a Communist Party. All these phenomena expressed, as well as contributed to, the fragmentation of a mass movement. So did the heavy casualties, for many of the men who had offered their services for the war and had gone out to fight were Labour men who had volunteered but who opposed compulsion: large numbers of the Australian Imperial Force voted against the conscription proposals.

In those twenty-five years, Australian radicals had shown much interest in the great debates of the Socialist International in Europe, as well as in questions of colonial unrest in Asia and even in Africa. Their level of information is astonishing and the same is true of the quantity and quality of their publications. Most of these men and women were self-educated.

Inspite of these mainly pacifist, internationalist streams, the main stream of Australian radicalism has long favoured a national defence effort, under Australian direction and control. In this, it has drawn on and continued the debate of the previous century and it has shown, like its conservative opponents, a close link between thoughts about defence and those about foreign affairs. As in any great movement, a wide variety of shades of opinion and of groupings has abounded here.

There existed, however, another kind of radicalism which was fundamentally isolationist. It is mainly known through the *Bulletin* school of writers. Here, radical nationalism was fused with xenophobia and racist ideas in often *simpliste* amalgams. The *Bulletin's* effect on nationalist thinking in the Australian Labor Party can be overplayed. In the Labour Party, it was exposed to other views.

VI

This, then, is a study of a major, continuing debate in Australian history. The ideas, attitudes and fears forming this debate are those that were seriously and repeatedly expressed in a wide range of mainly official sources: despatches, reports, parliamentary debates, evidence to commissions of enquiry, political platforms that emerged as enduring constituents. Other sources are restricted to occasional illustrations.

The major positions in this debate predate federation. But, on the whole, they were to find implementation in policy only at a much later date. Within one hundred years of the establishment of the sad settlement at Sydney Cove, a viable group of colonies had developed in Australia which, if of no great import in the world, was nevertheless making itself felt in it. In these colonies, questions about relations with the world found vigorous expression in a continuing debate which, of geographical necessity, had to become a debate about Asia, about relations with the countries of Asia: about Australia's Asian policies.

It took a further fifty years, from this first centenary, for an active Australian foreign policy to come into being. This slowness, and often conscious reluctance, are among the themes of this study. The sources for this hesitation are to be found in the conservative concepts which were mentioned above. They were sustained by the reality of a powerful Empire. The effectiveness of its ability to protect Australia was questioned by John Curtin in 1935, and it was Curtin who was Prime Minister when that contingency occurred. He then proceded to implement an Australian foreign policy which gave the debate a new dimension.

By the end of the nineteenth century - the decade of federation - the major positions taken in this debate had been established. This study must begin with an examination of their evolution to that stage. Any choice of a starting point contains arbitrary elements. Yet, unlike their subject-matter, works of history must have a beginning and an end. It seems appropriate to begin with the first attempt in Australia to intervene in the affairs of Asia.

Part One: 1839—1881
From the Opium Wars to the Defence Enquiries

THE GIPPS DESPATCH

T HE FIRST DECISION taken in Australia to intervene in the affairs of Asia was not carried out.

In July 1839, the Governor of New South Wales, Sir George Gipps, reported to London that he had acted on intelligence received 'via Singapore and Java, of the events which occurred in China' as it seemed 'that Captain Elliot, H.M. Principal Superintendant of Trade, was under constraint and threatened with immediate death by the Chinese authorities.'[1]

Gipps responded to these circumstances. Three naval vessels being in Sydney harbour, he invited the Captain, Sir Gordon Bremer, 'either to proceed with the whole of them or to despatch thither as large a portion of the force under his command as he . . . might think fit.'[2] In view of the frequent colonial alarms, it is significant that Gipps commented that, in his opinion, there was nothing in the colonies or the neighbouring seas that should stand in the way of such a proceeding.

Although exaggerated, the intelligence on which Gipps acted was accurate enough. There had been mounting tension between the Chinese authorities and the British, due to the highly profitable opium trade which had wide support in the reformed Parliament, the East India Company's monopoly of the China trade having been abolished by the 1833 Act to regulate the Trade of China and India. Under this Act, a Court of Justice had been created on Chinese territory - 'within the Dominions of the Emperor of China and the Ports and Havens thereof, and on the High Seas within one hundred miles of the Coast of China' to be held at 'Canton, in the said Dominions, or on a British ship or vessel in the Port or Harbour of Canton . . . by the Chief Superintendant.'[3]

The Chief Superintendant of British Trade and H.M. Commissioner and Plenipotentiary was Charles Elliot. He had been Protector of

Slaves in Guiana from 1830 to 1833. In the following year, he was seconded to Lord Napier who was then Superintendant and whom Elliot succeeded in 1837. Related to Lord Minto and to Rear Admiral Elliot, he belonged to the ruling Whig establishment. He appears to have been a competent and fair-minded administrator.

The same competence and incorruptibility may be ascribed to Elliot's Chinese counterpart, Lin Tse-hsü who had been appointed by the Emperor as Imperial Envoy or Commissioner — Kin-chae — at Canton, in a determined effort to stop the opium trade.

Lin Tse-hsü acted firmly. He threatened the Chinese guild, or *Hong*, merchants handling this trade with extreme penalties. He further demanded the surrender of all stocks of opium held by the foreign merchants. He insisted that they sign bonds to discontinue the trade, under penalty of death. As about twenty thousand chests of opium, then valued at U.S.$ 12 million, lay in the holds of foreign ships, a compromise offer was made - to surrender one thousand chests. Lin refused. He had the foreign factories surrounded with troops and ordered all Chinese subjects out of them.[4]

On 27 March 1839, Lin, according to an entry in his diary, received a note from Elliot through the *Hong* merchants, who had the monopoly of the foreign trade, saying that the English would surrender 20,283 chests of opium and were awaiting instructions about the checking of its reception. On the following day, 'Elliot', in Lin's words, 'invented reasons for delaying the surrender of the opium'.[5] But this time, the Chinese succeeded in enforcing their prohibition. On 13 May 1839, according to Lin's diary, 'the trenches . . . are being made to drain off the opium when it is destroyed'.[6]

This was the situation to which Gipps responded. In due course, it would lead to the opium wars. The details are well enough known and modern studies, using Chinese sources, have put earlier accounts into clearer perspective. Here we are concerned with the effect of Asian affairs on the formation of Australian attitudes.

Gipps, a son of a manse, had served in the peninsular wars and, at the time of the battle of Waterloo he was, we are told, detailed to look after the defences of Ostend. After the end of the war, he travelled in Europe. From 1824 to 1829, he was stationed in the West Indies and his reports on slavery were noted in London. We have seen that Elliot went to Guiana as Protector of Slaves in 1830.

Gipps spent some years in England, working with the Commissions on electoral boundaries and, in 1834, as Lord Auckland's private secretary when the latter was First Lord of the Admiralty in Lord Melbourne's first government. Auckland went to India as Governor General, arriving in Calcutta in February 1836. Gipps had, before that, been appointed, together with Sir Charles Grey, to serve as a member of Lord Gosford's Royal Commission in Canada, where he worked from 1835 to 1837. He was knighted within weeks of that appointment but he did not become a major until January 1837. Later in that year, he was appointed Captain General and Governor in Chief of the Colonies of New South Wales and Van Diemen's Land and their dependencies. He arrived at Sydney on 24 February 1838, to assume the government.[7]

In his earlier army life, Gipps had acquired some acquaintance with works of defence. He had gained his colonial experience in the slave-based plantation colonies of the Caribbean and in the divisive Canadian atmosphere of the 1830's. He had obtained rapid preferment from the Whigs. Their policies, especially in Imperial affairs, were clearly familiar to him.

Gipps had been Lord Auckland's private secretary when the Act under which Elliot was appointed was passed, and both men had been concerned with slavery in the Caribbean. Lord Auckland had now gone as Governor General to India. Although the Hon. Company had lost its monopoly of the China trade by the 1833 legislation, Auckland was nonetheless concerned in a wider sense with this enormous trade and its implications.

These developments and his personal connections were important in Gipps' background, and his action must be seen in this conspectus. At that time, an Australian colony could not, of course, pursue a foreign or defence policy of its own, distinct from Imperial policy. Yet, even a hundred years after Gipps' action, when such distinctions not only existed but played an important part in the debate, the conservative side in that debate was still firmly wedded to the principle on which Gipps had decided to act: an Imperial position being endangered, it was little more than a reflex action to mobilize the forces available in his fief to come to its help *aussi vite que possible.* Gipps had concluded his despatch - 'I trust that your lordship and Her Majesty's government will approve of what has been done in this emergency.'

They did indeed. The despatch had arrived in London just before
Christmas, 1839. It was circulated to the Foreign Office, the
Admiralty and the Board of Trade. Lord Palmerston was clearly
pleased and suggested 'whether it may not be expedient to communi-
cate Sir George Gipps' Despatch to the Admiralty and the Board of
Trade . . .'[8] But the Admiralty had already replied, to 'approve of
Capt. Sir J. Gordon Bremer having acceded to the recommendation
of His Excellency Sir George Gipps to proceed with the *Alligator*,
Herald and *Pelorus* from Sydney to China.'[9]

Bremer, however, did not proceed. His main interest lay in the
Port Essington Settlement where he was styled "Commander of
H.M. Settlements on the North Coast of Australia". In January
1840, the Colonial Office questioned 'the whole correspondence
going on in a very irregular manner . . . Sir Gordon Bremer is in
fact governing a colony, under orders from the Admiralty.'[10]
The pathetic fate of the abortive Port Essington settlement does not
concern us here.[11] It should only be remarked that, as their logs
disclose, none of the three ships went to China in 1839.[12] Bremer,
however, succeeded to the command of the India Station, in a
temporary capacity, on the death of Sir Frederick Maitland in
December 1839, until he was superseded by Rear Admiral Elliot -
Charles Elliot's cousin. Their careers crossed again in China, where
Bremer was sent in charge of the expedition arriving at Canton on
20 June 1840; and once more after Admiral Elliot was invalided in
November of that year, when Bremer acted until the arrival of Sir
William Parker in August 1841.

Bremer's own motives for not proceeding from Sydney to China,
in 1839, seem clear enough. It appears from the files that he had
attempted, on 14 September 1838, to resign his Commission in order
to accept an appointment in the Surveyor General's Department of
New South Wales.[13] Having apparently been refused, he continued
to concentrate his efforts on the Port Essington settlement.

Port Essington was one of the most hopeless Imperial ventures.
Yet, Bremer and some of his successors at Port Essington had
grandiose visions of another Singapore: a great *entrepôt* and a base
for forward movements into parts of Indonesia that were not as yet
under clear Dutch control. Raffles' ghost cast a strong spell: this
was to be the great Australian junction for acting on Asia.

The anti-climax of Bremer's failure to proceed to China in July

1839, may be amusing but it is not very important. In this context, the importance of the affair rests in Gipps' decision to intervene from Australia with what forces he could muster, in support of a British position in Asia, on the basis of a very clear notion of the policies he was serving. In this instance at least, political acumen compensated for the slowness of communications. In the failure to follow up, the latter played a decisive part.

Gipps viewed Asia as an arena for action and his post in Sydney as one from which such action, if need be, should be supported. In his position that was a reasonable view. In acting on it, he established a major precedent for the future.

The "Eastern Expedition" which Bremer was to command in the following years, not only succeeded in reducing Chinese opposition to the opium trade. It inaugurated a new period in the relations of imperial China and the Europeans and resulted in changing the course and rate of European penetration of East and South East Asia. A new era in world history had begun.

As a post-script to this affair, the similarity in the fates of the two original antagonists at Canton is worth mentioning. Commissioner Lin Tse-hsü's recall and disgrace, however unjustified, occurred in the circumstances of shock and defeat. Elliot also was replaced, as Lord John Russell admitted to the House, after repeated questioning, on 6 May 1841.[14] Russell's consistent reticence on the affairs in China may perhaps be explained by a critical and informed opposition[15] which had caused the withdrawal of the China Courts Bill on 28 July 1838 and came close to carrying a censure motion on the war with China on 9 April 1840, the voting being 262:271.[16]

The episode of the Gipps Despatch - which is all it turned out to be - involved no debate in Australia. The decision he took, however, provided the pattern of seeing Asia as an arena for action in support of the power responsible for, or guaranteeing Australia's security: the argument on which conservative diplomatic theory was to rest in the future.

INTRA-IMPERIAL DEBATE ON COLONIAL DEFENCE

The initial debate was essentially one between the Imperial government and their governors who were to express, with growing frequency, views held by prominent groups of colonists. An Austra-

lian debate evolved with the constitutional and political development
of the colonies, reflecting their economic and demographic development and social change. The earlier debate between British governors
and governments is relevant and important for its formative effects
on the debate within Australia.

Transportation of convicts to New South Wales was to end in
1840. In October of that year, Gipps referred to '. . . the disappointment, not to say alarm, which would be created . . .' by the abandonment of the works of defence just begun, adding:' . . . if this work
is not performed whilst yet the government has some convict labour
at its disposal, it must ultimately be executed by free labour, at an
expense of from ten to twenty times the amount of what it will
now cost.'[17] The sense of alarm and the worry about costs to which
Gipps referred, appear to have grown rather than diminished with
the economic viability of the colony, especially through wool and
gold, and the issue of fortifying Sydney harbour remained one of the
recurring subjects of despatches between Sydney and London, resulting in some limited fortifications. Gipps had raised these questions
several times although he was always very conscious of the fact
that the best way to succeed with Downing Street was to avoid
incurring expense.

In 1846, Gipps was succeeded by Sir Charles FitzRoy. FitzRoy's
correspondence with Earl Grey on the subject of defence stressed
the need for stationing Imperial troops especially on grounds of
internal security: 'There are many desperate ruffians among the
lower classes of the population of Sydney' he wrote in April 1847,
and he was 'much disposed to believe that the knowledge that there
is a strong military force at hand has much to do with the preservation
of public peace.'[18]

FitzRoy stressed that a local police force posed very special
problems, for the men of the class from which it would be procured
could obtain high wages as labourers or mechanics, leaving them a
considerable amount of time at their disposal and no real inducement
to enter a service 'which is irksome in its duties and subjects them
to the restraints of discipline.'

Not even Imperial troops were immune: '. . . Such is the demand
for labour that no soldier stationed in this colony finds the slightest
difficulty in obtaining a loan of money . . . to purchase his dis-
charge.' FitzRoy feared the consequences of 'the mob of Sydney

ever getting beyond the control of the executive power' in view of the great wealth in Sydney which, he was 'credibly informed amounted 'to nearly £700,000 in specie in the different banks of Sydney', exclusive of the funds of the Colonial government and the Military Chest. In November 1849, FitzRoy wrote that -

'. . . a considerable proportion of the population were originally transported to the Colony, and of the immigrants there are many who left home from motives of political discontent, and whose evil passion might again be easily roused if they were placed in circumstances which would give them even a temporary power of embarrassing the Government . . .'

It would be "unsafe and unwise" to entrust mechanics and labourers "with arms or to train them in their use, lest they should at any time be disposed to turn them to bad account." It was not only fear of desperate ruffians, but of the working class.

These reasons - great, readily accessible wealth and endemic insecurity - were also advanced in asking 'the mother country for protection against foreign aggression which the colonists are not in a position to provide for themselves.'[20] France and America were seen in this role, to be shortly joined by Russia. The source of aggression would always be seen in the Asian arena.

In his reply of 21 June 1850, Earl Grey agreed that 'prudence does prescribe the erection of works sufficient to protect the city of Sydney from predatory attack'. However, 'the great value of property it contains, and the wealth and prosperity evinced by the very large sums of money stated to be in the banks, afford proof no less of the ability of the colony to meet the expense of providing such protection than of the necessity of doing so.'[21] Earl Grey had sounded a note that was to recur in later despatches on this subject. If local prosperity made the colonies an attractive and vulnerable prize for attack, then local prosperity should provide the answer.

Again, at the end of January 1854, Lt. Col. Edward Macarthur, the Deputy Adjutant General in Sydney, submitted 'a plan for promoting the Defence of this portion of Australia, where - as in most communities whose population is not numerous - the difficulty is to combine measures for raising a National or Colonial Soldiery, in some mode that shall neither inconveniently engage the time of individuals, nor unduly press upon the Public Finances.' He proposed a scheme of voluntary 'Australian Fencibles or Militia',[22] operating on a part-time basis. Fear, and the need for some defence effort were again in the air. There were formal and informal petitions due to 'the present unsettled state of affairs in Europe' as the Sydney Chamber of Commerce had it in a Memorial to the Governor-General [23], requesting legislation to enrol citizens as volunteers.

That idea was fairly widespread. A sixteen-page document by one Mr. Charles Adam Corbyn 'two doors east of Robin Hood Inn - South Head Road', addressed to the Colonial Secretary in Sydney was circulated by FitzRoy's command.[24] In his paper, Corbyn expressed fear of invasion by the Russians of the 'Port and Harbour of Sydney, by a hostile naval force, this country being depicted in Europe as especially famous for its wealth and for its insecure and defenceless condition.' The author realised that the Russians could neither equip a major naval force to carry out the *coup de main* much-feared as a result of their reported presence in the China Sea, nor escape the Royal Navy if they tried, but he did believe a minor attack to be feasible, and he called for the raising of a volunteer force.

Meanwhile, a parallel development took place, more intimately connected with the Crimean War. In November 1853, a variety of propositions concerning the defence of Port Jackson had been sent to London by FitzRoy. By the time Downing Street replied - 3 June 1854 - England was at war. The reply promised a variety of arms and ammunition, but no troops: 'So great is the pressure upon the troops of all arms consequent upon the War, that it is impossible to send out either Sappers and Miners or half a Company of Artillery to assist, as proposed, in the construction of the works of defence contemplated.' [25]

It was therefore once more suggested that the troops be raised locally. In the opinion of the responsible officer in Sydney, Colonel Barney, this would be impossible: '. . . I have the honour to observe that no doubt can exist as to the value of such a corps . . . but . . . the extreme high price of labour seems to preclude the possibility of obtaining the class of men required . . .'

The pay of the Royal Sappers and Miners was five shillings per working day, and in Barney's view it would be altogether inadequate to induce colonial young men to enlist: an inferior mechanic could readily earn twenty-five shillings per day, and a labourer eight; they had also the option of working only so many days a week as might suit their purpose: under such circumstances it was hardly to be expected that men would enlist for service compelling them to work every day in the week, subject to military discipline, at a rate of pay not more than one-third of the rate then received by mechanics and labourers. Barney concluded: 'I am led to the conclusion that any attempts to raise a Corps of Sappers and Miners in this country would signally fail.'[26]

FitzRoy was succeeded by a highly competent engineer, Sir William Denison, and at length the Imperial government was pre- pared to 'assume that observations respecting the obstacle which at present oppose the formation of a Militia Force for the defence of the colony were well founded.' This despatch - Stanley to Denison - of 11 March 1858, continued: 'The force to be maintained by this country in the Australian colonies should be that which may be reasonably required for defence against possible aggression;' and, adopting Lord Grey's words, 'if a greater amount of force is required, the local legislature should make provision for the pay and allowances of an additional number of Her Majesty's regular Army'. The Imperial government was prepared to execute the duty allotted to it of serving distant possessions against foreign enemies; while, if troops were required by any Colony beyond the amount necessary for this purpose, they would readily assist to the best of their ability in furnishing those troops, if they could be spared, and provided the Colony would pay for them.

Stanley then raised a crucial point:

Your proposal . . . that the pay and allowances of the troops should be halved between the Mother Country and the Colony, . . . would seem difficult to adopt . . . unless your own further proposal were incorporated with it - that the Colony should possess, through the vote of its Legislature, the responsibility of determining the amount of force which should be maintained in it, whether in peace or in war. Her Majesty's Government do not, as at present advised, see in what manner this suggestion could be adopted, without compromising that independent action of the central authority of the Empire. The Executive in this country having full information as to its available force, and as to the different calls on that force in the various portions of the Empire, can alone be in a position to decide what force is required, and what force can be spared, for purposes of defence against foreign aggression, in each particular point. If every Colony were to assert a voice in this matter, as in your proposal it would have to do, I do not see in what manner the general defensive arrangements of the Empire could be conducted.[27]

The problem of Imperial control and the decision-making powers of self-governing colonies had now been raised. The British government would not and could not guarantee in advance of any possible contingency, how and where *their* troops were to be deployed. The colonies, on the other hand felt that, if they paid, that is, if they contributed to the upkeep of these troops, they had to be assured that the forces would be available when they were most needed. To colonial conservatives especially, the defence shield of Imperial forces seemed essential. They were prepared, at most, to contribute half the cost, and they wanted to be assured that they could rely on these troops in case of an emergency. The question of final control over defence forces was clearly vital to both parties to the correspondence. The British government favoured the establishment of local forces, as in the Straits Settlements and in Ceylon. Out of the defence problem at length there arose, among conservatives in the colonies, the idea of Imperial Federation, and, among the colonial radicals, the concept of Australian defence forces raised, financed and controlled by Australian parliaments.

For the time being, the Defence responsibility remained entirely with the British government, notwithstanding the marginal existence of colonial volunteer units.

The contingency of possible intervention on the confederate side of the American civil war was raised in a circular despatch to the colonies by the Colonial Secretary in Palmerston's last government, the Duke of Newcastle. He reassured the colonies in that despatch of 26 December 1861, 'that the best mode of affording protection will engage the anxious and unceasing attention of Her Majesty's Government.'[28]

When he advised the colonies on 22 January 1862, that the danger had passed, Newcastle sought to impress on them 'the necessity . . . of prompt and effectual preparation against contingencies, which, though happily no longer imminent, can never, in the present disturbed state of the world, be regarded as impossible.'[29] Writing in this vein, he was foreshadowing the Report of the Select Committee on Colonial Military Expenditure which reached the Commons on 4 March 1862.

That enquiry had been concerned essentially with colonies enjoying some form of self-government: the North American colonies, the Australian colonies, with the exception of Western Australia - still a receptacle for convicts under Governor's rule - as well as the West Indies, the Cape of Good Hope, New Zealand, the Mauritius and

Ceylon. The conclusions of that enquiry were summarized in a resolution of the House of Commons:

That this House (while fully recognising the claims of all portions of the British Empire to Imperial aid in their protection against perils arising from the consequences of Imperial policy) is of [the] opinion that Colonies exercising the rights of self-government ought to undertake the main responsibility of providing for their own internal order and security, and ought to assist in their own external defence.[30]

In the Australian colonies, the sense of dependence on British defence was still very strong, the views on necessary requirements disparate, and the enthusiasm for meeting the costs, subdued.

WITHDRAWAL OF THE BRITISH ARMY:THE LINES OF FUTURE DEBATE

The British Liberals returned to power under Gladstone at the end of 1868, committed to a major defence review, resulting in important reductions which were implemented without delay.

These decisions were especially unwelcome in New Zealand where military operations of some dimensions were in progress against the Maoris. The outcry was the greater since neither Gladstone nor Lord Granville, then at the Colonial Office, had much sympathy with a settlers' war, resulting from a policy of punitive confiscations of Maori lands. It should, however, be said that the policy of not using British troops in Maori wars had also been that of Lord Carnarvon, Granville's conservative predecessor, who had offered to leave one regiment in New Zealand, if the colony paid for it and if it was only used to garrison towns - not in the field against Maoris.[31]

The outcry co-incided with the foundation of the Colonial Society, the original name of the present Royal Commonwealth Society. Of its founders, many had made their fortune in Australia and retired to London where they tended to consider themselves experts, if not spokesmen on Australian affairs. Granville's biographer claimed that in the foundation of the Society, 'the hand of the Conservative party organiser could also be recognized.'[32]

Nevertheless, both Gladstone and Granville attended the inaugural dinner of the Society on 10 March 1869.[33]

A fortnight later, on 25 March 1869, Granville sent his despatch, advising the colonies of the government's decision, concluding that their forces in the colonies were 'capable of considerable reduction'.

Granville stated that, as far as Australia was concerned, such a reduction was almost forced upon the government by the total withdrawal of British troops from New Zealand which rendered it no longer possible to station the detached wing of a regiment in continental Australia. Orders had therefore been given to withdraw from Australia all infantry in excess of a single regiment.

Granville continued:

The principle that the Colonies should pay the full expense of their own military defence must now be considered as established in general, and it is actually applied to the two Crown Colonies of Ceylon and the Straits Settlements.

In Granville's view, no reason could be alleged why it should not be equally applied to the flourishing colonies of Australia. A careful enquiry was shortly to be instituted into the expense of the troops employed in the different British possessions, with the object of ascertaining the rate of colonial payment which would cover the full cost of these troops: 'You may therefore, at no distant period, expect a proposal founded on this enquiry; and it will be for the Australian Colonies to consider whether or not it is worth their while to pay this increased cost for the presence of a small body of Her Majesty's Troops.' The new arrangement would include Tasmania which would lose its advantage of 'receiving the services of Her Majesty's Troops without payment. The new arrangement would therefore apply to that island and its government should become a party to any colonial consultations on this subject.'[34]

Agreement proved as impossible among the Australian colonies as it was with them. New interests had grown which it was becoming impossible to ignore. The remaining British troops left in 1870.

In the ensuing debate, it became clear that, although the British military presence had been small, the void left by its absence would, to some, seem disproportionately large. In their views, a feeling of increased insecurity, fear, and a sense of being unready to cope with the problems of a region which they viewed as unfriendly and probably dangerous, came to be reflected. That position has never disappeared.

The British policy also caused unrest in the Colonial Society. A number of its leading members called a meeting, to be held in its rooms, with a view to organizing an unofficial colonial conference in London, preferably with official representatives from the governments of the Australian colonies. Strictly it was not an activity of the Society but the distinction was a fine one.

Granville parried this move with a circular despatch, drafted with evident satisfaction by the Permanent Under-secretary at the Colonial Office, Sir Frederic Rogers, to scotch a proposal which had, in any case, a widely hostile reception in Australia,[35] where other views had become articulate by this time.

The 1860's had been a time of great constitutional disputes which had shaken Victoria. This crisis began with disagreements between the government of the colony, supported by the radical majority in the lower house, the Legislative Assembly, and the conservatives who dominated, as they have continued to do, the Legislative Council. These disputes developed into a struggle with the Imperial government over their dismissal of the Governor, Sir Charles Darling, and their criticism of his successor, for both men took it to be their duty to act on the advice of the colonial ministers.

THE HIGINBOTHAM RESOLUTIONS

Throughout that crisis, the great jurist George Higinbotham had played an outstanding part, as Attorney General in successive Victorian governments. Higinbotham was not only a great jurist. He was, and was known to be, an incorruptible humanitarian, a man capable of applying his strongly-held principles to changing situations and yet remaining relevant and truthful in his observations. He had no great love of office. He resigned his cabinet post as well as his seat in the Executive Council of the colony in February 1869, as he had come to the view, after consideration of the House of Lords debate on the Victorian crisis,[36] that the course to which he felt committed was in fact, if not in law, blocked.

Higinbotham is perhaps best remembered for his support, as Chief Justice of Victoria, of the Melbourne Trades Hall Council, after the employers' refusal of a request for a conference in the great maritime strike of 1890. The man's measure emerges from these lines, announcing his support:

Law Courts.
The Chief Justice presents his compliments to the President of the Trades Hall Council, and requests that he will be so good as to place the amount of the enclosed cheque of £50 to the credit of the strike fund. While the United Trades are awaiting compliance with their reasonable request for a conference with the employers, the Chief Justice will continue for the present to forward a

weekly contribution of £10 to the same object.[37]

His portrait used to hang in the old Melbourne Trades Hall Council chamber. It has not been possible to discover its present whereabouts.

On 2 November 1869, Higinbotham, no longer a member of the government, introduced the resolutions in the Victorian Legislative Assembly which were at once linked with his name. It was an attempt to clarify the relations between the colony and the Imperial government:

1. That the care of the political rights and interests of a free people can be safely intrusted only to a body appointed by or responsible to that people; and that the Legislative Assembly declines to sanction or to recognise the proceedings (as far as the same may relate to Victoria) of the conference proposed to be held in London, at the instance of a self-constituted and irresponsible body of absentee colonists.

2. That the people of Victoria, possessing by law the right of self-government, desire that this colony should remain an integral portion of the British Empire, and that this House acknowledges, on behalf of its constituents, the obligation to provide for the defence of the shores of Victoria against foreign invasion, by means furnished at the sole cost, and retained within the exclusive control, of the people of Victoria.

3. That this House protests against any interference, by legislation of the Imerial Parliament, with the internal affairs of Victoria, except at the instance or with the express consent of the people of the colony.

4. That the official communication of advice, suggestions, or instructions, by the Secretary of State for the Colonies to Her Majesty's representative in Victoria, on any subject whatsoever connected with the administration of the local Government, except the giving or withholding of the Royal assent to or the reservation of Bills passed by the two Houses of the Victorian Parliament, is a practice not sanctioned by law, derogatory to the independence of the Queen's representative, and a violation both of the principle of the system of responsible government and of the constitutional rights of the people of this colony.

5. That the Legislative Assembly will support Her Majesty's ministers for Victoria in any measures that may be necessary for the purposes of securing recognition of the exclusive right of Her Majesty and of the Legislative Council and Legislative Assembly 'to make laws in and for Victoria in all cases whatsoever'. and putting an early and final stop to the unlawful interference of the Imperial Governemnt in the domestic affairs of this colony.[38]

Higinbotham spoke at great length in support of these resolutions, initiating one of the great set-piece debates in Australia on colonial-imperial relations. The Higinbotham resolutions were debated altogether on six days - on 2, 3, 10, 16 November and, in Committee, on 22 December 1869. The Chief Secretary attempted to soften the terms of (1) but his amendment was defeated 45:15. He attempted to amend the second resolution by inserting 'in concert with the Imperial authorities' but he failed, the voting being 40:21. (3) passed without comment. (4) was opposed by the government but it passed 40:18. Higinbotham offered to withdraw the whole of (5) if any one member or the government wished it to be withdrawn: it passed without comment.[39]

Higinbotham's supporting speech raised a number of points that have, over the succeeding century, recurred in this debate. He examined 'the occasion and circumstances' of the British refusal of military aid to the New Zealand colonists in the Maori war. Higinbotham was at pains to stress his respect for the Maori: 'I believe that the rising of the noblest race of uncivilised men known in the world against our New Zealand fellow countrymen has been, at least in part, occasioned by the crimes of English civilization.' Higinbotham's concern about this kind of issue was not new. In 1859, he had written, as editor of the Melbourne *Argus*, that 'the treatment of the Aborigines has from the commencement of the settlement of the continent been a standing reproach against the colonists.'[40]

In the present context, however, Higinbotham thought that it might be improper and presumptuous to press this part of the question. The fact was that the colonists of New Zealand had asked 'for the aid of English troops and for the guarantee of a loan to enable them to defend themselves' and that they had been refused both of these applications, the stated reason being that the privilege of self-government carried with it the obligation to provide for their own defence. Since this reasoning was undeniable, no matter why it was employed, it raised in Higinbotham's view the question: 'Shall these Australian colonies continue their connexion with the Mother country or not; and, if they do, upon what conditions?'

The 'outlying question' of union of the Australian colonies, which was pressed by Charles Gavan Duffy, had been omitted from the resolutions because the colonies would first have to settle it among themselves. Higinbotham was somewhat sceptical of it; it seems, from other evidence, that he feared any tampering with the British system of responsible government, which is of course unavoidable by the very fact of the division of powers in any federation.

He went on to the question 'whether we should not claim on behalf of these colonies exemption from hostile attack upon the

part of powers with which Great Britain may be at war.' That is,
whether they should claim rights of neutrality which Gavan Duffy
linked with federation. Higinbotham pointed out that it could hardly
be expected that foreign countries would readily and willingly accept
a principle which would deprive them of much of their power in
time of war against the country with which they were at war. It was
a question full of difficulties and one they could not then discuss. It
could only be discussed 'between the English Government and the
colonies on the one hand, and the Governments of all civilized
countries of the world on the other hand . . . at a sort of congress of
nations.'

Higinbotham was no secessionist. He hoped that 'the formal
connexion and still more the real and substantial connexion - between
Great Britain and her colonies, should continue for an indefinite
length of time to come.' But he also felt that any individual in the
community had to be free, if he pleased, to express 'his desire that
Victoria may be separated from the British Empire.' One should add
that the use of the word 'empire' was in transition at that time.
This was reflected in Higinbotham's own usage: at times, he spoke
of the 'Empire of England', in the sense of 'realm of England'; at
other times, he spoke of the British Empire and we tend to think of
the later usage, without being certain of his precise meaning.[41]
Higinbotham pointed out that the question of separation - 'of casting
off the colonies' - was freely discussed and considered in the British
Parliament and the English press and he could not see why it 'should
not be as freely considered in this country'. He wished for 'conditions
which render real connexion and sympathetic and lasting union
possible to be conceded freely on both sides.'

Having clarified his position, Higinbotham turned to the question
of defence, accepting without reserve the proposition that 'a people
that would be independent must be able to defend themselves'; but
he insisted that 'the English Government were bound to make a
contribution to the defence of English commerce in our waters which
might be affected in case of war.' For, any danger to the colony, in
time of war, would result from its connexion with England: 'If
English merchants send English ships to this colony, and, if this
colony, in consequence of its connexion with the mother country, be
involved in war with any foreign country, it is surely not unreasonable
to ask that England should defend from foreign aggression not

Victoria, but her own ships, while they are in our waters . . . it is an admission of the obligation of the empire to defend the interests of British commerce, so far as those interests may be affected by their position in our waters in a time of war with foreign countries.'

If this principle was accepted, Higinbotham would only limit it by one condition:

That either the land force or the naval force which is created and called into existence by our own means, and maintained at our cost, should be kept under our own control.

He could not see that anyone could raise a rational objection to that limitation which was prescribed, in his view, by prudence and self-respect. It was certainly prescribed by prudence. He asked what advantage could this or any of the neighbouring colonies gain by paying in time of peace for either a military or naval force which might be withdrawn in time of war? 'If a regiment or a ship of war kept here in time of peace be withdrawn in time of war, of what earthly use is it to us? And, if it is outside our own control, it may be withdrawn, and probably will be withdrawn.'

This question was not really settled until the second world war. The Fisher Labour government would establish the Royal Australian Navy which came under Admiralty control in 1914. In 1925, an Australian cruiser was attached to the China station of the Royal Navy, causing a serious parliamentary dispute about Australia's Asian policies and her relations with the Imperial government. The exchanges between Curtin and Churchill on the return of Australian forces for self-defence in 1941, are now well known.

In his pragmatic assessment of Victoria's defence needs, based on the then existing strategic situation, Higinbotham's position was far removed from the excited views often found in contemporary estimates:

I think it will be an advantage to us to alter the system, so far as that either the military or the naval defences which may be necessary for the protection of this country shall be wholly under the control of Her Majesty's Government for Victoria. I believe that the defences which we can create and maintain for ourselves will be abundantly sufficient for the purpose. We are situated at a remote corner of the world, and certainly no land force which could attack this country could attack it in such power as to be able to resist the weakest of our colonial defences upon land . . . But, if our land forces are not sufficient, we should increase them upon this condition and for this express purpose - that they be kept under our own control, as they are paid for by our own money.

Similar arrangements should be made for naval forces, including the ownership and staffing of ships. Higinbotham thought that 'this frank and full acceptance of the duty of self-defence is one that our fellow-countrymen at home may reasonably expect from us. On the other hand, we have a right to demand from our fellow-countrymen at home another condition - the condition on which the English government has based this demand that the colonies shall protect themselves - namely, that we shall possess the absolute and entire right of self-government.'

It was Higinbotham's major contention, his major reason for moving these resolutions, 'that while we possess by law, in this country, almost absolute and entire powers of self-government, we do not possess, and never have possessed, self-government in fact.' He contended that the colony enjoyed by its constitution and by law 'almost all of what are known as absolute rights of independent states.' As to the former, they were limited by 'a very anomalous condition . . . imposed upon us by the English government and the English Parliament, which enables an English minister - a foreign minister, I will say for this purpose - to advise the Crown either to accept or to reject any of our legislative measures.' Higinbotham stressed the lack of a foreign-affairs power: the relative rights of independent states. The Victorian government could not 'send an embassy' that could claim official recognition 'even to a neighbouring colony.' They could not make a peace or proclaim a war: 'This distinction between absolute and relative rights forms the clearest and most distinct description of the rights of self-government which this and the neighbouring colonies enjoy under their Constitution Acts.'

Colonial self-government was limited by Imperial action in three ways.

Firstly, by Imperial legislation which was prepared by the Colonial Office: he pointed out that the Colonial Office prepared all measures passed by the English Parliament relating to the colonies, and, 'by an ingenious device, they confound and mix together not only those colonies which are under the control of the Colonial Office, but colonies which enjoy the right of self-government under a responsible system.' There was usually in all these colonial measures a clause defining what a colony or a colonial possession should be, and having lumped together the forty-three colonies or colonial possessions of the British Empire under one distinctive title, they passed one sweeping clause, applicable to them all. But the effect of measures applicable to all colonies without distinction was that the English Parliament, at the instance of the Colonial Office, and in its disregard and inattention to colonial affairs, passed measures which really it had no constitutional right to pass at all because the English Parliament had already surrendered that power to the representatives of the people in these colonies. He did not believe that the English Parliament had any design or intention of interfering with their rights, but simply in its indifference, in its absorption in Imperial domestic?* affairs, it paid no attention to these colonial Bills. The result was that the Colonial Office could propose any Bill it pleased in relation to colonial affairs, and it was passed.

The second means of Imperial interference, 'its chief interference, the interference we have most to complain of' was the interference by instructions addressed to the Governor. These were the instructions, given the Governor under Royal sign-manual before assuming his office, for the entire period of his government.

The third were those sent to him by despatch.

It was Higinbotham's conviction that these instructions, 'except so far as they are authorized by terms of express legislation, are beyond the power of the Secretary of State to give.'

He drew these conclusions about the effects of this state of affairs on government and on popular attitudes to government in the colony:

We all know, though we don't like to say it, that responsible government does not exist. We don't govern ourselves, and we know it. We are all ashamed of it, though we don't dare to say it. The same sense of a want of respect extends from us to our constituents, and I believe that in time it will tend to degrade the national character, by extending this sense of shame and want of respect for our Constitution.

If *saeva indignatio* caused Higinbotham to overstate his case, he had nevertheless a case to state. He presented an incisive analysis of the bureaucracy in relation to any Secretary of State for the Colonies who, he pointed out, could not possibly be acquainted with the wants, interests, institutions and feelings of the forty-three colonies over which he was said to preside. If the minister only reigned, who, then,

*It would seem that Higinbotham here used *imperial* in the older sense, so that 'absorption in Imperial affairs', would signify *domestic* affairs. The distinction is important. See also above: 'colonies and colonial possessions *of* the British Empire.'

ruled? His answer included the phrase about Sir Frederic Rogers which was to become common coinage in Australia:

I believe it might be said with perfect truth that the million and a half of Englishmen who inhabit these colonies, and who during the last fifteen years have believed they possessed self-government, have been really governed during the whole of that time by a person named Rogers. He is the chief clerk in the Colonial Office. Of course he inspires every Minister who enters the department, year after year, with Colonial Office traditions, Colonial Office policy, Colonial Office ideas. His views form the law for his chief, while the chief writes in imperious, and almost imperial style, to the representative of the Crown in the colonies, and the representative of the Crown - the agent of the Colonial Office - rules over this very patient people.

Higinbotham continued with a peroration:

If we are free, let us have the rights of freedom under the form of Government which exists by law. If we are not free, then I say the sooner we cast off the obligations of an apparent freedom, and cast upon England the general obligation to govern us and to defend us, the better for us all.

In order to put an end to the malpractices which he had denounced, Higinbotham proposed an insistence upon direct correspondence between the colonial ministers and their British counter-parts, together with a complete refusal to deal in any other way, except in respect of reference of bills. His proposal amounted to civil disobedience within the law, by administrative or, as Higinbotham would have preferred, diplomatic means. He contended that the temporary 'suspension of diplomatic relations between these two countries' would hurt the colony little but would soon lead to the asking of some pertinent question in the House of Commons, the answer to which would reveal that the difficulty arose from the fact that the British ministers 'really could not find it in their hearts . . . to communicate with their brother ministers in the colonies . . . An answer of this kind would not be given without immediate renewal of diplomatic relations.' But, if it did not; if the British government were to instruct the governor to dismiss his advisers, the suspension would become permanent for no others would then be found 'who could be endured in office': Higinbotham's intellectual daring was based on his deep faith in parliamentary stability.

For Higinbotham, there was another aspect to this struggle for full self-government. He wished to safeguard the future relations between Australia and the mother country and, for this reason, it seemed essential to him that the government of this country should assert its rights. His one fear was that in one or two generations there would be millions of Australians without 'the feeling of kindred' of his own generation. They would not only be estranged and alien from the mother country, but hostile and inimical. It was to prevent such an unhappy consequence that the rights of both countries had to be adjusted:

I believe that by these resolutions . . . we shall be doing something more than merely establishing our liberties and rights; I believe we shall be establishing the rights and liberties of these Australian colonies.

Significant opposition to the Higinbotham resolutions did not come from the conservatives. It came from Charles Gavan Duffy who had the distinction of being the only Victorian parliamentarian to have held, and resigned, a seat in the House of Commons where he had represented Irish peasant interests. He had arrived in Australia in 1855 and was elected to the Victorian parliament in the following year. There, he began his career with the successful introduction of a Bill to abolish the property qualification for parliamentary candidates. His major political interests were land reform and federation of which he was an early advocate. He became a Minister in 1857, and Premier of Victoria in 1871, holding that office for a year, which was then something of an achievement, in view of the fragile condition of Victorian majorities. In 1880, he retired from colonial politics, to live on the French Riviera, where he died, after a fruitful further career as an historical writer and political commentator, in 1903.

Gavan Duffy was one of the major figures of nineteenth-century public life in Victoria, though he never lost his European roots. That fact stands out in the arguments he advanced in opposition to Higinbotham's second resolution, on 22 December 1869.*

To Gavan Duffy that resolution implied, firstly, that the half million of people in Victoria should declare that they were able and willing to maintain a war with such a nation as France, or such a nation as America: 'that proposition needs only to be stated to answer itself.' His second objection was:

That we shall pledge our lives and fortunes in a quarrel with any nation that the Foreign Minister of England thinks proper to go to war with, without the slightest relation to us . . . the proposal to hold us responsible for wars . . . over

* see page 30

the commencement, duration, or termination of which we have not the slightest influence - is a proposal to give up what is infinitely more important than any part of our local liberties or rights.[42]

Gavan Duffy claimed that 'all the wars that living man has seen in which England was engaged were the reverse of defensive wars.' They had been entered into with objects and designs with which 'the democratic people of this country would not have the slightest sympathy, such as the war which resulted in English colonies constituting themselves into the United States.' The next war in which England had been engaged, was a war 'to suppress democratic government in France.' He predicted that there might be a war in the near future as a result of probable French aggression in Belgium: 'Nothing is more certain than that England would interpose . . . because Antwerp is considered a menace to England if in the hands of an enemy.' This was a reasonable prognostication in 1869, even though the events of the following year disproved it: for, as a result of the Franco-Prussian war, Belgian neutrality came to be strengthened rather than weakened. He also considered war between Great Britian and Russia 'in the highest degree possible', as a result of Russian penetration of Persia for, should Russia take Afghanistan, the British Empire in India would be at her mercy. He asked:

But are the people in this colony to risk all that is dear to them in order to prevent Russia penetrating into Persia? I do not object that we should take our our full share of responsibility; but what I do object and refuse to do is to declare that we are perfectly prepared at our sole cost, and with our unaided force, to take our share in contests engaged in from interests wholly apart from our colonial interests, the beginning and the end of which are beyond our control.

Duffy proposed a negotiated arrangement, like that which Hanover had with England, when she was under the same Crown, whereby she was secured from engaging in war with any of the German states, because she had certain relations with the German Empire:

In the same way, I take it that the colonies of England might by negotiation, through the mother country with the great powers, have an international law agreed to by which the colonies - outlying states like this, practically independent, being connected with the mother country simply by the tie of the Crown - might not be considered necessarily engaged in hostilities with powers [with] which England went to war, unless the colonies voluntarily chose to associate themselves in the contest.[43]

These were intellectually and politically daring proposals and, though Gavan Duffy's opposition to Higinbotham's second resolution failed, they led to the establishment, in the following year of the *Royal Commission on Federal Union*, under the chairmanship of Gavan Duffy. In its first, and only, *Report*, he developed his ideas on neutrality anticipating the link between the concepts of federalism and neutrality very like that which was to play such an important role in the theoretical foundation of Edgar Bonjour's History of Swiss Neutrality.[44] The *First Report* of Duffy's Royal Commission is reprinted in the Appendix.*

Full sovereignty was slow to come and slower to be exercised in Australia; but the effects of the Higinbotham resolutions were to be apparent within five years, when Lord Carnarvon was considering the re-introduction of Imperial troops into the Australian colonies. Colonial conservatives had viewed the withdrawal with trepidation, and they charged the government with disloyalty to the mother country, for failing to make arrangements with the Imperial government for the retention of British troops. Thus, T.H. Fellows, Higinbotham's major conservative antagonist, in the Legislative Assembly on 16 June 1870:

No doubt there are members anxious to cut the last connexion between this colony and the mother country. At any rate, they are anxious that there should only be a nominal alliance without any reality. I regard the removal of the troops as one of the first steps towards accomplishing that fact.[45]

The Chief Secretary, Sir James McCulloch, pin-pointed the position of the nationalist radicals in his reply:

Our ambition should be to raise up, from amongst ourselves, a force that shall defend and protect our colony without our being obliged to look for our defences from persons outside, and without being dependent upon them for conditions which we have already stated we will not consider.[46]

There was, however, by 1870, another view of international life, based on an uncompromising opposition to war. It was expressed in the Victorian Parliament by the member for North Melbourne, J.G. Burtt, who objected to 'state aid to soldiers as much as . . . to state aid to religion,' not as an enemy of Christianity but as a Christian pacifist:

I believe not in the sword of man; I believe not in the over-running of right by might; I believe not in the making of widows and orphans and the waste of blood and treasure for the gratification of human ambition. I hold that war and the preparation for war are things altogether alien to the civilization of the nineteenth century; and if such a thing as a tax were imposed in this country for the maintenance of any warlike force - whether regulars, militia or volunteers - [I] would rather submit to imprisonment than pay a single penny for such a purpose.[47]

* Document No. 3

By 1870, then, the major Australian attitudes to the world were taking shape. The major positions in the debate of the next one hundred years had been taken.

THE CARNARVON PROPOSALS.

In 1874, the British Conservatives, more especially the Earl of Carnarvon, once again at the Colonial Office, attempted to undo what the Liberals had done. On 15 December of that year, he sent a despatch to Sir Hercules Robinson, then Governor of New South Wales, under cover of a private note in which he emphasized the 'very confidential nature' of his proposal '. . . also written so as to leave you free to show or read it in confidence to any of the leading men in New South Wales with whom you may think it expedient to communicate'.[48] In the despatch covered by this note, Lord Carnarvon stressed that he had always regretted the withdrawal of the troops from the Australian colonies 'and perhaps not less the manner in which that withdrawal took place'. He was now thinking of permanently stationing a regiment 'of say 500-600 men' in the colony which would, in his view, have 'an influence for good' and in a 'visible manner set up an external symbol of Empire'. But before making the attempt he would need to feel that he had 'the concurrence not only of the present government of New South Wales but of all other leading men on both sides of the House'.

The Governor asked Henry Parkes, then out of office, for his views which Parkes set down in a long letter - a document not only of the new radical nationalism but of a great deal that has remained valid on questions of stationing supporting forces abroad. It is significant that Parkes, in considering that problem, consistently referred to the British troops in question as 'their' forces, in strong contrast to the 'us' and 'our forces' that prevailed in conservative speeches on the Empire until well into the twentieth century.

Parkes feared that the mere annual expense of maintaining a regiment of infantry, or any equivalent of the Imperial forces, would be made a question of chronic public discussion renewed at every general election. It followed that a parliamentary majority under financial pressure might abrogate the agreement.

Parkes looked at the sources of discord between the colonial population and these forces: 'The unpopularity of the officer in command, or one or two flagrant instances of misconduct . . . would manifest itself in turmoil with which British authority would be associated.' This, he felt, could not tend to strengthen the Imperial connection.

Moreover, Parkes was frankly doubtful about the promise not to remove these forces 'in a season of national trouble'. He foresaw a hundred reasons for this: 'I do not see how any condition could be made which in the nature of things could be or ought to be binding in the unseen future.'

Parkes then launched into a discussion of some length, dealing with political principle and historical development:

In my judgment the step taken by the Imperial government in withdrawing the troops a few years ago was one of such national significance for both countries and has had too abiding an effect on the rapidly-developing character of the Australian communities to be now retraced.

He saw in it the acknowledgement by Great Britain not simply of the colonies' political freedom, but of their complete power to provide for themselves: it was the removal of the last symbol of Imperial authority in the management of Australian affairs.

Parkes admitted that the colony had not all at once succeeded in military organization, and he also conceded that 'persons of influence in the colony will be found to favour Lord Carnarvon's suggestions'. But he doubted 'that they would find the means of carrying them into effect'. He placed reliance on the ability of the colony to defend itself and, moreover, '. . . in another ten years these colonies will unitedly possess the numbers and all the elements of strength of a powerful State'. By 1875, Parkes was looking to federation.

But he did not conclude on this note. There were some further practical arguments to consider. Money would be spent mainly for the defence of Sydney and Melbourne; but the remote country districts and large inland towns, already jealous of any expenditure confined to the capitals (characterized as extravagant and useless) would be sure to object. Moreover: 'how could the troops be distributed among the widely-separated seaport cities with limited populations along the extensive seaboard of Queensland?'[49]

These problems did not disappear with the British troops.

Parkes was as aware of the decisive character of the change that had occurred as he was of the decisive character of his reply and he had this correspondence with the Governor printed in the Votes and

Proceedings in 1889, when he was pressing for federation.[50] The British correspondence is equally revealing. This episode depicts a turning point in the relations of both countries as well as in the debate.

Up to this point it was mainly a debate of colonies with Imperial governments of varying complexions. Now, it became a debate in Australia about Australia's relations with its Asian environment. In the last third of the nineteenth century, when imperialist competition reached hitherto unknown levels of intensity, it also attracted corresponding interest and concern in the Australian colonies where internal economic growth had begun to effect major social changes.

THE ASIAN ENVIRONMENT : FEARS AND ASSESSMENTS

The self-governing colonies of Australia now possessed defence forces but no foreign affairs power. It is hardly surprising that the old fears, combined with the new responsibilities led to a spate of enquiries dealing, by way of the defence issue, with estimates of real or pretended foreign dangers, as well as estimates of the cost of meeting them.

In 1876, the colonies, on the initiative of New South Wales, asked the British government to make a defence expert available, if possible Sir William Jervois. Jervois was a great military engineer. Between 1852 and 1855, he had designed and directed the fortification works at Alderney in the Channel, as a check on Cherbourg. It was the largest British defence project of the time and it led to his appointment as Assistant Inspector-General of Fortifications in the War Office, where he spent nearly twenty years. For most of this time - from 1857 to 1875 - he was also the Secretary of the Empire Defence Committee, and he had been Secretary of the Royal Commission on National Defence of 1859, leading to the legislation of the following year which resulted in the large new fortifications of the British coast, harbours and estuaries. Jervois' career included advice and planning of fortifications in many parts of the Empire - Malta, Gibraltar, British North America, Bermuda, India and Burma.

In 1875, he succeeded Sir Andrew Clarke - another Royal Engineer - as Governor of the Straits Settlements. Jervois' government in Singapore included the period of the so-called Perak War, a punitive action resulting from the murder of Mr J.W.W. Birch, the British resident of Perak. For this action, Jervois obtained forces from India as well as from Hongkong. Lord Carnarvon had been emphatic that the sole purpose of the action was to bring the culprits to justice: there was to be no extension of British responsibilities and the action was not to be a cover for a 'forward movement'. Carnarvon suspected that Jervois had cried 'wolf' rather too loudly, by obtaining more troops - and causing greater expense - than was necessary. These views found forceful and clear expression in despatches to Jervois.[51]

In the eyes of the Colonial Office, Australia would therefore be a more suitable scene for Jervois' undoubted ability.[52] He arrived in Australia in 1877 and, in October of that year, he became Governor of South Australia, an office which he held until 1883, when he became Governor of New Zealand. He investigated and reviewed the defence problems of the colonies with meticulous care, and a great deal of zeal, making numerous speeches and reports, and he succeeded in the adoption of many of his proposals. He delivered his *Preliminary Report on Defence, New South Wales* in 1877, in an atmosphere of renewed and heightened insecurity, due to suspicions about French colonial designs in Asia and the Pacific. On this occasion, Jervois discounted the likelihood of *major* actions against the Australian colonies. In the event of Great Britain being engaged with any of the great naval powers, the enemy would retain the most powerful portion of his fleet in European waters, or in the Atlantic, for the protection of his country or for operations in the immediate neighbourhood of hostilities. If he sent his fleet, or any considerable portion of it, on an expedition against the Australian Colonies, a sufficient part of the Home fleet would in turn be set free to intercept it. But 'he might no doubt despatch one or more cruisers to operate against our maritime commerce, or make a descent upon any of our colonial possessions; and the Australian Colonies, owing to their wealth and prosperity, would, if undefended at certain points, be tempting objects of attack.'[53] These views were hardly original.

Jervois shared the views of earlier and less highly qualified men that small raids might be carried out against the Australian Colonies who, owing to their wealth and prosperity, would be vulnerable to even the limited aggression he envisaged. However, as sources of attack, he mentioned, in addition to Russian and American Pacific bases, 'the French port of Saigon'.[54]

Why Saigon? The Straits Settlements had been involved in the
diplomacy of the great powers as a result of the Franco-Annamite
Treaty of 15 March 1874, which gave France exclusive consular
jurisdiction over all aliens resident in Annam and special rights, especially in customs matters over the port of Saigon. Jervois' predecessor
in Singapore, Sir Andrew Clarke had been sent a copy of the terms of
that treaty and the objections made by the British Ambassador in
Paris to the Duc Decazes. After further despatches, including a cable
in cypher, Clarke had replied, also by cyphered cable and, then, with
a full despatch. In his view, the exclusive privileges and general scope
of the treaty were 'injurious to us and probably no gain to the
French'.[55] He had been careful to say that the memorandum submitted by the British Ambassador to the Duc Decazes 'anticipates
and exhausts the objections which in the interests of general Trade
and Commerce I would have to offer on behalf of this Colony against
the terms . . . securing . . . for France exclusive rights and privileges
which she would hesitate to deprive other Nationalities from enjoying in common with herself when trading on her own soil.'[56]
Clarke understood British policy - and the pitfalls of causing inter-
departmental misunderstanding.

Clarke had given the value of the trade from Singapore alone - he
had no figures for Penang or Malacca - as 550 thousand Straits dollars.
He added that 'it was in the hands of some twenty Chinese firms
resident here'. It was still being conducted 'in junks, although of
late two or more steamers have been employed'. Clarke concluded
his despatch by raising the question of the status of Annam in international law '- although doubtlessly it has not escaped the attention
of Her Majesty's Government - that the Kingdom of Annam is not,
as has been alleged, an independent State, but . . . a dependency of
the Empire of China' and, in Clarke's view, the treaties 'would be null
and void unless they also received the ratification of the Emper-
or of China'.

There is however an earlier document, a memorial from 'leading
British bankers and merchants' in Singapore to the Foreign Secretary
which Clarke had transmitted to the Colonial Office, with his explicit
support, on 21 December 1874. In it, the Foreign Secretary had been
asked to appoint a British Consul at Saigon in succession to the
retiring incumbent, a Mr Caswell. The memorial spoke of large
British interests - in the rice trade of Saigon to Singapore, Hong Kong

and Japan, much of the grain being carried in British vessels. Further, the cotton manufactures 'consumed in Cochin China are nearly all shipped from Singapore and we think the absence of a consul would materially discourage the extension of this business'.[57] No mention here of Chinese firms, or of junks, or of the French treaty providing for a French monopoly of consular jurisdiction. The Foreign Office met the request for a consul shortly after receiving that memorial. French rights in Annam were recognised in August 1875.

That episode illuminates a good deal of the workings of the Empire and of the imperialist rivalries: what is stated or left unsaid in one situation and, in particular, the competence of Imperial governors in using the knowledge and experience gained in one colony, for a very different purpose, in another.

What Clarke had seen as an economic threat to Singapore, was interpreted by Jervois as a military threat to Australia. According to him, a squadron intended for such an operation as a limited attack on British colonial possessions, might consist of some three or four vessels, one or two of which would probably be armoured. It might issue from 'the Russian ports of Vladivostok or Petropaulovski, from the French port of Saigon, from San Francisco, or from some other quarter. Eluding our cruisers, and appearing suddenly [*sic*] before Sydney, Melbourne, Adelaide, or in Moreton Bay,' it might capture the merchant vessels lying in the harbours; intercept any of the numerous vessels conveying valuable shipments of gold; or under threat of bombardment, or after actually firing into one of the large towns, demand and obtain a payment of 'many millions of money'.

Jervois' appraisal tended, like most of his speeches and writing in the Australian colonies, to heighten their fear of being at the wrong end of gun-boat diplomacy. It involved highly debatable strategic assumptions, and some special pleading. Nevertheless, this passage does summarise various elements in colonial defence thinking which elsewhere often appeared in isolation. Jervois' hypothetical aggressors were the potential enemies of Great Britain at that time. He envisaged attacks launched from their Asian or Pacific bases. Jervois captured the long-standing colonial fear of being held to ransom for its ill-protected wealth, and its sense of isolation in an environment that seemed largely alien and hostile.

Another of the many enquiries into defence problems sat in Sydney in 1881. Concern for security had remained unmatched by a commensurate desire to pay for it. It may also have been motivated by the prestige attached to the new colonial defence responsibilities, unmatched though these were by a foreign affairs power. Enquiries seemed to become a substitute for action.

The *Military Defences Inquiry Commission* of 1881, was a Royal Commission chaired by the Chief Justice of New South Wales, its vice-president being Colonel Scratchley, who had come out with Jervois.

This commission was the scene for the juxtaposition of colonial fears expressed by some officer witnesses, and a rather more sober assessment by others, especially by Commodore J.C. Wilson. Through his secretary, he had presented a detailed memorandum to the commission, followed by his oral evidence.[58] By way of introduction Wilson had considered what enemy forces these colonies were likely to encounter. He added that it was almost superfluous to say that this paper was written under the suggestion that England retained her command of the seas, for were she to lose it, it would follow that the colonies would go too, and the defence and force required in that case to maintain independence of a foreign power would necessarily be totally different.

Wilson had basically the same potential enemies in mind as Jervois - Russia, the United States and France - but Wilson's list of ports likely to be a source of attack did not include Saigon. He confined himself to

Petropauloski, a distance from Melbourne of 5,900 miles
San Francisco,   "   "   "   6,800 miles
New Caledonia,   "   "   "   1,550 miles.

He remarked that New Caledonia 'need hardly be included, as no armament of any strength could be prepared or assembled without the knowledge of the colonies'. Once again, the possible enemies were those of Great Britain, reflected in the Asian-Pacific areas. By omitting Saigon and discounting New Caledonia, their number had, in fact, shrunk to two.

Commodore Wilson, moreover, considered that the only probable attack on the colonies would be by armed merchantmen. Questioned by the Commission, he most emphatically scotched any ideas of invasion. He began by stressing facts that apparently needed stressing - the nature of Britain's naval supremacy: 'For every cruiser that Russia could have sent to sea, we could send fifty. There is no such thing as want of vessels in England.'

The Commission was, however, determined to press its own concepts resulting in this dialogue: ꝓλ

COMMISSION: Do you think it possible for Russia, from the Amoor, or for America, from San Francisco, to send speedily a force large enough to land 5,000 men?

WILSON: Perfectly impossible, because the vessels could not carry coal. I doubt whether the Orient steamers could steam here, with ordinary bunkers, 6,000 miles, at full speed.

COMMISSION: How many vessels would be required to land a force of 5,000 men - bearing in mind the large transports nations have?

WILSON: It depends entirely upon the circumstances. France would send them over in three ships. One of our Indian troopships carries 1,200 men.

COMMISSION: Five of those, then, would be required?

WILSON: Yes; but that has no reference to artillery and cavalry, I think they could not possibly be carried in less than ten ships, and then you must have a covering squadron.

COMMISSION: Suppose they did not care about cavalry or artillery; say that they wanted to make a dash at Sydney, that they landed at Botany or Broken Bay and made a rapid march to Sydney - could it be done?

WILSON: All kinds of things could be done, but I think it would be as difficult as storming the moon. How could it be done without a covering fleet to protect them? If I knew that troopships were outside without a covering fleet, and you gave me a vessel like the 'Rotumahama', I would go and ram the lot of them without the necessity of firing a shot. There is no regular man-of-war that can steam 2,500 miles at full speed, the consumption of coal is so enormous; and that is the groundwork upon which I say that as long as England retains command of the seas attacks in force on these Colonies are impracticable. If you put six or eight inches of plate on a ship's side she cannot carry coal. She cannot carry the weights inside and outside too.

Wilson put forward a thoroughly professional appreciation of the new logistics dictated by coal-fired, and armour-plated, steam-ships. He showed that the presence or absence of coaling stations would largely determine the range of a nation's activities throughout Asian and Pacific waters. That his thoughtful and succinct appraisal went well beyond the conventions of professional naval expertise, emerges from later passages in his evidence where he relates defence policy to social structure:

In new countries, such as Australia and New Zealand, where all are hard-working men, struggling with nature for a livelihood, the presence of a permanent armed force supported out of their earnings, was always distasteful, not from any lack of military ardour, but from the feeling that such forces were living in comparative idleness, and not adding by their labours to the common weal. Such being the case, it was as well, in my opinion, whatever may be argued on the other side, at once to bow to and recognise as a fact, that a Permanent Military or Naval Force cannot under the present circumstances and condition of these Colonies, flourish.

Wilson recommended light, mobile forces based on gunboats and a certain number of torpedo boats for harbour defence rather than heavier 'ironclads' which would be expensive and would lead to 'centralising too much the defensive power'. He also recommended a Colonial Seagoing Defence Force of armed merchant vessels acting in concert with the Royal Navy Squadron for the defence of trade and exposed towns on the sea-coast.

Wilson stressed that confederation of 'all the Colonies on this Station, or even those belonging to Australia, including Tasmania, on the subject before us' would result in enormous savings and even greater advantages in efficiency and power. He was careful to confine his remarks to the matter under discussion, i.e. defence. He did not discuss political federation. He was also insistent in recommending a voluntary force. In Commodore Wilson's view, the instincts of the people were opposed to standing forces, but they appeared, on the other hand, to be singularly partial to the semi-military, such as their volunteers.

Wilson was not against 'a certain percentage of permanent force, especially of permanent artillery. You must always have a nucleus of good gunners in your valuable fortifications, and also [to] take care of plant in peace time.' Wilson believed the Commission should recognise that Australian colonies were so far removed from European complications that a tendency would always be shown to cut down the standing force, especially when there was a calm for a few years.

Now the Commission began to worry about the effect of defence measures on their pockets and convenience. They asked the Commodore whether he did not think 'that taking away men for a month's training would interfere with the working of the civil institutions here?' 'Well,' said he, 'it is a question of pounds, shillings and pence.'

There had always been an unresolved contradiction between the desire for defence, and its cost and inconvenience. Gipps had foreseen it in 1840. FitzRoy had referred to it and so had Barney in 1854. The withdrawal of British troops in 1870 had been due to disagreements about cost as much as to the rise of national radicalism.

Commodore Wilson's evidence was followed by Colonel Downes of the Royal Artillery. He was a witness after the Commission's own heart. His views would appeal to colonial fears and the urge for importance. This is how Colonel Downes saw Australia's security problem, on 15 March 1881:

Before giving my views as to the . . . strength required I must give . . . my opinions upon which I consider are the dangers to which Sydney is exposed from the attack of land forces. There are only two nations by which Australia is . . . likely to be attacked, namely France and Russia.

Downes thought that the former would have as its base of operations Saigon, the latter, Vladivostok and other ports in the same seas. He gave a vivid description of the Russian danger, stating that he had relied on 'the papers' and on 'information one has been able to gather' as his sources. Russia had been greatly augmenting her powers of attack in those seas ostensibly in order to be prepared for hostilities with China. She had at her naval stations in the Pacific, vessels designed to carry one thousand to two thousand men. Downes made no serious attempt to evaluate Russian political aims or strategic potential.

He had also noticed that the Russian government was forming a Pacific Commercial Steam Company, similar to a company in the Black Sea. 'These steamers are to go at a rate of sixteen knots per hour [*sic*], they are to be constructed so that if necessary they can carry heavy guns; naturally they will carry a large number of men, and they are built of steel.' Downes was furthermore concerned - as a danger ot Australia - about the Russian military colonisation of Eastern Siberia:

Russia has especially during the last two or three years, endeavoured in every way to get military and naval settlers in considerable numbers on these settlements in the China Seas. With such means at her command, Russia, in the event of war, will be able to prepare with her usual secrecy, and schemes fully worked out beforehand, a powerful force to attack these colonies; and in my opinion our first intimation of such an attack, after declaration of war, would be by the arrival of such a force on our shores.

Downes ignored Commodore Wilson's evidence about the logistics of such an expedition, sailing from Northern Asia to Eastern Australia, unnoticed by anyone, concluding that 'the forces of these colonies must be prepared *at any instant* to meet a serious attack . . . particularly . . . Sydney, a position of such immense value . . .' He assumed an attack force of 2,000 to 3,000 men, 'probably the latter number could be more correct', with six to eight guns. On this basis he proposed at Sydney and its immediate proximity a force of

3,000 paid volunteers, one hundred mounted rifles, an engineer corps of one hundred, and three batteries of field artillery, each battery to be composed of six guns. Downes added 'I am aware that this proportion of artillery is far in excess of [that] . . . in European armies . . . the moral strength gained by having this additional number of guns will far more than compensate for the very slight disadvantage . . .'

Colonel Downes had no views about the major coaling port of Newcastle, just one hundred miles North of Sydney 'from want of knowledge of the locality.' As a result of Jervois' work, a fort was, in fact, then being constructed there. Downes understood that it would effectually prevent a landing.

Downes had a poor opinion of the Royal Navy which he dismissed in these words:

The question will naturally be asked, 'Do you take no account of the English navy?' In reply to this, I should say that such vessels of the English navy as might be on the coast would in all probability be drawn away by false rumour or by false attack made upon some other point of the colonies, or looking after cruisers.[59]

Here we have almost a laboratory amalgam of service rivalries, special pleading, colonial romanticism and particularism, seasoned by splendid logic. The views expressed by Downes reflected much of the colonial insecurity and the sort of romanticism which prefers imaginary dangers to insignificance. The Vice-President of this Commission, Colonel Scratchley, a distinguished officer who had come to Australia with Jervois, expressed views much like those of Downes, with the same vigour.

CODA : NO HORSES FOR INDIA

The Indian mutiny provided the first occasion involving representative government in Australia in a question of military aid abroad.

In response to a request from the Governor General of India for a regiment of infantry and a company of artillery, Denison arranged for the despatch of the 77th Regiment, due to depart from Sydney to Hong Kong, for Calcutta. He also sought and obtained the consent of the New South Wales government for the despatch of a company of artillery which was quartered at Sydney, and the government agreed to pay for the horses to fit the company for field service.

In Denison's words [60], the matter had been "alluded to" in his speech at the opening of the parliamentary session and, in the Address-in-Reply, the Assembly assured him that they would have been glad, if necessary, to contribute to the expense of forwarding the artillery to India.[61] When the government introduced the resolution for the vote enabling them to spend £3,600 on 150 horses, its reception by the House induced them to drop the matter.

They were told that it was "a vote in aid of the East India Company," which, said another member, was one of the wealthiest Governments, having "plenty of means for purchasing whatever horses it required." A third added that they were called upon to vote this sum, not in aid of the sufferers of the mutiny but simply in aid of the East India Company; and, added a fourth, "it was nothing more than a vote in favour of a huge corporation." These speakers showed a remarkable command of the facts and of the interrelations between them.

It is impossible to say whether hostility to the Hon. Company alone would have caused the defeat of that measure. It came in the wake of severe spending cuts and at least some of those in opposition felt that their constituents would not stand for such a donation while essential development could not proceed.[62]

When Gipps had decided to aid an Imperial position, he had no parliament to consider. Denison, however, thought it either necessary or prudent to consult his advisers, now responsible to a parliament, before moving an Imperial unit. Stanley's despatch of 11 March 1858, which removed all doubt on that score, was then on the water. Imperial refusal to share control led to the removal of the British units twelve years later. These developments were followed by a period of enquiry and, then, by foreign adventures which formed the prelude to the federation of the colonies at the end of the century.

The episode of the horses has its own significance. For the first time, a parliamentary government in Australia had offered support for an Imperial military venture; and its parliament refused to vote the necessary funds. In future, governments would send volunteers as well as equipment; they would not always go to Parliament before doing so; but they would take care to create the necessary atmosphere. 108 years were to pass before conscripts would be sent into battle in Asia.

Part Two: 1882–1900
Foreign Adventures and Federation

NEW GUINEA ANNEXATION FEVER :
PLANTERS' COLONIES OR FREE SOCIETY?

PROPOSALS for the importation of coolies from India and China arose in New South Wales in 1837, as soon as it became clear that the transportation of convicts from Great Britain would come to an end and, with it, an assured source of cheap manpower. One such proposal is reproduced in the Appendix*.

None of these schemes succeeded. However, a sizable immigration of Chinese took place during the gold rushes, leading to clashes of often tragic proportions, followed by diverse forms of exclusion and restrictive legislation in the various colonies. These matters have been covered in several good monographs.[1]

Attempts at Indian coolie immigration were revived, unsuccessfully, in Queensland, after its separation from New South Wales, in 1859. At separation, Queensland formed a self-governing colony of some 25,000 Europeans in a territory of 554,000 square miles.

Large stretches of land along the coast of Queensland seemed very suitable for the development of a plantation economy. The first Governor, Sir Charles Bowen had attempted to establish cotton-growing plantations when the cotton shortage, due to the American civil war, created an urgent demand at Manchester. Although cotton failed, sugar did not. In both cases, the assumption had been that cheap manpower from Asia and the Pacific Islands would be available.

After meeting Imperial objections of form, proposals for Indian coolie immigration were enacted in 1862. At Brisbane and Ipswich, in southern Queensland, workers petitioned against that legislation,[2] the Ipswich petition being remarkable for its intellectual vigour.

After the usual preliminaries, it began by stating that legislation of such importance to the future material interests and moral well-being - 'as the introduction of a Helot class of labourers into the Colony should have been reserved for the Royal Assent rather than

*Document No. 1

have been immediately assented upon by . . . the Governor of Queensland.' It proceeded to claim virtual violation of the Constitution and, further, that 'the majority of the Colonists of Queensland' were 'decidedly opposed to the introduction in the manner proposed of Hindoo labourers and residents, as foreign to our customs and policy and adverse to our best interests as a nascent country'. Their use of the term 'Helot class' reflects a social awareness far beyond the ethnocentric talk that has so often buried intelligent debate on this subject.

The petitioners further expressed fears that the proposed immigration would be the prelude to 'enormous and unbearable social evils and to frightful and devastating diseases . . . as proved by their prevalence in the Mauritius consequent upon their introduction of Coolie labour'.

 They dismissed the argument that coolies were required for the development of the tropical parts of Australia as special pleading, as shown by the 'house-building, road-making and other labourious pursuits being carried on in summer as well as winter in those very parts'.

Moreover, they said, cotton *had* been raised by 'European labour without the assistance of Coolies', two hundred bales of which were going to be sent that year from Queensland to Great Britain. Cotton-picking was neither arduous nor did it take place in the hottest period of the year.

But the rub was economic: 'That if Coolie labour were dearer than British, no thought of its employment would be for a moment entertained, it is therefore evident that the idea of cheapness is one that is dominant in the minds of those wishful to inundate the Colony with [it]'.

Here we might stop and marvel at the intellectual audacity of those Ipswich mechanics who argued, in 1862, in terms of social cost: the idea of cheapness, they said, was 'exceedingly erroneous, arrived at by merely counting the *prima facie* costs of such labour, without reckoning for its concommitants, such as special and appropriate education for Coolie children' - education for Coolie children? - 'increased police for the suppression of fearfully augmented vice, enlarged and fresh hospitals for the cure of diseases, some of which are fortunately unknown amongst us at present, - all of which when duly met, will shew Coolie labour to be doubly expensive as compared with British', not to mention the deterioration of the quality of the society: 'the presence of Coolies amongst us in great numbers would entail woes which no money can compensate'.

Finally, the petitioners pointed to the distress experienced in parts of Great Britain and urged large-scale immigration, assisted by 'the local and Imperial Governments'.

This extraordinary document, reproduced in the Appendix*, was forwarded together with the Petition of the Brisbane Mechanics Institute by Bowen to the Duke of Newcastle, on 18 July 1862.

The covering despatch occupies fourteen pages and, being complementary to the Petitions covered by it, it demands some attention.[3] In it the Governor assured the Lord Duke that no spectre was stalking Queensland: 'The Brisbane petition was presented to me by a deputation of respectable citizens and loyal subjects of the Queen, as indeed are all classes of the inhabitants of this Colony'. How he received the Ipswich petition, Bowen did not say. He did not feel that too much should be made of their arguments, claiming that he was 'informed on all sides that these and similar petitions [sic], are really got up by a few individuals, generally without any stake in the country, who seek to make political capital by trading on the prejudices of the mass of the working men in our towns . . .'

Deprecation of radical argument by this means was not original even in 1862, but it serves to establish the social significance of this debate. The Governor went on to spell out its economic character. These 'working men . . . now regard the introduction of Asiatic labour into Australia with feelings akin to those which the mass of the working men at home formerly regarded the introduction of machinery into England'.

But, Bowen assured the Colonial Secretary 'the more intelligent and far-seeing of the working classes and the whole body of employers perceive and acknowledge the material advantages which cannot fail to accrue both to the Colony and to the Mother-Country from the establishment here of large plantations of cotton and sugar, by the help of coloured labour, for the field work.' He said that all reasonable men of every side - thus excluding the petitioners - further admitted that if the resources of the vast intertropical districts of Queensland were to be developed at all, they had to be 'developed with the help

*Document No. 2

of Asiatics of some race . . .'

He argued that, 'if capitalists and trading companies are not permitted to introduce Indian labour under proper regulations and supervision' there would soon be worse to come and they would 'ere long
deluge Northern Australia with Chinese, Malays, Polynesians, Mela-
nesians, and hordes of other barbarians, under no regulations or
supervision whatever'.

Comment seems superfluous. I know of no document that
delineates the class interests in the debate on coolie immigration
more clearly.

It remains to indicate that in his reply, Newcastle, or, rather, Rogers
instructed Bowen to inform the Petitioners opposed to the employment of Asiatic labour in the colony that no sufficient grounds were
shown for depriving Queensland of a supply of Indian labour if the
community at large desired to have it - the local legislature being
the only exponent of the will of the community.[4]

Legislation did not lead to Indian coolie immigration into Queensland. The urban opposition seems to have been effective. The government offered land grants and export premiums for cotton growing
and it agreed to reserve public expenditure for the immigration of
Europeans. At the other end, neither the Manchester interests nor
the private planters would meet the full cost of indenting coolies
and nothing more was heard of that scheme for twenty years.

As Bowen had predicted, the failure of the coolie immigration
scheme led to the importation of large numbers of Pacific Islanders
as a work force for Queensland's plantations.

For the next twenty years, that labour supply seems to have been
adequate to the planters' needs. But by the 1880's, the combined
effects of more effective British supervision of the recruiting activities
in the Pacific and an expansion of the sugar industry due to rising
demand, resulted in a manpower shortage in the sugar industry. This
co-incided with a speculative proposal for the construction of a
'transcontinental railway', from the Charleville to the Gulf of Car-
penteria at Point Parker, to be built under the Railway Companies
Preliminary Act and run on private capital, financed on the land-
grant principle. The promoters of that scheme, known to contemporaries as the *syndicate*, had the support of the Premier of Queensland, Sir Thomas McIlwraith, himself a businessman with large
plantation interests in Queensland and elsewhere. Indeed, some of

his political opponents identified him closely with that syndicate. It was further claimed in the Queensland parliament that the transcontinental railway syndicate was pressing for a supply of cheap labour which, it was said, 'must inevitably result in reducing the wages at present paid to labouring men in this colony.'[5]

In these conditions, McIlwraith attempted to revive the 1862 legislation to import Indian coolies. There were also plans to import Chinese labourers. The considerations advanced by McIlwraith in favour of coolie immigration and his view of the society he hoped to develop in Queensland, are well reflected in his Roma speech of 1883, reprinted in the Appendix from the *Sugar Planter**. That journal carried, in the same issue, a warning by the Rev P. Macfarlane against attempts to obtain manpower from New Guinea:

I should be exceedingly sorry to see the 'traffic' begun and carried on in New Guinea as has been amongst the South Sea Islands.

That it might be conducted in a manner calculated to benefit both planters and natives was my firm conviction twenty years ago, publicly maintained against considerable opposition, and embodied in a 'leader' in the *S.M. Herald* after an evening spent with the editor. And this is till my opinion, whilst emphatically condemning the conduct of some of those engaged to procure labourers.

As to the prospect of obtaining 'hands' (as we should say in Manchester) from New Guinea, I fear 'the play would not be worth the candle'. A vessel might sail along a New Guinea coast-line of a thousand miles without getting fifty volunteers for the plantations in Queensland. In the Papuan Gulf, and along the banks of the Fly river, the natives are numerous but wild and treacherous. Those in Torres Straits and the adjacent New Guinea coast who can be induced to work for foreigners, are employed by pearl shellers and beche-de-mer fishers. Along the coast of the S.E. peninsula they are more tractable, unwilling to leave home. In the vicinity of China Straits, where we have a prosperous mission conducted by native evangelists from Maré and Lifu the natives have begun to manifest a disposition to see the white man's country. Some are engaged in beche-de-mer vessels and have visited Cooktown. A few might be induced to go to Queensland from the S.E. peninsula, and if treated kindly would bring back a good report of the land, which would probably lead others to go. Thus, as I said twenty years ago, the thing would right itself if the natives were legitimately obtained. However, I cannot advise you to risk any expenditure in attempting, at present, to get labour from New Guinea.

The planters' interest in manpower 'recruited' in New Guinea was linked to the demand for the annexation of non-Dutch New Guinea, on the familiar grounds of forestalling some other power.

*Document No. 4

That proposal was advanced in the eighteen-seventies and the British view then was that, since the main beneficiaries of annexation would be the Australian colonies, they should meet the cost, then estimated at £15,000 a year. This the colonies would not do and opinion was divided, even in Queensland. That had been the situation between 1874 and 1882, when rumours of foreign interest in New Guinea were revived. McIlwraith offered the Colonial Office aid in taking possession of it, and in meeting the expense of administration.

Without awaiting a reply from Whitehall, he then instructed the Queensland police magistrate at Thursday Island to take possession of New Guinea and 'adjoining islands' from 141° to 155° East, well into the Solomons: latitudes were not specified, other than Netherlands New Guinea. The Union Jack was hoisted at Port Moresby on 4 April 1883. It should be added that the Queensland parliament was not in session and when it was recalled on 27 June 1883, McIlwraith confessed that he had delayed its meeting for fear of the Opposition criticism weakening his hand, if not defeating his government.[7]

The news of the attempted annexation reached London twelve days later, where it had a mixed reception. The colonies, although self-governing, did not possess a foreign affairs power. The British government could, and did, disallow this annexation. Although Gladstone - who was then in office - was opposed to it, the answer was by no means a foregone conclusion, and its formulation took almost three months.

Gladstone's opposition to this adventure was strengthened by the views of his old friend Sir Arthur Gordon, then High Commissioner for the Western Pacific who, at that time, happened to be in England. Gordon had been instrumental in making the restrictions on the 'labour trade' more effective. He shared Gladstone's opposition to Imperial enlargements; and he wrote to him on 20 April 1883, when the news came to be known. Gordon considered the annexation, under any terms, 'somewhat immoral; because we shall, without the consent of these people, take from them their independence, and I fear . . . other and perhaps even dearer rights . . .'[8] Gordon was especially hostile to the proposed annexation by Queensland: 'In no case do I think the rule of a vast native population can be safely entrusted to a small, and for the most part ignorant, and selfish oligarchy, of another race, having interests directly opposed to those of the natives themselves.

But there is a special unfitness in the case of Queensland . . .' which Gordon summarized under three headings.

First, there was the inability of the Queenslanders to distinguish between Queensland aborigines and New Guineans. The former were nomadic 'without laws, property, or agriculture' whilst the latter lived in settled agricultural communities, looked to their property rights and built well-made houses. Gordon did not think that Queenslanders were likely to respect any facets of their civilisation.

His second reason, worth quoting in full, concerned Queensland attitudes to non-Europeans:

The habit of regarding the natives as vermin, to be cleared off the face of the earth, has given the average Queenslander a tone of brutality and cruelty in dealing with 'blacks', which it is very difficult for anyone who does not *know* it, as I do, to realize. I have heard men of culture and refinement, of the greatest humanity and kindness to their fellow whites, and who when you meet them here at home you would pronounce to be incapable of such deeds, talk, not only of wholesale *butchery* (for the inequity of *that* may sometimes be disguised for themselves), but of the *individual* murder of natives, exactly as they would talk of a day's sport, or of having had to kill some troublesome animal. This is not the spirit in which to undertake the government of native races. (Gordon's emphases.)

Gordon's third point concerned the 'labour trade' which, in his view, should not be left to the sole regulation by the Queensland Parliament. He wrote:

The chief industries of Queensland require black labour . . . It is imported from various islands and groups in the Pacific. There are, at present, restrictions on its introduction; and the appointment . . . of a Committee of which I am a member, has created a not ill-founded alarm that the imposition of yet more stringent precautions against kidnapping and other abuses will be recommended. If New Guinea becomes a part of Queensland . . . the labour trade along the shores of New Guinea will be a coasting trade, with which no Imperial legislation can interfere and no Imperial authority can supervise, or check. Whether those who are directly interested in the employment of immigrant native labour are those to whom the regulation of its introduction can be most fitly committed I need not ask.

Gordon also showed something of the paternalism of this Liberal view, in asking Gladstone not to depart from the 'most wholesome precedent - that where large bodies of natives, and a small number of whites are brought together' their government should be directly responsible to the Imperial government 'and able to bear itself impartially between conflicting interests'.[9]

There was a mixture of motives in the colonies as there was in London. The planters wanted a regular supply of manpower free from the impediments which British supervision in the Pacific involved. It is likely that the enthusiastic support which McIlwraith received from the Victorian government led by James Service, was not unconnected with existing Melbourne financial interests in the Queensland sugar industry. Fears of imperialist competition and strategic fears also played a part. It is noteworthy that Alexander Stuart's government of New South Wales took a rather more detached view than either Service or McIlwraith. These differences seem to have reflected the state of vocal public opinion, as well as divergent economic interests among the colonies.

On 13 June 1883, Service submitted the draft of a cable to Stuart which Service wished to send to the Victorian Agent General in London if Stuart took similar action. It reflects a particular outlook of that time: 'Pacific Islands annexation or protectorate necessary for Australian future. Colonies willing contribute expense. In interests of natives British philanthropists should support; England should do for Australia what Australia cannot do for self. Great dissatisfaction if England fails to secure our future.'[10] Agitation for annexation of the New Hebrides, the Solomon Islands, and possibly other islands, had been mixed up with Queensland's attempted annexation of New Guinea. In fact, five days before, on 8 June, Stuart had cabled his Agent General to urge the 'Imperial Government's occupation as infintely preferable to risk of foreign; but we have no knowledge here of any foreign movement being imminent.'[11] The rider is the more important, as Service, in Melbourne, had claimed to have a credible report 'that *French occupation is imminent* and will be accomplished unless prompt action be taken'.[12]

Lord Derby announced the disallowance in the House of Lords on 2 July 1883 in reply to a motion 'for further papers, relating to the proposed annexation of New Guinea,' moved, from the opposition benches by Lord Lamington. It is worthy of remark that his views were not dissimilar to Gordon's, whom he quoted with approval. Lamington also referred to Commodore Wilson who was close to Gordon and in whose view 'it would, undoubtedly, be best entirely to stop what is known as the Polynesian labour traffic.' Lord Lamington went on:

It is said that New Guinea had iron mines, gold mines, and so on; but was that a good argument for annexing it? The same kind of argument might be used for breaking into a rich man's house.[13]

He hoped that the government were not disposed to sanction this policy of annexation. But the Earl of Carnarvon, among others, took the opposite view, in support of the colonial annexationists:

When the question was raised in 1876, he [i.e. Carnarvon] as Colonial Secretary, had no fear of the action of any Foreign Power; the Government had taken the precaution to satisfy themselves; they stated so publicly, and their confidence was justified by the results; but a great change had occurred since that time. It was impossible for us to shut our eyes, and still more for the Australian Colonists, to whom this was a matter of life and death, to shut their eyes to the recent action of France, whose rulers had publicly proclaimed their desire to have a Colonial policy, and who were taking action in Tahiti, the Congo, Tonquin, Madagascar, and possibly other parts of the world. The establishment of a Penal Colony by France or any other Power on the Southern Coast of New Guinea would be simply an intolerable nuisance, and the establishment of an armed fort would be a menace to the Australian Colonies. Torres Straits would cease to be English territory, and the result would be to throw an enormous military burden on the Australian Colonies.[14]

In his reply, the Earl of Derby, who seemed to have enjoyed 'the interesting conversation which has been carried on on the other side of the Table', praised the recently established system.

Giving to the Agents General for the self-governed Colonies what I may call a *quasi*-diplomatic character and position [which] has made it much more easy than it formerly was for any person holding the Office which I have the honour to hold to obtain accurate and constant information as to the opinion which prevails in the Colonies themselves on local matters.

Derby was not, however, prepared to discuss generalities about the desirability of annexations or whose responsibility they ought to be. He continued with the words that were to become famous - if occasionally misunderstood. They were not those of a little Englander:

Speaking generally, I should say - and I think it is the universal feeling of this country - that our responsibilities are already heavy enough, that our Possessions, scattered, as they are, over every part of the world, are sufficient to require the utmost care and vigilance, and that it is not desirable to increase either the one or the other.[15]

Lord Derby opposed the view that 'a colony should be left free in its external policy'. There was a wide difference between this and the administration of its internal affairs:

Whatever a Colony does with regard to its own affairs affects principally - indeed almost exclusively - those by whom the legislation is undertaken. But when you come to the question of external policy and of annexation, or of extension, other considerations come in, since the annexation even of an island in the Pacific may raise a question of foreign policy in which the Imperial Government is very deeply concerned. I do not think, therefore, it can be denied that questions of this kind are questions on which the Imperial Government ought to have, as it actually has, a controlling power.[16]

As for Lord Carnarvon's argument about French designs, 'it seemed to me to cut both ways and rather tell against his case than in favour of it':

If the French Government, whether with or without the will of the French people, have already undertaken two considerable Colonial expeditions, and, in all probability, have involved themselves in two Colonial wars, that is about as good a security as we could have that they will be not in a hurry to have a third complication of the same kind on their hands.[17]

Lord Derby chided Queensland for failing to ask for Imperial sanction by cable for their so-called act of annexation which would not have involved a delay of more than twenty-four hours. He felt that they seemed to have entertained 'a reasonable apprehension that the sanction they asked for would not be granted'. The effect of the action of the Governor of Queensland was simply null, his authority being territorially limited and since New Guinea was not a newly-discovered country, possession by right of discovery could not be claimed either. And, 'we are not prepared to undertake the annexation of New Guinea'.[18]

Lord Derby supported his decision with some of Gordon's arguments but he left the door ajar:

If . . . anything is to be done in the way of conquering and administering New Guinea, one thing is clear - that it must be done by the Imperial Government, or by the Australian Colonies acting together, or by both those agencies combined. New Guinea is too important to be made the Dependency of any Colony. I can quite understand the Australian feeling as to the Coast of New Guinea being a country which lies within the scope of British influences and interests. I purposely use vague and general language; but undoubtedly we should not view it as a friendly act if any other country attempted to make a settlement on that Coast.[19]

Of the fear of aggression so often expressed in Australia, Lord Derby thought that they underrated their own powers and their own importance. But he accepted as a fact the view that these fears were 'a general opinion . . . among a great majority' - which, on

Gordon's estimate, they were not.

Lord Derby advised the Administrator of Queensland on 11 July:

Her Majesty's government . . . are unable to approve the proceedings of your government in this matter. It is well understood that the officers of a colonial government have no power or authority to act beyond the limits of their colony, and if this constitutional principle is not observed serious difficulties and complications must arise.[20]

Had there been any evidence of an intended foreign threat 'the views and proposals of the colonial government could have been placed before Her Majesty's government by telegraph' and if the circumstances had really justified immediate action it could have been taken without a delay of more than a very few hours. It was therefore regretted that the Queensland government should, without apparent necessity, have taken on themselves the exercise of powers which they did not possess. The British government was, moreover, convinced as a result of its own enquiries that no foreign power was about to establish itself on the shores of New Guinea, and there did not seem sufficient reason to believe that a white, lawless population would establish itself from Australia in the island.

In any case, the British government did not see any justification for occupying the whole island, even if there were reasons for securing its shores, since it was certain that the large population 'of whom little or nothing is known . . . has given no sign of a desire that their land should be occupied by white men. It would require exception- ally strong reasons to justify the annexation of these tribes and their territory'. In the absence of these, a grave responsibility would be incurred to do this to 'a large coloured population which would certainly resist subjugation and has apparently nothing to gain by it'.

It was evident that Gordon's letter to Gladstone had had its effect. There was more to come. Even if it had been shown that the extension of the Queen's sovereignty to eastern New Guinea had become necessary, the proposal that it should form part of the colony of Queensland would be open to strong objections. The colony already comprised an immense territory. The capital lay a thousand miles from the southern part of New Guinea; it was governed 'by a Parliament which represents the white population, whose interests are altogether different from those of the coloured races, aboriginal and imported, within the colony'. It was known that there had been difficulties with the labour traffic and other questions affecting native interests and these had 'often of late been the subject of much comment'.

Lord Derby's reference to the sugar planters' aims, which follows, carried the clear implication that these had not been mentioned officially; that he had had to go to the press to find out:

It has been stated in the press that one reason for which some persons in Queensland desire the annexation . . . is the facility for obtaining a large supply of coloured labour for the sugar plantations without going beyond the limits of the colony. It is no doubt generally understood that the natives of New Guinea would not willingly accept or be suitable for labour engagements at a distance from their shores, but the fact that the suggestion has been made indicates a special difficulty which might present itself if the request of the colonial government were complied with.

Finally, Lord Derby suggested joint proposals from the Australasian colonies, expressing the hope that they might unite for this if not for other purposes, and he offered to put one or more deputies of the British High Commissioner of the West Pacific on the New Guinea coast, if 'Queensland, with or without the assistance of the other colonies, is prepared to meet the cost'.

Upon receipt of advice from Lord Derby, the Victorian Premier, Mr Service, stated that 'the action of the Queensland government took us all by surprise. We could not well understand the principle on which they went to work'. But theirs was a step in the right direction 'for the purpose of annexing New Guinea, not to Queensland, but to the British Empire' in order to prevent 'it ever being occupied by any hostile nation'.[21] On 11 July Service moved, in the Victorian Parliament:

1. That, in the opinion of this House, it is essential to the future well-being of the Australasian colonies that New Guinea and the Pacific Islands lying between New Guinea and Fiji should be annexed to the British Crown, or that England should establish a protectorate over them.
2. That concerted action on the part of the Australasian colonies is desirable, in order to accomplish the result.
3. That this colony is willing to contribute its proportion of the expense entailed by such annexation or protectorate.
4. That a message be sent to the Legislative Council, inviting their concurrence in these resolutions.[22]

He referred to the French government which used 'one of the islands in the Pacific' for the deportation of convicts. Transportation had caused feelings of strong indignation in Melbourne thirty years before when they had 'compelled' the Imperial government by the almost threatening attitude they assumed, to cease emptying all the gaols into this city and this colony. But many of the French deportees, who had escaped to Australia, were not just ordinary criminals: '. . . many of them are people who go about with the one object of subverting society in every rational shaped in which it *check* exists'. They were, in other words, survivors of the Paris Commune, but in the words of Service, 'the refuse of European nations'.[23] His second reason was fear of sudden attack.

Service was, however, taking a longer view and his demand for British annexation or a British protectorate was supported by the argument that 'we in these colonies certainly do not want another Europe established in Australasia'. He went on:

We don't want to have a variety of nationalities represented here, each one armed to the teeth against the other, and causing an enormous expenditure of life and treasure, which has been shown in the old countries of the world to be an absolute necessity, with human nature constituted as it now is . . . Our annual revenue is six million pounds, and if we were to set aside two million pounds of it for our defences - for soldiers and sailors - where would our railways and water reservoirs be? . . . We should look forward and take such action at the present time as will be calculated to bring about that state of things when, at all events, future generations will be able to 'beat their swords into ploughshares and their spears into pruning hooks'. This is really what we want to look forward to, and not that we shall be subjected, or that future generations shall be subjected, to the condition of things which has made life almost intolerable in Europe.[24]

There was no opposition to the Premier's resolutions only a suggestion, which he accepted, to add 'including the New Hebrides'[25] after the word 'Fiji'. A further suggestion to include Dutch New Guinea was ignored, as was a demand that 'Victoria will . . . go in for having a considerable share of that territory' - which indicated the competitiveness among the Australian colonies as much as the material reasons for annexations. The Victorian Parliament asked the Governor to forward the resolutions to Lord Derby.[26]

There was, then, no opposition to the New Guinea adventure in the Victorian parliament. Though Service was careful to dissociate himself from the Queensland attempt at unilateral annexation, once it had failed, that is not what he had said to McIlwraith when he heard of his *coup* - though, even at that time, he spoke with differing emphasis, depending on his audience.

According to the Melbourne *Argus* of 19 April 1883, Service had been quick to react to cabled reports from London, 'that the Imperial Government were likely to be influenced against the step' of Queensland's annexation of New Guinea. He cabled the governments of New South Wales and South Australia, suggesting that they join Victoria in instructing their Agents General in London 'to support promptly and earnestly the action of Queensland'. He appears to have cabled the Victorian Agent General without awaiting the replies of the other colonial governments that he had solicited. McIlwraith had had the same idea, as that report in the *Argus* also quoted a telegram from McIlwraith to Service, asking for just such action to which the latter replied that he had already taken it. Service concluded his telegram to McIlwraith: 'I thank you in the name of the people of Victoria for the action taken'.[27]

However, in the Victorian Parliament, more circumspect language was used. On the same day on which the *Argus* carried the above-mentioned report, Parliament was prorogued and, in the Prorogation, that is in a government statement, the Governor said:

The proposed annexation of New Guinea to British territory has been received with great satisfaction by the people of Victoria, and my advisers have taken prompt action to support the Government of Queensland in urging that course on the Imperial Government.[28]

'Proposed annexation . . . to British territory' and 'action to support the Government of Queensland in *urging* that course on the Imperial Government': these terms carry rather a different implication from the published telegram sent by Service to McIlwraith.

On the following day, 20 April, the conservative *Argus* carried a leading article, objecting to Queensland's methods, outlining, in low key, the possible dangers due to Italian, Russian, German and French interests in New Guinea, and expressing the hope that the Imperial government would take action to protect it.[29]

In the Parliament of New South Wales, the colourful radical politician Buchanan raised the matter, in a somewhat confused passage, on the adjournment on 14 November 1883.[30]

The most interesting opposition to the New Guinea affair was that of the Sydney *Bulletin*.[31] It is the more remarkable for its attitude to England which was not always as mellow as on this occasion: 'The New Guinea business', its editor said on 14 July 1883, 'is not likely to have any serious effects on the relations between the Australian colonies and the Mother Country'. In his view, the amount of real interest felt by the colonists was very small and he did not believe that there was a 'spark of irritation everywhere. The affair will neither hasten Australian independence nor precipitate federation'. Significantly, writing at Sydney, in the view of the *Bulletin's* editor, there was no financial loss involved and 'as sense is not obscured by interest or greed, the fact is fairly appreciated that the snub was invited'. Though New Guinea was, no doubt, a magnificent territory, Australians were not stinted in the matter of territory. Were the Imperial government to take steps to limit the inflow of people or capital, 'there would be an instinctive sense of injury. That would truly be a crippling blow. But — additional territory!'

The political excuse for the annexation was chiefly 'fudge'. There was 'surely nothing so terrible in the idea of having neighbours'. Nor was this the way to avoid having any:

Even admitting, however, that danger would be involved in having the settlements of a foreign power planted close to our boundaries, the plan for annexing half of New Guinea is precisely the worst step which could be taken . . . without New Guinea, Australia is self-contained, and shares with Great Britain the grand advantage of being moated by the ocean. For Australia to annex southern New Guinea would be just as if Great Britain seized or incorporated Belgium or Hanover. It would be to pass the moat, and [to] substitute an imaginary line on the map for the real demarcation and barrier of the sea.

Rather than being removed further from foreign neighbours, Australians would 'jostle the Dutch, and approximate to the Spaniards in the Phillipines and to the French in Tonquin. In *Bulletin* geography, Java was 'quite as close to New Guinea as New Guinea is to Queensland. Politically and strategically, the position of Australia would be no better'.

On the other hand, the Germans, the Italians or the French might step in and appropriate the island, and the need of any of them, in his view, was greater than Australia's. The Italians, because they found it 'hard to live in their own country'. The French because they were successful colonists although it was fashionable to affirm the contrary: their colonizing enterprises had been crushed, not by internal failure, but by the supremacy of the British Navy.

Unless it be contemplated that our own countrymen shall appropriate the whole globe, we must submit to having neighbours somewhere. And it does seem ridiculous that, while we are screaming 'Keep your distance!' - we should be stepping out towards the very people we warn off.

In the New Hebrides, the *Bulletin* said, Presbyterians and other clergymen had laboured for a number of years; they had invested several hundred thousands of pounds in native souls and they seemed to regard those islands 'as forming a kind of appanage of the Kirk'. But for the frequency with which 'the pretensions of sectaries have plunged the world into war' that claim would be 'too preposterous for consideration'. Nevertheless the thing was a little farcical:

The two great nations, France and England, have mutually entered into a solemn undertaking not to seize [the] New Hebrides. And a clique of reverend busybodies work upon a Presbyterian premier of [a] dependency of one of the contracting Powers to induce him to urge the Mother Country to break her plighted faith and dishonour herself - for the love of GOD! Mighty pretty morality this missionary politique.

In the *Bulletin's* view, there was 'a lot of Phariseeism and some flavour of cowardice' about all the fuss: 'what harm would it do us to have Italian, or French, or Spanish, or German, or Dutch neighbours? We English are the salt of the earth, forsooth, and must not have our native world tarnished by rubbing shoulders with any other people. This is fudge unqualified'.

The editor went on to make two points. The first concerned the effects on the Australian community of rubbing shoulders with a different kind of settler - implying the *settlement* of New Guinea and, presumably, other Pacific islands, by colonising European emigrants. On that assumption, the editor reached this conclusion:

Nothing would be more likely to stimulate progress, to enlarge the scope of ideas and the variety of methods, than the interchange of ideas which would follow the establishment close at hand of quite a different sort of settler. The United States owes its grand intellectual freedom and progress, in no slight degree, to the chafe of systems and survival of the soundest ideas, consequent on the admixture of nationalities by universal immigration from all parts of the civilized world.

The *Bulletin* scoffed at the argument of fear, as Buchanan had done: not from a pacifist position but, rather, aggressively:

. . . are we Australians so degenerate, so unworthy of our sires of war-proof [*sic*] that, with all the advantages of numbers, and comparatively settled establishment, we are to shiver in our shoes because a handful of foreigners, wearing fierce mustachios, squat down over the way, and on our route to our tea-market?

The only difficulty was that, once again, penal colonies would be established:

There is just one solid objection to foreign nations having a whack in the Southern Hemisphere, and that is the risk that they will again imitate our own style of colonization, as they have once already done in New Caledonia. The era of convict settlement should have passed away. But we cannot cry with the force of lung which would otherwise be ours, because we have up to this very hour been quietly tolerating in our own continent the identical thing which we are or pretend to be horror-stricken that the French should think of. Western Australia is still a penal settlement, just as much as New Caledonia is. How, then, can we consistently make it a *casus belli* that another nation should do far away what we have not objected to our own nation doing close at hand?

It is not proposed to analyze this logic or the use made of facts. The significant thing is that the journal was bent on proclaiming, loudly, the emperor's lack of clothes. The *Bulletin* has the distinction of having exposed the claims advanced in favour of annexation; that, in fact, there were two alternatives to having neighbours: one was to annex the rest of the world and the other, to remain self-contained and sharing "with Great Britain the grand advantage of being moated by the ocean." The *Bulletin* also advocated "the admixture of nationalities by universal immigration" for which it praised the United States and to which, it said, America owed, in no small degree "its grand intellectual freedom and progress" - an idea reflecting nineteenth-century European radical thought, but one that was to become ever less popular in Australia, and in the *Bulletin* until the great transformation of the 1940's of which the post-war immigration movement was but one aspect.

There was, of course, no mention of Asians or Polynesians, or of their rights: it would be hard to deny the racist and often xenophobic character of the *Bulletin,* which is one reason why the attitude displayed in the foregoing article towards other European nations is so notable. The same issue carried a piece of pure antisemitic propaganda and another, opposing votes for women. The radicalism of the *Bulletin* was that of nationalist populists. It was predominantly inward-looking and that, too, makes the article remarkable.

It is the more so, since parliamentary opposition to the affair was so limited. In Victoria, there was none. In New South Wales, Buchanan referred to it, without much clarity; the Premier, Sir Alexander Stuart, had his doubts and reservations but he was too discreet a politician to announce them publicly.

JOHN BULL: "HALLO THERE! JUST DROP IT, NOW!"

From the Sydney *Bulletin*, 14 July 1883.

In the same issue, there was also the cartoon reproduced here, displaying a similar critical attitude to the motives of the Queensland government as well as a detached understanding for the British position. Oddly, though, the French are here pictured as coming from the West, through Torres Strait, presumably from Indo-China, rather than from New Caledonia.

The parliamentary situation in Queensland was complicated by the fact that the McIlwraith government was fighting for its life. The major attacks were aimed at its proposals for coolie immigration and the support given by the government to the proposed large land-grant railways.

The Governor's speech contained the paragraph on the Annexation, found in the Appendix, which stated that 'New Guinea and the adjoining groups of Pacific Islands must form part of the future Australian Nation.'[32] Contrary to the fears expressed by McIlwraith, Samuel Griffith, the Leader of the Opposition, went out of his way at that belated meeting of Parliament on 27 June 1883, to support the principle of annexing New Guinea, in his speech on the Address-in-Reply which, in other respects, was most critical of the government he hoped to replace. The main burden of his attack was directed against the proposals to introduce Indian coolies and Chinese labourers, and against the railway syndicate.

Eight days later, on 5 July 1883, the Premier was obliged to inform the House of the Imperial disallowance of his Annexation, the subject of a cable he had received from the Queensland Agent General in London - 'which, I think, entails upon me the duty of making a sort of statement to the House. The telegram is as follows:

June 3rd 1883

Lord Derby in House last night disallowed annexation States the [that?] other Powers making settlement would not be viewed as friendly act Prepared to extend to New Guinea the power of High Commissioner Unable to obtain interview today.[33]

McIlwraith then read a cabled report in that morning's Brisbane *Courier* which gave a more detailed account, including Gladstone's statement to the Commons.[34] He went on to repeat the relevant section of the Governor's speech, reminding the House that it had had 'the hearty approval of the Leader of the Opposition', and that the Speech had been adopted without amendment. In his view, the Imperial government's action had been inimical to the interests of Queensland

and the other Australian colonies. He continued:

. . . so far as Queensland is concerned - and the other colonies too - I look upon the annexation of New Guinea to British territory - or, at all events, to Queensland territory - as an accomplished fact. I question - and with all modesty I do it - the legality of the decision of Mr Gladstone when he says that our action was null and void. I believe that it was perfectly legal, and that we were fully entitled to annex the island without the formal sanction of Great Britain.[34]

Maybe, McIlwraith wished to cover his embarrassment that way. Griffith came to his aid with the briefest of statements: 'I regret that the Imperial Government has not seen fit to sanction the annexation of the island of New Guinea which I approved of, as I have said on a previous occasion. Beyond that I do not think it a fitting time to enter into the matter.'[35]

McIlwraith was, however, severely attacked from another quarter. Mr, later Sir James, Garrick a parliamentarian of some prominence, began by charging that it was unconstitutional 'for the Premier . . . to . . . say that he did not call the members together because he thought they might defeat his views'.[36] Garrick outlined his own views of the essential function of the opposition in constitutional government. Turning to the New Guinea question, he said that he had not thought the Premier would have the hardihood to tell the House that he defied it: but he had also defied the Imperial government, and he had received exactly the sort of reply that Garrick had thought he would:

What fear was there of danger from a foreign power interfering with New Guinea? And even if there was, why not let the Imperial Government act in a matter which might involve her in some difficulty which might have affected Queensland also?

Garrick went on:

The Premier has been inaugurating - has been establishing - a navy, and now, forsooth, he is determined to have a foreign policy. That seems to me to be his idea. He has a ship or two in the way, and now he is going to inaugurate a foreign policy. But can we undertake the protection of New Guinea? Could we defend even a mile of her coast? The action should at least have been a federated one between Queensland and the other colonies; but the Premier consults nobody, and that has been his policy all through. He acts in defiance of us and of the Imperial Government, without consulting us or the rest of Australia on a matter which might have involved us and the Imperial Government in very serious difficulty. I say that up to the present time, with the information which he has afforded to the Home Government, they could have given no other answer than they have done.

McIlwraith made no attempt to answer Garrick. Instead, he used his right of reply for an untenable attack on the other Australian colonies which even the most elaborate embroidery of the facts would not cover:

Had the New Guinea and Queensland question stood alone, I believe the answer would have been favourable; but when the other colonies went on to annex more territory the Government thought fit, under pressure at home, to take a different course than they would otherwise have taken. I think that it is unfortunate for us in respect of the New Guinea question that the southern colonies proceeded to annex certain of the Pacific Islands; but when they did take action there was no other course that we could in honour pursue than to back them up as they had us. I agree that a great deal may be done by federal action, and that we shall be able to work out a remedy either by that or some other course. I believe that New Guinea will be annexed.[37]

The McIlwraith government lingered on for a further five months, until its defeat at the polls. It was then replaced by a Liberal government under Griffith who proceeded to introduce legislation to repeal the 1862 Act. However the Legislative Council succeeded in delaying the repeal until 1886, when that legislation, having caused much unrest without, however, leading to coolie immigration to Queensland, disappeared from the Statute Book. The legislation authorizing private railways met a similar fate.

Intercolonial agreement between the governments of New South Wales, New Zealand, Queensland and Victoria resulted in a very detailed submission to Lord Derby, on 21 July 1883, running to some 5,500 words.[38] In that document the historical, economic, political, diplomatic, strategic and legal arguments for annexation were set out.

The New Guinea question was linked to the demand for annexation or protectorate in the Western Pacific. The latter was based on the fear about French intentions, due to a proposed French law to transport convicts to certain Pacific islands, and the connected fear about the future of the New Hebrides.

But on the subject of their own future, the colonies were less certain: 'The large question of Federation which your Lordship has here raised is one on which the colonies have not made up their minds, and is one of too grave moment to be decided even under the sway of the strong feeling which now exists among them respecting the policy that ought to be pursued in the Western Pacific.' This, however, ought to be no bar to joint action with the Imperial government in the Pacific.

The Colonial Office replied at Lord Derby's direction on 31 August 1883, recognizing the care and ability of the Agents General account.

Their historical account did not appear exceptionable; at any rate, it was not reviewed in detail. But copies had been sent to the Admiralty as well as to Sir Arthur Gordon, who, as we have seen, was then High Commissioner of the Western Pacific.

Turning to their enquiry 'as to the extent to which the claims of foreign powers in the Western Pacific have been recognized by Her Majesty's government', they were told, somewhat coldly, that 'His Lordship is disposed to doubt whether there is really so much uncertainty or absence of information in the Australasian colonies as you seem to apprehend'. They were told that 'the claims and interests of other countries constitute a very serious impediment to that "complete jurisdiction" which' they had asked England to assume. 'Her Majesty's government have not before them any evidence that the governments of the Australasian colonies have sufficiently considered the extent of the responsibilities which the annexation or protectorate of these islands would involve, and they are far from being satisfied that the assumption of those responsibilities is necessary or justifiable'.

Regarding New Guinea, the Agents General were referred back to Lord Derby's despatch of 11 July, and invited to submit united recommendations, furnishing also an effective guarantee for such expenditure as may be incurred. They were invited to do the same, if they wished, in respect to any other islands not already connected by treaty or otherwise with foreign powers.[39]

Regarding the French penal settlement, they were advised that the matter had been taken up with the Foreign Office.

This exchange led to the Intercolonial Convention - the so-called 'Annexation Convention' - of November and December 1883, mainly at the initiative of Service who obtained reluctant agreement from Alexander Stuart by offering to hold it in Sydney, thus making Stuart its chairman. Stuart wrote rather more frankly than in formal communications to Saul Samuel, the New South Wales Agent General in London:

For my own part, I have not felt any strong desire to see the annexation policy carried out. I believe it would be far preferable if some arrangement could be come to whereby none of the maritime powers should annex any of the islands; but so detrimental to colonial interests would be their occupation by foreign powers, that, rather than leave such a contingency open, I would urge as strongly as anyone that the Imperial government should annex them; and thus it is that I telegraph to you to join with the other Agents-General in urging the Imperial government to take some action in the matter . . . In New South Wales there is a marked contrast between the feelings of the masses of the people and that which obtains in Victoria and Queensland . . . it would be a hard task to get up upon this subject the enthusiasm which is displayed by our neighbours . . .[40]

This attitude was all the more remarkable in view of the large proportion of the Western Pacific trade with New South Wales, compared with Victoria and Queensland. The following figures for that trade from 1871 to 1880, were given in the Agents' General submission[41]:

Colony	Vessels	Tonnage	Imports £	Value Exports £	Imports & Exports £
New South Wales	1,305	395,391	2,147,858	2,726,227	4,874,085
Victoria	187	67,725	162,095	110,647	272,742
Queensland	320	47,390	2,899	83,800	86,699
New Zealand	908	349,681	705,223	548,187	1,253,410
Totals	2,720	860,187	3,018,075	3,468,861	6,486,936

Gladstone requested Gordon's diagnosis. The latter expressed his views on the 'annexation fever' in a letter to the Prime Minister on 8 October 1883:

The Australian agitation for sweeping annexations in the Pacific is, I believe, to a great extent unreal, and does not reflect the genuine feelings of the working and thinking part of the community.

He added that in so far as the desire was genuine, it was to a great degree due to a real, though unreasonable fear of the influx of criminals into Australia from convict stations, which foreign powers might establish in the Pacific, and to 'a strong *jingo* feeling', in which a vague sentiment that it was a fine thing to extend Australian dominion was combined with great ignorance of actual facts. He went on to identify the interest groups behind the agitation:

But, in addition to those influenced by these rather hazy views, are two small but powerful classes, who have a direct interest in annexation, and who work on the passions and prejudices of those who have none. I refer to the sugar growers of the North, and to the shop owners engaged in what is called the island trade. These are both very powerful interests, which every colonial politician will seek to consolidate and propitiate, if he can do so without offence to other sections of the community.[42]

One voice of protest reached the 'Annexation Convention'. The Royal Hawaiian government lodged a formal protest, through the Hawaiian consul at Hobart. Dated 'Iolani Palace, Honolulu, August 28, 1883', - i.e. fifteen years before its final annexation to the United States - it expressed the wish of the Hawaiian government that 'instead of annexation in the Pacific, that the few great powers, viz. England, France, Germany and America, should join in a protectorate over the islands and archipelagoes in the Pacific'. It pointed to the existence of such protectorates in Samoa 'making that archipelago quite an independent state, and recognized as such by European diplomacy'. The Hawaiians showed an awareness of the problems of the Pacific territories in relation to the rivalries of the great powers:

Whereas His Hawaiian Majesty's government being informed that certain sovereign and colonial States propose to annex various islands and archipelagoes of Polynesia, does hereby solemnly protest against such projects of annexation, as unjust to a simple and ignorant people, and subversive in their case of those conditions for favourable national development which have been so happily accorded to the Hawaiian nation.

The Hawaiian people, enjoying 'the blessings of national independence confirmed by the joint action of great and magnanimous states', which were ever ready to afford favourable opportunities for self-government, could not be silent about or indifferent to acts of intervention in contiguous and kindred groups which menaced their own situation. The Hawaiian people, it went on, encouraged by favourable political conditions, had cultivated and entertained a strong national sentiment, which lead them not only to cherish their own political state, but also inspired them with a desire to have extended to kindred, yet less favoured communities of Polynesia, like favourable opportunities for national development.

It was seen as the duty of the Hawaiian government to proffer to kindred peoples and states of the Pacific an advisory assistance to aid them in securing opportunities for improving their political and social conditions: 'His Hawaiian Majesty's government, responding to the national will and to the especial appeals of several Polynesian Chiefs, has sent a Special Commissioner to several of the Polynesian Chieftains and States, to advise them in their national affairs'. And the Hawaiian government, speaking for the Hawaiian people, 'so happily prospering through national independence, appealed to the Governments of great and enlightened States', that they would recognise the inalienable rights of the several native communities in Polynesia to enjoy opportunities for progress and self-government, and would 'guarantee to them the same favourable opportunities which have made Hawaii prosperous and happy, and which incite her national spirit to lift up a voice among the nations in behalf of sister islands and groups of Polynesia'.[43]

Although it did find its way into the records of the Convention, the voice was, of course, ~~not heeded~~. *ignored*

The Intercolonial Convention of 1883 was remarkable for two things: it succeded in agreeing on a series of resolutions regarding New Guinea and the Pacific which were cabled to the Colonial Secretary by the Governor of New South Wales on 5 December 1883;[44] and it agreed on a draft forming the constitutional basis of the Federal Council of Australasia.

We may, at this point ask, why did Lord Derby disallow the McIlwraith move?

Three factors emerge:

1. Although the Colonial Office appears at first not to have been greatly perturbed by the Queensland move and the prospect of unrestricted recruiting of manpower from New Guinea for the Queensland sugar plantations, it did object to the attempt at an independent foreign policy, an objection which was strengthened by the additional colonial demands for wide annexations in the Pacific.

2. This view was hardened by Gordon's advice, stressing the unfitness of the colonial establishment for the administration of New Guinea, and supporting Gladstone's hostility to imperialist adventures, at a time of diverse British commitments - in Burma, Malaya and China to mention but three 'forward movements' in Asia, quite apart from major preoccupations in Egypt and Southern Africa.

3. Foreign Office advice about the intentions of Germany, based on official statements by Bismarck which were misconstrued in

in London and which may have been misleading, encouraged the slowness of the Colonial Office in this matter. Once German intentions were revealed by German annexation, in 1884, Britain felt obliged to placate Bismarck, rather than find him in support of France in the Egyptian question, which was vastly more important to Downing Street than New Guinea.

The future of Eastern New Guinea - that is, the part unoccupied by the Dutch - had been under discussion within the Colonial Office since the early 1870's. In 1871, R.G.W. Herbert had become its Permanent Under-Secretary. He was not only related to Lord Carnarvon; he had also been the first Premier of Queensland. It is not surprising that Carnarvon valued his advice and, indeed, as one historian has put it, Herbert 'had, until his retirement in 1892, an influence upon Colonial Office relations with Australia which has yet to be assessed.'[45] In a minute to Carnarvon, Herbert stated, on 26 March 1874: 'I do not think there is any hope of us being able to keep clear of interference with New Guinea'. But he did insist that the Australian colonies who wished to force the pace in this matter, and who would be the main beneficiaries from such interference, should also share in the cost. In the 'interesting conversation' on 2 July 1883, in the House of Lords, preceding Derby's statement, Carnarvon had favoured annexation. He, too, feared foreign designs - but only from France. There was no mention of Germany.

When the unilateral annexation by Queensland became known in London, Herbert seems to have been less shocked by the annexation than by McIlwraith's method. It is possible that, given a Conservative government, the action might have been ratified as a British annexation, but in this speculation it must be remembered that Herbert *also* considered the action of Queensland most improper.

A year later - in 1884 - it was Derby who felt that, in view of Bismarck's implicit rejection of an 'Australian Monroe doctrine', and his proclaimed intention to protect German traders in Africa and the Pacific, the New Guinea question ~~was urgent~~ *assumed some urgency*. Derby therefore recommended annexation to the Cabinet meeting of 5 July 1884. The Prime Minister, Mr Gladstone, was opposed, and the item was adjourned to the next Cabinet meeting on 6 August, when it was agreed to. Three days later, Cabinet reversed its decision, when Granville, the Foreign Secretary, learnt of Bismarck's interest in the Pacific: Cabinet wished to placate Bismarck, and the protectorate was limited to the Southern part of Eastern New Guinea. Any idea that Herbert or Derby might have had of rectifying this decision later, was dispelled by the announcement, without prior warning, of the German protectorate, on 19 December 1884. Derby then attempted to extend the British protectorate to Huon Gulf of the North coast of the island, but he had to agree to a withdrawal to the line 8° Southern latitude in the face of Gladstone's and Granville's insistence that Bismarck's attitude in the Egyptian question was crucial.

Two things are remarkable. The first is that the German action was, to say the least, hastened by the clamour in the Australian colonies. In March 1884, Count Hatzfeld explained to the British Ambassador in Berlin 'that the attitude assumed by the Australian authorities in regard to the annexation of the unoccupied portions of New Guinea and the neighbouring islands was stirring up the "envy and cupidity" of the German colonial party . . .'[46] It produced the familiar urge to move before someone else did, which also accounts, at least in part, for Bismarck's extreme deviousness. The second point concerns precisely these methods. Once again, as with McIlwraith, the British government objected primarily to Bismarck's method.

It was Alexander Stuart who had foreseen that the great noise made by the colonies or, as he put it - 'the prominence which has been given to the subject will of itself cause some nation to take it up as a strong strategic point in the future domination of the seas'.[47] It was for these strategic reasons, which 'in the event of a European war, [would be] most disastrous to Australia, and therefore for British interests' that Stuart, on 1 August 1883, reluctantly supported annexation.

THE BISMARCK DIMENSION

For Bismarck, as for Granville and Gladstone, the New Guinea affair was important only as one item in a complex diplomatic situation. Moreover, there were domestic political questions of the greatest importance. Bismarck was faced by a hostile majority in the Reichstag and the socio-economic distribution of forces had changed decisively since he had defied the Prussian diet in the 1860's. Furthermore, Bismarck feared that, if those conditions persisted when the aged Emperor Wilhelm I was succeeded by his son Friedrich, with Queen Victoria's daughter as Empress, a 'German Gladstone' cabinet might indeed eventuate and, moreover, lead to too close an identification of German interests with those of Great Britain.

It was basic to Bismarck's policy that relations with England (as with Russia) must never be allowed to deteriorate below a certain level, or for too long. After the victory of 1870, he realised that, no matter what the terms of the settlement, sooner or later a *revanchiste* party would succeed in France, to threaten the rickety structure of his Reich. Although he would probably have preferred softer conditions of peace than those imposed at Frankfurt, terms which would have given him greater diplomatic flexibility, he was deeply pessimistic and regretful about the chances of a successful diplomacy with France. Emotive talk about the *Erbfeind* had no room among his diplomatic concepts. The nature and the state of relations with the other two major European powers was, therefore, all the more crucial to his diplomacy. A serious or a permanent break with either of them would have been viewed by him as a fatal catastrophe.

However, having supported British policy in the Egyptian crisis without any tangible advantage, he felt the time ripe for practical recognition of that support. He was fond of saying that, in public life, nothing is done *pour les beaux yeux*; that to ignore that maxim was dangerous, and could only lead to counter-productive results. So, he decided to be a little disagreeable to the British - for a while.

There were a number of factors inducing him to do so. The domestic aspect has been mentioned and it should be added that the political and economic pressures had grown very substantially, in conditions of prolonged depression. Bismarck had said before, as he would say again, that he had a profound dislike for formal colonies: *ich bin kein Kolonialmensch*. Colonies simply meant jobs: they would be a form of outdoor relief. How deeply Bismarck's whole economic ideas (and policy) had been affected by the *laissez-faire* ideology, is often over-shadowed by the undergrowth of his authoritarian conservatism in politics.

The question of his attitude to colonies is a very complex one. In October 1870, Théophile Gautier *fils* went as an emissary of the

Empress Eugénie from London to Versailles, carrying proposals to
the King of Prussia and, more importantly, to Bismarck. Among
her proposals was the cession of Cochin-China to Germany. According to Gautier, Bismarck, who had listened thus far without
interrupting his visitor, moved his shoulders and, prompted by the
old instinct of Prussian parsimony, not yet replaced by Imperial
German megalomania, said, with a touch of humility: 'Oh! oh! la
Cochinchine! C'est un bien gros morceau pour nous; nous ne sommes
pas assez riches pour nous offrir le luxe de colonies!' [48]

There is also a well-known excerpt from a despatch of 11 February 1873, by Lord Odo Russell to Granville [49], with Bismarck's
claim that many colonies had been offered to him and that he had
rejected them all:

"Colonies would only be a cause of weakness, because colonies
could only be defended by powerful fleets and Germany's geographical position did not necessitate her development into a first-class
maritime power . . . and [Bismarck] only wished for coaling stations
acquired by treaty from other nations."

That extract has to be seen in its context, a Bismarckian mon-
ologue. He had asked Russell to an after-dinner *tête-à-tête* "to
smoke a pipe", in order to seek his co-operation in "contradicting
calumny", spread in England by the Queen of Holland, that "Prussia
sought to annex the Netherlands with a view to acquiring colonies
and a fleet for Germany." The very thought that such an idea might
find credence in England would have sufficed to fill Bismarck with
alarm and he put himself out to discredit the rumour, adding complaints about "his Imperial master", even "for resisting the
introduction of a system of administration under a responsible
Premier," adding that he foresaw no difficulty in persuading the
Crown Prince "to follow the good example of England . . as the best
for Germany."

Although Bismarck protested rather too much, the core of his
statement has an intrinsic significance in revealing his awareness of
the dimensions implicit in a colonial policy: its relation to sea-
power and the consequent rivalries with existing maritime powers.
Among these he reckoned - in 1873 - besides England, the United
States and France. It is hard to believe that, eleven years later, he
would have forgotten all this, or, that he would suddenly have been
ready to run the risk of a long-term colonial policy. His preference
for informal empire had been very strong and I share Wehler's

view [50] of Bismarck that he foresaw a German colonial empire would be run by bureaucrats with neither the training nor the aptitude for the task. The hypothesis, that he saw a colonial policy as a temporary expedient, fits Bismarck's political theory and his policies, though it is hardly susceptible to proof. That, once begun, a colonial policy would be driven forward by powerful economic forces in German society and thus become irreversible within that system, was a development he would neither have foreseen nor wanted to foresee, for this faith in his own ability to undo what he had done, was very great.

Once Bismarck had decided to ally himself to the colonialist lobby, in 1884, he acted in a manner, the deviousness of which left a lasting impression in London. It is arguable that Gladstone and Granville would have been co-operative, had he acted differently. Even though he did not, they acquiesced. But, had he sought to obtain colonies with British co-operation, one of his reasons for supporting the colonialist lobby would have been defeated. Such Anglo-German co-operation at that point would not have fitted into his aims: to divide his domestic opponents by buying some of them off without incurring domestic liabilities, and to create a limited deterioration in the relations with England in order to neutralize anglophile circles at home, including those around the Crown Prince. Bismarck had no intention of allowing his relations with Great Britain to deteriorate too much or for too long.

His primary colonial interest lay in Angra Pequena - South West Africa, or Namibia. The very names reflect its history. It is a reasonable assumption that the Australian clamour about New Guinea suited his purpose. In the case of Angra Pequena, the opposition in the Cape Colony played a similar part and here, in the 'South Seas', there were the makings for a ready-made disagreement with England - of just the right proportions. It was a *casus classicus* for making support dependent on an awkward rather than a vital issue and, at the time, it worked.

About the clamour in Australia, Bismarck said two things: the British government had to decide whether the clamour of the colonists was more important to it than the friendship of Germany. If, however, the colonies were really so independent as to be beyond the control of the British government - and in 1883-4 he did not seem to believe that - then 'we would have to establish a legation

with English colonial governments of this sort'.[51] On a later
occasion, Bismarck asked the German Ambassador in London,
Count von Münster, to tell Lord Granville plainly 'that we could
not agree to keep two accounts about our relations with England:
one with the Foreign Office where we can only book friendly remarks to our credit, and another one with the Colonial Office
where we are debited with disadvantages (Schädigungen).'[52]

On 20 October 1886, Count Hatzfeld, Münster's successor in
London, said in a hand-written private letter to Herbert v. Bismarck, on the Samoan question: 'We must find a formula for the
concessions which we desire enabling the [British] government to
accommodate us without causing them difficulties with Australia'.
Here, Bismarck *père* put 'correct' in the margin. Hatzfeld went
on to say that that point was 'a dangerous cliff in the present
state of the relations between England and her colonies'.[53] Clearly,
Bismarck had revised his views about the position of the Australian
colonies.

There had for long been views in London anticipating the future
secession of the colonies of settlement in one or two generations.
They were no secrets of state. Dilke said as much to Herbert von
Bismarck, and Derby had used very similar language to Sir Arthur
Gordon: 'All my observations on the tempo and the tendency of
the colonial mind lead me to the conclusion that within the next
generation or two, we in England shall have nothing to say in Australasian affairs'.[54]

Dilke said he had wished to keep hands off New Guinea: that
had not been possible 'because of the absurd line our colonies
take.'[55] The German annexation was, in Dilke's view, a mistake
and 'you will have grave difficulties there in the distant future'.
He went on:

Australia is growing tremendously in power and population. In one or two
generations, the time will come when - maybe after seceeding from us -
it will feel itself as strong as the old European powers; will want to wage
war to clear out all foreigners from its neighbourhood. Germany will hardly
be able to wage war at such a great distance and then find itself in the fatal
situation to evacuate New Guinea. But that is your affair.

There was, however, another and greater consequence attendant
on Bismarck's change of policy. Bismarck had succeeded in attaching
the German middle classes to his system and, hence, opposition

from the political parties representing their interests would remain limited and nominal and pressure for internal reform, the preserve of the Social Democrats, the S.P.D. The S.P.D., however, remained beyond the pale in the Bismarckian state. The foundation was thereby laid for a policy of imperialist expansion, leading to the construction of a first-class navy, in necessary competition with Great Britain, and thence, in stages, along the road to 1914.

The crucial decision was taken by Bismarck for short-term domestic and diplomatic reasons. Bismarck seems to have had the view that his actions were reversible at (his) will. The consequences of this action took thirty years to mature. It may very well have been possible to conduct a more sophisticated and a more subtle foreign policy, had Bismarck 'educated' his successors and had Wilhelm II made use of such people. Whether it would have been possible for them to avoid the challenge to England which the decision to construct a major navy for the protection of the German overseas empire implied, may be doubted. The other *gaffes* of Wilhelmine diplomacy, the weakness of its critics, the economic necessities of its aggressiveness and the sclerotic political structure of the *Reich*, make one rather doubtful. Bismarck's short, successful and decisive flirtation with colonialism proved to have been among the foundations for the later policies.

It is unlikely that he saw it in this light. There is much that suggests that Bismarck did indeed regard his policies as reversible. Towards the end of his rule, he felt that the German Constitution of 1871 - his handiwork - no longer suited his purposes; he considered its dissolution: being a compact between the German princes, they might then agree to another compact. This is by no means the only, though maybe the most extraordinary, example of his theory of history.

There were, however, some who did foresee the general direction of the journey on which this colonial adventure was bent. Among them was Count Münster. In 1885, Münster wrote to his friend Werthern, then Prussian Ambassador to Bavaria, at Munich:

Bismarck, who used to have a calm and sound judgment about overseas affairs, has suddenly, about a year ago, somersaulted . . . and inaugurated a colonial policy which is going to cost us a great deal of money, cause us many embarrassments, lead to many disappointments and losses and which is going to weaken rather than strengthen our power.

Münster's greatest fear was that Germany and England would, as a result, 'tear each other to pieces'.[56]

Australian troops occupied German New Guinea in August and September of 1914 on behalf of the Imperial government. It became an Australian Mandate at Versailles. In 1975, the whole of Papua New Guinea achieved independence, as a sovereign state within the Commonwealth of Nations.[57]

DEFEAT OF THE PLANTERS

The opponents of a plantation society in Queensland, a society based on un-free, non-European manpower, insisted that to base the sugar industry on free Australian workers was not only desirable as an economic and social goal but perfectly feasible. With the help of government subsidies, their policy was beginning to succeed in the 1890's, a decade of unprecedented economic depression and of great class struggles - which were perhaps worst in Queensland. Yet, the forces in the Queensland Parliament were also changing and the planters, having lost control over it, had expressed their preference for crown-colony status to that of parliamentary government at Brisbane, by petitioning for separation - an unsuccessful rearguard action which, though it failed, marked the depth dividing the contending social forces.

Attempts at using Malayan, Javanese, Indian, Japanese and Chinese manpower, evoked even more determined opposition from the working class of the colony, than the use of 'kanakas' had done. There was an implicit realization of Asian ability and competence, as well as the threat of a larger labour pool: a fear that hard-won improvements in working conditions might easily be undermined by a supply of competent and versatile workers who, even if not indentured, would be content with much poorer working conditions and be beyond the scope of trade union organization.

Most of the Australian colonies had for long had legislation to restrict Chinese immigration, though there were considerable legislative and administrative differences from one colony to another.

The 1890's also saw the first hesitant steps towards the Anglo-Japanese alliance of 1902: the Anglo-Japanese Commercial Treaty was signed in 1894. Japanese commercial expansion affected Queensland most among the Australian colonies, firstly in pearl fishing and then in sugar cane production. Alone among the Australian colonies, the Queensland government accepted the general provisions of the Anglo-Japanese treaty, together with a special assurance from the Japanese government that the 'Law for the Protection of Emigrants' would, in effect, restrict the flow of Japanese manpower to those industries. Dissatisfied with the operation of this arrangement, the Queensland government attempted to enact restrictive legislation, involving 'racial' definitions. The Acts were: the Pearl Shell and Beche-de-Mer Fisheries Act, 1899; the Aboriginals Protection and Restriction of the Sale of Opium Bill, 1899; the Sugar Works Guarantee Act Amedment Act, 1900. The first confined the renewal of pearl fishing licences to British subjects; the second specified that Asians could not employ aborigines; the third sought to limit government financial aid to sugar mills employing European manpower.

As a result, there was active Japanese diplomatic opposition especially to the last two Acts. Royal Assent was withheld from the third, in deference to the Japanese government. The Imperial government's reasons were those outlined in Joseph Chamberlain's famous speech to colonial Premiers which was read into the Commonwealth Parliamentary Debates on the first Immigration Restriction Bill by Alfred Deakin, then Attorney-General, on 12 September 1901.

In Chamberlain's view, the Central Sugar Mills Bill of the Queensland Parliament embodied a disqualification based on a place of origin which was, principally a distinction of race and colour. Any attempt to impose disqualifications on the basis of such distinctions, besides being offensive to a friendly power, was contrary to the general conceptions of equality which, he said, had been the guiding principle of British rule throughout the Empire. Disqualifications by educational tests, such as were embodied in the immigration laws of various colonies, were not a measure to which the government of Japan or any government could take exception on behalf of its subjects; and if the particular tests were not regarded as sufficiently stringent, there was no reason why more stringent and effective ones of a similar character should not be adopted. The main reason for Chamberlain's opposition stemmed from a major shift in British foreign policy:

. . . besides being contrary to the general policy on which the British Empire is based, the Bill is objectionable as embodying a provision which is peculiarly offensive to Japan, a power with which His Majesty's government is, and earnestly desires to remain, on friendly terms.

Chamberlain argued that the Bill not only excluded Japanese from certain employment; but in excluding them placed them 'in the general category of Asiatic races', without any consideration being paid to their state of civilization, a proceeding which was not agreeable to the Japanese government, as the Consul at Townsville stated in his letter of 6 November 1899, to the Chief Secretary of Queensland.[58] British policy was to prevail but a divergence of attitudes and interests remained.

By the time the federation campaign had reached its height in the second half of the 1890's, it had become clear that sugar would be produced in tropical Queensland by workers of European origin. The industry was being reorganised, with the help of government subsidies, from a plantation economy to one based on *farms* supplying sugar cane to capital-intensive central mills, established by the government as well as by private capitalists. Having realized that they had lost the struggle for an industry based on an unfree, non-European workforce, they decided to support the federation movement which, though based on a restricted immigration policy and aimed at a 'white' Australia, at least guaranteed a protected nation-wide market against foreign sugar, all of which was produced with cheap manpower. They also proceeded to produce it outside Australia, e.g. in Fiji, by means of such an unfree, Asian workforce.

There was wide agreement between the parties about the necessity for restricting immigration, although there was considerable variation of emphasis, both in respect to the reasons and to the warmth of their support. As a result of Queensland's experience, and in deference to British foreign policy, the Commonwealth Parliament restricted immigration without specifying 'racial' grounds. Therefore 'White Australia', which has played so large a part in political debate, was not an article of law.[59]

THE SUDAN ADVENTURE

After the New Guinea adventure, further schemes for enlarging the sphere of influence had little practical effect other than to demonstrate the existence of considerable and diverse pressure groups in the Australian colonies with imperialist intentions of their own. The power to make foreign policy remained firmly in the hands of the Imperial government. The latter had, however, for a considerable time promoted a policy of colonial self-defence, and it had more than once hinted at the advantages of federation.

Defence, therefore, and not merely home defence but the raising of contingents for overseas service, became to those pressure groups the avenue by which foreign policies and the definition of a colonial role in Imperial affairs could be obliquely achieved.

The question of the colonial contingent to the Sudan provides valuable evidence of the bases upon which these policies proceeded. The Mahdi's revolt in the Sudan was the occasion of the first offer of locally-raised forces for purposes of Imperial defence, following the fall of Khartoum and the death of General Gordon.

Although offers of South Australian, Victorian and Queensland units were politely refused by the British government, that of a New South Wales contingent was accepted. W.B. Dalley, an active supporter of Imperial federation, was acting Premier while Stuart was ill, and his minutes and cables give a very frank and clear picture of the strategic and political thinking on which his policy was founded.

The imminent evacuation of the Sudan, before the New South Wales contingent had had an opportunity to earn military glory or to suffer serious losses, seemed to add to the fervour with which these ideas were expressed. Dalley stated in a minute ~~for his~~ cabinet, on 27 April 1885:

Our purpose was to assist the arms of England wherever our help was needed. The evacuation of the Soudan by Imperial troops renders the presence of our contingent there unnecessary; but it is manifest that if our aid was ever necessary its necessity is not diminished, but on the contrary, from the alarming news received each day, England is menaced with heavier engagements and larger perils. It is not to be thought of that, by reason of a change of military policy, probably essential to the safety of the Empire, which abandons a particular position, that our relation to the Empire is any way changed. Wherever our contingent can be useful it should be available to the Mother-country. This was clearly our intention in organising it and despatching it . . . It is unnecessary to avert to the way in which our conduct . . . was appreciated and approved all over the world . . . It is simply impossible for us, because of the evacuation of the Soudan, to call back the troops which we have offered for the help of England. It would be unfair to the soldiers themselves, to the reputation of this country, whose action has been the subject of universal praise and of the gratitude of the Empire.[60]

Corp. It should be added that his cabinet approved.

During the days preceding Dalley's cabinet minute, there had been an exchange of telegrams between Sydney, London and the Sudan. On 23 April, Dalley sent a cable to the New South Wales Agent General in London 'to ascertain from the War Office what will be the destination and employment of the contingent if Imperial troops are withdrawn from Egypt',[61] and another, marked "confidential" to Colonel Richardson who commanded the force at Suakim: 'If Soudan evacuated, ascertain what your movement will be and inform me at once. What about contingent serving in India, if deemed necessary by Imperial authorities?'[62]

The colonial government explicitly placed the contingent at the disposal of the War Office, in any sphere of their Imperial interest. Richardson's reply held several surprises. For one thing, it revealed that the officers in the contingent did not receive retiring allowances as in the Imperial service. For another, 'majority opinion' was, according to Richardson, that 'present service practically concluded with present war, therefore contingent should volunteer afresh'. But, he added, having mentioned the question of status in relation to Imperial officers, that 'most would volunteer in any case'.[63]

The reply from London, giving the British response to the suggestion of using the contingent elsewhere, was more significant. On the 24th, the Agent General cabled:

Confidential. Have again seen Lords Derby and Hartington. Am to inform you that it is impossible to state at present the destination of the troops now at Suakim . . . As it is not probable that they will be called on for immediate active service in Africa, and as the Colonial Contingent may be required for the defence of their own Colony, Her Majesty's Government will, under the altered circumstances, be guided by the wishes of your government. Reply. Position regard to war unchanged.[64]

The oblique reminder by the British Liberals that colonial troops should be used for the defence of the colonies was lost on the Empire loyalists in Sydney. The British had to become very plain. On 12 May 1885, Dalley received this despatch from London:

Lord Hartington desires me to say that the aspect of affairs now being peaceful, he thinks it would be unfair, after the good services rendered by the contingent, to keep it a moment longer than necessary in such a climate . . . and suggests whether time had not arrived for your government to consider the subject of the disposal of the force. Instruct.[65]

The suggestion that the New South Wales contingent ought to be repatriated was at last carried out, at British expense.

Opposition to the Sudan adventure arose for a variety of reasons and from men holding diverse views.

 Buchanan made a very blunt attack on the government on 17 March 1885, ~~whose~~ proceedings he described as 'wholly criminal'. He referred to the 'height of folly' that had penetrated the whole of Sydney society for the past month. In his view, it was 'an occasion the importance of which it is impossible to exaggerate . . . It has been scandalous in its illegality. There has not been a shadow of an excuse for it - unprincipled, paltry, in every way contemptible'.[66] On the constitutional issue, less radical and less excitable men agreed with Buchanan.

Buchanan was also right in his assumption that Sir Alexander Stuart, who was ill, had been unaware of those decisions. Buchanan attacked the use made of the concept of loyalty by the government and its supporters in order to create great excitement in the community. In his view, the whole undertaking of enlisting 'soldiers to fight in a foreign quarrel' and of having 'sent them out of the country', was illegal and unconstitutional and the excuse that England had been 'in a death struggle' was false. But that was not the point:

If it were true, and even in an emergency that could befall England, it was no part of our duty to send her any troops. If we understood our duty as colonists, we should know that our duty is to defend ourselves against attack by repelling invaders, and we have no duty cast upon us to do anything else.

Buchanan then launched into a long attack on British policy in Egypt, in the course of which he said that the

Arabs are fighting for their liberties just as much as the Scotch in Wallace's time, or the Italians under Garibaldi. What patriotism, then, is it for our soldiers to go and fight against those patriots, who have never done them any harm, and desire to them no harm?

He advocated separation on the same grounds that had been used in the great Victorian debate, fifteen years before, that 'every enemy of England becomes an enemy of ours'; that British naval expense was so enormous that many British statesmen would, in fact, prefer 'that all her colonies were separated from her'.

Turning an old argument to a new purpose, he said:

The same danger did not exist in olden times when we were not great, wealthy, and populous as we are now. We were not of much importance then, but we are now; the plunder of this country would be an enormous booty; it would be a splendid thing for an enemy to bear down on us and destroy us, and as surely as we live that will be done some day. England's enemies now know that in the Pacific Ocean she possesses a country of untold wealth, and would not one of the first acts of an enemy at war with England be to seize these colonies? It is in consequence of this that I have always advocated separation from England. Let us establish ourselves in a separate community, and not be involved in any danger through any of England's wars. In case we separate from England she may go to war with whom she likes, and we should have nothing to fear from any of her enemies. The security which we should thus have would be of infinite and transcendent benefit to us, and England would find that she would be saved an enormous amount of expense. I am not standing alone in advocating this.

In Buchanan's view, the connection with England would not stand the test if its interests ran counter to those of Australia: 'you will soon see how completely you are involved in self-interest - how completely the interest of this country will swamp and drown any such feeling as this loyalty about which we have heard so much'.

He questioned the implications of the decision to send that contingent of 500 men to the Sudan: 'Will it end with this one act or shall we not be bound to interfere in all of England's quarrels!'

When the matter came up again in September 1885, Buchanan added little that was new - but for his epic description of the contingent's exploits in the Sudan:

They went to the front and had a most desperate encounter with 200 donkeys and about as many nanny-goats. This was the solitary exploit of the contingent. Writers have described how they encountered these goats after one of the most magnificent marches on record. They suddenly turned a corner and discovered this formidable body of goats and donkeys, standing, as they say, at bay. It was in the course of this battle, in this most important and terrible emergency, that the war correspondent of the *Sydney Morning Herald* received his leg wound. I believe the contingent came out of this terrible encounter leaving the whole host of the enemy dead on the field, with the exception of three goats and two donkeys, which they brought home with them, and, greater folly than all, one of the donkeys was made a major-general. But they came home. Nothing but noise, tumult, and sensation would suit the Government, and therein lies the key to the childish, puerile, empty, senseless policy by which they were actuated. They wanted a noise; they wanted to set people talking about the thing, and the whole world to be ringing with the news of it. Bismarck was to be flabbergasted; Russia was to hide its diminished head for ever, and shrink into nothingness. And all this was to be brought about by this terrible contingent.[67]

Buchanan persisted that the government wanted a noise:

They came back as I have said, and in order to keep up the noise, the talk, and the tumult, they would not let the men go ashore quietly and disperse to their homes; but in spite of a most frightful storm of rain - a far greater storm than the men had encountered in the Soudan, except perhaps their engagement with the goats - they were marched through the streets for no purpose whatever except that of creating a sensation. The action of the Government in that particular was as contemptible and disgraceful as it was cruel to the men.

The most prominent opponent of the Sudan adventure was Sir Henry Parkes who began by stating his preferences:

I want this country to establish its reputation by the splendour of its resources, by the soundness of its commercial policy, by its efforts at planting a free people within the land, and by its sober spirit in avoiding any meretricious military display. I want this country to be known as a community of solid, sensible British people, where the people of the three nations may mix as British-Australians, and where their object will be the industrial progress of the country. But I maintain that this military business has never received the approval of this country, and I venture to predict that, whatever else is shown, the general election will show that the great body of the people never were in favour of it.[68]

He considered the despatch of soldiers to have been a great mistake:

I believe that if England stood in a position of peril the British feeling in these colonies is so strong that we should hazard our lives and our property in the cause of the old country. But England has never been in a state of peril; she has never needed our assistance.

Parkes reverted to the earlier distinction between support for imperialist wars and support for the British Isles, were they to be threatened. He also wished to show the very improper ways in which that assistance had been forced upon the Imperial government:

We know well enough that when the thing was first broached his Excellency the Governor telegraphed to London as follows:-

This Government offers her Majesty's Government two batteries field artillery, with one battalion of infantry to be transported by Orient steamer, and undertake to land force at Suakim within thirty days after embarkation. I strongly urge it may be accepted. Refusal would be deeply felt in the Colony.

Now I say that his Excellency was not justified in sending that message to the Imperial Government, and I say that he stepped out of his proper course; he exceeded his power, and violated the position of strict neutrality which he ought to observe as the representative of the Queen; but this telegram has been partly suppressed. How do we know what the other words are which have never seen the light of day of which we have never had any intimation? It is no wonder that the Secretary for State hesitated at giving a direct negative;

he did not want to displease the Australian colonies, he did not wish to do anything which would be so 'deeply felt', and he is told by the Queen's representative - most improperly told by him - that a refusal would be keenly
felt by the people. I do not believe a word of it.

Parkes' objection to the Governor's actions went further. In the
view of Parkes, the Governor's position was to observe 'a strict
neutrality between contending parties', which, as Parkes proceeded
to show, Lord Augustus Loftus had not done:

But this is what his Excellency chooses to say:
There is a certain party here of which Sir Henry Parkes may be called the
leader which is exciting opposition to the policy of my Government —
My Government! He must have thought he was at St Petersburg.
in respect to the sending of troops to the Soudan.
I am sorry his Excellency could not express himself in clearer English. How
could the sending of troops to the Soudan be part of the policy of his Government, I should like to know? It was a simple transaction; there was no policy
about it. They are not going to keep up a system of sending troops to foreign
countries, I suppose. It was, in fact, an erratic leap from a settled policy,
and the language does not describe the transaction.

Sir Henry Parkes objected to the 'unfair manner' in which the
Governor misrepresented the state of public feeling in his despatches.
As further evidence of that claim he pointed to various newspaper
cuttings which the Governor had despatched to London, to show
that the 'press of Sydney highly approved the course which had
been taken, and considered it as the opening of a new epoch
for the Australian colonies'.

Parkes then turned his attention to another aspect of the affair.
He objected to the growth of the military forces; but he would not
have objected to their use for the promotion of federation:

If this Government ever was in favour of federation, if they ever had a well-
settled feeling on the subject, what a grand opportunity they have lost! If
there was really a disposition to aid the mother country by a military contingent,
what a grand opportunity they missed! I do not say that the time was ripe
even for this, but if they thought it was what would have been more statesman-
like - what would have been grander in its conception and more impressive
to the world than communicating with the rest of the colonies and forming a
a small federal army to be at the service of the Crown if the Crown wanted it?
That would have been a noble act.

Instead, Parkes asserted, they rushed into that thing 'without
reflecting', apparently afraid that the governments of the other
colonies would get the start of them. That, as we know, was true and

*Loftus had been H.M. Ambassador at Vienna and at St
Petersburg.

it indicates a deal about the prevalent political mentality. Certainly Parkes did not want his small federal army 'to be sent away on the spur of the moment but ready whenever the Home Government said their services were required'. From this, and other evidence, it is clear that Parkes wished to harness the defence question to his campaign for federation, rather than federalism to the military.

As for the failure to obtain parliamentary sanction, the 'real gravity' lay in 'the incurring of an expenditure unlike in principle to anything which had ever been considered before . . . the expense was incurred for a thing which in principle was never debated before'. Of public opinion Parkes said:

Public opinion in this country resides with men who do not go to banquets. It resides with the men who are on their farms, who are in their shops, who are at their counters. It resides in the men who are the plodding, unseen workers of the country. They are the men who give effect to public opinion.

In reply to Sir Henry Parkes, Baker, who sat on the cross-benches, pointed to the thanks expressed by the Crown to the people of New South Wales and to those of the British Parliament to the troops in the Sudan: 'Is all this nothing for such a young colony? I say that it is a great feather in the cap of the country'. He felt that, though the number of troops involved had been very small and that they could have had very little effect upon the issue of the war, had it continued, yet, the effect upon the future relations of England would be very great:

There had previously been a settled conviction in the mind of foreign nations that the colonies of Great Britain had become a burden to her; that, although she derived advantages from their commerce, yet if war occurred it would be found that the colonies would be a sore burden and trial to her strength. It was said in foreign countries that when England became engaged in any great war the colonies would sever their connection with her; but that impression has been changed since one of the colonies (its action being indorsed by the other colonies) came forward to the assistance of the mother country. Instead of foreign powers thinking that the colonies will be a source of embarrassment to England they see that they will be able and willing to assist her. The sending of our few troops to the Soudan may not of itself have very greatly impressed a nation like France or Germany; but it would concern them greatly if when England was engaged in a great war Canada, Australia, and all the other dependencies of the empire were to unite in sending an army of ten or fifteen thousand men into Europe at a given point. That is the possibility which has been indicated by our action.[69]

The other speakers in this debate, worth mentioning, were

O'Mara[70] and Garvan. O'Mara's contribution is reproduced in the Appendix.* Garvan made two points worthy of mention. He maintained that, from the moment the troops had left our shores, they became 'representative Australians' and, as such, beyond criticism:

> I have no sympathy whatever with that keen criticism or that cheap wit which endeavours to throw discredit upon representative Australians wherever they go. Whether they acted well or ill, for all future time the conduct of the contingent will leave its impress upon the history of New South Wales and Australia.[71]

That view has interesting implications, some of which are still lingering on.

Garvan's second point amounted to a further condemnation of the government 'for having committed the country to a participation in the Soudan war without giving this Parliament its privilege and right of first discussing whether it was a prudent course to take'. In his view -

> it was a matter deserving the most serious consideration of the Government whether it was desirable to remove from the neutral position we had previously occupied with reference to European countries; that the fact of engaging even in the remotest way in any of the contentions of Europe became a matter of the most supreme importance; that no greater, graver, or weightier subject could ever have been considered by the Parliament of this country; and I condemn the Government for having committed the country to a participation in the Soudan war without giving this Parliament its privilege and right of at first discussing whether it was a prudent course to take. There is no doubt in my mind that from the natural development of the colonies Australia will in the not very distant future become an independent country. In that independence I see no lack of loyalty or patriotism to the country from which we sprang.

Garvan compared, as was the fashion, Australia with 'the other great colony which has developed into a nation, namely America' to say that America was England's greatest protection against 'unjust invasion by any great power', and a free Australia or Australasia would be a greater protection to the British Isles than she could be as a colony. That view implied 'no deviation from sound patriotism or true loyalty to the country from which we sprang'.

Garvan's view, then, stood half-way between that of Parkes and, say, Buchanan's. His concept of neutrality, however mistaken on the facts of the colonial position, is nevertheless worthy of note.

The Sudan adventure was significant for a number of reasons.

*Document No 5

It was the first expeditionary force sent from Australia, and, as a result, it caused the first debate on the desirability and the propriety of raising and despatching such forces overseas. In that first debate, the 'loyalist' taunt that, to raise any question about such proceedings was tantamount to treason, arose, never to disappear. Certain other positions also came to be fixed. Some fifteen years earlier, in the great debates in the Victorian parliament, as also in the subsequent First Report of the Victorian *Royal Commission on Federal Union*, a theoretical distinction had been raised between involvement in wars resulting from British expansion overseas and Australian support for the defence of the British Isles.

This distinction received further support in the debates on the Sudan expedition and it marked future divisions between those who would oppose involvement in the former but not the latter, such as Sir Henry Parkes and others opposed to any involvement abroad. Among this last group another distinction was emerging, between anti-English Irish nationalists, and anti-imperialists who considered the cause and effect of the wars in the capitalist system so interwoven, and its foreign policies so indivisible as to make distinctions between them impracticable. This latter approach tended to blend into that of pacifists whom we first noticed in 1870.

However, the distinction between Irish nationalists and anti-imperialists must be treated with great caution, like all tribal and ethnic distinctions in politics. For one thing, opposition to English rule in Ireland was no Irish monopoly - radicals of most shades shared in it. For another, many Irish expatriates in Australia shared in the broader concerns, opposing capitalist and imperialist policies, not simply from tribal animus, but because they disapproved in general of what they had experienced in a particular situation - and situations tend to be particular manifestations of general conditions.

Lastly, to bracket the Irish nationalists as a separate group would be to ignore the fact that there were politicians, like Dalley, who were Irish in origin and sentiment but as strong in their support for the British Empire as any other imperialists in Australia.

These ideological distinctions and implicit divisions developed into major political positions over the next thirty years and, in the destructive orgy of the first world war, they were to play their part in rending the Australian polity.

Their consequences, like the taunt of disloyalty, have never disappeared, and they remain as obstacles to a rational debate on foreign policy in Australia.

The Sudan expedition may have been a black farce. Yet, the resulting debate served to clarify political positions which would remain significant in future debates. These positions had been developing over a generation. Dalley's expedition, with all its tawdry banality, provided the occasion for classical disputation about political facts.

[margin note: Australia's position in the world.]

The desire for an Imperial role found renewed expression in the despatch of colonial contingents - all of them raised from volunteers - to the Boer War and, in 1900, as part of the British units participating in the international action to suppress the 'Boxers' in China. Neither conflict had a direct relevance to Australia's security - or to that of the mother country.

These actions did not reflect the only significant section of colonial opinion at this time. The Boer War caused considerable public debate and the despatch of colonial contingents did not go unquestioned.[72] A vocal working class press had come into being and the defeat of the great strikes in the early 1890's, had led the trades unions into political action. Labour Parties were founded in the various colonies in quick succession. In 1893, Labour gained control of the cross benches in the New South Wales Parliament, thus being able to exert concessions in return for support. It was also the beginning of a period, rich in Labour and socialist writing, theorizing and debating in Australia. Of the new journals, *Tocsin's* very name - from the Paris *Tocsin des Travailleurs* of the June days of 1848 - proclaimed its heritage and position. It was the organ of the Labour Party in Victoria and later became the *Labor Call*. In Sydney, the *Worker*, renamed the *Australian Worker* in 1913, remains as the journal of the Australian Workers' Union, for many decades the largest and most influential trade union in Australia. It reaches very remote places, being mailed to every member of the union. There were numerous other Labour publications, of more local influence, or of shorter life. The rise of the Labour movement signalled a change in Australia's political culture.

FEDERATION FOR DEFENCE?

Federation of the colonial defence establishments had been advocated by General Jervois, Admiral Wilson, and others at the major defence enquiries. Political federation of the Australian colonies had been suggested by the Colonial Office from the time of Lord Grey to that of Lord Derby.

In the Colonial Office and, later, the Commonwealth Office, federative proposals and policies have, for more than a century, played an important role, still awaiting historical analysis.

In Australia, the first, if qualified success came in response to Derby's suggestion, contained in the refusal to ratify the Queensland attempt to annex New Guinea.

The first formal move had been taken by the 'Annexation Convention' in 1883 towards the establishment of the Federal Council of Australasia. It was not an elected body and only represented participating colonial governments.

The Federal Council was boycotted by New South Wales and, but for one session, by South Australia. Sir Robert Garran had called it a 'mouse'[73], pointing to the fact that it was left with 'scanty legislative power, no executive power, and no power to raise revenue . . .' It did pass some legislation dealing with pearl-shell and *bêche-de-mer* fisheries which was politically and economically significant, affecting relations between Europeans and non-Europeans, including the operation of Asian-owned and operated industries in Australian waters.

In Garran's words the Federal Council 'eked out an inglorious existence till superseded in 1901' by the Commonwealth of Australia.

The expert information on which the 'defence argument' was based, had come from the many reports of Jervois, and evidence of other specialists. Then, in 1889, Major-General J. Bevan Edwards was brought out to report on the defences of each of the Australian colonies. The most famous use of his report was made soon after its publication by Sir Henry Parkes in his Tenterfield oration, linking the Edwards findings emphatically to the cause of political federation.

Edwards appended to each of his individual colonial reports, proposals for Australian defence, recommending 'an organisation, which will not only enable the different colonies to combine for mutual defence, but lay the foundations for a sound military system'. He recommended the federation of the forces, a federal military college, federal munitions factory, gun wharf and ordnance store but, like his predecessors, he was careful not to draw any political conclusions.

Edwards went to great lengths to stress the importance of railways. Before the completion of the railways linking Adelaide, Melbourne, Sydney and Brisbane, it had, he said, been impossible for the colonies to co-operate for defence; and this was not even then possible on account of their different organisation, and because the colonies could not employ their forces outside their own borders:

Railways are now such important factors in war that no combined operations are possible over a large area without them. The break of gauge which exists between the colonies would be fatal to the celerity of movement . . . If, therefore, full benefit is to be derived from the railways, a uniform gauge must be established . . . No general defence of Australia can be undertaken unless the distant parts are connected with the more populous south and east of the continent.[74]

Edwards was especially concerned about Western Australia and about Port Darwin; the loss of the latter would cut off all telegraphic communication with the rest of the world: '. . . Standing as it does face to face with the teeming populations of Asia, and connecting Australia by means of its cable with Singapore, it has become a harbour of the first importance . . .' The 'teeming populations of Asia' - as distinct from European colonial powers in the region - had become part of the defence argument.

Edwards recommended the protection of Darwin by two or three guns and a small force to enable a fast steamer to shelter there, and be employed in keeping up communications through Singapore with the outside world. In his view, the interests of the whole continent, therefore demanded that the railways to connect Port Darwin and Western Australia with the other colonies should be built as soon as possible.

A federal constitution was drafted in a series of intercolonial conventions, meeting as parliamentary delegates in 1890-91, and, on an elected basis, in 1897-8. One of the more remarkable facts is the discrepancy between the strong use made of the defence argument, appealing to the fears of the electorate, and the evident unwillingness of the Conventions, to transfer the railways to the

Commonwealth. The railways were important to colonial governments and parliaments for political as much as for economic reasons. There was no question of transferring them to the Commonwealth of Australia.

On the other hand, Western Australia made its membership of the new Commonwealth of Australia conditional on most explicit promises, that its railways would be linked to those of the eastern States, as the colonies were to be known after federation. These promises are reflected in sec. 51 (xxxiii and xxxiv) of the Australian Constitution, conferring limited legislative powers on the Commonwealth Parliament for the acquisition, construction and extension of railways of, or in a State by the Commonwealth, with the consent of that State.

The Trans-Australia Railway, linking Western Australia with the eastern States, was built between 1912 and 1917, and some further standard gauge connections have been constructed, now linking all State capitals, except Adelaide, which is linked to Melbourne by a broad-gauge line. But the systems remain separate, adding to the strategic problems of domestic defence, not to mention other disadvantages. The spur line, running south from Darwin has never been linked with the Australian railway network.

The importance attached to defence among the priorities faced by the constitutional conventions in the 1890's, may be gauged with some precision by their treatment of the railway question. Despite the very explicit advice of experts like Jervois and Edwards, responsibility for the colonial railway systems remained, with their differing gauges, with the States.

Perhaps the lack of discussion of the External Affairs power will seem even more extraordinary than the Conventions' treatment of the railway question. The elective Conventions had inherited a draft constitution from their appointive predecessors of 1891, including, among the legislative powers of the federal parliament 'External Affairs and Treaties'. There was no great debate on this subject. Beyond agreement to include it at each session of the Conventions, the only discussion of the External Affairs power took place at the Third Session at Melbourne, on 21 January 1898. There was an amendment proposed by the Legislative Council of New South Wales, to omit the words 'and treaties', and, at the suggestion of Edmund Barton (who would be the first Prime Minister of the Commonwealth), the words were omitted. This transaction takes up barely half-a-column in the *Report*.[75] Compared with the long debates of many details, some of which appear now trifling, this smooth despatch of the External Affairs power is worthy of remark - especially, if it is remembered that the distinction between colonial status and sovereignty in Australia remained ambiguous for many years to come, whilst the sole foreign affairs power of the British Empire was that exercized by the British government, and the channel of communication for Australia continued to be the Colonial Office, supplemented, after 1910, by the Australian High Commissioner in London.

THE FEDERAL COMPROMISE

The nineteenth century had seen rapid development, especially in eastern Australia. The steady growth of investment opportunities in the pastoral and agricultural sectors had received an enormous fillip as a result of successive mineral booms. This, in turn, enabled a rapid expansion in the public sector to take place, especially in transport and communications. The spreading pattern of settlement tended to follow rather than precede these life-lines in Australia. The price of such rapid growth and relative prosperity may have been the continuing sense of insecurity and isolation. The concern with defence forces, fortifications and Imperial protection was continuous throughout the century, even if more pronounced among the propertied classes.

It was through this concern that the Asian environment within which the continent is set, first entered the calculations of the colonial governments: Britain's enemies were Australia's enemies; but the avenue of danger lay through their Asian possessions. The sources of danger followed the fluctuating course of Great Britain's relations with other powers, whether in Europe, North America, Africa, or in Asia. Therefore colonial governments took alarm at real or imagined threats from Russia, France, the United States of America and, later, Germany. They gave support to Imperial engagement in China and in Africa.

The United States had been at war with Great Britian in 1812, and there was a moment, fifty years later, during the Civil war, that they came close to war again. Even in the earliest colonial *of the Australian colonies,*

period, America was also an important trading partner. As late as the 1880's, it still appeared as a possible aggressor in defence assessments.

Russia, Britain's ally in the Napoleonic wars, was its enemy forty years later in the war, fought in alliance with France, for the control of the Dardanelles, which for both powers was a precondition for the building of the Suez Canal. As this was also a period of expansion by Russia in North East Asia, fears of Russian aggression, obvious in China and Japan and understandable even in Singapore, also found expression in Australia and led to the fortification of Sydney harbour against the Czar's navy.

It must be remembered that the colonial governors and their military advisors were Imperial officers and that for them every outpost had Imperial significance. Their careers took them to many parts of the world - outposts of the British Empire. Their perspective was to look at local developments in the light of Imperial strategy and commitments. Colonial politicians tended to look through the other end of the telescope. This same consideration applies to their relations with the Colonial Office.

Although France had been an ally in the Crimean war, it was in competition with Great Britain in Egypt, in East and South East Asia, and in the South West Pacific where, for the first time, certain colonial interests were distinct from and different to British interests. Saigon appeared as a potential threat to Sydney first, because of a possible clash of Anglo-French interests in South East Asia and in Egypt, but then because Australian interests wished to elicit British action against France, or to forestall her in the South West Pacific.

This last reason was one also used in the New Guinea adventure. The German occupation may have been precipitated not least by the volume of the colonial clamour. This thinking had led to the one attempt at an independent foreign policy by direct action in the colonial period. It failed. Finding this avenue closed, colonial interests in support of this action returned to an extended use of defence as a substitute for foreign policy. They raised troops for British colonial wars, not only from Imperial loyalty but in order to win the 'gratitude of the Empire' and, through the Imperial connection, to enhance their role in world affairs - and in Australia.

The second consequence of the New Guinea adventure was to

harness defence arguments to the federation movement. *Defence* was a powerful argument of conservative origin and at least, in part, radical adoption, whereas, *White Australia* was of radical origin and general adoption.

Defence contained many seeds of future differentiation between conservatives and radicals over questions about the proper nature and functions of Australian defence forces.

The exclusion movement, on the other hand, in association with the tariff Wall of Protection, led to an extraordinarily insulated but also a very homogeneous society. Because of the success of these policies, Australia was able to develop a broader economic base than would otherwise have been the case. The pressures in the nineteenth century against restrictions on immigration were neither liberal nor humanist: they would not have led to the creation of an open, pluralist society. On the contrary, they were aimed at the creation of a plantation economy with the narrow economic base and the rigidly stratified society peculiar to such systems. Because of the isolation afforded society and the economy by the measures of restriction and protection, Australia is now in a position to evolve as a pluralist society. It is indicative of this evolution that immigration reform became a radical demand in the second half of the twentieth century.

In the 1880's and 1890's, a specific defence programme alone would not have brought success to the federalists because the protagonists of this cause were, indeed, small pressure groups and their agitations and alarms sounded hollow when attached to definite objects. It was, however, useful in promoting federal enthusiasm in support of other arguments.

The exclusion movement was a very different matter. It did have a mass basis of acceptance. It was linked to militant demands for political participation and social reform and for an active responsibility of government in social and economic development. Its opponents were a numerically small group of large employers and of planters. A major part of the middle class - both urban and rural - was willing to support 'White Australia', perhaps more on grounds of ignorance and prejudice than from class interest. For the workers, the order of motives was reversed.

Federation was a compromise of major social forces. The federal movement, though it had a radical wing, was essentially middle-class and largely opposed to working-class aims. In the Conventions, Labour played no significant part but it is hard to doubt that its existence outside, as a growing political force, had a deep effect on the men who drafted the Constitution. Its limited list of legislative powers and the position of the Senate, reflected the enduring separatist loyalties and interests of the colonial politicians who framed it, and ensured the future frustration of Labour governments, attempting to enact their policies of economic and social change.

The Commonwealth of Australia Constitution Act embodied the first Dominion constitution including an external affairs power, as well as a defence power. It remained to be seen to what use they would be put.

Part Three: 1901–1941
Commonwealth within the Empire

FAR EASTERN ALARMS

THE AUSTRALIAN Constitution was the first Dominion constitution to contain a clear foreign affairs power. British apprehensions on the dangers to the unity of the Empire which this implied, proved to be unfounded. There was no rush to exercise this power. Mistakes did not arise from its premature or hasty application.

Australian governments stressed Australia's loyal support of, as well as reliance on Great Britain - the mother country of which many Australians spoke as 'home'. A Prime Minister - Hughes - would say in Parliament in 1919: 'We are more British than the people of Great Britain'.[1] Even in 1939, a Minister for External Affairs would assure the House, with great satisfaction, that 'all that is of the least importance upon foreign affairs is known in Canberra a few hours after it has been handled by the British Foreign Office'. He went on to explain that the Commonwealth government had four channels of advice always in operation. Officers of the External Affairs Department with direct access to all Foreign Office sections, 'despatch with speed the most important news'; the British Dominions Office communicated a somewhat fuller story; the High Commissioner in London reported at once on his consultations with British Ministers; and the many representatives abroad of the Commerce Department added information of particular interest and value to Australia. Further, it had become the practice, with the concurrence of the British government, for the Commonwealth to address communications direct to the embassies, legations and consulates in every foreign country upon matters of Australian concern.[2]

Even in 1939, Australia had no diplomatic establishment beyond that described by the Minister.

The whole period since federation has been one punctuated by debate between conservatives and radicals, the former taking their stance for the first fifty years, behind the Royal Navy and, later, behind the American shield; while their opponents, if not free from a similar sense of insecurity, revealed through their speeches and actions a more 'australocentric' attitude.

Seen from the outside, the dichotomy between the written external affairs power and the less visible restrictions on its exercise, during the decades of acceptance of British leadership, has often appeared very advantageous to the dominions. Bismarck had commented on the degree of British consideration shown to the self-governing colonies (who had no external affairs power at all). At first his comments were incredulous and sarcastic; later, he, too, took account of them. In 1910, Professor Manes, a German economist who had visited Australia, would comment:

The peculiar intermediate position between an independent state and a dependent colony enables Australia to entrench itself behind the British government and to declare that Australia's foreign policy is made in England, whereas foreign states are told in England that Australia is so independent that England may not interfere with its policies. In fact, the latter view has shown itself to be correct sufficiently often, especially in Australasia's xenophobic legislation, which has affected the interests of other British subjects or allies very considerably and which will no doubt one day lead to a most consequential conflict between English and Australian interests.[3]

Manes met many leading figures of the day, including Deakin and Fisher who both impressed him. Though of necessity impressionistic, his study is valuable for his insights from a point of view rarely heard at that time. He was a liberal nationalist and it is remarkable that his analysis of the Australian Labor Party is mistaken in ways similar to Lenin's, of like vintage. Manes expected also that Australian and New Zealand expansion in the Pacific would be a fruitful source of future international conflict. He may not have known of the long-standing dispute with the Imperial government on this subject.

The old loyalties to the mother country and the Empire were subject to novel tensions in the decade of federation. The Anglo-Japanese Commercial Treaty of 1894, was followed by the Sino-Japanese war. The Peace of Shimonoseki, in the following year, was amended under pressure from France, Germany and Russia. 1895 was also the year in which Roentgen discovered the x-ray; Engels published the third volume of *Das Kapital*; and Freud and Breuer, their *Studies in Hysteria*. In 1898, both Gladstone and Bismarck died. It was also the year of the Spanish-American war,

as a result of which the United States became a power in the Pacific
Ocean, having gained the Philippines and Cuba from Spain, and
finally annexed Hawaii. Russia obtained Port Arthur. In 1899, the
Boer war was begun, and in the following year, the European
powers suppressed the 'Boxer rebellion' and, joined by the United
States and Japan, agreed on the policy of the open door in China.
In the same year, 1900, the second German Navy Bill was passed,
providing for an enormous expansion. Splendid isolation was dead.
In 1902, Great Britain entered into a formal alliance with Japan.
In 1904, the Russo-Japanese war, for the control of Korea and
Manchuria, began, leading to the first Russian Revolution and
Japanese victory. The twentieth century had been inaugurated.

Australians found it increasingly difficult to decide what to
applaud and what to fear. During the Russo-Japanese war, they had,
on the whole, voiced support for Japan but its victory was followed
by an abrupt change of mood. The old fears went to work in their
most exaggerated form. The defeat of Russia in North East Asia
might be welcomed. But, were not the victors as dangerous - even
though allied to the mother country - and were they not geographically closer? Moreover, they had defeated one of the great powers -
and they were Asiatics. In that atmosphere, the growth of American
power in the Pacific was widely applauded and the more strident
American attitudes on Asian and Pacific questions found a warm
response in Australia, leading to Deakin's invitation to President
Theodore Roosevelt, to send the American fleet to Australia, in the
course of their cruise to show-the-flag in the Pacific.

Roosevelt was not above confusing the problems arising from
Chinese and Japanese immigration in the western States in his
oratory, which was more emotive than his diplomacy. The latter
was concerned with the rapidly developing American interests in
China and the strategic interests of a great power which the
Pacific cruise was designed to promote. None of these considerations
applied to Australia.

In Australia, insistence on the immigration question reflected
a multi-faceted sense of fear of possible dangers. Immigration control,
the enforcement of the white Australia policy, was carried out by
the Australian government by means of the dictation test which
proved an effective method for deciding whom to admit. Working-
class fears were predominantly economic, overlaid with a dislike of

the alien. Among the middle classes, the latter was the predominant motivation, fuelling the fear that a powerful Japan, though allied to the mother country, was a danger both to the 'white Australia' policy and to a 'white' Australia - a distinction that was not always preserved.

British assurances and references to Japan's record in this matter had little effect. In that context, it is worth noting that an early source for this infusion of the immigration question into considerations of foreign affairs, was a despatch from the British Minister at Tokyo to the Foreign Office of 26 December 1894, that is, after the victory of Japan over China, but before the peace of Shimonoseki.

The Minister, Le Poer Trench, assumed that the terms would include a large indemnity, the appropriation of which, he said, was already under discussion, the 'Military party' having declared that a great portion of it would have to be devoted to an increase in the navy. A strong Japanese navy, Trench felt, might 'at any time constitute a menace not only to Hong Kong and Singapore, but also to the Australian colonies and Canada'. Indeed, especially to the latter, as there was no great probability of differences arising with Japan at Hong Kong or Singapore, except in case Japan were at war with a third power, when matters of contraband and cognate subjects might crop up.

But, Trench thought, the case was different where Australia and Canada were concerned:

There exists a strong inducement for the migration of Japanese labourers and artizans to the Colonies in the great difference of wages - the wages in our Colonies being many times greater than they are in Japan, where they are extremely low - and, if adequate facilities are afforded, that inducement is likely to be effective.

Such facilities as now exist will almost certainly be very greatly increased as soon as the war is terminated. A large number of merchant steamers which have been purchased by Japan for the purposes of the war will then be thrown out of employment, and it is proposed to utilize them by the establishment of new lines of steamers to the Australian ports and elsewhere. Emigration agencies exist in Japan, and their energies will no doubt, with the increase of facilities, be directed in that quarter, and the prospects of a labour difficulty arising there under such circumstances cannot be said to be remote.

Canada may possibly from its climate and other circumstances not offer the same attraction as Australia, but the same difficulty may arise there also.[4]

Trench had a more detailed memorandum prepared on the same subject which he transmitted to the Foreign Office on 11 January 1895; and both documents were at length communicated to the Colonial Office. The latter must have assumed with some justification that the Foreign Office attached some weight to the views expressed by Trench - which they probably did. In any case, the Colonial Office requested and received twenty-five copies of the Trench despatches and the memorandum, for transmission to the Governor General of Canada and the Governors of the Australasian colonies.[5] The infusion, or confusion, of the immigration question with power politics therefore predated federation and received a measure of respectability through these diplomatic documents.

was justified to assume q ?

The Japanese disliked the discrimination and the unequal status which allowed colonial residents to benefit from their status as British subjects under the Treaty, while Japanese citizens were subject to colonial immigration legislation. The Japanese expressed their dislike of that situation repeatedly. However, they never used the Alliance to change it - even at a time during the first world war, when their advantageous position might have tempted them to do what many Australian politicians had for long expected of them.

In the United States, the infusion of the immigration question into foreign affairs was connected with the perfectly absurd proposition of a great Japanese military threat to the North American Pacific coast. This was intellectually cognate to the fears expressed in the course of the debate in colonial Australia, the difference being that it was put about by a major power whose President wished to mobilize racist fears in order to promote his imperialist foreign policy at home.

Theodore Roosevelt's aggressive flamboyance undoubtedly had a certain appeal in Australia, and it fitted Deakin's policy: within Australia, in order to popularize military and naval expenditure and, towards the Imperial government, in his endeavours towards greater independence, for instance, by the creation of a separate, Australian navy.

In the event, some of the sting of the cruise of the American battle-fleet in the Pacific Ocean was removed by the Japanese decision to invite the U.S. fleet to visit Japan - where officers and men apparently hugely enjoyed the lavish Japanese hospitality.

When the Japanese invitation became known in London, Hardinge *as Puccini had anticipated four years before, in his Madame Butterfly.*

ital.

wrote to King Edward VII:

The Japanese government have been very clever in inviting the American fleet to Japan, as they have thus robbed the cruise in the Pacific of its element of danger, and as the Americans are to leave behind them their cruisers and destroyers, their battle-ships will, while in Japanese waters, be hostages for their good behaviour. We sent yesterday an invitation to the American fleet to come to a port of Great Britain if convenient, and offered them any facilities they might desire at British colonial ports.[6]

That last offer was to cause some problems in various places because of the enormous requirements, especially of coal, by that huge fleet. However, the visit to Japan - which the cruise was to have antagonized - was not without success.

In any case, the American government knew as well as the Japanese that the British government was not prepared to use the Anglo-Japanese Alliance for a confrontation with the U.S. Navy and that Great Britain would only agree to maintain naval superiority over European powers. The implications were known, considered and accepted by the major powers in question.

But Australia was no major power. It lacked the means even to monitor, much less to evaluate British diplomacy, let alone that of other powers. Deakin's motives, forcing the British government to pass his invitation to Washington, were, no doubt, mixed - as were Theodore Roosevelt's, in sending that huge fleet on a tour around the globe.

Deakin's actions were, in the end, as little appreciated in Washington as they were in London where all the departments involved had hesitations about his project: the Admiralty, because they would have liked to avoid it but saw no way of doing so; the Colonial Office, because they disliked Mr Deakin's style as much as his methods; and the Foreign Office, because 'the visit of eighteen battleships to a British Colony is a matter of Imperial political importance which should not be decided by the Colony alone'.[7] It would be tedious to enumerate their reasons. But it is relevant to add here those of the Colonial Office for not administering the reprimand which, the Foreign Office felt Mr Deakin deserved, much less giving the above details why such unilateral interference in international affairs was considered irregular: 'Lord Northcote [the Governor General of Australia], had 'so many difficulties with Mr Deakin that they did not much like to increase them'.[8] What,

then, would they have done, had there been vital reasons of state
for doing so? However, Sir Edward Grey's commonsense prevailed:
We must offer to telegraph Washington and ask the C.O. to let us know if
they concur. It will never do to let it be supposed that we made any difficulties
about this.[9]

Meanwhile, however, Deakin had gone to the press and to American
diplomats, in order to make very sure that his invitation would be
noticed. His procedures pleased no one. Finally, Lord Bryce, then
Ambassador at Washington, cabled Grey the American acceptance,
adding that 'Mr Root privately expressed regret that a premature
acceptance of the invitation should have appeared in the Press
without the knowledge of the Department of State'.[10] It was not
quite the splendid diplomacy Mr Deakin may have thought it to
be, but it had raised the possible alternative of an American policy.

The invitation was accepted, the fleet came to Australia under
Admiral Sperry, and went from Australia to Japan. During its
Australian stay, there was a great deal of romantic oratory about
cousins and brethren, and common destiny and such - but little by
way of analysis of the workings of any international system,
its alliances, competitions and conflicts. The question of compat-
ibility of American friendship and Empire loyalty came to be noticed
more clearly later.

A novel set of fears was also voiced during those years: the fear
of military attack by China which was said to be arming; and by
India, 'seething with discontent'. This did not, then, play a major
part in the debate. But it was there and would continue to play a
part in the formulation of concepts that were to grow in importance
in later years.

The alarm about India arose at the time of the Morley-Minto
reforms, providing a set of ingredients not previously heard from
Australian Empire loyalists, including that of opposition to British
policy in another part of the Empire. On 16 September 1908,
Senator Lieutenant Colonel Cameron, speaking in support of the
government's proposals for compulsory military training, said:

We [*sic*] are about to give India a larger measure of self-government than the
country has hitherto had. That this departure is looked upon as a very serious
matter, the statements both of those who have to deal with the civil side of
the Indian government, and those who have to deal with the military side of it,
are sufficient to show. They look upon the situation with serious misgivings. I
have the highest military authority for the statement that this new policy is a

mistake, that it will lead us into serious trouble. My authority is Lord Roberts
. . . If this new policy be carried out as it is about to be, an enormous
responsibility will be thrown upon us in Australia. Can we in this country
look at this Indian question without feeling that in the event of trouble arising
there, the first brunt of it must of necessity fall upon us? We cannot get away
from that position. If trouble should arise in India, as the result of the new
policy that is about to be adopted, and we are not able to help the Mother
Country in her difficulty, or her extremity - if we cannot come to her
assistance with trained and efficient troops - what must inevitably happen to
us in Australia? Do honorable senators think that we shall be able to maintain
our White Australia policy? Do they think we can maintain our institutions if
the Mother Country fails to maintain her power in India? I say that *we here are
part of an Imperial people. We must think imperially, and we must act
imperially.* This problem of India is indissolubly mixed up with the question of
the defence of our own hearths and homes. The holding of India as part of
the Empire is indissolubly mixed up with the very question of our military
ability to exist.[11] (Emphasis added)

The attitudes and alarms voiced by Senator Cameron rested on
the implicit assumptions that greater self-government for India would
lead to trouble; that Britain would have to re-assert her authority by
military means; that Indian independence - which the reforms did not
even envisage - would pose a serious threat to Australia; that
Australia would be centrally involved in such Imperial military forces
and that compulsory military service for Australians was an appropriate, indeed essential, measure in the light of these contingencies.
Cameron favoured conscription specifically because of an Imperial
need and this view was to be sharply challenged in the great conscription referendum campaigns during the war. Cameron's conception of
Australia's Imperial destiny and his views on 'the natives of India'
were equally repudiated by radicals in 1908. For instance, the *Worker*
had this to say about the *Awakening of the Colored Races:*

The races which are not White begin to think of following in the white man's
track. The talk everywhere, in the Brown and Yellow countries as well as in
the white countries, is of reform of constitutions, of parliamentary government.
Japan has now a Labor movement. The new Chinese Emperor's title has been
chosen to indicate that he will promulgate a constitution. Representative
government has been conceded and withdrawn, and now fights for its recognition
in Persia. Some sort of reform has been wrested by the Hindoos from the
dominant white man. A Sultan of Turkey has solemnly driven in state to open
a free Parliament. All these phenomena point to the conclusion that the
colored races have an idea of trying government by the people . . . If the

colored races should persevere in the upward path and learn the lessons of Liberty, undoubtedly it will profoundly affect their racial types. Equally, without doubt, it will lead to a wide disturbance of existing arrangements. There will be then no possibility of a white race insisting on governing a black race 'for its own good'. The cry for a 'White Australia' would be matched by just as insistent a demand for a Brown India.[12]

We do not know whether the anonymous writer of those lines believed in ideas of race; whether he used it as a form of speech; or whether he was simply adapting himself to currently fashionable jargon. What is clear is that he thought that conditions, which man could change, would change societies: his perspicacity is impressive.

The above was no isolated piece. ~~Among the~~ longer articles on *There were* such subjects, ~~of which there was also~~ a constant trickle of news *as well was* items in the working-class press, *India's Troubles*, published by the *Worker* on 10 July 1909* bluntly stated that the lines on which 'our Eastern Empire' was governed might have been well enough a hundred years' ago, but they had become impossible:

Millions of these people perished of famine, while the British sahibs battened upon the wealth that India produced. And scarcely a groan was heard from their lips, though the land was a charnel-house that the Union Jack waved arrogantly over, and the British sahibs feasted riotously amidst scenes of hunger and horror.

Scarcely a word of complaint did they utter, though those whom famine spared were weighed down under the burden of an intolerable oppression, condemned to unremitting toil for the merest pittance, denied all hope of constitutional redress.

The beasts in the jungle are better off than the Indian ryot, whose very name is a byword for the lowest condition of human wretchedness.

Remember, now, that the Hindus are also a proud people, and you'll begin to understand the situation in India.

There is reason for that pride. They are an ancient race, of honourable history. When we were barbarians their civilisation was a world's wonder. Art, poetry, and science flourished there, when Europe was sunk in ignorance. They have a moral code as exalted as our own, a philosophy as profound. And they were thousands of years in front of us.

India had fallen from her former glory, and degenerated, when the British trader came, and turned a profitable market into an Empire of Greed.

Suffering and sorrow, the *Worker* said, had awakened the spirit that had made India great in the old days and 'we are witnessing the reincarnation of a people'. India demanded self-government:

India is demanding control of her own destiny. India is tired of being the slave of a useless aristocracy trampling her under the feet of an alien contempt.

* Document No. 8

India is demanding what even Persia and Turkey have had to be granted - what no nation now with an atom of self-respect will willingly forego - the right of self-government, the right to direct its own affairs and mould its own future, according to its own will and its own genius.

This right, this guarantee of national development, which America conceded to the Filipinos as soon as the Star-spangled banner was unfurled above them, Great Britain has withheld from India for one hundred and fifty years. She has treated the Hindus worse than the negroes of the United States who have at least been given a voice in the government of the country.[13]

That's what's the matter with India.[13]

Racist myths about the 'Yellow Peril' enjoyed a wide circulation in Australia, fostered by the otherwise iconoclastic *Bulletin* as much as by the conventional press. An alternative view, based on the social and economic realities in Asia, found expression in the working-class press. This approach informed the article *The Yellow Peril* which appeared on 14 May 1914, in the *Australian Worker*, and which is reprinted in the Appendix.* It dealt with the huge investment from Europe and the United States, taking place in China, which was leading, by way of the grossest exploitation of the Chinese, mostly of women and children, as in the days of the industrial revolution in England, to enormous profits. Therein, the *Worker* saw a looming danger for the workers in the developed countries:

This attempt of European and American capitalists to capture the patient, industrious, much-enduring, rice-eating millions of China, and turn them into wage slaves who will count themselves passing rich on a shilling a day, is the real Yellow Peril.

The workers of Europe and America are discontented. They are enlightened and comparatively high-spirited.

Their demands for higher wages and better conditions are becoming more and more insistent. Not even with bludgeons and bayonets can they be beaten into a state of passive servitude.

But if the capitalists of the West can transfer their works to the East, and obtain control of the cheap and servile labor there, the Western workers will be confronted with a danger greater than any which has yet beset their path.[14]

DEFENCE AGAINST ENGLAND'S ALLY, JAPAN?

The question of compulsory military service focussed opinions on a specific aspect of policy. Conflicting attitudes had arisen in the very first years of federation over the question of conscription. Ignoring for the moment the pacifist wing of the Labour movement,

*Document No 7

agreement on the principle of conscription covered a deep disagreement about its purposes. The conservatives were concerned with 'our Imperial responsibilities'; the Labour supporters of conscription, and some Liberals, on the other hand, wanted to raise Citizen Defence Forces to defend Australia. The idea gathered momentum following the Russo-Japanese war, on the wave of fear of Japan.

Following earlier attempts in 1901 and 1903, the enabling legislation was introduced in 1909 by the Liberals under Deakin, but not implemented until the succeeding Labour government under Fisher had considered the recommendations contained in Lord Kitchener's *Memorandum on Australian Defence,*[15] to see what was, in the British expert's view, required.

Kitchener here concerned himself solely with the defence of Australia. His reasoning seems, in some respects, to anticipate Curtin's who raised this contingency from 1935 on, and had, as Prime Minister, to face it as a reality in 1941-2. In 1910, Kitchener began, of course, with the axiom held by the British government that the Empire's existence depended primarily upon the maintenance of adequate and efficient naval forces. As long as this condition was fulfilled, and as long as British superiority at sea was assured, then it was an accepted principle that no British dominion could be successfully and permanently conquered by an organized invasion from overseas.

But in applying this principle to Australasia, Kitchener said, considerations of time and space could not be disregarded. The conduct of a great war depended upon the calculated and proper combination of naval, military, and diplomatic forces. Kitchener stressed that it was quite conceivable that in the future, as in the past, national considerations might require the concentration of British naval forces in one or other theatre of operations. It followed that, in areas remote from such a concentration, the British naval forces might find themselves for the moment inferior in strength to an actual, or potential, enemy. In such a situation, although the ultimate British superiority at sea might not be a matter of doubt, some time might elapse before its command of the sea was definitely assured in all waters. As Kitchener saw it, therefore, it became the duty of all self-governing Dominions to provide a military force adequate, not only to deal promptly with any attempt at invasion, but also to insure local safety and public confidence until the

British superiority at sea had been decisively and comprehensively asserted. For this reason it had recently been agreed that the Home Forces of the United Kingdom be organized in such a way as to compel an enemy contemplating an invasion to make the attempt on such a scale that he would be unable to evade British naval forces. The same arguments applied to Australasia, and its land forces should be calculated and organized on this basis. Kitchener's recommendations rested on the Defence Bill of 1909, emboyding 'the principle that every citizen should be trained to defend his country'.

The legislation, which was passed in 1910, provided for conscription for home service - not for service overseas. It was far from universally accepted and it led to a large number of prosecutions. Likewise, Alfred Deakin had worked towards, and the Fisher Labour government had established, the Royal Australian Navy, in opposition to conservative proposals to donate a battleship to the Royal Navy or to pay Britain a subsidy for naval protection.

These very considerable defence efforts were largely justified on the basis of the fears expressed about the mother country's ally, Japan, whose victory over Russia in 1905, had been followed by a veritable cataract of fear and abuse from Australian printing presses, mobilizing the most primitive of political emotions: tribal feelings of 'race'.

By 1911, it was felt in London that something had to be done. Sir Edward Grey wrote on 27 January 1911, in a private letter to his cousin Albert, that the Australians required 'a good deal of education', for 'the logical conclusion of denouncing the [Anglo-Japanese] Alliance would be that Australia and New Zealand should undertake the burden of naval supremacy in China seas. This they are neither willing nor able to do'.[16] This expression of Grey's view is the more valuable for being given in confidence, to one very close to him.

The coronation of George V, attended by the heads of all Dominion governments, served also as the occasion for an Imperial Conference. Grey addressed them at a meeting of the Committee of Imperial Defence on 26 May 1911, treating them 'to a lengthy exposition of British foreign policy - a more detailed survey, in fact, than he ever gave his colleagues'. He made a deep impression on most of the Dominion politicians, including Fisher, but that does not seem to have affected Australian views on Japan. Senator Pearce, the Minister for Defence in Fisher's government, told Grey that it was considered degrading in Australia to have an alliance with an Asiatic country:

I think the Prime Minister of the Commonwealth [of Australia] will agree with me that the Japanese Treaty has been most unpopular in Australia . . . We in Australia are undoubtedly nervous as regards the Japanese, because perhaps we are nearer than any of the other Dominions, with the exception of Canada, to Japan, and they undoubtedly, until the passing of our Immigration Act, were coming in at a very rapid rate to our northern ports and rapidly acquiring a footing, and, in fact, to-day on Thursday Island they outnumber the white population many times over. We also think that as the northern portion of our continent is practically unpeopled there is a grave temptation to such a crowded country to get a settlement there. The feeling in Australia is certainly very nervous as to the Japanese Treaty and as to any extension of it. I know that when it comes before the public that the Treaty is to be renewed, unless that point is fully made public at the same time, namely, that it does not affect our position as regards immigration, there will be a strong outcry against the renewal of the Treaty, because it has always been immensely unpopular in Australia. There has been this feeling in Australia too, that to a certain extent it degraded the position of the Empire to go into a Treaty with an Asiatic country. Perhaps people living in other parts of the Dominions do not quite know the feeling there is in Australia towards the Asiatic peoples and cannot appreciate it, but I think it only right in telling you what is the feeling there towards this Treaty.[17]

Pearce, it should be added, was a political survivor who was again Minister, for External Affairs, twenty-five years later.

in a conserva- government [handwritten margin note]

On 17 March 1914, Churchill, then First Lord of the Admiralty, once again explained the situation in a memorable speech on the Navy Estimates, addressed as much to the Southern dominions as to the House of Commons.[18] He said that these remarks about the Pacific and navy 'policy connected with the great dominions there' were the most important part of his speech. He re-iterated the *credo* of British strategy - that no European power would or could invade or conquer New Zealand or Australia unless the British navy had been destroyed:

The same naval power of Great Britain in European waters also protects New Zealand and Australia from any present danger from Japan. While Japan is allied to Great Britain, and while Great Britain possesses a sufficient margin of naval superiority, Japan is safe from attack by sea from the great fleets of Europe. In no other way in the years that lie immediately before us can Japan protect herself from danger of European interference. It would appear that the reasons which have led Japan to contract and renew the alliance will grow stronger with time. The growth of European interests in China and the general development of European navies on a scale greater than Japan can afford to imitate will lead her increasingly to rely on that sure protection which British naval supremacy can so easily afford. The obligations of Great Britain to Japan under the alliance are not limited to preventing an armada being dispatched from European waters to alter suddenly the balance of naval strength in the China Sea. We are bound to maintain in these waters a force superior to any other European Power, and consequently any danger to Japan arising from a gradual increase of European squadrons in the Far East is also provided against.

Churchill felt that the implications of British policy, as of the contingency of its failure had to be made plain in some detail. Not only had Japan been a good ally, the alliance was useful to both sides:

Quite apart from the good sense and moderation for which the Japanese Government have become renowned, and quite apart from the great services mutually rendered, and the advantages derived by both Powers from the alliance, there is a strong continuing bond of interest between them on both sides. It is this bond that is the true and effective protection for the safety of Australia and New Zealand, and this bond depends entirely on the maintenance of British naval supremacy. If the British Fleet were defeated in the North Sea, all the dangers which it now wards off from the Australasian Dominions would be let loose. If the victorious European Power desired any territorial expansion or naval stations in the Pacific, there would be no forces which Australia and New Zealand could command which could effectively prevent it. If Japan chose to indulge in ambitions of empire or colonisation in the Southern Pacific, she would be no loser so far as the European situation was concerned. But we should have lost at a stroke the means both of making our friendship serviceable and our hostility effective. There are no means by which, in the next ten or twelve years, Australia and New Zealand can expect to maintain themselves single-handed.

Churchill then drew a conclusion of the available alternative - if, indeed, it was an available alternative - that may be read, with the advantages of hindsight as an unintended prophecy:

If the power of Great Britain were shattered on the sea, the only course of the five millions of white men in the Pacific would be to seek the protection of the United States.

It is not suggested that Churchill meant to taunt the Australian politicians when he set out to force them to confront this reality. He went on to deal with the assumptions of strategic planning on which the concept of a united Empire was based. Given those assumptions and that concept, his conclusions were inescapable.

He praised the 'profound wisdom' of New Zealand's policy: 'In giving a splendid ship to strengthen the British Navy at a decisive point, wherever that point may be', the Dominion of New Zealand had shown great insight. The implication for Australia, which had refused to follow that policy and had, instead, insisted on developing its own navy, could not be lost on anyone. Churchill, however, spelled out the strategic implications of the alternatives, as he saw them:

Two or three Australian and New Zealand 'Dreadnoughts', if brought into line in the decisive theatre, might turn the scale and make victory not merely certain but complete. The same two or three 'Dreadnoughts' in Australian waters would be useless the day after the defeat of the British Navy in Home waters. Their existence would only serve to prolong the agony without altering the course of events. Their effectiveness would have been destroyed by events which had taken place on the other side of the globe, just as surely as if they had been sunk in the battle.

Churchill insisted that the dominions were 'perfectly free'; that the Admiralty's responsibility ceased when the facts had been placed plainly 'before Ministers and those to whom they are responsible'. That is to say, in Churchill's view, the Admiralty had a 'responsibility' to place 'the facts' before the public of the dominions. Though he showed little enthusiasm for the centrifugal implications inherent in the policy of developing dominion navies, he was at pains to display some understanding for the motives leading to their creation:

The Dominions want to have their own ships under their own control, cruising in their own waters and based on their own ports. They want to have something they can see, and touch, and take pride in, with feelings of ownership and control. These feelings, although unrecognised by military truth, are natural. They are real facts which will govern events.

It was, he said, easily understood that the difficulties of enlisting the active co-operation of the dominions in naval defence by means of ships they rarely saw, and which were absorbed in the great fleets of Britain at the other end of the world, were insuperable. Therefore, the Admiralty had 'co-operated loyally in the development of the Australian fleet unit. We regard the effort which the Australian Commonwealth is making as heroic, and we will leave nothing undone to make it a complete success. A thoroughly sound arrangement has been made between the Admiralty and the [Australian] Government relating to the use of the Commonwealth fleet in war'.

Churchill based his assumptions for naval strategy on the unity of the Empire. With that view, it was logical to think in terms of

one large Imperial navy, put to use where it was needed, supplemented by smaller local naval units for the defence of local bases
and maritime trade routes. Any capital ships the dominions might
have or acquire would help to provide an Imperial squadron as 'a
really strong and effective naval force - not one or two ships
isolated on particular stations - which will be able to move rapidly and freely about the world, bringing aid wherever it was needed
in time of war'.

The response in Australia was, at best, mixed. The government
of Sir Joseph Cook - the Liberal-Conservative *fusion* - made angry
retorts but some major newspapers, notably the Melbourne *Age*,
wrote in a way, less hostile and more realistic, about the role then
played by Japan, which found a ready response in the working-
class press. The *Age* reported Churchill's speech on 19 March
1914,[19] and discussed it in a leading article on the following day.
Though otherwise very moderate, it did not dismiss the possibility
of a Japanese landing 'on our Northern shores'. But it did refer to
the Japanese threat as a 'bogey'.[20]

On 2 April 1914, a fortnight after Churchill's speech, the
Labor Call carried a major article by the Labour parliamentarian
Frank Anstey, under the title *The Spooks of Imperialism.*[21]
Since Federation, wrote Anstey,

> we have put up £30,000,000 in preparation for war . . . Sometimes the
> bogey has been Russia, then France, then Germany, then back to Russia;
> but since the defeat of Russia in Asia, it has been Japan. For years the
> Japanese menace has been a scare heading in the daily press.

He emphasized that his paper had shown since 1908, that Japan
was economically incapable of waging another major war for a
generation to come without courting 'industrial ruin and internal
revolution'. Yet, awful pictures of an almost certain invasion by
Japan had been conjured up by the assiduous work of politicians
and the press.

Now, said Anstey, quoting the *Age*, Australia was being told
that the 'apprehension of a Japanese invasion of Australia' was
'a mere unsubstantial bogey' and that the navies of Japan and
Australia were to work in alliance in the Pacific. He asked: 'Where
are we now? The jingoes must fake an enemy from somewhere . . .
What will they do next?'

The answer was provided within four months.

WAR

The outbreak of war in 1914, engendered a sense of crisis hitherto unknown in Australia. A general election was pending and, though W.M. Hughes suggested that it should be cancelled and a coalition government formed, it was held on the scheduled date, 17 September 1914, resulting in the government's defeat. Andrew Fisher became Labour Prime Minister for the third and last time.

Speaking on 1 August 1914, at the Victorian country town of Colac, Mr Cook, the Prime Minister had said that if there was to be war - 'if the Armageddon was to come - you and I shall be in it. It is no use to blink our obligations. If the old country is at war so are we.' It was not even a matter of choice but of international law. The consent of Parliament was, of course, a very proper thing to have were the time opportune and Parliament sitting:

Our self-government must extend, of course, to the complete control of our army and navy; but in times like this our resources must be placed where they are needed to be ready at once if the necessity arises.

I hope there shall be no need for our brave men to leave our shores, but I am perfectly certain if the need arises we shall see a response as spontaneous and complete as at any time in our history. There will be no lack of volunteers. My impression is that if war breaks out the trouble will be to get our men to stay home. Good luck to the spirit that prompts them.[22]

Two days later, on 3 August 1914, Cook announced:

The Government has decided in the event of war to place the Australian vessels under the British Admiralty. We have also decided, in the event of war, to offer to the Imperial government an expeditionary force of 20,000 men of any suggested composition to any destination desired by the home government, and the cost and despatch and maintenance will be borne by the Commonwealth Government.[23]

The Minister of Defence, Senator Millen, said that this force would not be drawn from the citizen army. On 8 August 1914, the acceptance of the offer by Britain was reported. Cook said: 'We propose to send . . . at the earliest possible moment and we will organise at the earliest possible moment'.[24]

Although Andrew Fisher had made his famous pledge to stand behind the mother country 'to the last man and the last shilling',[25] this was not the attitude of the entire Labour movement to the war.

On 6 August 1914, the *Australian Worker* published an article *Australia's Duty*, setting out an alternative viewpoint, holding that the war, having been precipitated by the capitalists of Europe, it behoved all in Australia who believed in peace to keep their heads steady, and to decline to be drawn into 'the raging vortex of Jingoism'.[26]

They agreed that, as a part of the British Empire, Australia was involved in any war waged by Great Britain. That was one of the penalties of the Imperial connection: 'It implicates us in the international policy of the British ruling class - that class whose greed has brought one-third of the British people to the lowest depths of degradation and suffering'.

The duty of patriotic Australians, they said, was to defend Australia - 'to hold this soil free from invading feet, and its flag unsullied by hostile hands'. But it was also the duty of patriotic Australians to protest against inflammatory utterances of armchair firebrands who sat at ease in their suburban villas, and yelled for ships and men to be sent on expeditions abroad. Every man and every ship might be needed in Australia and all that they were called upon to do was 'to keep this portion of the British Dominions inviolate'.

The *Australian Worker* continued:

The working classes of the nations have no quarrel with one another. They have done one another no hurt or harm. They have nothing to gain in any shape or form from this war, however it may result.
But they have a vast deal to lose. The rivers of blood poured out will be drawn from their veins. The immense sums of money wasted will be wrung from their labor.
Their homes will be destroyed. Their crops will be ruined. Their women will be dishonored.

Only the big capitalists would reap advantage from the war which, the *Worker* said, they had deliberately provoked, scenting profits in the ghastly horrors of the battlefield. The *Worker* concluded:

This gigantic war is the culmination of the foul wrongs that Capitalism has inflicted on humanity for a century past.
In order that we may come through with our national sovereignty unimpaired, it is absolutely essential that every ship and every man we have should be consecrated to the safeguarding of our own shores.

The publication of this kind of view in the organ of Australia's largest trade union at that time, had its own significance; but the *Australian Worker* was neither alone, nor did these views constitute the expression of a party-line manipulated by some all-powerful central committee. One of the longer articles by John Curtin, Australia's Prime Minister in the second world war, which appeared in the *Labor Call* in October 1914, will be found in the Appendix.*

This strong and literate tradition of socialist, internationalist and pacifist thought, carried for the most part by men and women who were self-educated, had strong affinities with the Socialist International. Paradoxically, although it was not until 1965 that the A.L.P. affiliated with the International, its influence was more deeply and more consciously felt in the early years of this century, when formal links were lacking.

CONSCRIPTION AND LIBERTY

On 27 October 1915, Mr W.M. Hughes succeeded Andrew Fisher as Labour Prime Minister of Australia. Fisher went to London as Australian High Commissioner. Hughes visited Great Britain, France and the battle-fields, and enjoyed a certain popularity in Britain as a result of his flamboyant, martial speech-making.

On his return, Hughes was determined to introduce conscription for overseas service. Aware of the strong opposition within his own party, he would not hold a Labour Party Federal Conference to discuss the matter, nor would he allow a vote to be taken in the parliamentary party on a Conscription Bill. He had determined to take the issue direct to the people, by means of a referendum. Cabinet agreed to this step only after much compromise, by a majority of one. The referendum was bitterly fought. Indeed, it is still regarded as a climactic struggle in Australian political life; one in which the links of political allegiance were forged by a developing colonial society, in the heat of the controversy around this fundamental question. New alignments emerged from the struggle, splitting the governing Labour Party. The question put was:

Are you in favour of the Government having, in this grave emergency, the same compulsory powers over citizens in regard to requiring their military service, for the term of this War, outside the Commonwealth, as it now has in regard to military service within the Commonwealth?

The answer returned on 28 October 1916, was:
     Yes - 1,087,557; *No* - 1,160,037.

* Document No. 8

After the defeat of this referendum, the Prime Minister, followed by some twenty-four out of sixty-five members present, left the Labour Party Room, to form a new government supported by the former opposition. Among those following Hughes was Pearce, who had instructed Sir Edward Grey on Australian racism.[27] The new government used its war emergency powers extensively under the Labour opposition's militant attacks, which were all the more bitter for being directed against former comrades and friends. For many years, public debate was affected by these issues and the composition of the anti-conscriptionist movement is well worth examining.

At one end of the spectrum were the Australian Catholics of Irish descent, who regarded this as an English War and of no concern to the Irish, some averring that any weakening of England would advance Irish interests. In their opposition to conscription, they were led and encouraged by the Archbishop of Melbourne, Daniel Mannix, who had arrived from Ireland in 1913. At the other end of the spectrum were the international socialists, who opposed the war as imperialist. To this view also, Archbishop Mannix occasionally gave a benign nod.

Between these groups, there were many who were either pacifists on moral or religious grounds, or who were opposed, for similar reasons, to compelling youths into the trenches. There was also a strong feeling in the community that Australia was doing enough, if not more than its share, in the Allied war effort. As well as these articulate views, there was a good leavening of 'know-nothing isolationism', and of people who were opposed to conscription on grounds of private convenience.

A second conscription referendum was held on 20 December 1917, the question put being:

Are you in favour of the proposal of the Commonwealth Government for reinforcing the Australian Imperial Forces Overseas?

The reply: *Yes* - 1,015,159; *No* - 1,181,747.

The previous sources of opposition were strengthened by certain contemporary factors which contributed to the increased negative majority. The events of the Russian Revolution gave impetus to the opponents of the war. The atrocious losses on the western front did not fail to have their impact. Vindictively suppressed strikes at home and a fierce censorship, fractured the very sense of national unity which the government had been at pains to create.

The parliamentary atmosphere of that period may be gauged by the following episode. In 1917, Hughes decided to hold a secret meeting - not a session - of Members of Parliament, presumably in order to air his views on Japan. Members were invited to that meeting on the condition that they bound themselves 'not to reveal anything of a character which they cannot, and do not obtain from the usual sources of public information . . . Any gentleman who finds he has conscientious objections, or apprehends any danger from the course proposed, can save himself by staying away from the meeting.' A Labour member, Mr Fenton, commented:

It would seem that in Australia, in this Commonwealth or National Parliament, we are called upon by the leaders, so-called, to maintain secrecy or silence in regard to subjects that are being discussed and have been discussed in the public journals of other countries nearly ever since the war began . . . We are asked to be silent, although if we go into the library we find in the magazines there articles contributed by some of the best brains in the world, including the brains of Japan, dealing with the very subject which we are not allowed to discuss. These matters are dealt with elsewhere in the most open manner, and without any apology; and, altogether, I think that there is too strict a censorship in Australia. Take up any British journal, whether it be the *Times*, a Labour paper, a Socialist paper, or a magazine, and we find that almost unlimited latitude is allowed in the discussion of questions in relation to the war. Public addresses by public men in Great Britain, no matter to what party they belong, have the freest possible circulation . . . In reference to Japan, particularly amongst writers and editors, a triangular controversy has been going on ever since the war began in respect to trade and treaty questions, and this controversy has been contributed to by Japanese, British, and American writers. If these questions are discussed in the journals to be found on the table of the Library, and in every library in the world, why should secrecy be observed here? In my opinion, this hush-up business makes the public suspicious that there are being kept from them things they ought to know.[28]

Hughes relied heavily on the special powers of the War Precautions Act, and thus produced a qualitative alteration of the role of government in Australia. In doing so, he created many enmities on both sides of the House, as well as in the community at large, which festered long after 1923 - the year he was forced to resign the Prime Ministership and the leadership of the Nationalist Party which he had created after leaving the A.L.P.

Australians had to learn anew that to question the policies or motives of those in power could be dangerous; that war-time censorship could be used for domestic political warfare; that men might be detained for being of Irish or German *origin*; that the very detainees might be offered their release in order to break strikes - and would, for the most part, refuse. Members of Parliament of the decimated opposition had to spend much of their time on pains-taking questions and provision of proof in such cases, and on complaining about the severity of a political censorship, far in excess of what was thought necessary in Britain; in braving threats, abuse and the kind of propaganda sheltering behind the very censorship that was to change the political culture of the Commonwealth. Debate, equated with argument, was now dangerous. Families were split over the issues, as were most other social organisations.

The results were far-reaching. In the second world war, it took a great deal of irrefutable, heart-rending evidence to convince sceptical Australians of the truth about Nazi ferocity because of their revulsion against the grotesque propaganda of the first world war. The fear of debate and its consequences lingered in Australian society long after that time. Under Hughes, the atmosphere and standards of politics reached lowest level, that time, and that was to have long-term effects.

In the last year of the war, Hughes, now accompanied by Cook, once more went to the United States and England, participating in occasional meetings of the Imperial War Cabinet. Hughes then succeeded in obtaining a place at the table of the peace conference where he displayed great concern about the disposition and future defence significance of German New Guinea in particular and the whole settlement of the Pacific region in general.

THE WAR AIMS DEBATE

There were two, inter-connected, international questions of importance to Australia during the first world war: Australian estimates of and attitudes to Japan, and the disposition of the German possessions in Melanesia and other parts of the Pacific Ocean.

Immediately after federation, the British government had pressed for the transfer of British New Guinea to Australia, a move for which there was wide support in the Australian Parliament. However, J.C. Watson who then led the Labour Party in the House and, three years' later, became the first Labour Prime Minister, had ounded this note of caution:

> . . the motion [to transfer New Guinea to Australia] . . . involves the whole
> question of whether we are to set up, at this early stage in our career, a
> Monroe doctrine for Australia. I can quite understand the desire to have this
> doctrine . . . But . . . it is idle in the connexion to quote the United States,
> because years ago, when the Monroe doctrine was announced there, that
> country even then was a power as far as population, wealth and resources
> are concerned. We here in Australia are not such a power as America then
> was.[29]

Watson had not been impressed, either, by the defence argument: whatever evil was likely to arise from the settlement of New Guinea by a foreign nation had, it seemed to him, already arisen. The great danger that was always pointed out was that of foreign powers getting military or naval bases near Australia: New Caledonia and the New Hebrides, for instance. But in the case of New Guinea, both Holland and Germany had already between them a fair proportion of the territory. Therefore, so far as one object of Australia's taking possession was concerned, it was beside the point. Those two powers were already established in New Guinea, and 'any advantage which that possession may be to them from a tactical stand-point is available now'.[30]

Fisher, who had favoured Australian control over New Guinea as well as an Australian Navy, nevertheless expressed similar views about the potential defence value of New Guinea for Australia.[31] Curtin's view in 1914 was less gentle.[32]

Shortly after the outbreak of war in 1914, German New Guinea was occupied by Australian forces on behalf of Great Britain.[33] The British invitation to occupy German New Guinea included the provision that —

any territory now occupied must, at the conclusion of the war be at the disposal of the Imperial government for purposes of an ultimate settlement.

On the question of Japan, the Australian government were caught on the horns of a dilemma, largely of their own making. It is unnecessary to retrace the history of the relations between the powers in East Asia and the Pacific, the subject of a number of competent studies.[34] I am here concerned with certain facts pertinent to the debate in Australia.

On 3 August 1914, Sir Edward Grey cabled the British Ambassador in Tokyo, Sir Connyngham Greene, to —

warn Japanese that, if hostilities spread to Far East and an attack on Hong
Kong or Wei Hai Wei took place, we should rely on their support.35

That is to say, Grey was preparing the ground to invoke the
casus foederis. Out of concern about neutral reactions, especially
American and Dutch suspicions, shared in Canada and Australia,
he expressed second thoughts resulting in the unsuccessful attempt
to hedge the Japanese in, by limiting the scope of their participation
in the war. The results of this episode had unfortunate results in the
long term, for they were no more forgotten in *Gaimusho*, than Bismarck's behaviour over colonies had been in Whitehall.

At any rate, Japan sent Germany an ultimatum which resulted
in the Japanese declaration of war of 24 August 1914. Japan also
issued a statement about her intentions, in order to appease the
suspicions of other powers and the dominions in the Pacific.
Meanwhile, Grey had recovered his usual common sense and he
had cabled Greene on 20 August 1914:

Japan cannot go into this business for nothing: if Germany is beaten Russia
France and ourselves will all get something somewhere & the Japanese
cannot be told that there is nothing for them anywhere.36

Japanese war aims were centred in the former German possessions
in China and the North Pacific. Although the British government
did not undertake to support these claims officially until February
1917, they were aware of them. They had, indeed, ensured that the
Governor General of Australia, Sir Ronald Munro Ferguson (later
Lord Novar), would acquaint his Ministers in general terms of the
fact that the German Pacific colonies would be divided between the
British and the Japanese Empires at the equator, which, Munro
Ferguson assured Harcourt in January 1915, he had already done.
This ~~question~~ is of some importance, in view of Hughes' later
statements.

In 1916, Great Britain sought further naval assistance from Japan.
The Japanese government suggested that they might be able to make
four cruisers and four destroyers available and, on their part,
made a number of requests, including Australian adhesion to the
Anglo-Japanese Commercial Treaty of 1911. Like every other power,
Japan was pursuing her 'interests' but, unlike the others, she nursed
a deep grievance, based on 'racial' discrimination - especially
where Australia was concerned.

Protracted negotiations between Hughes, Grey and the Japanese

Ambassador in London ensued in the spring of 1916. In the course of these, Hughes insisted on the inclusion of the Australian-occupied islands in the South Pacific in an Australian shipping monopoly. As a consequence, he had to accept a similar Japanese monopoly North of the equator.[37] Although there was then no formal agreement on the future of the German possessions, their *de facto* division in the Pacific between the British and the Japanese Empires at the equator, assumed a negotiated character through Hughes' diplomacy in London in 1916.

As for the naval assistance requested by Britain, it was given without Japan 'insisting on her price'.[38] A similar situation arose in the following year, as a result of urgent Admiralty pressure on the Foreign Office for greater Japanese assistance. Now, the Japanese government asked for the formal agreement on their claims to Shantung and the Pacific islands North of the equator. Once again, Japan acceded to the British request for naval assistance without awaiting a reply to their requests: the *Tsukishima* and *Viitaka* would be based on the Cape of Good Hope to chase German raiders in the South Atlantic and the Indian Oceans. The *Akashi* and two flotillas of destroyers would be despatched to the Mediterranean.[39] It should be added at this point that Japan was supplying large quantities of equipment and ammunition to Russia, though they steadfastly refused all suggestions for sending expeditionary forces to the Western or the Russian fronts.[40]

The British government decided to give the assurances asked for by Japan, provided that New Zealand and Australia would agree: there was no loss of British interests involved and the Japanese were in occupation. It would therefore be preferable to agree now gracefully than to squabble later. Moreover, perhaps as an afterthought, it was considered that 'the possible entry into the war of the United States increased the necessity in regard to Japan and Shantung and the occupied islands North of the equator in order to avoid negotiations in the subject with another power'.

Both the Australian and the New Zealand governments agreed and the British government then advised the Japanese government:

His Majesty's Government accede with pleasure to the request of the Japanese Government for an assurance that they will support Japan's claims in regard to the disposal of Germany's rights in Shantung and in possessions in islands North of the Equator on occasion of a Peace Conference, it being understood

that Japanese Government will, in eventual peace settlement, treat in th
same spirit Great Britain's claims to the islands South of Equator.[41]

;he|

Hughes was, therefore, not only aware of the situation ~~and~~ ha
approved British policy. More than that, by insisting on the exclusiv
Australian control over coastwise shipping in the islands South of th
equator and, consequently, by Japan to the North of it, he ha
taken an active part in settling the dividing line between the tw
empires in the Pacific. The surprise in the Foreign Office at hi
volte face at the end of 1918, is therefore understandable when, or
4 November 1918, he wrote at length to Lloyd George, re-openin
that matter and demanding the whole of the former Germai
possessions in the Pacific Ocean: North as well as South of th
equator. Hughes claimed that the islands North of the equato
were 'most important to Australia from the point of view both o
defence and of possible offence'.[42]

The Foreign Office felt that a reply was indicated. They wer
not amused. A detailed reply, setting out the history of this affaii
was drafted and carefully amended by Balfour who had succeede
Grey at the end of 1916. Though it was not sent, it is a documen
of intrinsic value which, together with the letter from Hughes
is printed in the Appendix. So much for the facts of internationa
history. What about the debate in Australia?

In Australia, the question of Japan had been divisive since th
first Anglo-Japanese Alliance - and the division did not necessaril
follow party lines. Anti-Japanese attitudes did not disappear witl
the activation of the Alliance in 1914. For instance, while Fishe
was still Prime Minister, an opposition member complained in th
House about the absence of the Japanese flag at public function
when allied flags were flown, enquiring whether this was due t
government action. Fisher, of course, replied that it was not, an
that 'the government . . . recognizes equally and alike all who ar
associated with us and would not willingly insult any nation.'

~~(Emphasis added.)~~

Not much later, on 4 August 1915, J. H. Catts, at that tim
possibly the Labour member best informed on world affairs, asked
Is the Minister of External Affairs aware that, in January, Japan issued a
ultimatum to China, and that, as the result of the negotiations, there has bee
a compulsory military unification of Japan and China, practically unde

*Document No 10

the dictatorship of Japan, and that thereby the balance of power in the Pacific has been radically altered? It is stated in the press that the British Government were consulted; and I should like to know whether the Minister of External Affairs has been in any way informed in regard to this matter; and, if so, whether he can inform the House as to the actual position?

The Minister: I have no recollection of the Department having received the information to which the honorable member refers. I did see in the press vague statements of which the honorable member has conveyed the substance, but I do not think that we have any official knowledge that the steps taken, or alleged to have been taken, by Japan have actually been taken.

Mr J.H. Catts: They have: it is all fixed up.

The Minister: I shall make further inquiries, and let the honorable member know.[43]

Catts had referred to the Twenty-one Demands, but the real interest in Australia centred on the Pacific rather than on China. Cook, then Leader of the conservative Opposition, had put that view as early as 15 April 1915:

There is a whole crop of questions regarding the Pacific which call for careful and resolute treatment. There is, for instance, the future control of our tropical Pacific Islands. These are a great responsibility for Australia, but one, I believe, that we shall be able to shoulder; indeed, we should be glad to have the opportunity of assuming any responsibility arising out of the acquirement [sic] of these islands, for, in my judgment, they should never have belonged to any other country but Australia . . . Japan, too, has made some changes in the Pacific, and there may be questions of a diplomatic character arising which can only be settled around a table at the proper time. Some prominent journalists in the Old Country are saying that the British people desire no territorial acquisitions as the result of the war. That may be so, speaking broadly and generally, but I venture to say that we in Australia expect some little additions to our territorial possessions in the Pacific.[44]

On this issue, Empire loyalty clearly had limits - those of a separate, Australian, imperialism. But even at the end of 1916, Hughes, in Parliament thought it would be prudent of him 'to refrain from expressing any opinion on that matter'.[45]

However, after the conscription referendums and the consequent political changes, talk of an Australian Monroe doctrine in the Pacific came to be renewed. The Japanese occupation of German possessions in the Pacific North of the equator became the basis for demands for the *annexation* of German New Guinea and other, more expansionist plans: the doctrine described by Hughes as 'Hands off the Pacific'. Hughes and his colleagues were not alone in pursuing their peace aims during the war. It was a concommitant of the war and a consequence of the policies that had led to its outbreak. Talk of Monroe doctrines was not a plagiarism unique to Hughes: Viscount Ishii had used it also in 1917, in describing his view of Japan's role in China, in his talks with President Wilson and Lansing. What was unique was Hughes' support while he was Prime Minister for sowing fear and hatred during the war against the very ally who was supplying the naval escorts for Australian troopships and other convoys.

It would seem that this was one of the reasons for inviting members to secret meetings, as indicated by the remarks of Dr Maloney, the Labour member for Melbourne, in the debate on 14 June 1917, referred to before:

If I understand the Prime Minister aright, I take it that the question of Japanese relations will not be brought in at all at the meeting to-morrow. If I am wrong, I enter my protest at once, and object to a noble ally being insulted, not so much by actual statements, as by innuendoes.

Maloney stated that this view of Japan's being subjected to insults and slanders were 'the words of the [Japanese] Commander-in-Chief as well as the words of one of the great statesmen Premiers of Japan . . . The people of Australia should know the worst, so that they may face it. If it is that Japan is a danger to Australia, let the people know it. I do not think she is, and I protest against any insult being offered to her'.[46]

The disposition of German possessions in the Pacific acquired fresh urgency in the debate, as a result of the American entry into the war and President Wilson's war aims of which Senator Millen, the government leader in the Senate said: 'Our latest Ally has made it tolerably clear that she is little disposed to continue a war merely to enable one country to acquire territory at the expense of another.'[47]

It was curious as well as typical that the Ishii mission to Washington was seen by the Australian government as dealing with the status of those islands taken from Germany by the might of the Japanese arms, naval and military. Not a word here about China - though in fact there is not a word in the Ishii-Lansing exchange of notes about the Pacific. Yet it was that issue which, in the words of Senator Millen, 'is something that has grown out of this war which has a very great bearing on our future, and in connexion with which our American cousins ought to know what I might call the innermost thoughts of the administrators of Australia's affairs'.

The disposition of the German possessions was not a subject of any unanimity. A resolution -

That the restoration of the captured German Colonies in the vicinity of the Australian Continent will constitute a standing menace to the safety of this country, as well as to the future peace of the world [48]

was opposed in Parliament by the Labour Party under six heads which may be summarised in this way:

1. It was not worth prolonging the war for these islands;
2. this resolution was in clear contradiction to Wilson's peace aims of no annexations, no indemnities, and the freedom of the high seas;
3. against what enemy would occupation of the islands give protection? It had become impossible under the system of secret diplomacy to foresee, over a period of ten or fifteen years, which countries would be enemies and which allies;
4. Australia already held more territory than she could develop; external territories would create onorous international responsibilities;
5. annexation of former German colonies would involve Australia more deeply in the colour question;
6. the inhabitants of those islands should be empowered to say under whose flag they wished to live. [49]

The concern for the welfare of Asian and Pacific peoples had never quite disappeared during the war. In 1918, the Labour Party took up the plight of the Indian workers in Fiji, working for the [Australian] Colonial Sugar Refining Company. The conditions of those workers was such that even the vice-regal Government of India was perturbed. It was felt in the Labour Party that 'by representations to the Imperial government or by pressure upon the Colonial Sugar Refining Company' some alterations should be brought about.[50] Finlayson had raised this matter in the House and went on to link it with the 'policy of Australia in regard to the Pacific . . . we should surround ourselves with such a protection of friendly nations as will secure to us, so far, at any rate as the Australian possessions in the Pacific are concerned, a fair and reasonable opportunity in peace and security'.[51]

Meanwhile, Hughes had made a speech in New York in which he enunciated the 'Australian Monroe Doctrine in the South Pacific'.

Hughes advanced the same arguments as are set out below in his speech on the Second Reading of the bill ratifying the Treaty of Versailles. In New York, he concluded:

. . . You understand that unless the Allies are triumphant peace will be worse for Australia than war. Our destiny, like that of your Western States, lies in the Pacific . . . We therefore seek America's steadfast co-operation, and we are committed by inexorable circumstances to the doctrine, 'Hands off the Pacific'.52

Finlayson had quoted from that speech and, against a barrage of interjections, set out to demonstrate the contradictions between the position of Hughes and those of Lloyd George and Wilson. He claimed that speech-making about terms, both by the Germans and the Allies, had contributed to the lengthening of the war. Finlayson was not opposed to future expansion: 'I have', he said, 'a most hopeful opinion of Australia in future dominating the Pacific. [But] are we prepared, at this present time, to accept this tremendous responsibility?' He questioned the wisdom of over-extension of administrative capacity.

THE DEBATE ABOUT VERSAILLES

On returning to Australia, Hughes reported to Parliament, in his Second Reading speech to the Bill ratifying the Treaty of Versailles. Among other things, he said:

Perhaps there are very few Australians who realize that New Guinea is greater in size than Cuba, the Philippines, and Japan, except Sakhalin, all rolled into one, that it is only eighty miles from our northern shores and that those who hold it hold us. Recollect that our coast line is so vast that to circumnavigate Australia is a voyage as great as from here to England, and no five million people can possibly hold this continent when, eighty miles off, there is a potential enemy. Well stretched out from New Guinea there are New Ireland and New Britain. There are literally hundreds of other islands stretching out and out, every one of them a point of vantage from which Australia could be attacked. The possession of those islands was necessary, therefore, for our safety. We sought to obtain direct control of them, but President Wilson's fourteen points forbade it; and, after a long fight, the principle of the mandate was accepted. Then the nature of the contest changed, and, since the mandate principle was forced upon us, we had to see that the form of the mandate was consistent, not only with our national safety, but with our economic, industrial, and general welfare.53

Hughes said that he had sharply rejected President Wilson's

'open-door policy'. He had told the British Empire Delegation at the Peace Conference, in 1919, that if the 'open-door principle' operated, the former German territory in New Guinea would become Japanese or German within ten years. As an effective barrier against hostile (particularly Japanese) penetration, Hughes wanted the white Australia Policy to operate throughout the Bismarck Archipelago, which Australia wanted for purposes of defence. The extent of Hughes' display of determination on this point may be measured by his blunt statement to Lloyd George and other Cabinet members: 'As regards the Pacific Islands, my attitude is that if anyone wants to shift Australia from them, they will have to come and do it'.

The continued Japanese presence in the Marshall and Caroline Islands after the war, was a further source of anxiety to Hughes. Together with New Zealand, he instituted an elaborate negotiation, whereby, as Mr Austen Chamberlain put it: 'Australia and New Zealand held that it would be better to allow Japan to exclude us from the islands north of the Equator, in order to have the right to exclude the Japanese south of the Equator'.[54] That was Mr Hughes' version.

The Parliamentary Leader of the A.L.P., Mr Tudor, took the view that it did not matter very much whether this Parliament agreed, or not with the Peace Treaty, which would, in his opinion, in any circumstances be signed by Great Britain: 'Of course, it is probably better that all the Parliaments of the Dominions which were represented at the Peace Conference should have an opportunity to discuss the Treaty'.[55] Tudor deplored the fact that, in spite of the high-sounding phrases, neither disarmament nor an end to secret diplomacy were in sight, and he pointed to the A.L.P. peace proposals of June 1917, preceeding the British Labour Party Peace proposals by six months and Wilson's fourteen points by seven, and he applauded the creation of the I.L.O.

It was left to Catts to deflate Hughes' claim to statesmanship and Catts was probably closer in his views to the Prime Minister than many other Labour members, on such subjects as Japan, 'White Australia' and Australia's Asian policies. He had played an active role in the recruiting campaigns for the A.I.F. but he had opposed conscription and remained in the Labour Party. Now, he flatly denied what Hughes had claimed: 'The Prime Minister gained nothing at the Peace Conference, seeing that the disposition of the

Pacific Islands was determined in 1915, 1916, and 1917'.[56] He
believed that Hughes 'apparently gave the islands away in 1915
and then went and kicked up a shindy in France in 1919 to mislead
the people of this country'.[57]

Catts had a strong grasp on the facts available to him. He produced
the texts of the Anglo-Japanese exchange of letters, constituting
the agreement of 1917, as well as the Franco-Japanese correspondence.
His sources being questioned, he revealed that they were 'records
produced before the Foreign Relations Committee of the American
Senate'. His assertions are supported by the Foreign Office *résumé*
of negotiations, printed in the Appendix.

He vehemently attacked 'what had been done to China as one of
the greatest blots on civilization. As shown by the French correspondence, China was induced to come into this war for the advantage
of the Allies; to release 40,000 tons of German shipping for the use
of the Allies, China was induced to declare war on Germany.
The only reward China received has been her despoliation right and
left . . . I mean that to hand over 36 million defenceless Chinese
in the province of Shantung to Japan, for the simple reason that
China, being practically unarmed, was not in a position to fight, is
a disgraceful blot on civilization'.[58]

Catts supported the abortive American proposals for the internationalization of all the former German Pacific possessions and
the creation of a buffer state which, he said, Hughes had turned
down by representing in Paris that mass indignation meetings had
been held throughout the length and breadth of Australia, pro-
testing against internationalization - an entire fabrication. Catts held
that the American solution would have been preferable to the
Japanese presence in the Marshall, Caroline and Ladrone groups.

Ignorant of the earlier understanding about the inapplicability
of the Anglo-Japanese Alliance in any dispute between the United
States and Japan, Catts expressed grave fears that under the Treaty
of Versailles, by virtue of the sanctions provided in the League of
Nations Covenant, Australia might be forced to fight against the
United States. That fear we have encountered in pre-war years at
the time of Admiral Sperry's visit. Catts quoted the American
opposition to the Shantung provisions of the Treaty, and pleaded
for accepting it only with reservations: he said that he had asked
Sir Joseph Cook what would happen supposing America refused to

ratify this violation of China, and war broke out between Japan and America? 'Under this League of Nations we should be called upon to fight for Japan against our cousins in the United States of America'.

That Peace Treaty, Catts urged, ought to be received with some qualification in this respect. There was no power on earth that would make Australia fight for Japan against America. It would be as well to face that fact to-day, 'before we sign the Treaty which commits us to such an impossible condition'.

We have been told to-day by the Minister for the Navy that if we sign the Treaty, and refuse to fight for Japan, our commerce will be blockaded, and we shall be regarded as outcasts and pariahs, and ridiculed as a people not prepared to accept our Treaty obligations. If such is possible under the Treaty, we had better face the position now than face a worse position in years to come.

Catts was asking for qualifications to the Peace Treaty under three headings: 'so far as to safeguard our American-Australian friendship, so as to show that we are not a party to the settlement of Shantung, and do not agree to bringing Japan 3,000 miles towards these shores, and thereby endangering the White Australia policy'. He added:

I say that Germany in the Ladrones, the Marshalls, and the Carolines would be a preferable neighbour to Japan. I would rather have a white race as a buffer between this country and the hordes of Asia than set up an aggressive coloured race in the islands - I would [not] open the gate to practically 400 million of the Asiatic agony to come to our very gates.[59]

His deepest fears and chief objections were racist. If any one belief can be described as ideological in Australian public life until the second world war, it was the fear of Asia and the unquestioned need for 'White Australia'. An accusation of doing anything to neglect this dogma, was met with emphatic denial; often with a counter-charge. Indeed, Hughes, in his speech in this debate, made much of his struggle to have the White Australia policy accepted before agreeing to the Mandate:

Remember that this is the only community in the Empire, if not, indeed, in the world, where there is so little admixture of race. Do you realize that, if you go in England from one county to another, men speak with a different accent; that if you go a few miles men speak with a different tongue; that if you go from one part of France to another, men can hardly understand one another? Yet you can go from Perth to Sydney, and from Hobart to Cape York, and find men speaking the same tongue, with the same accent . . . We are all of the same race, and speak the same tongue in the same way. That cannot be said of any other Dominion in the Empire, except New Zealand, where, after all, it can be said only with reservations, because that country has a large population of Maoris. We are more British than the people of Great Britain, and we hold firmly to the great principle of the White Australia, because we know what we know . . .

Hughes quoted Baron Makino as saying that the Japanese were a proud people and had fought by Australia's side in the war; that they regarded it as intolerable that they should not be treated as the equals of Australians and other races. Hughes stated that he had replied he would be one of the first to recognise them as 'our equals'. He hoped that they would always remain friends and Allies. He recognised to the full what they had done in the war. No one had a greater admiration than Hughes for the habits of industry and perserverance of the Japanese 'race'. Australia was bounded by the same ocean and hemmed about by the same conditions as was Japan. 'But', Hughes added, 'the history of your people has its roots in far different soil. I hope they will always be our friends and Allies . . . We hope that not only with Japan, but with all nations, we shall remain for ever on terms of the most perfect friendship. We claim the right, however, to say in regard to Australia who shall enter and who shall not'.[60]

That was also a crucial part of Catts' view of the world. We have just seen how traditionally socialist and internationalist views could be found side by side with this fear-inspired racist ideology.

Catts' views are also remarkable, but by no means atypical, for joining his belief in the necessity of a 'white' Australia with a strong concern over injustice done to Asians in Asia - in this case to the Chinese. 'White' Australia had economic and social origins, and these were its rational bases. But it also had strong non-rational aspects, as do the communal tensions elsewhere.

The clearest statement of internationalist pacifism in the memorable Treaty of Peace debate came from Frank Brennan who, in 1929, would become Attorney-General in the Scullin government. He restated Tudor's view of Australia's status in this matter:

As a matter of fact, the Commonwealth has no status in regard to the signing of the Treaty beyond that of a Dependency which is necessarily bound by the action of the Imperial government and of the British Parliament. I recognise that the Imperial government have naturally been disposed to flatter Australia with the suggestion that she entered the Peace Conference, and became a party to the Peace Treaty, as a nation. But we know that that is a mere compliment

Commonwealth within the Empire

to her, a mere attempt - and perhaps not an unnatural one - to pander to the vanity of some of those who pretended to speak at the Conference for the whole of the people of Australia.[61]

In fact, this very vanity - and insistence - undoubtedly assisted the movement towards a full Dominion foreign affairs power,which became effective in the Statute of Westminster, 1931, but it was ~~which however~~ not adopted by Australia until 1942. In the course of his speech, Brennan vigorously presented an alternate view of the course of the negotiations, an opposing ethic and the opposition concept of Australia's proper role:

. . . at the conclusion of the struggle, which we were assured had been fought for purely defensive purposes and for the establishment of right against might, we should find ourselves at a Peace Conference, which was summoned to give effect to the points laid down by President Wilson, arguing, bargaining, and contending for more territory to be added to the already over-large territory which we Australians possess. Of course, members of the Labour Party had more than once ventured to say that it was this lust for conquest which played an important part in inflaming the minds of men and thus prolonging the war. It was not until the very end of the struggle, until we have actually entered into the Peace Conference, that it became apparent, from the unblushing admissions of those who represented us, that we had really had in view the hated spring of evil annexation . . . Members of the League agree that the manufacture by private enterprise of implements and munitions of war is open to grave objections. There is not a Labour man in Great Britain, France, Germany or Australia, but has scathingly denounced this practice of building up fortunes for capitalists out of the manufacture of these engines of destruction, and not so long ago, while the war was in progress, it was a matter of public scandal that the very bishops in the House of Lords were drawing dividends from the private manufacture of these very things. The Covenant of the League of Nations, if it does not expose it, at least condemns it, and promises us some reformation for the future . . . Who were those who gave their best efforts to the eloquent denunciation of secret diplomacy? Some were those for whom the Prime Minister (Mr Hughes) has manifested so deep a contempt, the pacifists, the anti-militarists, the Socialists, and Labour men, of whom he was once one. Those were the men who, in the face of bitter opposition, denunciation, calumny, and cowardly attack of every kind, persisted in pointing out that as long as the destinies of nations were left to the secret and aristocratic channels of diplomacy, so long would we have no guarantee of the peace of the world; and they said these things and argued them, and proved them before the blood of the world's people began to flow. After it has flowed, it is admitted by the distinguished representatives who assembled at Versailles that Labour, Socialism, and Pacifism were right.[62]

The Australian Parliament's ratification of the Treaty of Versailles, officially closed the period.

The spectrum of opinions, ideologies, theories and doctrines finding accommodation within the A.L.P. has always been a very broad one. A very military-minded man such as Hughes, who had pressed for compulsory military service since federation and who, in August 1914, wanted to stop the general election to be held on 5 September of that year, in order to form a coalition government, made his career through that party. So did people of very different views, including pacifists, socialists and internationalists.

We have seen something of the views expressed at the beginning of the war in the *Australian Worker* and in *Labor Call*. They had, at that time, also reported the murder of Jean Jaurès and a canard, that Karl Liebknecht and Rosa Luxemburg had been shot by order of a German court-martial, as a result of Liebknecht's vote against the war credits and - horrible prediction - of Rosa Luxemburg's agitation against the war among soldiers. Memorial meetings had been held in Melbourne for these three Socialist leaders. Once this 'news' about Liebknecht and Rosa Luxemburg had been discovered to be false, the working-class press speculated freely on its authorship and on the motives for putting it about.

In spite of the heavy censorship and other wartime obstacles, a degree of international news was published in the Australian working-class press throughout the war - including news from and about Asia. The *Australian Worker* carried news about the Russian Revolution from the pen of John Reed, the later author of *Ten Days that Shook the World*. They were assiduous in providing information about the Labour movement in many countries, including China, as documented by the article on *China and the Social Revolution*, by the National Secretary of the Socialist Party of China, Professor Chiang K'ang-Hu, which is reprinted in the Appendix*.

The war itself, with enormous Australian casualty lists, the subsequent split in the Australian Labor Party, followed within a few years, by the foundation of the Communist Party, greatly sapped the intellectual originality and strength of the Labour movement and affected deeply the course of its later development. The loss of spontaneous internationalism, rather than manipulated expressions,

*Document No. 9

whether Communist or otherwise, was considerable but it was not complete.

A small but significant instance was provided by an episode at the 1924 Commonwealth Conference of the A.L.P. Maurice Blackburn, a leading Labour theorist and one of the most honest men ever to come into politics, read a letter from Dr Omero Schiassi, an Italian scholar and Socialist living in Melbourne, asking Conference 'to express . . . this sense of solidarity with the working class of Italy now being oppressed by 'Fascist' domination and ferocity and to pay a fraternal tribute of sorrow to the memory of G. Matteotti . . .'[63]

Two things are remarkable. The first, that in Blackburn's apparent judgment of the state of knowledge among his fellow delegates, he thought it prudent to explain 'that Matteotti was not a Communist but a Socialist'. The second, that Conference passed a motion in the requested sense. If the Labour Party had lost much of its intellectual strength and international awareness during and after the war, it had not lost it all. A residue remained alive to be re-activated by the opportunities of government in the nineteen-forties.

A similar loss of intellectual strength occurred among the middle-class nationalists. Until 1914, men of Deakin's stamp had pushed Australia's position within the Empire steadily towards a more independent position. To some extent, Hughes had continued that work; though provocative of speech, he was conservative in action. He would not establish diplomatic relations with the United States, as requested by the Senate in 1917 and later. When the renewal of the Anglo-Japanese Alliance was discussed in the Imperial Conference and, then, in the Washington Conference, Hughes opposed the, ultimately successful, pressure of the United States and Canada, preferring the security proffered by a Japan allied to Great Britain to other alternatives.

Subsequent conservative governments in Australia continued through the nineteen-twenties and thirties, to sail in the wake of Imperial policy. They displayed no interest in questioning that policy, much less in developing one of their own. The search and pursuit of political independence and of a distinct Australian foreign policy devolved on the Labour Party.

During the 1920's, concern tended to centre on economic problems and Australia retreated behind progressively higher tariff

barriers. A Tariff Board was set up to review claims for protective
assistance and to advise the government. An effort was made to
diversify production - particularly in the field of secondary industries -
and to supply a ready labour force by encouraging immigration, as
well as to survey and develop the country's resources. To these ends,
the Development and Migration Commission and the Council of
Scientific and Industrial Research were set up.The scale of government
borrowing was greatly extended to meet the costs of these undertakings, with the result that the public debt, exclusive of war debt,
rose from £443 million, to more than £980 million in nine years.

In this period of predominantly economic concern, questions of
foreign policy and of security tended to be submerged. But not
altogether. One such exception was the debate about the Washington Conference, when Hughes felt that Australia's security would be
best served by the continuation of the Anglo-Japanese Alliance
which, however, was buried at Washington.

The debates showed once more that there were wide differences
of opinion but only a partial understanding of Australia's international position - as a dominion that was as yet not sovereign.
Brennan stressed this point:

We cannot have it both ways; we cannot, on the one hand, be constantly
boasting of the eternal glory of our association as a part, and a subordinate
part, of the Great British Empire, and, on the other hand, expect complete
recognition as an independent nation.[64]

H.M.A.S. *BRISBANE* AND THE MAY THIRTIETH MOVEMENT

The affair of the *Brisbane* was of a different kind. It demonstrates
the wide gulf between the approach of the conservatives and that of
the radicals to Asia as well as to the relations with Great Britain and
the disposition and control of Australian defence forces.

Mr S.M. Bruce - later Lord Bruce of Melbourne and Westminster
Gardens - had succeeded Hughes as Prime Minister in 1922. He was
perhaps best known for his slogan 'Men, Money, Markets'.

In 1924, he agreed to provide H.M.A.S. *Brisbane* for the
China station of the Royal Navy, then preparing to 'deal with trouble'
resulting from the strike wave and widespread unrest in the major
Chinese ports.[65] It was reminiscent of Gipps' action in 1839. But
it was not taken by a British governor. It was taken by the govern-

ment of the Commonwealth of Australia and the *Brisbane* did go
to China. Parliament was not informed.

H.M.A.S. *Brisbane* was a light cruiser of the Royal Australian
Navy, built during the war at the Cockatoo dockyard in Sydney. Of
5,400 tons, she was armed with eight six-inch guns and one three-
inch gun. She was of very shallow draught, of eighteen feet, her
measurements being 430' x 50'.

It was not until after the bloodshed of 30 May - and the consequent
newspaper publicity - that some information was forthcoming. The
Brisbane had been despatched in February to the China station,
apparently because her shallow draught enabled her to be taken eighty
miles upstream the Yang Tse-kiang from its outlet. The government
had avoided all discussion and there was a temporary exchange with
a Royal Navy vessel. On 24 June, Brennan asked from the Opposition
front bench:

(1)   Is the Australian warship *Brisbane* or any Australian warship operating
      in Chinese waters in connexion with the industrial disturbances in
      Shanghai?
(2)   Where, and in what capacity, are the major vessels of the Australian
      fleet operating at present?[66]

The reply provided by the Minister for the Navy, Sir Neville
Howse, on the following day, stated:

(1)   The H.M.A.S. *Brisbane* left Australian waters in February to be attached
      to the China station as an exchange cruiser, the H.M.S. *Concord* being
      attached to the Australian squadron [*sic*] in lieu. I have no knowledge
      of the *Brisbane's* present detailed movements, but she is due back at
      Thursday Island about the middle of August.
(2)   They are *en route* to Hervey Bay, Queensland, for exercises, and are
      due back at Sydney on 9 July.[67]

That night, Brennan raised the matter on the adjournment. He
quoted the question and answer, adding - 'I venture to say, and I
say it with the concurrence of my Leader, that the answer is totally
unsatisfactory'. Brennan then referred to lengthy newspaper reports
of the events leading to, and following the thirtieth of May, without,
however, mentioning the date which had not yet become known as an
historical landmark. It was claimed that the Australian fleet, consisting of *Sydney, Adelaide, Stalwart, Anzac,* and *Tasmania* had
left Sydney for a winter cruise, and might proceed to China, if
necessary. Furthermore, 'in addition to the *Brisbane,* H.M.A.S.
Vindictive . . . is on the China station, is also commanded by an

Australian officer, Captain G.F. Hyde'. Brennan continued:

The complaint which I address to this House, and particularly to the government, is that, whatever the detailed circumstances may be, the fact is outstanding that an Australian battleship is being employed as part of the British squadron in Chinese waters, against Chinese in their own country, and in a war which is primarily an industrial war.

Brennan stressed the peculiar suitability of the *Brisbane* for operations upstream mentioned above:

I am well aware that, technically, there is no war. I am concerned not with technicalities, but with actualities. To the honour of the Labour Party be it said that the one thing for which it has stood more sternly and strongly than for any other is that the Australian Navy and the Australian Army shall not be employed in any industrial conflict in Australia. If they should not be so employed in Australia, certainly they should not be so employed in foreign territory . . . I cannot imagine any action that would more gravely shock the Australian conscience than that we should so employ our navy . . .

Brennan made it plain that his grievance was, in the first place, that this thing had been done at all, and, secondly, that it had been done secretly. It was said that the *Brisbane* had been exchanged for the British ship *Concord*. If there were any circumstances in which an Australian vessel might be exchanged for a British ship for naval operations of a serious character anywhere, all the reasons for it, and the conditions attending it should have been disclosed to the House. In the peculiar circumstances of this trouble in the East, the duty of the government to explain the position fully to the House was particularly urgent: 'I hope and believe that this House, and I am sure that this party, will not agree in any circumstances to take part in this fight against the Chinese proletariat'. He said that one could not know in what way this matter might develop. The trouble was industrial in its origin, and it was largely nationalist in its development; the great Chinese Republic was awakening, and, for his part, he wished it well: 'We on this side of the House sympathise deeply with the people of this great republic in the age-long conflict during which they have been ground down by their depredators from other so-called civilized countries, who have taken every advantage of China's weakness, and have used their strength to despoil their victims'. Brennan said the British Empire was not guiltless, but duty, like charity, began at home. He asked the Prime Minister to do what he should have done before, namely, 'to take us into his confidence in this whole matter of the *Brisbane* and the Australian

Navy.'[68] Charlton, the Leader of the Opposition, immediately rose in support of Brennan who, he said, had 'rendered a service to his country'. He said that, if the Prime Minister should claim that he had no jurisdiction over the *Brisbane* because of the exchange, an explanation of this kind would not be satisfactory to the people of Australia: 'We created our navy for the definite purpose of defending Australia, and not for the purpose of going to other countries to interfere in their affairs'.

The chief significance of the affair, in Australian terms, is to be found in the approach and policy of the government, its attitudes to the British government, to Asia, and to Parliament and, equally, in the attitudes of the Opposition. It had been Bruce who arranged for R.G. Casey to sit in Hankey's Cabinet office to keep the Australian government *au fait*.

Almost two years later, as the situation in China neared the revolutionary crisis of 1927, the Leader of the Opposition, Matthew Charlton, addressed a question to the Prime Minister, in an attempt to discover whether any representations had been made by the Imperial government regarding the position in China; if so, would the Prime Minister disclose the nature of the negotiations and the government's reply? Bruce would not. He replied that his government had been kept informed of the actions of the British government in China, adding: 'But I think the honourable gentleman must see that it would be impossible for the Commonwealth government to publish communications outlining the course that the British government was proposing to take in an extraordinarily delicate and difficult situation'.[69]

A week later, the Deputy Leader of the Opposition, Frank Anstey, tried again, without obtaining greater enlightenment from the Prime Minister. Anstey then asked a supplementary question, whether the government had been 'consulted on the Imperial policy in China, in accordance with the principles enunciated by the Prime Minister in his report on the Imperial Conference, or has been merely "fully informed" as to what has taken place, as he stated in his reply to my previous question'.

Bruce replied:

The usual practice of consultation has been followed in this case. The British government advises the Commonwealth government of its contemplated action, and it is open to this government or that of any other dominion to assent or dissent. In the absence of dissent it is taken that the governments consulted have no desire to express any view. The honourable member will recognize that, in some cases, it has been quite impossible for the British government to consult the dominions, because immediate action has been necessary to safeguard British lives and property. Except in such cases, the fullest opportunity for consideration and consultation has been given.[70]

If the Prime Minister's reply was hardly helpful to his questioner, it has some use for the historian as a statement of Australian conservative concepts of Imperial and foreign relations, after the Imperial Conference which had produced the Balfour Report - the basis of the later Statute of Westminster - unsought by, and unwelcome to Australia's conservative establishment. That it involved a clear choice made by the Australian conservatives, emerges from the fact that, when the alternative was put to Bruce in June 1924, whether Australia wanted 'a foreign policy distinct from that of H.M. Government' or 'an endeavour to link up more closely with H.M. Government on all matters of Imperial relations with foreign countries', Bruce opted for the latter.[71]

LABOUR DEFENCE POLICIES AFTER 1918

The Labour Party, strongly opposed to foreign intervention, nevertheless remained concerned about national defence. Curtin had demanded the development of air defences as the economically and strategically most rational form of protection at the 9th Commonwealth Conference of the A.L.P. in 1918. Charlton had advocated defence by air power and submarines in 1923.[72] By 1924, its federal platform referring to Defence, demanded 'convertible factories for small arms, munitions, aeroplanes . . . air forces . . . fortifications . . . submarines, and adequate above-water craft, and mines'. It desired the 'utilisation of the Bureau of Science and Industry for the purpose of standardisation of railway and motor rolling stock and materials' - certainly novel thoughts at that time. In 1928, the party's new leader, J.H. Scullin, amplified the A.L.P.'s defence policy in his policy speech on 4 October:

Defence must be bound up with production and general development. Let me illustrate: an air service linking the interior of the continent with our coastal settlement may be employed in normal times for the transport of passengers, merchandise, and mails, and as a means of drawing the people together by rapid and effective communication. If the worst should come and war eventuates then such training and experience would be invaluable to the men engaged in such a service.

If the time has not yet come when we could apply the words of the Prophet, 'beating our swords into ploughshares and our spears into pruning hooks', at least our munition factories should ring in the long days of peace with the making of machinery necessary for the development, alike of our primary and secondary industries.[73]

In the 1928 election, Labour once again failed to obtain a majority; but they did succeed in the following year.

In 1929, the Australian Labor Party won a federal election for the first time since the split over conscription, and a Labour government took office under the leadership of Scullin. The election had been remarkable as the first in which Labour had succeeded since 1914, and as the one in which an outgoing Prime Minister, S.M. Bruce, was defeated in his own electorate.

However, the Scullin government took office in October 1929, the month of the Great Crash. They lacked a Senate majority and were faced by the shock wave of the world depression which hit Australia with great force, creating economic conditions of a complexity and severity unknown before. Like other governments, their deflationary policies made matters worse rather than better. Without freedom of action in Parliament, or over the Commonwealth Bank - whose Board they could neither control nor change - and, least of all, in their international financial relations, they became first the prisoners and then the victims of this crisis. In this turbulent period, the Defence Minister, Mr Chifley, did move, however, to abolish compulsory military training. Japanese aggression in Manchuria caused hardly a ripple in Parliament.

The federal Labour government were defeated in a manner reminiscent of the end of the British Labour government in the preceeding year - except that it was not the Prime Minister who changed sides. After holding office for twenty-seven months, under conditions of very great difficulty, it gave way before a new conservative alignment, led by J.A. Lyons, a former Labour Premier of Tasmania, who crossed the floor of the House in 1932, with some like-minded colleagues. The new grouping called itself the *United Australia Party* (U.A.P.) and held office, mostly in coalition with the Country Party, until 1941.

Emerging from the crisis of the depression, Australia found new sources of concern in world events. There was much debate about tariff policies, protection and Imperial preference which, for a time, led to a trade policy - the *Trade Diversion Policy* - especially hostile to the United States and to Japan.

THE LATHAM MISSION

In 1934, the Minister for External Affairs, Mr, later Sir John Latham led the first Australian diplomatic mission to Asia. Latham was about to leave Parliament and take up his appointment as Chief Justice of the High Court of Australia. His very thoughtful report reflects the conservative attitude that Australia does and should sail in the wake of England. It is in some ways a curious document. Latham rightly stressed the Eurocentric nature of Australian contemporary thinking: 'We have adopted European phrases and the ideas that correspond to them. From our childhood we have been accustomed to read, think and speak of the 'Far East'. It is the Far East to Europe . . . but we must realise that it is the 'Near East' to Australia'. It took the wit of Menzies to coin the phrase *Near North,* four years later. Latham continued:

It is inevitable that the relations between Australia and the Near East will become closer and more intimate as the years pass. Therefore, it is important that we should endeavour to develop and improve our relations with our near neighbours, whose fortunes are so important to us, not only in economic matters, but also in relation to the vital issues of peace and war. It is in the highest degree improbable that anything which we do will lead to war in the East; but if war takes place there on a major scale, it is bound to affect Australia profoundly whether or not the Commonwealth is actually engaged in that conflict. The whole of our interests, therefore, lie in doing everything in our power to prevent the risk of war in the East from becoming a pulsing reality.

The Latham mission had visited 'The Dutch East Indies, Singapore, Saigon in French Indo-China, Hong Kong, Shanghai, Nanking, Tientsin, Peiping, which was formerly Peking, and Canton. We also visited Japan and the Philippine Islands'. Latham reported that it was remarkable to see how anxious people were to obtain information with respect to Australia, and how the absence of any authoritative source of information handicapped not only Australian trade, but also prejudiced the general position of Australia. The British diplomatic and consular representatives had done most valuable work in helping

Australian interests, but they did not have the detailed knowledge which would enable them to correct misstatements and remove misapprehensions which had often become part of the mental stock of a particular people.[74]

Nonetheless Latham proposed no change in this state of affairs. He pointed out that 'Canada . . . is well represented in the East'. But Latham preferred to rely on arrangements made through the British Foreign Office for his mission's despatch and reception. The Mission had received a Japanese request for diplomatic relations:

Upon that subject I had a frank conversation with Mr Hirota, which is summarized on page 24 of the report. I represented to him, first, that very few diplomatic matters arise between Australia and foreign countries - I may add, the fewer they are, the better. 'Happy is the country that has no history' is a well-known saying. To-day, I say, the less diplomacy a country has the better are its chances of happiness. The less the Ministers for Foreign Affairs have to do the better for the world. Secondly, I told Mr Hirota that when any diplomatic matters arose we always had the ready and willing service of the British diplomatic officers, and in many cases their representations would have more weight than ours. I said, further, that the institution of diplomatic relations with Japan would raise a very big problem for us. In the case of Japan it would mean only the addition of another representative to the diplomatic corps, but in the case of Australia it would mean the establishment of a diplomatic branch of our Public Service, and if we sent a Minister or ambassador to Japan we should have to reconsider the nature of our representation in London, and whether we should send representatives to other capital cities, such as Paris, Washington, Rome and Nanking. The matter could not begin and end with the appointment of a diplomatic representative to Tokyo. I also added that it was the intention of the Government to send a Trade Commissioner to Japan. After hearing me, Mr Hirota agreed that there was no need for diplomatic representation by either country in the other. Possibly there is room for difference of opinion on this subject, but I think that I stated the general view of Australians.

This sums up the conservative pre-war attitude in Australia. In his introductory remarks, Latham had said that 'this Mission was a novel enterprise . . . almost without precedent in any other country'. This is probably true. Here was a government free to conduct its external affairs, but unwilling to do so. Yet, this mission brought Australia a little closer to it. Latham, a very rational thinker, was prepared to look at the assumptions underlying traditional ideas, and he was clearly pleased that many of the people in the countries he had visited in Asia 'regarded this visit as the first recognition in this area of the world of a common human interest in mankind'. In the following years, a rudimentary External Affairs Department came into existence.

Shortly before the war, Lyons took the initiative to establish diplomatic relations, at legation level, with Japan and the United States. These posts were established in 1940. But they did not seem to affect, and perhaps did not have time to affect, government thinking a great deal. It was to remain largely a matter of form, if an important one. There is only limited evidence of independent approaches or ideas. [76] Indeed, the conservative outcry at Curtin's invitation to Roosevelt, and at the subsequent ratification of the operative parts of the Statute of Westminster in 1942, seems to underline this point.

The period preceding the outbreak of war, was notable for the growing political concern with Japan which, after its invasion of Manchuria, its withdrawal from the London Naval Conference and the League of Nations, began war in China proper - then known as the *China incident* - and drew closer to the European axis powers, Nazi Germany and Fascist Italy.

Mussolini's war against Abyssinia, with the sanctions issue; the Spanish civil war; and the expansionist threat of Nazi Germany, created new debates on foreign affairs in Australia. They not only showed up major divisions between the government and the opposition, they also showed marked division within the conservative coalition, as well as within the Labour Party. This is especially true of the Spanish civil war, which revealed the first signs of the polarising conflict between right-wing Catholic Labour men and Stalinists who supported 'left-wing' groups within the Australian Labor Party and in the unions. At that time, however, neither pressure group was effective in shaping Labour policy. Among the government parties, the divisions, less open, were over-shadowed by the traditional policy of following the British government.

THE CURTIN PROPOSALS

In matters of defence, the U.A.P. government held to the policy followed in the first world war - co-operation with and support for Britain involving, in case of war, an expeditionary force, based on army units, as well as naval support.

The A.L.P. advocated a completely new policy, propounded by

John Curtin who had succeeded Scullin as its parliamentary leader. It concerned itself first of all with the defence of Australia and its territory and, for the first time in Australian political thought, it considered the probability of Australians being faced with the need to defend themselves, by themselves, in Australia.

For this purpose, Curtin stressed the need for concepts of mobile defence, especially a strong air force. He had propounded this idea since 1918. Even in 1935, when Curtin proposed it in Parliament, it seemed all very new and very improbable, but it drew on the tradition of the A.L.P. which had established conscription for home defence and the Royal Australian Navy before the first world war. These new concepts were developed by a fine and fertile brain with an originality and consistency of thought that was to surprise many in 1941, when Curtin, who remained a convinced pacifist, became Prime Minister two months before Pearl Harbor.

Speaking on the Defence Estimates in 1935, Curtin expressed his basic view that not sufficient money was being spent on the Air Force and too much was devoted to the Navy. He held the view that any naval force Australia might possibly afford would be inadequate to defend it: 'There is no disloyalty to Australia in expressing the view that the increased expenditure on the Navy will be of less service and less economical, having regard to what it will secure, than would increased expenditure on the Air Force'.[77]

A year later, during the debate on the Defence Estimates in 1936, Curtin was much more explicit. He pointed to the weakness in the strategic concept of naval defence based on Singapore, which would require naval forces of a magnitude which Australia could not provide and which, in war-time, Britain could not spare. Relying on the authority of Lords Jellicoe and Beattie, Curtin also quoted Admiral Webb as saying:

We are not only an Asiatic power in the widest sense, but also a European country with all Europe's complicated troubles and responsibilities at her door. That being so, to imagine that we are going to uncover the heart of the Empire and send our fleet or the best part of it thousands of miles into the Pacific with only one base for our supplies and damaged ships is to write us down as something more than fools. The British people would not tolerate it.

Curtin proceeded to make the further point that, according to the Treaty of London, 1930, the naval forces of Great Britain had to

include the Royal Australian Navy. Were Australia to double or
quadruple her naval units, the home fleet would be correspondingly
reduced. That was part of an international agreement, which
demanded that the whole of the naval forces of the British Empire
were to be considered as one unit, and if Australia were to spend
more on naval organization under the terms of the treaty, that
expenditure had to be taken into account and included as a representative part of whatever was Britain's fleet in accordance with
that agreement.

The capacity of the naval forces of the Empire to ensure the security of this
continent is open to very grave doubt. Another British admiral has said that
the loss of Australia during a war would not be vital, and that if the Empire
Navy were successful in the main struggle, Great Britain would again reconquer
Australia at its leisure. That is not a nice situation for us to be in![78]

Curtin went to some pains to deflate the notion that, in time of
war, Australia could rely on naval forces based on Singapore. Five
years before the event, he emphasised that 'History has no experience
of the situation I am visualizing', and his analysis of the likely
outcome of hostilities was so accurate that it merits quotation at
length.

Someone interjected: 'It is imagination'. 'No', Mr Curtin rejoined,
'it represents a reasonable examination of the possibilities of the
situation'. Great wars in which Australia's security would be
imperilled would not be European wars. They would be wars in the
South Pacific. The delay in despatching the British fleet to Australia's
aid would be bound to be prolonged. This delay would provide
an enemy with the opportunity to capture or damage the Singapore
base: 'It must be obvious to any thinking person on the face of
these considerations that Australia's danger is more than a mere
hostile tip-and-run raid. Some may argue that with the main fleet in
European waters light cruisers based at Singapore and augmented by
the Royal Australian Navy would be a deterrent against anything
but raids.' He went on:

Let me examine that aspect of the question. Singapore is well placed for the
defence of India and the trade routes of the Indian Ocean, but it is nearly
3,000 miles west of a direct line from Japan to the eastern coast of Australia, as
far as Gibraltar is across the Atlantic from New York. The great expenditure
by the United Kingdom on the base at Singapore was dictated by no paramount
consideration for the security of Australia but was influenced very profoundly
by the desirability to ensure the integrity of India from hostile cruisers. That

a naval unit based on Singapore which would obviously be weak in relation to
Japan's naval strength would be a real deterrent to any hostile overseas intentions
on Australia is contrary to all naval history. From my reading of naval history
there is nothing so inferior as an inferior fleet. If a nation has a fleet that cannot
conquer it would be better off without one. Britain's Grand Fleet bottled up
the German High Sea Fleet for practically the whole of the war . . . Rather
than a deterrent, an inferior force at Singapore, pending the arrival of the
main British fleet, would be much the same as von Spee's squadron in the
Pacific Ocean; it would be chased across the ocean and sunk.
Therefore, much more than minor raids is to be feared. What then is the possible
extent and object of more extensive offensive operations? The political object
of a probable enemy would vary between the enforcement of a demand or a
policy of territorial conquest. The first step would be the capture of Hong
Kong and/or Singapore, but as long as the principal Australian ports remained
intact there would remain in the mind of an enemy the lurking possibility of the
eventual arrival of the British fleet to use these ports as a commencement of
operations to recover step by step the losses sustained. It is true that these ports
are capable of being used as, or of being transformed into, first-class naval
bases to re-establish British interests; but a long delay would be inevitable. It
might be that the enemy would consider a major attack on Australia essential
to the elimination of British sea-power, even if he had no intention of remaining
in permanent occupation of the country. Hence our provision for local defence
should contemplate the possibility of a major land and air attack.[79]

What is striking in Curtin's analysis of 1936, is its soundness and
originality. Lacking the advantages of government and access to
confidential information about the state of the Imperial defences of
Singapore and the Pacific, Curtin foresaw with remarkable and
detailed accuracy the flaws of British strategy, as it applied to
Australia, and the main-lines of Japan's strategy - apparently before it
had been developed - and the impact of both on the defences of
Australia. In the event, it was the United States which used
Australian bases 'as a commencement of operations to recover step
by step the losses sustained' and it did so on Curtin's invitation.
Even in 1936, he was advocating a more fraternal attitude towards
America than was possible under the existing hostile trade policy.

On the outcome of a blockade, Curtin was moderately optimistic
but he added that 'our land and air forces . . . are . . . essential . . . in
the prevention of a blockade'. Likewise, he came to the conclusion,
in 1936, that carrier-based air attacks would not be a source of undue
apprehension in the Australian context.

The threat, then, would be land-based air attacks and 'a combined
land and air attack', and in this context he expressed his regret at the

lack of progress in developing the infrastructure: 'Our differing railway gauges, for example, are an insuperable obstacle to the efficient transportation of our men'. An interjection by the Minister that 'Transportation could be done by air nowadays' - which, in 1936, it certainly could not - helped Curtin's argument. The enemy, Curtin foresaw, would aim at a quick decision. It was, therefore, unlikely that his main attack would be at any place the loss of which would probably not effect Australia's national life. While, therefore, a minor landing at a remote place could not be left out of reckoning, sound strategy would demand that his principal attack should be made against one of Australia's vital centres. 'This would place it within the areas of our transportation system. Our forces must of necessity be mobile and highly trained for offensive action.'

He summed up his consideration under these six points:

(1)   A really effective central system of Imperial defence, with the Royal Australian Navy a unit thereof, did not meet the requirements for Australia's safety. Local defence had to supplement it.

(2)   Australia required a greater degree of self-containment and self-reliance in defence than had obtained hitherto.

(3)   The principal means available to Australia for attaining greater local security were land and air forces.

(4)   Australia's land forces should be organized, equipped and trained on such a basis as would enable them, if necessary, to expand into a field force that would compel an enemy to use his maximum available shipping when he would still be inferior to our force before a second convoy of reinforcements arrived.

(5)   Australia's air force should be developed on the basis of the tasks required to be performed in reconnaissance and as a striking force, and later in direct conjunction with the land forces.

(6)   The development of Australia's capacity to produce munitions locally, both by munitions factories and elsewhere was an essential element in the attainment of self-reliance.[80]

His final point, however, referred to the economic bases of a defence policy, development of Australia's economic capacity and an end to a trade policy designed expressly to discriminate against the U.S.A. - 'our neighbour across the Pacific Ocean' upon whom 'we should look with a degree of fraternity', and against Japan about whom 'I say that this Parliament should hesitate, not once, but several times, before putting into operation a policy which is capable of being misunderstood, to use no stronger word, by that country'.[81]

John Curtin was far ahead of his contemporaries in his thinking.

He avoided being drawn into making gestures about fascist aggression in Europe - about which he felt strongly - but which, he believed, Australia had not the means to affect, and which might only lead to the depletion of Australia's defences and the division of its society.

The events which Curtin anticipated, developed very much as he had foreseen. The preparation which he had advocated from the opposition benches, remained undone. The reasons were largely to be found in the profoundly different views held by the governing conservative parties about Australia's stature and future role. Defence concepts and foreign policies provide a sensitive gauge of this variance.

1939

Lyons died on 7 April 1939, and Menzies succeeded him as Leader of the U. A. P. He became Prime Minister on 26 April 1939. He had opposed the Lyons decision to establish Australian legations in Tokyo and Washington in January.[82] In an international affairs debate on 9 May, he said that as a first condition of Australia's independence, it was vital that "the integrity of the British Empire" be preserved. But for all his identification with the British Empire, Menzies now accepted this crucial distinction:

I believe that the Pacific is of all zones in the world the zone in which our risks are primary risks and our responsibilities are primary responsibilities. Consequently, as I have already indicated, this government proposed to take the necessary steps as soon as may be, not only to establish closer diplomatic contact with the United States of America and with Japan - those two great and friendly powers in the Pacific - but also to do everything that it can to increase our cultural relationship, our personal contact with them, to improve all of those things which go to make up a real and personal understanding.[83]

For all his difficulties in understanding the non-British world, Menzies has the credit of establishing Australia's first diplomatic relations - with the United States and Japan, and then with China. He furthermore searched for and appointed outstanding men to head these missions: R.G. Casey (later Lord Casey) to Washington; Sir John Latham, on leave from the Chief Justiceship of the High Court, to Tokyo; and an able political thinker, Sir Frederic Eggleston, to Chungking, the wartime capital of China.

There was no surprise in the fact that, when war broke out in September 1939, Australia was involved because Britain was involved. A special issue of the Commonwealth of Australia Gazette, published on Sunday 3 September 1939, stated that the Commonwealth government had been informed that Great Britain was at war with Germany, and this was printed above the announcement of a formal Proclamation of a State of War.[84]

When Parliament met, on 6 September 1939, the Prime Minister made a detailed statement, tracing the events that had led to the outbreak of war. Mr Menzies began by saying:

On Sunday last, the 3rd September, shortly after 8 p.m. Australian time, the Prime Minister of Great Britain announced that the time limited by a notification to the German government had expired and that Great Britain was at war with Germany. An hour or two later, a proclamation was issued in the Commonwealth of Australia, declaring the existence of a state of war in Australia. In order that hon. members may have before them, and in order that we may have on record, some accurate statement of the affairs leading up to this tragic consequence, I am today laying on the table a White Paper, which contains the relevant documents exchanged between the governments, together with such explanatory matter as may serve to connect one document with another. Nobody can foretell the course of events. Nobody can foretell how this war is going to be fought, what special dangers Australia may encounter, or what are the best services which we can render Great Britain and the Empire; but we do know that we are together in this struggle, and we are confident that our unity and determination, being based upon justice, are bound to succeed.[85]

Following a detailed *résumé* of the White Paper, Menzies concluded with a promise about the quality of public life in war-time:

However long this conflict may last, I do not seek a muzzled Opposition. Our institutions of parliament and of liberal thought, free speech and free criticism must go on. It would be a tragedy if we found that we had fought for freedom and fair play and the value of the individual human soul, and won the war only to lose the things we were fighting for. Consequently, I shall welcome criticism, but I do want to emphasize that our great task, however long this struggle may endure, is in common. If we remember that, all criticism will find its right place and its true perspective.

As the honourable member opposite has suggested, we have no bitterness against the plain and private citizens of Germany and I hope we will not feel called upon, at any stage, to disfigure what I believe to be a noble cause by any hymns of hate. We are in this war to win it and as quickly as possible. My prayer is that it may be won so quickly as to permit a just peace, a peace that will really end war and not a peace which will sow the dragon's teeth of bitterness and hatred and distrust.[86]

In contrast to the bitterness of the first world war, political life during the second world war remained moderate and Menzies has the credit of setting the tone at the outset.

Granted the context, however, there are aspects of his speech which demand further comment. Speaking as Prime Minister of Australia in Parliament on such an occasion, he hardly referred to the significance of the conflict for Australia. Fascinated by the inter-play of great power relations, he assumed that it would be generally understood that, as he had so often said, Australia's interests were Great Britain's, and that Australia was at war if, and because Britain was.

In some ways, therefore, the most interesting aspect of this great speech lies in what was left unsaid: the assumptions upon which it rested.

Replying for the Labour opposition, Curtin spelled out the implication, that Australia was included in the British declaration of war. Although he supported the war, his speech and the Labour Party's policies showed that there were differences of approach of far-reaching consequences. Curtin made the following statement, supported unanimously by the federal parliamentary Labour Party - at that time, an achievement in itself:

The Australian Labor Party affirms its traditional horror of war and its belief that international disputes should be settled by arbitration.

It deplores the fact that force, instead of negotiation and discussion, has plunged the peoples into war. It believes that resistance to force and armed aggression is inevitable if attacks on free and independent peoples are to be averted.

In this crisis, facing the reality of war, the Labor Party stands for its platform. That platform is clear. We stand for the maintenance of Australia as an integral part of the British Commonwealth of Nations. Therefore, the Party will do all that is possible to safeguard Australia and, at the same time, having regard to its platform, will do its utmost to maintain the integrity of the British Commonwealth.

As to the conduct of Australian affairs during this unhappy period, the Australian Labor Party will preserve its separate entity. It will give support to measures having for their object the welfare and safety of the Australian people and the British Commonwealth of Nations.

We take the view that these measures should include the immediate control by the Commonwealth government of all essential raw materials and the resumption by the government of the factories associated with the production of munitions and war equipment.

There must be a rigid control of commodity prices and house rents so that war-profiteering will become impossible.

Interest rates must be kept within bounds, and the monetary system re-adjusted so that the National Debt be kept as low as possible.

The democratic rights of the people must be safeguarded to the maximum. The very minimum of interference with the civil liberties of the people should be the objective of the government in carrying through its measures for national security. To ensure that this be done, it is essential that the Parliament of the Commonwealth should remain in session. [87]

Curtin drew the distinction between the Nazi dictatorship and the German people and linked the rise of that *régime* to the reluctance of the democracies to make concessions to the Weimar Republic: 'it is idle at this juncture, to argue in respect of what might be some of the features of the Treaty of Versailles. There is no point now in harking back to lost opportunities when perhaps other courses might have produced a different development in Germany.' [88]

The speeches of Menzies and Curtin at the outbreak of the second world war are of major significance. Each was an outstanding exponent of the views of his political tradition; each provided an eloquent restatement of the approach to defence and foreign affairs, characteristic of his respective tradition.

The juxtaposition of their views under the stress of incipient warfare, provided an impressive contrast of the two main attitudes which have dominated Australian thinking about the world for a century - the conservative and the radical.

This was to be the last great occasion on which Australia *automatically* followed a major British decision.

BUSINESS AS USUAL

Following the outbreak of war the government announced on 15 September, the raising of volunteers, which became the Second Australian Imperial Force and, as its name implied, was to serve the Empire, for the most part in the Middle East.

When war broke out in 1939, Curtin and the Australian Labor Party had supported Australia's participation, but they were critical of the government's economic policy of *Business as Usual* during the *phoney war*; of a military policy which viewed Australia's effort as ancillary to Great Britain's; and of the increasingly authoritarian style of the Menzies government. The Labour Party did support the Empire Air Training Scheme. Under the impact of the Nazi victories, the A.L.P. held a Special Federal Conference in June 1940. It passed an important resolution on defence, largely reflecting Curtin's thinking.

It set out as Labour policy 'complete and indissoluble unity with the Allies in the war'; complete government control over 'the entire resources of Australia' including those of 'all productive and financial organizations'; absorption of 'all idle employable labour . . . into industry'; provision of an adequate system of physical training throughout Australia and complete participation in the Empire Air Training Scheme; necessary provision for reinforcement for the Australian forces overseas - 'the extent of European participation by the volunteer army to be determined by circumstances as they arise, having regard to the paramount necessity of Australia's defence'. The ideas which Curtin had propounded had been accepted by his party.[89]

Other relevant resolutions included references to trade union rights, a war-profits tax, regular consultation of Parliament, civil liberties, the maintenance of the Labour Party's 'integral identity in the people's interest' and a demand for a National War Council 'including representatives of Labour . . . to advise the government in respect to the conduct of the war and in preparing for the post-war reconstruction'.[90]

This policy stood in contradiction to the government's *Business as Usual.* Few Australians would then have foreseen how completely it would replace not only the government's policy but its men.

In March 1940, a by-election had to be held for Mr Casey's seat (Corio), following his appointment as Australian Minister to Washington. This the government lost to the A.L.P. and thereupon Mr Menzies discovered the merits of a great coalition - a 'National' government.

The Labour Party consistently refused to join such a 'National' government, but Curtin suggested to the Prime Minister the establishment of an advisory war council implementing the resolution passed by the special conference. Menzies asked for a letter giving the conference resolution 'together with a summary of the view which Mr Curtin had placed before him'.[91]

Curtin wrote:

The purpose of the War Council is to ensure that there would be opportunity for collaboration, having regard to the national interests, in order that the conduct of the war could be carried out with the greatest speed and efficiency and the least amount of friction.[92]

That was on 24 June 1940. Menzies showed little interest. He replied, on 12 July 1940:

Cabinet is of the opinion that no good purpose would be served by the constitution of the National War Council of an advisory kind.

He offered the Labour Party 'five or possibly six seats'[93] in a Cabinet of sixteen ministers.

Curtin said of this reply:

Not only must there be agreement in the major objective of the war, an agreement which already exists, but there would need to be agreement in major policy as a foundation for a National government that was to be a National government and not a miniature Parliament in which debate would be continuous.

Further, having regard to the absolute powers which the government now has, it is my view that it is imperative that the Parliament should be alert and efficient to protect the people against the misuse of those powers and Parliament could not succeed in this fundamental obligation unless there existed in it an effective, patriotic and rationally-behaved Opposition.

I am willing to do all I possibly can for Australia and for the men and women who live here, and also for the unborn children, but I refuse to desert the great body of Labor to prop up political parties of reaction and capitalism. Whatever this war may bring, Labor will give its maximum co-operation. But to be merely a part of a government would destroy Labor and would be a disaster to Australia.[94]

In the general election which followed in September 1940, Menzies made a great deal of his desire to establish a National government. The poll reduced the government majority to two Independents, and it brought Dr Evatt into the House, who had resigned from the Bench of the High Court of Australia, to contest the Barton seat, as well as Chifley who had been out of Parliament since the fall of the Scullin government. Menzies repeated his offer of a coalition and, rather than offer five or six seats in Cabinet, he enquired about the Labour Party's terms. Instead, on 21 October 1940, the parliamentary Labour Party carried a resolution in favour of a National War Council. It was established two days later. Menzies nevertheless continued pressing the Labour Party for a coalition, but to no avail. The Labour Party, and especially Curtin, had a very realistic anticipation of the dangers inherent in such a course: 'The establishment of a National government would promote disunity . . . I say without hesitation that a National government, which is a coalition of government and opposition, would stifle constructive criticism and thus weaken the war effort'.[95]

After a great deal of acrimonious strife within the government parties, the Prime Minister, Mr Menzies, was forced to resign in August 1940. The leader of the Country Party, Mr (later Sir Arthur) Fadden, led the conservative coalition as Prime Minister until October when, after further, rather squalid squabbles, the two Independents crossed the floor of the House, having indicated their willingness to support a Labour government. The coalition had disintegrated before it had collapsed.

Part Four: 1942–1949
Australia in South East Asia

THE GREAT TRANSFORMATION

IN 1939, Australia was at war because great Britain was at war with Germany. No embassies had to be closed because none existed. There was no diplomatic corps in Canberra: as in colonial and dependent territories, the most senior foreign mission was a Consulate General, in Sydney.[1] The Australian government was still relying on the Foreign Office for advice and information, as well as for diplomatic representation. There was no Australian declaration of war. The government announced that it was to be business as usual.

In 1945, Australia provided the British Commonwealth Member on the Allied Council for Japan[2], the Commander-in-Chief of the British Commonwealth Occupation Force[3] and the President of the International Military Tribunal for the Far East.[4] The revolution in the conduct of Australia's diplomacy reflected by these facts took place during and as a result of the second world war.

We have seen that, whatever his reservations, Menzies carried out the Lyons decision on becoming Prime Minister in 1939, and, as a result, Australian legations were established in Washington, Tokyo and Chungking. Menzies had been opposed to the principle of separate Dominion representation abroad, as the following letter to Lyons of 5 January 1939, indicates:

. . . [The] solution, of accrediting an Australian Minister to Japan, is not one that I like; my feeling is that if each Dominion begins separately to accredit diplomatic representatives to foreign powers, grave divisions in our foreign policies will begin to appear and a serious blow will have been delivered to British unity. My feeling is that the right course is for us to direct an urgent despatch to the British Government, pointing out that we have a direct and vital interest in the Japanese position and that in consequence we expect that, before any decisions of policy in relation to advancing money to China or otherwise are made, we will be given the fullest opportunity of expressing our views.[5]

Whatever interpretation one chooses to adopt about the policies of Menzies, his political practice or its motivations, it would be hard to dispute that his views on Imperial unity were central to his political cosmology and their justification of splendid simplicity: Australia's security was based on the power of the Royal Navy, on the power of the British Empire and, therefore, the closest co-operation by Australia with Great Britain was imperative. Twenty-five years later, when the role of Imperial protector had been assigned to the United States, Menzies would express himself in ~~almost identical~~ terms.[5] His consistency on this fundamental question qualified him as a classical proponent of the conservative view in the debate.

Consequently, the establishment of those first three legations was an exception to his settled principle of Imperial unity in international affairs, rather than a point of departure.

It was left to Curtin and Evatt to implement the great change in the political theory and diplomatic practice which was to transform Australia's international relations and her Asian policies.

LABOUR GOVERNMENT AND THE PACIFIC WAR

John Curtin became Prime Minister on 3 October 1941.[6] Two months later, on 7 December 1941, Japan entered the war with the raids on Pearl Harbor and Malaya having occupied Indo-China in August of that year. Curtin was now faced with the very contingency which had haunted his thinking for years.[7]

The extent and the speed of the Japanese advance produced something of a traumatic shock among many Australians. It was also the source of an epiphany: the unthinkable contingency proposed by Churchill in March 1914, had arisen: 'the only course . . . would be to seek the protection of the United States'.[8]

It is true that, apart from Australia, there was no suitable base outside the United States for holding and reversing the advance, and that was the foundation for Curtin's famous appeal of 27 December 1941. In his historic invitation Curtin said:

The Australian government, therefore, regards the Pacific struggle as primarily one in which the United States and Australia must have the fullest say in the direction of the democracies' fighting plan. Without any inhibitions of any kind, I make it quite clear that Australia looks to America, free of any pangs as to our traditional links or kinship with the United Kingdom. We know the problems that the United Kingdom faces. We know the constant threat of invasion. We know the dangers of dispersal of strength. But we know, too, that Australia can go and Britain can still hold on. We are, therefore, determined that Australia shall not go and shall exert all our energies towards the shaping of a plan, with the United States as its keystone, which will give to our country some confidence of being able to hold out until the tide of battle swings against the enemy. Summed up, Australian external policy will be shaped towards obtaining Russian aid and working out, with the United States as the major factor, a plan of Pacific strategy along with British, Chinese and Dutch forces.[9]

Curtin's words caused an uproar of indignation among Australian conservatives, as if they were a betrayal of British heritage.

Roosevelt accepted Curtin's invitation and South West Pacific Area Headquarters were established in Melbourne, under the command of General MacArthur. Reviewing this situation in March 1945, in the Charter Address to the University of California, Dr Evatt pointed out that 'the position of General MacArthur in Australia ... has been unique. He is an officer of a foreign friendly power with his headquarters ... and his base organization located in the country of another government which has continued to exercise all its sovereign powers, but assigned to him its combat forces which for long constituted the great bulk of his command'. Evatt went on to stress that 'the position both of General MacArthur and Mr Curtin was obviously one of great delicacy and could have been fraught with possibilities of trouble and difficulty ... It was a remarkable experience for Australians to be entrusting their forces to an officer of another country in Australia itself'. However, MacArthur had always shown special regard for Australian rights: 'The most cordial relations have been maintained and ... there has been the closest consultation between the Commander-in-Chief and the Prime Minister ...'[10]

Of the military situation confronting him on his arrival in Australia, MacArthur said in his memoirs:

The immediate and imperative problem which confronted me was the defence of Australia itself. Its actual military situation had become almost desperate. Its forces were weak to an extreme, and Japanese invasion was momentarily expected. The bulk of its ground troops were in the Middle East, while the United States had only one division present, and that but partially trained. Its air force was equipped with almost obsolete planes and was lacking not only in engines and spare parts, but in personnel. Its navy had no carriers or battleships. The outlook was bleak . . .[11]

He decided to move a thousand miles forward into eastern Papua, and to stop the Japanese on the rough mountains of the Owen Stanley Range in New Guinea: to fight for Australia beyond its own borders. If successful, this would save Australia from invasion and give him an opportunity to pass from defence to offence, to seize the initiative, move forward, and attack:

This decision gave the Australians an exhilarating lift, and they prepared to support me with almost fanatical zeal. As a matter of fact, throughout the war, the most complete co-operation existed not only with the Australians, but with the other nationalities under my command.

But problems arose from another quarter. According to MacArthur, just at this time, Churchill had presented Roosevelt with the thought that the Japanese intended to halt their advance on Australia and would, instead, launch an attack on India.

On 8 May, MacArthur sent an outline of the situation, as he saw it, to President Roosevelt. In his view, the Japanese would not undertake large-scale operations against India at that time. Although India was undoubtedly within the scope of their military operations, MacArthur considered their postponement would be 'strategically advisable' to Japan. The military requirements for a decisive Indian campaign were so heavy that it could not be undertaken under those conditions. On the other hand, a continuation of the Japanese southern movement at that time, would give added safety for their eventual movement to the West.

In view of this situation, MacArthur deemed it of the 'utmost importance to provide adequate security for Australia and the Pacific area . . . to be followed at the earliest possible moment by offensive action'.

Even allowing for the usual military special pleading, the events proved that MacArthur's evaluation had been correct. In his words, the 'Japanese did not concentrate against India, and continued their drive southward, closing in on eastern Papua'.

Curtin's five-year-old prognosis had become a fact. The Churchill view reflected the type of strategic thinking that Curtin had pinpointed in 1936: if Australia falls it can be retaken later. As Curtin had said: 'This is not a nice position for us to be in.' [12] Curtin had foreseen it and he succeeded in preventing it.

However, the ~~Americans~~ U.S. government did not see any long-term implications in their acceptance of Australia's invitation and in the close war-time co-operation in the Pacific. Evatt had become convinced of the need for a regional defence arrangement including the United States but, however much he tried to interest Washington, he failed to obtain an adequate response. It took the collapse of the American post-war policy in China, and the Korean war, for the *ANZUS* Pact to be signed, as re-insurance for the Japanese Peace Treaty. A form of regional defence arrangement, the Manila Pact - creating *SEATO* - was achieved after the fall of Dien Bien Phu, in 1954, But that was far different from the kind of association proposed by the Labour government in the 1940's.

In 1941, the Curtin government had found that there were formalities necessary to clear the way for an independent foreign policy which the events were forcing on Australia, and which the Labour government was intellectually prepared to take. Separate Australian declarations of war on the Nazi sattelites were logical expressions of the Labour government's purpose and policy. Curtin cabled the Australian High Commissioner in London on 3 December 1941:

In the event of a state of war coming into existence with Finland, Rumania or Hungary, at the instance of His Majesty's Government in the United Kingdom, His Majesty's Government in the Commonwealth of Australia will adopt the following procedure to declare and proclaim a state of war in the Commonwealth of Australia and its Territories . . . This procedure will be in accord with the now recognized status of the Commonwealth of Australia in its international relationships as evidenced by the Balfour Declaration and other authoritative declarations. The view of the Commonwealth Attorney-General is that . . . it is desirable to express with clarity the unbroken chain of prerogative authority from His Majesty to his Representative here, making it clear at the same time that in relation to the Commonwealth and its Territories, His Majesty is acting exclusively on the advice of his Ministers in the Commonwealth of Australia. . .[13]

Following the news of the Japanese attack, Curtin sent this further cable:

7737. Please submit to His Majesty a recommendation for the issue to the Governor-General of an instrument in similar terms . . . substituting Japanese Empire . . . His Majesty may take this telegram as representing the advice of His Majesty's Minister in the Commonwealth.[14]

On the 9th, the Minister for External Affairs, Dr Evatt, instructed the Australian Chargé d'Affaires in Tokyo by cable:

To inform the Imperial Japanese Government immediately that a state of war exists and has existed between His Majesty's Government in the Commonwealth of Australia and the Imperial Japanese Government as from 5 o'clock in the afternoon, 9th December, 1941.[15]

For the first time, an Australian government had acted in the forms and accepted the duties of a sovereign state. Australia's new diplomatic position found unsought recognition from the Imperial Japanese government by their declaration of war on Australia, through their Minister in Canberra. Consequently, Australia entered that war recognized as a sovereign participant by friend and foe alike.

The operative sections of the Statute of Westminster were ratified in 1942. Of this, the eminent jurist Sir Robert Garran, who had been Solicitor General from Federation until 1932, wrote in his memoirs:

The Adopting Bill was introduced by Dr Evatt, as an urgent matter, and its introduction at that time was objected to by practically the whole of the Opposition on the grounds that it was the tail-end of a session, that at a critical stage of the war it would divide the Australian people, and that it would help German propaganda as to the unity of the Empire. A motion for postponement was moved by Hughes, and many of the Opposition who followed him in the debate seemed to confuse the declaration of status, which was past history at least twenty-five years old, with the enactment of the liberation of Australian Parliaments from certain doubts and limitations of power. The debate developed quite an extraordinary amount of heat, and eventually Hughes's motion was only defeated by a majority of four, but when that had been disposed of, the second reading was carried with only seven dissentients, and the committee and third-reading stages were gone through without a word of discussion. The proceedings in the Senate were practically an echo of those in the House of Representatives. Of the predicted storm not even a ripple on the surface resulted.[16]

Australia had been put on a footing for total war. Towards the end of 1942, Curtin felt the need to obtain more troops for the Pacific war.

EXTENDING THE MILITIA'S RANGE

Curtin was a pacifist. He had fought in the struggles against conscription during the first world war and he had, at that time, developed his first theories of defensive war. He was now determined to defend Australia against invasion, and to defeat the invader. One of Curtin's first actions as Prime Minister had been to insist, against Churchill's will, on the recall of two of the three Australian divisions from the Middle East, for this purpose. Before they could be landed in Burma or Java, the Japanese were there. Hence, the bulk of the force returned to Australia, but two Brigades were disembarked in Ceylon which was thought to be the next Japanese objective. It is said that while the troops were on the water - as at certain other times during the war - Curtin hardly slept: not because of his disagreement with Churchill about their return, but because he feared their loss in a naval action. The sense of personal responsibility for their lives weighed heavily on him.

The Prime Minister was a Labour leader who, for all his detestation of war and violence, was one of Australia's most original thinkers on questions of defence. He was faced with the problem of obtaining more troops, conscripts if need be, for service outside Australia and to do so without creating great dissension in the country or in the Labour Party.

From the moment Labour took office, there had been a constant stream of noisy demands for conscription which Curtin had resisted in his way:

I will not in any way try to suppress opinions which are contrary to my own, but, at the same time, I ask the people of Australia to give due weight to an unfortunate experience in the history of this country during the last war . . . A controversy about conscription at this stage will not add one man to the fighting forces of Australia, but will merely give comfort to the enemy.[17]

Now, the situation was very much changed. The fight was a fight for the immediate defence of Australia, and Curtin said it was absurd to let the militia fight side by side with the volunteers and the Americans to a point on the map, but no further. Yet, there were traditionalists in the Labour Party reacting more powerfully to old concepts than to new facts and, unless great care were taken, the 'unfortunate experience during the last war' would be repeated with disastrous consequences. It was to Curtin's merit that he was able to obtain the troops and keep his party and his country united.

John Curtin had been the architect of Labour's unity. He had succeeded Scullin as leader of a party defeated at the polls and split in several ways. He had led it back to power. He had experienced the earlier split, caused by Hughes' divisive use of the conscription issue in the first world war. He was as determined to keep Labour and Australia united as he was convinced of the need for the conscript forces.

At the Commonwealth Special Conference of the Australian

Labor Party on 17 November 1942, which he attended as a member
of the Western Australian delegation, Curtin said that the problem
of Australian defence was a strategical one. If an area was vital to
Australian strategy, then that area would be the one to which
Australia had to give full weight. The present difficulty could be
circumvented by a proclamation annexing strategic islands, but that
would be an abhorrent action. At the same time, were that done,
it would be permissible to send the A.M.F., i.e. the conscript units,
to those islands. United States and Australian forces which were in
areas outside Australia should be released from doing work which
A.M.F. pioneer battalions could do.

He had opposed participation by Australia in overseas wars all
his life, and, Curtin argued, he did not now ask for that, but for the
definition of Australian territory to be extended to cover areas vital
to Australia. If the war went well, the United States forces would go
North, and those forces must be replaced by Australian forces in
areas not now Australian territory. The United States had saved
Australia, and the government had had a desperate fight to get aid
for Australia. Curtin said that he did not want to live those
months again. Now the position was that a barrage of criticism in
Australia and the United States was directed at Australia that it
would have Americans defend Darwin, but not Australians fight for
the Philippines. He was asking Conference to make certain that
islands outside the political administration of Australia, but strategically vital to Australia, should be denied to the enemy by the
strength Australia could put there. Because of the debt of gratitude
owed to the United States, Australia should be able to say that
Australian resources would go on with them and maintain supplies
and bases to them from islands close to Australia which, if not held,
could be bases for the enemy to attack the United States forces.[18]

Curtin gave an explanation of Japanese strategy in the Pacific
and Indian oceans, and of the constant threat to North West Australia.
Strategically, his motion was commonsense, 'and it had to be done'.
Further, the A.M.F. had seen action, but he defied anybody to
amend the Repatriation Act to cover them. It was the first time,
he pointed out, that Australia had had to fight for itself within the
Australian area.[19]

Curtin preserved the distinction whereby, as far as possible, the
conscript forces - the A.M.F. - were to be used for logistic support

of the volunteer units - the A.I.F. - a Labour concept flatly opposed by the conservatives when in office.[20]

who did send conscripts to fight in Vietnam?

Following Curtin's statement to the 1942 A.L.P. Federal Conference, Mr Calwell immediately raised a point of order aimed at excluding the subject: 'The request was one for conscription for overseas service, and Conference should not even entertain a debate on such a request, which in any case, was not an urgent one'.[21]

Consequently, the question of using conscript troops in the South West Pacific Area was remitted to the State Executives of the A.L.P. The Conference was adjourned and correspondence passed between the Federal Executive and the State Executives.[22]

When the Conference re-assembled, John Curtin moved:

That, having regard to the paramount necessity of Australia's defence, as set out in section 5 of the special resolution adopted in June 1940, by Federal Conference, the Government be authorised to add to the Defence Act, in the definition of the Commonwealth which at present defines the territories to which this Act extends, the following words:- 'and such other territories in the South West Pacific area as the Governor General proclaims as being territories associated with the defence of Australia'.[23]

Unfortunately, for the historian, there is hardly a record of the ensuing debate. In general, A.L.P. Conference Reports consist of summarized rather than verbatim accounts of debates. However, in the Report of the adjourned portion of this Conference, we find little more than a list of delegates 'supporting' or 'opposing' the motion. The chief opponent was still Arthur Calwell who was also the Minute Secretary. The motion was carried by four States to two, the opposing States being Queensland and Victoria.

only the barest

- and he

The measure reached Parliament, as the Defence (Citizen Military Forces) Bill, on 29 January 1943, three weeks after the passing of Curtin's motion by the Special Conference of the A.L.P. It defined the area to which the Citizen Military Forces could be sent as one 'bounded on the west by the one hundred and tenth meridian of east longitude, on the north by the Equator and on the east by the one hundred and fifty-ninth meridian of east longitude'. It therefore excluded Malaya, the Philippines and Borneo. Several members of the opposition attempted, in different ways, to widen its scope and to embarrass the government, but their only effect was to display the extent of their fragmentation. In the end, they all voted for it. Among Labour members, Calwell criticized and questioned the urgency of the measure, as he had done at the

Singapore

Conference. However, only Maurice Blackburn stood out, because for Blackburn this was a matter of overwhelming principle.

Blackburn first proposed an amendment to make the legislation subject to a referendum. Having failed to do so, he attempted to limit its operation to conscripts over twenty-one, on the grounds of his belief that boys under that age should not serve in the tropics.

Curtin would have none of it, but he expressed his respect for his old comrade in these words:

I understand the reasons which have moved the honourable member for Bourke (Mr Blackburn) to submit the amendment [for a referendum]. They are entirely consistent with the views that he has held all his life. He is opposed, of course, to the principle underlying this bill, and I respect his views. However, this change has become one of necessity in the light of what is required for the effective activities of the Australian forces, particularly in New Guinea at the present time, and I am not able to countenance any procedure that will permit of longer delay.24

Maurice Blackburn was, then, alone in opposing the passage of this legislation through Parliament. His rift with Curtin was not only painful; it was a true tragedy for both men, each seeing his stand in terms of inevitable necessity, following logically from past conduct and historical position. The logic of events had forced them apart; yet, this hour was a test of their greatness.

Within a brief span of time, Australia had been developed as a major base in the Pacific war, no longer in danger of siege or, as many had feared, of invasion. Australia had succeeded in making a very complete effort. The people had remained united, as had the Labour Party.

PLANNING FOR PEACE

Within six months of the special conference decisions, the A.L.P. won its greatest election victory, despite the assumption by a large part of the press of the function of opposition which the distracted conservatives were hardly in a position to fill.

By that time - 1943 - the Labour government began to pay increasing attention to problems of post-war reconstruction at home and the future problems of Australia's security. The Treasurer, Mr Chifley, assumed the office of Minister for Post-War Reconstruction, in addition to his existing duties, when that Ministry was created in December 1942. His appointment symbolized the im-

portance attached to the problems of peace by the government. *trs.*
Post-war reconstruction had been one of the major subjects of the
resolutions passed by the Special Commonwealth Conference of
the A.L.P. after the fall of France in 1940.

In the next few years, the guidelines of Australia's post-war foreign
policy emerged, and, throughout a subsequent period of twenty-
three years of conservative government, with a very different value
system and an equally different political style, these guidelines
remained valid in certain important respects.

They may be summarised in this way: Australia is a medium-
sized power, bent on industrial development and social justice,
situated in the South Pacific, in close proximity to South East Asia.
It desires close and friendly relations with its Asian neighbours,
with Britain and the Commonwealth, and with the United States.
The Australian Labour government welcomed the India Independence Act, and other decolonizing measures carried out by the
British Labour government. It lent its good offices to the Indonesians *trs.*
and to the Israelis. It had laid the foundation, in 1941-2, to Australian-
American friendship and co-operation. All these initiatives were, at
the time, deplored by the 'parties of resistance', to use Hancock's
term, led once more by Menzies after the 1943 elections.

While the war was still raging, the Australian government tried
to prepare the ground for a post-war regional security system,
which would include the United States. In this they were unsuccessful. *failed/*
As a first step towards this aim and to strengthen the voice of both
Dominions, the Australia-New Zealand Agreement was signed in
1944. Here was a policy application arising from wider concern.
On 9 February 1944, Curtin said during an international affairs
debate in Parliament, that the agreement 'provides the basis for the
development of a more extensive regional understanding with all our
neighbours in the Pacific'.[25] Introducing the Agreement, on the
following day, Dr Evatt added:

In the view of both governments, the time had arrived for making a beginning
with plans for the South Pacific . . . we have been entering a new phase,
that of organising victory and of ensuring post-war stability . . . At any rate,
the Australian and New Zealand governments believe that it is necessary to
formulate plans for the post-war arrangement in the Pacific lest the fruits of
victory be lost.
The Australia-New Zealand Agreement foreshadows an organisation for the
welfare of the less advanced peoples in our part of the Pacific. This is an

earnest of our joint intentions in regard to the native peoples committed to our care.26

In the same sense, Evatt worked for inclusion in the Charter of the United Nations of 'the first general international declaration of colonial policy', as Attlee stated in presenting the Charter to the House of Commons for ratification:

The colonial powers who have signed this Charter recognise the principle that the interest of the inhabitants of non-self-governing territories are paramount and accept, as a sacred trust, the obligation to promote to the utmost, within the system of international peace and security established by the present Charter, the well-being of the inhabitants of these territories. They undertake to ensure, with due respect for the culture of the peoples concerned, their political, economic, social and educational advancement, their just treatment and their protection against abuses. They undertake also to develop self-government, that is to take due account of the political aspirations of the peoples and to assist them in the progressive development of their free institutions, according to the particular circumstances of each territory and its peoples, and their various stages of advancement. Provision is made for the regular transmission to the Secretary-General of information relating to the economic, social and educational conditions in these territories. Here the delegates of the government of Australia made a very substantial contribution in the adoption of this Article.27

Attlee laid great stress on the value of the work done by the Australian delegation under the leadership of Dr Evatt. It had been largely due to his initiative that the Economic and Social Council, originally conceived as a subsidiary part of the world organization, was transformed into a principal 'organ of the United Nations. Under Article 56, all members pledged themselves to take joint and separate action in co-operating with the organization for the achievement of these purposes'. The raising of standards was not a matter that should wait for international agreement. In Attlee's view, the Conference also owed a great debt of gratitude to the New Zealand Prime Minister, Mr Fraser, who had chaired the committee responsible for drafting the chapters on colonial policy and trusteeship.

Under Curtin and Chifley* and, more specifically, the Minister for External Territories, E.J. Ward, the foundations were laid for the policies that made independence possible for Papua and New Guinea in 1975. Colonel J.P. Murray, Administrator of the Territory from

*Curtin died on 5 July 1945, and was succeeded by Chifley eight days later.

1945 to 1952, ~~in a paper read~~ in 1968 ~~at a seminar of the Uni-~~
~~versity of Papua and New Guinea~~, said of these policies.

The Curtin and Chifley Governments in 1945 were as relevant to the future
of Papua and New Guinea - in a more restricted range - as was the Attlee
Government in relation to India and Ceylon. These governments enacted
and administered policies in keeping with the principles enunciated at San
Francisco where Dr Evatt and his staff contributed to the evolution and
achievements of the U.N.O. Charter.[28]

The role played by Evatt at San Francisco in the fight for the
rights of the lesser nations in the United Nations' Organization
does not require recapitulation in this context.

The end of the war did not mark a turning point in Australian
foreign policy, or in the Debate. Policy had been worked out during
the war, and the Opposition had never ceased to attack it. The period
from 1941 to 1949 may be considered as a continuous whole.

Although a policy could be worked out in advance, its detailed
application could not. There were too many imponderables. Of
these, the war-time transformation of the South East Asian societies
and their political conditions, was to have a major effect in the post-
war world and in particular, on Australia's Asian policies / ~~our chief~~
~~concern here.~~

THE ANTIQUITY OF ASIAN STATES AND STATECRAFT

The study of the evolution of Australia's Asian policies would be
incomplete without some description of the region with which they
were concerned. One is made sharply aware of the need for this
when a historian of the stature of Golo Mann can write, in the opening
paragraph of his *History of Germany since 1789*:

. . . the genius of Europe has given much to the world: things good and evil,
generally things that are both good and evil - among them the state and the
nation. Elsewhere, in Asia and Africa, nations and states did not exist in the
past. They are being produced and reproduced there today, and the forms
invented by Europe are used as weapons against Europe. This is not unjust
or humiliating provided we do not misunderstand it.[29]

In the following pages, a very brief sketch is given simply to
indicate the antiquity of political, diplomatic and commercial
institutions in Asia. The Eurocentric view explicit in Mann's
introduction became a reality for most of Asia only during a relatively

brief period from the nineteenth century to the outbreak of the second world war. This was the span of effective Imperial domination of Asia. Before that lay between two and three millenia of recorded civilization where concepts of, and reflections on, the state, legality royalty and religion were *Leitmotive*. In these centuries, too, were formulated the institutions for the regulation of society at all levels. Whether transactions were political, commercial or diplomatic; whether they were between villages, city-states or empires, they were, and are, conducted according to strong notions of propriety and legitimacy.

Kauṭīliya, Machiavelli's peer, had probably formulated his *Artha sastra* in India in the -4th century. The recensions of decisions and correspondence from the period of the warring states in China show a sophisticated *Realpolitik* at work from the -5th century. State-craft and its exposition in parts of India and China are as old, if not older, than those in the Hellenic world, in the South Eastern tip of Europe.

Archaeological research has begun to pick up traces of trade in stone beads and pottery during the -1st millenium in many parts of South East Asia. It illuminates our view of trade arteries over land, mountain passes, rivers and sea, to remember that these were pioneered as long ago as the pre-historic period.

With the passage of time, trade routes were greatly elaborated and extended. Without doubt, long-distance trade, together with local agricultural efficiency, and the control over a strategic section of a route, were the major factors in pushing communities over the threshold from prosperous villages into city states.

Two widely separated sites, Beikthano in central Burma and Oc-eo on the Mekong Delta, present evidence of a degree of urbanisation starting from the +1st century, that certainly imply sophisticated societies, in contact with other sophisticated societies. In the latter case, trade objects from as far afield as the Roman Empire and China have been found side-by-side with local ornaments and utensils of quality and taste.

With trade came diplomacy. China was interested in the luxury wares of the West and, of necessity, in the status, organization and reliability of the *entrepôt* kingdoms that conveyed those goods in the India-China section of the great Asian maritime route. These were the kingdoms of South East Asia which were recorded by the Chinese as Fu-nan and Tien-sun or Tun-sun.

The first Chinese embassy was sent to the 'Southern Seas' between +245 and +250. At the court of Fu-nan, the envoys K'ang-t'ai and Chu-ying, sent by the House of Wu, also found in residence a mission from the Indian court of Murunda. Thus, records of the diplomatic relations of South East Asian states with China and India, respectively, go back to the mid-third century, while the relations themselves, with India at least, were probably considerably older.

From a variety of Asian sources - Chinese records, South East Asian stone inscriptions and manuscript chronicles, Indian stone inscriptions, copper plates and epic literature - there emerges a mosaic picture of diplomacy over sixteen hundred years under whose conventions treaties of royal friendship, imperial patronage, neutrality, non-intervention and alliances in the event of attack were formulated and enforced.

As in Europe in the mediaeval period, embassies were *ad hoc* undertakings and non-resident, in the modern sense of the word. The entourage of the envoy was, however, frequently numerous and his mission would involve at least six months' residence in the place of his assignment, in order to allow for the cycle of the seasons. In the case of China, the conditions of foreign trade were at times tightly regulated. Foreign missions approaching the capital were liberally furnished with offerings known to be favorably regarded there. These were meticulously recorded in Chinese departmental registers as 'tribute'. During a period of variable length, the credentials of the ambassador, the status and wealth of his sovereign and his and his envoy's equivalent status within their domestic hierarchy were assessed by Chinese officials. Once a mission had been authenticated and accepted, with its goods, a tacit understanding existed that an exchange of equally desirable goods would, in due course, take place. The largesse dispensed by the Chinese court was registered as 'gifts'.

To send a mission well provided with goods was no guarantee that diplomacy or trade would ensue. The Lord of Satsuma's envoy to China in the 14th century was carefully investigated and dismissed with a scalding reproof to his lord for his presumption in attempting direct diplomacy instead of approaching through the highest political institutions of his own land.

Religion was frequently pressed into service for diplomacy: the Japanese court found it expedient to appoint the heads of monasteries under royal patronage to lead their missions to China. This seems to have been done in the belief that fraternal links with influential Mahayanist Buddhist monasteries in China would indirectly ease the process of establishing the mission's credentials. Among the Theravada countries of South East Asia, the use of royal abbots and monks as ambassadors seems rather to have reflected a world picture in which royal, religious and economic elements were unitary and not distinct. The last king of the *Pagan* Empire sent his royal monk to negotiate delays and compromise with Khublai Khan, whose forces were making raids into Upper Burma and were to conquer the capital shortly afterwards.

Diplomacy between Thailand and Burma was still being conducted through the abbots of the royal monastic foundations on the eve of the third Anglo-Burmese war which was to overthrow the Burmese monarchy.

But for the intense diplomacy of South East Asia - by peaceful and other means - the European powers would have found it much harder to establish their small bastions of power during the sixteenth, seventeenth and eighteenth centuries, by exploiting and manipulating regional tensions to their own advantage.

The net result of the European powers' economic policies, in the period of their heaviest influence on colonial territories during the nineteenth century, had been to link a small segment of local production to world trade cycles - often with large financial consequences for the metropolitan power. For the countries concerned, however, this meant only a fragmentary connection between their economies and world markets. It was this segment of the economy which gave the decisive impulse to total production.

JAPANESE POLICIES AND THEIR CONSEQUENCES

Many observers have commented with surprise on the deleterious effects of Japanese occupation on rice production which was still connected with subsistence levels of production, during the war. At first sight this impact would seem paradoxical, but on closer analysis it becomes clear that falling production figures in this field reflected a decline in the whole economy, together with a decline in social and political morale in the latter stages of Japanese ascendancy. It is, therefore, necessary to isolate the economic, social and political consequences of the Japanese occupation insofar as they have played a major determining role in later developments in the region.

The political forms assumed by Japanese dominance in the countries of South East Asia depended on the conditions in which it was achieved. As these varied greatly, so did the political forms of Japanese control which were to have lasting consequences for the post-war developments of the countries concerned.

In Indo-China, Japan established herself shortly after the fall of France in 1940, by agreement with the French authorities at Hanoi and, in August 1941, by a far-reaching agreement with those at Vichy. In legal and administrative terms, Japan therefore shared power with the French colonial administration and the independence movements remained underground. Their situation was barely affected by the Japanese *coup* of 9 March 1945, ending French authority and leading to the internment of French citizens and the establishment of local puppet *régimes*.

In Burma and Indonesia, on the other hand, the Japanese supplanted British and Dutch authority as a result of military conquest. Whatever their reservations, the Japanese sought the political co-operation and support of the leaders of independence movements, whose response varied greatly. Some had looked to Japan as a liberating force against European imperialism, an attitude that can be traced back to the Russo-Japanese war. Aung San, the young Burmese leader who fled to China and Japan in 1940-41, wrote:

. . . A warrant of arrest was issued for me, and I went underground in August 1940. The warrant aroused the students of the country, and their protests caused its withdrawal.
But the time had come to strike, and I slipped out of the country - to Amoy in China - to search for contacts and aid in Burma's struggle for freedom. I stayed in the International Settlement in Amoy for about two months, at which time Japanese agents came and arranged for me to go to Tokyo.[30]

The experiences of occupation and collaboration government were, however, to expose the limitations of this form of 'Asian solidarity'. U Thant has recorded his administrative experience of this period:

I was not happy at all. It was much worse than the British system. There were too many advisers. They called themselves advisers but they really ruled.

Life in Rangoon grew pretty hot. Not only the bombing. I was the target of Japanese suspicion. I was thought to be pro-British.[31]

To add to Burmese difficulties at this time, there was an outbreak of intense hostility between undisciplined remnants of Burmese forces and Karens in the Irrawaddy delta area.[32] This deepened the social dislocation already apparent at this time.

In Indonesia, Sutan Sjahrir's priorities reflected his intellectual stature. He related the events in Asia to those in Spain and the effects of Hitler's decisions to the Indonesian struggle. On 25 March 1938, he wrote from his exile at Banda Neira:

I have now come to the conclusion that the situation in the world has changed so much that opposition to the Dutch rule can no longer be the primary task of Nationalist propaganda or of the Nationalist movement itself . . . More profound antitheses have now come to the fore, which overshadow and deprecate the conflict between Holland and Indonesia . . .[33]

He then went on to write of the essential preconditions for genuine co-operation between the Netherlands and Indonesia against the common threat of militaristic expansion in both the Eastern and the Western hemispheres. He was under no illusion about the brutality contained in the Dutch imperial system; he had tasted it. But Sjahrir also valued the qualities nurtured by European culture and he hoped to bend it selectively to the service of his country. On 31 December 1936, he had written:

The West is now teaching the East to regard life as a struggle and a striving, as an active movement to which the concept of tranquillity must be subordinated. Goethe teaches us to love striving for the sake of striving, and in such a concept of life there is progress, betterment, and enlightenment . . . Forms that the struggle take indicate the development and refinement of the individuals who are engaged in the effort.[34]

Sjahrir refused to collaborate with the Japanese occupation governments but seized the opportunity to organise socialist strength underground.

Japan's own policies in relation to the region must be viewed in the perspective of its China policies. Its attempts during the 1930's, at decisive penetration of China, remained incomplete by the time of the outbreak of war in the Pacific.

Japan's interest turned to South East Asia for several reasons. One was to eliminate European powers, particularly from the mainland, in order to improve Japanese chances of overwhelming resistance in China. Another was to gain access to the primary sources of wealth in that area, in particular to oil, for the benefit of Japan's own industrial expansion. Finally, when the tide of war began to run decisively against Japan, it became increasingly interested in promoting independence movements in the countries concerned which might prevent the re-assertion of European colonial authority and economic benefit. The stated aims of the Great East Asia Co-Prosperity Sphere were:

1. The countries of Great East Asia, through mutual co-operation, will ensure the stability of their region and construct an order of common prosperity and well-being based upon justice.
2. The countries of Greater East Asia will ensure the fraternity of nations in their region, by respecting one another's sovereignty and independence. and practising mutual assistance and amity.
3. The countries of Greater East Asia, by respecting one another's traditions and developing the creative faculties of each race, will enhance the culture and civilisation of Greater East Asia.
4. The countries of Greater East Asia will endeavour to accelerate their economic development through close co-operation upon a basis of reciprocity, and to promote thereby the general reciprocity of their region.
5. The countries of Greater East Asia will cultivate friendly relations with all the countries of the world, and work for the abolition of racial discrimination, the promotion of cultural intercourse, and the opening of resources throughout the world, and to contribute thereby to the progress of mankind.[35]

These policies had appeared in earlier form, from 1939 onwards. At first, they had envisaged a bloc formed by China, Manchuria - *Manchukuo* - and Japan. As collective Japanese cabinet opinion veered among the rival pressures exercised within it, policies towards the European powers and the United States were by no means static. By early 1940, the 'Southern Territories' - South East Asia - had, for their strategic resources, been included in the concept of a 'Greater East Asia', as a major object independent of, or, at any rate, the equal of, Japan's existing China policies.[36] By late 1941, the aims of this programme were defined to effect the quickest possible control by restoring public order, acquiring important resources for military purposes, and making the operational forces self-supporting. Economically, the document relating to the 'Principles of Economic

Policies for the Southern Area' delineated three objectives: obtaining resources vital to prosecuting the war; establishing the Great East Asia Co-Prosperity Sphere as economically self-sufficient; and building up Japan's economic strength by means of the first and second devices.

The principles of the Great East Asia Co-Prosperity Sphere stressed issues, such as liberation from European imperialism, Asian solidarity, and economic co-operation, which were likely to find ready acceptance in South East Asia. As events were to show, however, through the combined pressures of military conflict and the structure, as much as the limited capacity of the Japanese economy, Japan was not able to realise the broad aims of the Great East Asia Co-Prosperity Sphere, nor was it able to fill the economic vacuum left by the European colonial powers which it had displaced. Vietnam, Thailand, Burma, Malaya, Indonesia and Singapore were, in varying degrees, isolated from their former markets, without provision of an adequate substitute.

The second stage of Japan's planning required the occupation forces to become self-sufficient and to perform the vital task of pressing local economies and man-power into the service of the Japanese war effort and of Japan's concurrent industrial expansion. It was at this point that their strategy did not realise its objectives. When the occupation administrations realized the difficulties in obtaining deliveries, they began to apply a variety of pressures which were to have important long-term consequences in all three spheres: economic, social and political. Furthermore, unable to maintain complete naval supremacy, the Japanese could not maintain regular shipments of primary produce and strategic supplies to their metropolitan industries.

The Burma-Siam railway was conceived as one way to keep supplies flowing on land routes. Yet this substitute channel for goods became itself a voracious consumer of those elements most precious to the local economies: manpower in the shape of large forced-labour contingents as well as European prisoners.

Japanese engineers provided the following statistics. The railway involved four million cubic metres of earthwork; three million cubic metres of rock shifting; fourteen kilometres of bridgework construction, including the great lattice construction over the Khwae Noi - all completed within ten months 'after hastening six or seven months without mechanical aids'. The labour force comprised 330,000. These included 270,000 forced labourers on 'contracts' from Burma, Thailand, Indonesia and Malaya and 61,000 Allied prisoners of war. The total mortality lay between eighty and one hundred thousand men, of which 12,399 were Allied prisoners of war, including 6,318 British, 2,646 Australians and 2,490 Dutch. It must, however, be remembered that the British figures include a large number of Indian and other Asian servicemen and the Dutch a relatively larger number of Indonesians. Consequently, the total toll among the Asian workers was even higher.[37] The railway devoured good faith, co-operation and respect, as well as essential materials.

In every case, the degree of Japanese authoritarianism increased at the expense of local powers. Food grains were acquired, under mounting pressure, for the needs of the occupation forces and, in some cases, for the Japanese home market. Inadequate attention was given to the needs of local populations. Throughout the region, living standards declined. Areas of land under cultivation shrank, ageing rubber trees were not replaced, average local consumption of rice fell - all clear signs of Japan's failure to provide an economic impetus and leading directly to a decline in social and political morale.

This decline was accentuated by the increasing pressures brought to bear on the civilian populations. Labour contingents were compulsorily drafted for projects essential to Japanese war strategy. Coolie labour* was legally based on a six-month contract system. In practice, the wartime labour conditions were such that this limitation was rarely observed. In the absence of imports, the price levels of consumer goods universally rose. This inflationary tendency was reflected and accelerated by the printing of occupation currencies. The two groups of the populations most severely affected were estate workers and urban dwellers. The former were thrown out of employment in vast numbers and the latter caught in the grip of a run-away price inflation: economic dislocation spread to affect that most traditional of all enterprises - rice production. In Malaya, production figures fell from 338,000 tons in 1939, to 225,000 tons in 1946.[38] In Burma, the South had a surplus of rice but no export markets, while the North endured famine and could not gain relief.

In certain other ways, the period of Japanese occupation was to generate significant forces for future growth. In particular,

* *Romusha*

political and military organisation were to be deeply affected, in ways which varied from country to country. These developments must be placed against the specific background of the war period in each country in order to be adequately assessed.

BURMA

Burma's geographic situation is of primary strategic significance. Its territories extend far South along the western side of the Malay peninsula; bordering, there, on Thai territories. There is the long eastern border with Thailand and to the North, Burmese territories rise high into Central Asia, possessing long common borders with Yunnan and touching on Tibet. These border regions are ruggedly mountainous. The terrain plays an important part in the cultural and political separatism of the communities who live there. Settlement is fragmented into remote mountain valleys and mountainside cultivation is pursued under conditions which restrict it to subsistence levels. The western borders flank 800 miles of Indian territory over slightly less precipitous terrain. Thus Burma possesses some of the northernmost territory in South East Asia, while at the same time reaching far South along the Malay Peninsula towards insular South East Asia. It stands in direct strategic relation to the two great states which have traditionally, and continue to exercise their influence over the region; China and India. In this regard also, it differs from other South East Asian States.

Among the countries of the South East Asian peninsula, Burma was possibly the one to suffer most extensive war damage. It was a scene of combat at the beginning of the Pacific war, a two-pronged resistance to Japanese attack being staged by British troops and Chinese forces under the American General Stillwell. Bomb damage was heavy in the cities during the first stages of Japan's aerial attack and the policies of the retreating British included the destruction of installations of strategic importance. This, together with the flight of Indian labour, laid Burma's ports idle, and set the pace for economic run-down. Then, in the final phase of the war, Burma was again the theatre of heavy, exhausting combat, when the returning allies faced most determined and able resistance from 150,000 Japanese troops. It has been estimated that Burma, the Philippines, Poland and Greece suffered more extensive war damage than any other countries. These facts, arising from the strategic importance of Burma's geographic position, combined with the general consequences of Japan's imperialist policies, to create economic problems of singular intensity. The Burma-Siam railway which had devoured men and morale on such a scale, was over-taxed carrying military supplies from Siam into Burma. The records of the 9th Railway Regiment showed more than 180,000 tons of supplies and equipment moved into Burma from Thailand between January 1944 and December 1944. In December 1944 alone, 115 trains carried supplies to Burma. In the following month, the figure dropped to sixty and thereafter, the activity of the railway declined.[39] It could not serve trade needs of either export or import which might have alleviated economic distress.

A *Burma Central Government* under the pre-war Prime Minister of Burma Dr Ba Maw was created by the Japanese occupation force. It subsumed the existing administrative structure, but paired it at every significant level with Japanese advisers. This situation, besides creating the tension and despondency referred to earlier, brought into being a true mirror situation which should be examined closely. There was administrative dualism in the system instituted by the Japanese. Burmese administrators had to take public responsibility for policies originated by the Japanese, and enforced by their advisers in the Burmese structure. U Nu, who was a senior Minister at this time, wrote:

[People] thought we could set everything right with a mere stroke of the pen. And when I saw how little I could do I was so ashamed to meet them that I used to go up to my room in the office by the back stairs . . . The whole time since I took up politics, I have never felt so miserable. Before then I might be thirsty but I was happy; I might be hungry but I was happy; in jail or out of jail, I was quite happy. But now it was a case of a golden palace and an empty belly, as the saying goes.[40]

As the tensions of the political and economic situation worsened, sections of the Burmese administration went secretly into active opposition to the Japanese and so worked to undermine the power they appeared to serve. In the last period of the war, therefore, political reality in Burma was a mirror image of appearances.

Militarily, the situation was equally complex. Aung San had been appointed by the Japanese to lead the *Burma Defence Army*, which succeeded the *Burma Independence Army*. Groups of that loosely organised force had reawakened old and bitter conflicts in the Delta between Burmans and Karens. As Dr Ba Maw recorded, these lasted for weeks and culminated in a mass slaughter.

Aung San was, in the period 1944-1947, to make unique advances in healing the wounds of Burma's minority groups, and to allay, for a time, their centrifugal tendencies.[41]

He possessed the confidence of the Japanese occupation authorities, but their influence was reinforced in the new Defence Army by a dual system of Burmese Officers and Japanese advisers, similar to that of the civil administration. The Japanese trained this army with the aim of using it as a supplementary force to their own military efforts. After 1 August 1943, when Burma was officially declared independent and recognised as such by the Axis powers, the army was called the *Burma National Army*. In the military sphere as in the civil, a mirror situation developed whereby the army, trained by the Japanese for use against the allied powers, was in fact to be deployed by Aung San and Ne Win against the Japanese, in co-operation with the Allies.

These two forces, civil and military, were aware of each other's disaffection because of the close contacts between their leaders. On 1 August 1944, on the pretext of celebrating the first anniversary of Burmese 'independence', the activists met at U Nu's house to plan for real independence. The group achieved a united front truly remarkable in the history of political fragmentation in Burma. The unwieldy name, *Anti-Fascist People's Freedom League*, was soon abbreviated to A.F.P.F.L. The front united the leaders of the national army - Aung San and Ne Win; the Burma Revolutionary Party - Thakin Mya, U Kyaw Nyein, U Ba Swe; the Communist Party which had broken away in 1943 - Thakin Soe and Thakin Thein Pe. U Nu was a member of no party but linked to the others by earlier bonds in the political leadership of the Rangoon University Students' Union, during the twenties and thirties.

Underground contact with Allied forces in India and China was established and secret stocks of food and arms prepared. The mirror situation was at its clearest during the last year of the war. When the Allies began the re-invasion of Burma, Aung San led his army into the field against 'the enemy'. Japanese advsiers accompanied the force on their march North, confident, until the very last moment, of the target of their actions. After a pause at Prome, a farewell the advisers, Aung San led his army into the jungle and began his campaign against the Japanese.

The history of Indo-China since the second world war, has provided examples of a similar process of secret disaffection and preparations for action which are the reverse of the apparent situation. The term 'subversion', often applied to this process, compels one to stand within the situation and on one side only, but viewing the whole situation, the term used here - 'mirror situation' - is intended to stress the reversed role of public institutions as well as the great importance traditionally, and still, attached to the power of surprise in public affairs.

The A.F.P.F.L., a direct response to the Japanese occupation, was to remain the dominant factor in post-war Burmese political life for two further decisive years at least. Under Aung San, it achieved an exceptional level of national solidarity embracing even Karen, Shan, Chin, Kachin and Arakanese representatives. This fact, together with the calibre of the leader, figured largely in the course *the difficult* of negotiations with the Attlee government which culminated in the grant of Burmese Independence in 1947.

Even before the tragic assassination of Aung San in the same year, there were some signs of disunity in the League. The first came from Thakin Than Tun, leader of the White Flag Communists and Aung San's brother-in-law. The loss of Aung San reopened communal tensions. He had possessed a unifying influence of singular force. In the years since that time, the process of differentiation among the components of the old A.F.P.F.L. has gone further and the same is true of the centrifugal tendencies among the minority groups outside that conspectus. In the later record of changing governments and their search for viable economic and foreign policies, it is significant that until the year of writing, power has circulated among men from 'the thirty comrades' of Rangoon University days, whose power base today lies in differentiated factions formerly linked by the A.F.P.F.L., but whose formative political experience was acquired during the Japanese period.

THAILAND

The position of Thailand or Siam[42] differed from all the other territories occupied during the Japanese thrust of 1941-2, because

Thailand was a sovereign state, maintaining diplomatic relations with the major powers and most other countries.

In the nineteenth century, it had been in Siam that British and French forward movements came into conflict and it was not least due to Siamese diplomacy that the kingdom survived. Although it lost some territories to both powers, it did retain its sovereignty with all that follows in terms of continuous, unbroken development. It was the one state to succeed in retaining its independence in South East Asia throughout the colonial period and it did so by its own neutralization, a matter I have discussed elsewhere.[43]

With the coming of the second world war, Thailand faced a very serious situation. Even under the Prime Ministership of Philbul who was known for his pro-axis, pro-Japanese sympathies, the Thais were not anxious to be too close to Japanese and they certainly wished, if they could, to retain the independence of their state. On the other hand, the Japanese Emperor had, in 1938 'directed the army staff not to consider any moves over Thai territory without negotiating the prior approval of the Thai government'.[44]

In August 1939, the French had proposed a non-aggression pact to Thailand. The Thais were willing but raised the long-standing problem of the Mekong river border. These negotiations prospered until the fall of France. Non-aggression treaties had been signed on 12 June 1940, at Bangkok, with Great Britain and France and, on the same day, in Tokyo with Japan. However, the Thai-Japanese agreement provided that the two countries should exchange information and should consult upon matters of mutual interests'.[45] The treaty with Britain was ratified and the necessary instruments were exchanged on 31 August 1940. The French treaty remained in abeyance over the border negotiations which were not progressing. There is some evidence that by the beginning of October 1940, Philbul indicated to the Japanese that he was determined to 'see that problem through' and that he would or might allow the Japanese to cross Thai territory and that he might consider providing supplies for their forces.[46] This evidence is, however, not only uncertain: it is also disputed and, beyond referring to its existence and its status, there is nothing to be done with it at this point. I feel that F. C. Jones was probably not far from the truth in writing that 'of her own choice, Thailand would have preferred to remain neutral and even Luang Philbul might have elected to resist the passage of Japanese troops through his country had he been assured of greater initial assistance. The Japanese had hoped that Great Britain would become the initial violator of Thai neutrality in order to secure a shorter defence line in the Malay peninsula.'[47] This view is born out by Direck Jayanama [48] who was Deputy Foreign Minister and then Foreign Minister during this crisis, an office which he resigned on 8 December 1941. Other Thais who were in a position to know at first hand have confirmed this view to this writer with circumstantial details.

Allied support for Thailand depended almost entirely on what the British could spare, the Americans taking the view that Thailand was, in fact, in Japanese hands.[49] On 25 November 1941, the British Ambassador in Washington passed on a report that, unless practical aid was given to Thailand, it would indeed pass under Japanese influence.[50] The Thai Minister in Washington re-inforced these views and warned that a Japanese attack was imminent.[51] On 29 November 1941, the Japanese Ambassador/sent a message to Tokyo, warning against a possible Japanese infringement of Thai territory and advising in favour of landing troops in British territory 'which would almost certainly force Britain to invade Thailand'.[52]

In the evening of 7 December 1941, Direck Jayanama was advised by the Japanese Ambassador, ~~Tsubokami~~, that Japan had declared war on the United States and Great Britain and demanded transit rights for its forces, across Thai territory. Direck pointed out that Thai neutrality was well known and that they could not assist either side. It then appeared that Japanese forces had, in fact, landed at several points on the Thai coast - and we now know that what Thai forces there were, put up a courageous resistance. Direck pointed out that the Ambassador knew perfectly well that in case of any forces entering Thailand an unambiguous order provided for extreme resistance and that this order could only be counter-manded by the Supreme Commander. Philbul being out of town, it was agreed to adjourn till next morning. When the Thai Cabinet met in the morning, the matter was discussed and the decision reached, however reluctantly, that Thailand was in no position to resist Japan and that Allied help ~~was~~ unavailable, ~~Therefore,~~ resistance would have to cease.

It now becomes important to point out that the Japanese had put three alternative propositions to the Thai government: to provide simple military transit through Thailand; to include the possibility of a treaty of friendship to serve the defence of Thailand; and, to provide for an alliance, to fight Great Britain and the United States. After discussion, the Thai government decided on the first of these - simple right of transit.[53]

In the wake of the Japanese occupation, a Treaty of Alliance was signed on 21 December 1941. Thailand declared war on Great Britain and the United States on 25 January 1942. After some delay, the Swiss government was able to advise H.M. government accordingly. They took the information *au sérieux* and a declaration was published in the *London Gazette* of 6 February 1942, to the effect that a state of war had existed between the United Kingdom and Thailand as from 25 January 1942. Subsequently, the Australian government published a notice proclaiming a state of war between Australia and Thailand as from 2 March 1942.[54]

The United States ignored the Thai declaration of war as one issued by an occupied country. The Free Thai movement then came to have its centre in the Thai Legation in Washington. Although the British co-operated with it, they never gave it full recognition.

A mirror situation developed in Thailand much as it did in Burma. People in high office would keep up appearances as far as the Japanese were concerned but they would help the resistance in many different ways.

Although the Japanese restored former Thai territories held by the British and the French to the Philbul government, that government became so unpopular that it was forced to resign in 1944. The political pressure, the conscriptions for forced labour - though less fierce than in other South East Asian countries - and the economic decline combined to have their effects.

INDONESIA

Java fell to the Japanese in March 1942. It had been one of the major objects of their advance into the region because of its strategically important natural resources.

There had been considerable planning before the campaign was undertaken, concerning the Japanese administration of the Indonesian archipelago. Accordingly, Java came under the command of the

16th Army, based on Jakarta; Sumatra under Singapore-based 25th Army; while Borneo, Celebes and the Eastern islands came under the administration of the Japanese Navy.[55]

The political and military consequences of the Japanese administration require further attention. The most influential Indonesian leaders had been exiled by the Dutch from 1934 on, to outlying parts of the archipelago. Sjahrir and Hatta had been imprisoned first at Tanah Merah - the swampy, fever ridden camp in central New Guinea - and then on the small island of Banda Neira until late in 1941 when, just before the Japanese invasion, they were permitted to return to Java. Sukarno was not. As in Burma, the Japanese forces were anxious to strengthen their power-base by co-operation with local nationalists. Hatta and Sukarno accepted the opportunity; Sjahrir and Sjarifuddin did not. Though lacking real power within the Japanese administration, the Indonesian leaders who worked with the Japanese used the opportunity for strengthening their organisational bases and addressing themselves to a wider audience than they had ever had access to before. An important development of this time was the official use of the Indonesian language, standardised by nationalists in 1937 but limited in circulation until this time.

It accorded with Japanese policies to foster nationalism because of its anti-European implications, but these attitudes, together with lively and diverse political groupings, predated the Japanese period. Under the Japanese, the parties, nationalist and Muslim alike, received new impetus. That did not always reduce the traditions of rivalry and internal tension which were already marked in the 1930's. On the contrary, these continued and in some cases became heightened during this period.

Mass youth organisations were encouraged and trained in traditions of militant nationalism. The civil administration was now open to Indonesians at levels formerly closed to them. This social change embraced, not only members of the traditional Indonesian administrative *élite* - the *prijaji* - but also recruits from the militant youth groups, whose outlook tended to be quite different. These factors played their part later in the problems of internal factionalism and swollen numbers in the Indonesian bureaucracy.

From late 1943, the Japanese administration set up auxiliary armies in Java, Bali and Sumatra. The Indonesian officers at this time, comprised two basic types - the Dutch-trained and those trained by the Japanese forces. To these, a third element was to be added in the days of the post-war independence struggle - the new officers of the guerrilla army. General Nasution has noted how the divisive effects of these different influences expressed themselves in terms of intra-service rivalries and political-professional style.[56] From the same period originated the revisions in Japanese policies regarding Indonesian independence. With the first strong signs that its lines of occupation were over-extended in the light of the re-emergence of Allied strength in the Pacific, Japan began to consider ways of securing these territories from returning to Dutch control. At first, this appears to have involved only a 'high-level autonomy for Java.'[57] From 1943 until July-August 1945, there were at least six policy documents relating to this question, recording the successive revisions of policy which took place, more under the pressure of changed external circumstances than through internal political evolution which, however, was also taking place both above and below ground.[58]

 Economically, the period of the Japanese administration coincided with the fragmentation of production and exchange. Divorced from its pre-war trade outlets, the Indonesian economy was not supplied with an adequate substitute in the war-time capital investment or trade channels from and to Japan. Throughout the archipelago, production levels dropped to subsistence agriculture, plantation industry was run down, man-power was dislocated through these conditions as well as the forced-labour contingents and exchange suffered through the monetary policies of the occupation government. Particularly during the last year of the war, there was active discontent which showed itself in rural insurrections and urban unrest. It was at this time that the underground independence organisations gained much strength among the urban population.

By March 1945, an Investigating Committee for the Preparation of Independence was officially sanctioned and in early August, the Indonesian Independence Preparatory Committee openly began its work under the leadership of Sukarno and Hatta. On 17 August 1945, the Republic of Indonesia was proclaimed, three days after the Japanese surrender.

In briefly recapitulating the political evolution of the modern Indonesian state, one might select certain factors as playing a major role in determining its borders, and its structure. Though the Dutch penetration of the archipelago began in 1605, at Ambon, it was a slow, indirect and fragmentary process. The consolidation of a centralised Dutch administration - whether by direct or indirect means - was not finally accomplished until 1911. The Japanese struck at and defeated ~~this~~ authority at its centre, Batavia (Jakarta), in March 1942, and thereby succeeded to the entire area. When, in 1945, the Indonesian independence leaders proclaimed the Republic of Indonesia, they too claimed their right of inheritance to these borders whose historical legality, like the borders of so many other states in Asia, was based on the actions of the colonial powers.

The short-lived Japanese empire in South East Asia forcibly removed European colonial authority from the region. In Indonesia, the Dutch, like the French in Indo-China, did not succeed in reasserting their authority by force of arms in the post-war period. During the war, Indonesian political life had been released from the restraints characteristic of the Dutch period. The change that came about was ~~not~~ free from internal tensions, nor ~~was it~~ untrammelled by the occupation government, but the Japanese ~~did~~ release political and social forces much ~~bigger~~ than anything deliberately planned under their programme for encouraging local nationalism, and irresistible ~~because they were~~ widely-supported ~~indigenous forces~~ which rapidly assumed a revolutionary character in the face of a colonial come-back. As in Burma, all the Indonesian nationalists had used the period of Japanese rule to further, as far as possible, their own independent aims.

Returning Dutch colonial authorities assessed the Indonesian resistance as an artificial product of Japanese influence, and, as a result, they underestimated the indigenous strength and revolutionary character of the Republican government. This was all the more an error when placed against the fact that the first Prime Minister of the Republic was Sutan Sjahrir who, as leader of the underground and leader of the Socialist Party, the P.S.I., had ~~not~~ co-operated with the Japanese and possessed a moral and intellectual stature and parliamentary expertise which it was difficult to ignore.

In the course of the following years, to 1949, the Republic of Indonesia was to demonstrate its diplomatic and military ability to the world. The policies of the Australian government towards ~~this problem~~ were decisively altered by the course of the struggle between the colonial and nationalist ~~powers~~ in Indonesia. For

Australia, this conflict was to become highly significant. The government's fresh concept of Australia's place in the South East Asian environment was translated into major diplomatic initiatives, leading to a new phase in the Debate.

Together with India, the Australian government played a constructive part in bringing this conflict to its solution. This cardinal fact has deeply affected the later course of Australian-Indonesian relations.

THE AUSTRALIAN DEBATE ON DECOLONIZATION

When the French, but more especially the Dutch, attempted to restore their power in their colonies by methods that were unpopular in Australia, a climate of public opinion favouring policies designed to further Indonesian self-government developed. The actions of the British Labour government, giving independence to India, Pakistan, Burma and Ceylon by agreement, backed by statute, tended to foster this attitude - especially since Burma's refusal to remain in the Commonwealth served to stress the authenticity of the freedom of choice exercized by the other three Asian members in retaining this connection. There were, of course, Australians to whom 'Britain wasn't Britain anymore'. It was for this type of Empire loyalty that Menzies spoke at that time in Parliament:

When I read in my newspaper that on the 20th February last, the Prime Minister of Great Britain, Mr Attlee, had made his dramatic and historic statement on India, my first feeling was one almost of shock . . . It may seem to me, as indeed it does, that to abandon control of a people who have not yet shown a real and broad capacity for popular self-government is to do a disservice to them. We do not greatly serve a people when we throw them into a state of self-government before the majority of them have become fit to undertake this extraordinarily delicate and difficult task.[59]

He said a great deal more outside the House but eventually he came to live with the new world although he has never disguised his regret at the passing of the old - or of what he felt the old world to have been.

The same conflict arose over the Indonesian independence struggle. It arose in a less clear-cut form, over a much longer period. The very fact that the liberation of British Asia took place by agreement and was placed on the British Statute Book made opposition to it quixotic and short-lived. This goes as much for the Australian

'Empire loyalists' as for the Australian Communists whose discomfiture at the moral victory of British socialism, that is, at the agreed transfer of a great colonial empire by Act of Parliament, was amusing to watch.

The Indonesian case was different and infinitely more complex. The Dutch were Australia's allies. They were known as a brave, democratic people whose record in resistance to Nazi tyranny was unsurpassed. What other people had, under the terror of Nazi occupation, carried out spontaneous mass strikes against the deportation of the Jews? And, in the period in question, 1945-49, the tragedy summed up by *Auschwitz* was very much in the news. Moreover, the Dutch had been fighting side by side with Australians. Unfortunately, that story had its blots. It was marred, on the one hand, by accounts - possibly exaggerated by the bitterness of defeat - of poor co-operation and, on the other, by Dutch treatment of 'their natives', including Indonesians in the Dutch forces. Added to the confusion was the fact that at least some of the Indonesian leaders had co-operated with the Japanese. However historically absurd, they were labelled *Quislings*, which was not without political effect in Australia.[60] In any case, the Netherlands Indies, as Australia's nearest neighbour, had great strategic and economic significance.

To this thought, another concept was added, dear to Australian supporters of imperialism as well as to Australian supporters of Communist power - who share an admiration for force and 'toughness': it was the curious and *simpliste* notion that there was a single mystical phenomenon, called, *The Asian Revolution* and that all nationalist movements in Asia were Communist, or necessarily led to Communism.

All these factors, the strength of democracy in the Netherlands, the desire for powerful and friendly neighbours, a regard for Dutch interests as well as a growing and active sympathy for the Indonesians, whom considerable numbers of Australians had come to know during and after the war, combined to create a plurality of views and issues, for which there were no precedents.

In 1945, the Australian government assumed that Dutch colonial authority would be restored but with increased Indonesian participation, as indicated by Queen Wilhelmina, during her exile in Britain.

In that famous, carefully-prepared broadcast on 6 December,

1942, the first anniversary of Pearl Harbor, she had spoken of a round-table conference that might lead towards a commonwealth in which the Netherlands, Indonesia, Surinam and Curaçao would participate, with complete self-reliance and freedom of conduct for each part regarding its internal affairs, but with readiness to render mutual assistance. If, as the wartime Prime Minister of the Netherlands, Professor Gerbrandy has stressed, there was no promise of independence, there was a strong suggestion of self-government and an oblique reference to a foreign affairs power:

It is my opinion that such a combination of independence and collaboration can give the Kingdom and its parts, such as Indonesia, the strength to carry fully their responsibility, both internally and externally. [61]

Towards the end of the war, Dr Evatt and probably his colleagues in the cabinet considered such terms reasonable. Evatt certainly wished to maintain 'the wartime friendship with the Dutch'. These assumptions were to alter in the course of the ensuing struggle.

The question of the origins of Australian interest in the Indonesian independence struggle is central to the history of Australia's Asian policies and to the transformation of Australian attitudes towards Asians. The whole problem requires further research of detailed factual questions and of the relations of major issues within this development.

As a result of the Japanese attack on the Indies, considerable numbers of Dutch and Indonesians had been evacuated to Australia, where they remained for the duration of the war. Among the Dutch *colons* [62], military as well as civilian, political and social views predominated that were distasteful to many Australians. There were also several hundred Indonesian political prisoners from the concentration camp of Boven Digul in West New Guinea, which Sjahrir has described in his letters [63]. Significant numbers of ordinary Australians now had contact with Indonesians and they learnt something of them, of their problems, and of Dutch colonial policy. This pragmatic experience proved to be stronger than old beliefs based on abstract generalizations.

On 18 May 1945, nine days after the end of the European war, when Allied concentration on the Pacific war was reducing the question of its outcome to a question about its length, a very thoughtful Labour parliamentarian, Allan Fraser, raised one aspect of the Indonesian problem in Parliament. Indonesian seamen, employed in Australia by Dutch authorities, might find Allied victory a mixed blessing:

> These Indonesians are very much afraid of what may happen to them after the Japanese forces have been driven back and the Dutch regain possession of their own territories. It is admitted by them that prior to the war neither political nor trade union organization was permitted in Indonesia. But during the war, Indonesian seamen in Australia have, for the first time, gained some measure of freedom of expression and enjoyed reasonable standards of living. They now say that they have cause to fear that they will soon have to return to the extremely unsatisfactory conditions under which they existed prior to the war, and more-over, that action will be taken against those who have shown any progressive political spirit during their stay in Australia.[64]

The problem Fraser had raised, reflected much greater issues than may, at first sight, have been apparent.

Four months later, on 23 September 1945, some of these Indonesian seamen decided, at Brisbane, against taking three Dutch vessels to sea, unless a number of economic grievances were settled. Their demands related to pay and allowances withheld by the Dutch, and to the fixation of a monthly minimum wage and a maximum working week.[65]

On the following day, 1200 Brisbane dockers met and decided to support these demands and to endorse a recommendation of the executive of their union, the Waterside Workers' Federation, not to supply labour for Dutch ships in port, pending a guarantee satis-factory to the Indonesians.[66] That ban did not apply to the unloading of ships or to the Dutch hospital ship *Oranje*. Its aim was to prevent the Dutch from shipping military equipment to Indonesia. They then crossed the threshold to political action by demanding that the "Dutch government in Australia should not interfere with the goverment at present established by the Indonesian people them-selves."[67] The dockers' action was endorsed by the Disputes Committee of the Trades and Labor Council at Brisbane and it spread rapidly to other States and to other unions, especially to those under Communist control.

Much has been made of that, to the detriment of another, equally important fact that, for once, Australian Communists acted on their own initiative and in disregard of Soviet policy: to Moscow as to Washington, Western Europe was then far more important than Asia, and there was, then, no Soviet support for Indonesia. Diplomatic relations between the two governments were only established in 1954, that is after Stalin's death. Bruce Grant has been right in saying that the ban on arms shipments to Indonesia "had a startling effect, drawing attention not only to the issues involved, but to the political sophistication of the waterside workers." [68]

Though Chifley's approach was cautious, careful study of his early parliamentary replies suggests sympathy with the Indonesians. At length he responded to the able and realistic recommendations of the Indonesian representative in Australia, Dr Usman Sastroamidjojo, as well as to other evidence showing that the Indonesian government had a mass following and that they were not Communist.

With these facts established, their long experience in domestic politics made the Labour leaders singularly aware of an element often overlooked: the need to avoid polarizing the conflict. In this case, if support for the non-Communist Indonesian independence leaders against the Dutch had not been given, the mandate for the independence struggle would eventually have fallen to the Communists. These attitudes were hardened by Dutch attempts to capitalise on the bitter political campaign waged against the Chifley government in the Australian press. In view of the use made by Dutch officials in Australia of this press campaign, Chifley stated in the House, in reply to an opposition question, on 3 July 1946:

I am not aware of any lack of cordiality between the Dutch and Australian peoples. I am, of course, cognizant of a certain degree of feeling between representatives of the Dutch government on the one hand and myself and the Minister for External Affairs on the other hand, in consequence of statements that have been published by Dutch Ministers. I do not consider that that has disturbed in any way the good feeling that exists between the Dutch people and the people of this country. [69]

On 21 July 1947, the Dutch launched the so-called first 'police action' against the Indonesian republicans. Thereupon, Dr. Sastroamidjojo, who had been received, though without full diplomatic status, appealed to the Prime Minister, acting as Minister for External Affairs in Dr. Evatt's absence, to refer the case to the Security Council. After some consideration, Chifley agreed. It is probable that his decision was strongly influenced by India's announced intention to do the same. [70]

For the Chifley government, friendship and co-operation with India, as with Britain and the United States, were axiomatic without being blind. Political and personal sympathies between Chifley and

Nehru, aided their mutual understanding. It was a policy as much concerned with the relations with Australia's emerging Asian neighbours - a moving into South East Asia - as it was with her traditional British and war-time American allies. It was a policy making full use of direct and multi-lateral contacts. Support for the Commonwealth and the United Nations was not a matter of lip-service but one of policy.

On 30 July 1947, Chifley announced:

> The Australian government has instructed its representative in the Security Council to draw the attention of the Security Council to the situation in Indonesia under Article 39 of the United Nations Charter. Australia has taken action ten days after hostilities commenced in Indonesia, because, in accordance with Article 33 of the Charter, the parties to any dispute are obliged to seek a solution by negotiation or mediation.[71]

Chifley stated that his government had made strenuous attempts 'in consultation with other governments, particularly Britain, the United States and India' to bring about a solution. But 'further delay is not justified because of the loss of life being sustained'. To Chifley this was more than a phrase. He pointed out that in the past, his government's policy had been to urge an investigation under Article 34 of the Charter before decisions were taken in the case of a dispute. However, this situation differed from any previously brought before the Security Council: 'Hostilities are being carried on. Investigation is not required to establish the crucial fact, and, before the Security Council determines further action, it is essential that hostilities cease.'

Australia had drawn the attention of the Council to the situation in Indonesia under Article 39, as this would enable the Council to order a cease fire and then take 'such further steps as are necessary to restore peace'.

Being a very realistic sort of humanist, Chifley was also concerned about the effectiveness of U.N. machinery. He stressed the fact that this was 'the first time that this article had been invoked and it is the hope of the government, in taking this action, that not only will hostilities cease, but that the Council will prove its worth in dealing quickly and effectively with a situation of this kind'.[72]

In conclusion, Chifley emphasised that 'no attempt will be made to prejudge the issue, and discussion of the merits of the case will be avoided'. Chifley was always in favour of lowering the temperature. The Australian representative on the Security Council would ask first to terminate hostilities, and second, without discussing the merits of the situation, that both parties act upon Article 17 of the Linggadjati Agreement providing for arbitration by a third party 'or, failing that, the matter should be referred to the Chief Justice of the International Court'. Chifley hoped that if no procedural issues were raised 'there should be a good prospect of an immediate cessation of hostilities, and an immediate negotiation between the two parties with the assistance of a third party of their own choosing. Members of the Council should not therefore have to arbitrate or to pass judgement on the merits of the case'. He added that, since the Republican government of Indonesia was not then a member of the United Nations, this procedure would be contingent on an Indonesian undertaking to observe the obligations and duties of the Charter, and especially to observe Article 25, which obliges members to carry out the decisions of the Council.[73]

Before looking at the result of the Australian action in the Security Council - which, after long debates, led to the establishment of the Good Offices Committee - we should see what the Australian opposition had to say about it. Its tenor and approach may be gauged from Menzies speech to the House on 24 September 1947:

So far as Australia is concerned the nearest problem to us, geographically speaking, is the problem of the Netherlands East Indies; and if we are to be judged by results, then I want to say plainly that this Government has accepted a policy in relation to the Netherlands East Indies formulated by the Australian Communists, which is a policy of driving the white man out of the Netherlands East Indies just as their policy is to be pliant and complaisant in respect of elements which would drive the white man out of South East Asia and, indeed, out of the whole Asian continent. If that is our policy, then it represents what a great commentator once described as the very ecstasy of suicide - that we, a country isolated in the world, with a handful of people, a white man's country with all the traditions of our race, should want to set ourselves apart by saying to our friends here and there, as in the case of the Dutch, who have been great colonists and our friends, 'Out with you, we cannot support you'. The moment there is any trouble we automatically say we are in favour of the rebels. If that is to be our policy, then we shall be a very lonely country.[74]

Compared to this reliance on old fears as the main motive for the need for 'powerful friends', Labour as a government showed resilience and resourcefulness in using all possible channels in the pursuit of an active foreign policy. One of its main aims was to prevent the objectively absurd and politically dangerous considerations of 'race' from playing too great a part in world affairs - especially in

Asian affairs. Its policy was designed to take Australia into the South
East Asian region, as a country of that region.

The United Nations debate leading to the establishment of the
Good Offices Committee in Indonesia, reflected a growing
immobility of forces in the United Nations, arising from the *impasse*
between the powers throughout the world.

The establishment of the Committee was proposed by the United
States. It was a far cry from the Australian demand for immediate
arbitration. But it was a step in the right direction.
For Australia, another thing had been achieved. Australia's
position in South East Asia had been clarified. The Netherlands
nominated Belgium to the Good Offices Committee, and Indonesia
nominated Australia. This was a break-through in Australia's Asian
relations. The Australian government had opted for regional co-
operation with its newly independent Asian neighbours who
welcomed that policy. It was developing a new diplomacy as a
country with a democratic European tradition, opposed to
Communist aggression, actively pursuing friendly relations in Asia.

Australia was represented on the Good Offices Committee, at first
by Mr. Justice Kirby, and then by Mr. T. K. Critchley, a highly
competent career diplomat whose work made a major contribution
to Australian-Indonesian relations.

Finally, the Good Offices Committee succeeded in obtaining some
sort of temporary accord: 'the Dutch were permitted to retain the
areas they had wrested from the Republic, which included the most
important estate and mining areas in Java and Sumatra. When in
January 1948, the pressure of the United States chairman of the
Good Offices Committee resulted in the signing of a second negotiated agreement, the Renville Agreement, the terms merely reflected
the weaker military position of the Republic. Meanwhile Sjahrir had
left the Prime Ministership . . . [and] there was a considerable rise in
the strength of the Indonesian Communist Party'.[75]

Chifley confessed on 9 November 1948, that he had never believed
'that the dispute has been handled satisfactorily . . . . The Communists
are now adding to the difficulties there. That could have been
avoided if the right steps had been taken in the early stages'.[76] In
September 1948, a Communist rising - the Madiun affair - was
suppressed by the Republican government within a month.

In the face of Dutch determination to act on Churchill's dictum 'what we have, we hold', the work of the Committee was drowned in blood in the so-called second 'police action', beginning on the nineteenth of December 1948. Two days later, Chifley announced:

The Good Offices Committee has reported to the Security Council that the Netherlands have violated both the order to cease fire and the order to negotiate. The Security Council must now therefore decide what action it should take to ensure its instructions are carried out.

Cabinet endorsed action taken associating Australia with the United States in raising the matter at an urgent meeting of the Security Council in Paris. Australia will call for an immediate cease fire, the return of the Dutch forces to previous demarcation lines, and action by the military observers to prevent reprisals or executions. Meanwhile, the Australian representatives at Paris are instructed to discuss with other members of the Security Council, particularly Britain and the United States, what further steps should be taken to bring about a permanent solution to the dispute, for example, whether the Security Council should order an immediate election with a view to establishing a legislature along the lines proposed by members of the Committee of Good Offices; whether the full sovereignty ultimately envisaged by the Dutch should not be granted with much less delay than the Dutch contemplate; whether in the event of continuous disputes the United Nations should not consider a trusteeship agreement.[77]

Chifley's patience was exhausted. Diplomatic courtesies had simply been a prelude to further aggression. It was apparently to underline where Australia stood that its representative made a fierce attack on the Dutch government in the Security Council, with the desired effect on world opinion.

Australia also participated in the Conference on Indonesia at New Delhi on 23 and 24 January 1949, sponsored by the Indian government.[78] For the first time since decolonization, independent Asian countries met to confer about a major Asian problem. Australia's participation proclaimed her position, tempered the anger, and contributed to some 'de-racialization' of the issue.

This last point was as important to Nehru as it was to Chifley. Announcing this Conference in Delhi on 20 January 1949, Nehru had said:

I should make it clear that we do not wish to consider this, or any other problem, in a spirit of racialism. Racialism has been, and is even today, the policy of some other countries. We in Asia, who have suffered so much from it, are not going to encourage it, believing as we do that it is not only a negation of democracy, but is also the seed of conflict.[79]

Within Australia, there was nothing bi-partisan about these policies. The conservative parties attacked the Chifley government fiercely, using hysterical language. They claimed that its policies were pro-Communist. In fact, the government's policies contributed to the viability of the non-Communist forces in Indonesia and elsewhere in Asia. Harold Holt who succeeded Menzies as Prime Minister in 1966, reflected conservative thinking in this speech from the Opposition front bench in the House, on 16 February 1949:

In recent years, and particularly in the post-war period, there has been a remarkably rapid development of Asiatic nationalism, inspired in many instances and to a considerable degree by Communist propaganda, Communist tactics and Communist workers. That development represents a real threat to the security of the Australia people . . . Does any person in this country imagine where our interests would lie and who our friends would be if, as a result of Communist-inspired activity, the tide of Asiatic nationalism were to roll in this direction? Does not that mean that Australia, while giving full support to the admirable objectives of the United Nations, and lending the weight of its own support to the development of that organisation, it must line itself up effectively with those who support the democratic institutions and the way of life for which we stand?[80]

This, in embryo, is the concept of the 'downward sweep of China' and the consequent need for great and powerful friends. Small wonder that Holt was still accusing the Labour Party in 1962, blaming it for allowing the Waterside Workers to harrass the Dutch during the Indonesian independence struggle.[81]

Not only Australian conservatives have made a great deal of the role of the Communist-controlled Waterside Worker's Federation in influencing the policy of the Chifley government. The Chifley government could have broken the ban on Dutch arms shipments. The cost would not only have been grave economic dislocation; it would also have been to the benefit of a cause the support of which would have ensured Australia's long-term isolation in Asia, and one which many Australians were finding increasingly distasteful.

FOREIGN AID

By December 1949 major gifts to Britain amounted to £45 million. Australia was the fourth largest contributor to *UNRRA*, the U.N. Relief and Rehabilitation Administration set up in Europe and Asia, especially China. But the time was ripe for a new approach. The 1948 Commonwealth Conference of the A.L.P. carried a series of resolutions, breaking new ground and laying down new guide-lines that have not lost their validity. Expressing support for the United Nations and the purposes and principles of the Charter, three clauses were passed, formulating the Labour approach into policy:

Joint action by the British Commonwealth of Nations to bring about peace in the world based on justice and better conditions of life for all peoples. Active promotion of economic welfare and improvement of living standards throughout the world.

Active co-operation with the governments of the Pacific and South East Asia to assist in the economic and political development of these areas by means of regional arrangements and by means of direct technical, educational and material assistance. [82]

These resolutions were an early expression of the purposes of ECAFE, which the Chifley government supported; and the Colombo Plan which got its name from the conference of British Commonwealth Foreign Ministers held at Colombo in January 1950, a few weeks after the change of government in Canberra.

Labour governments in Australia had, since 1941, laid solid foundations for an Australian foreign policy. In 1940-41, Menzies had taken the first, hesitant steps in establishing Australian diplomatic missions in Tokyo, Washington and Chungking because of Australia's 'primary risks and primary responsibilities' in the area. But he was neither then, nor later, anxious for independent action. It was the Labour government which appealed to the United States, insisted on separate Australian declarations of war, a voice in major decisions in war, including the return of Australian troops to defend Australia, and at the armistice and after.

The Curtin and Chifley governments were active parties to international co-operation. They ratified GATT in spite of opposition within their ranks and from the 'parties of resistance'. They supported the British withdrawal from India, Burma and Ceylon and established cordial and active relations with the new Asian governments. But the crucial test arose over the Indonesian question. The Chifley government were faced with the alternatives of supporting the restoration of the colonial power, or of giving the Indonesians a chance. Their far-sighted decisions gave the Chifley government the opportunity to demonstrate the feasibility of a flexible, realistic and independent Asian policy. Their support for Western values and interests, where both were really at stake, was never in question. Chifley's despatch of RAAF units in support of the airlift for the

relief of West Berlin, during the Soviet blockade of 1948-9, may
serve as one typical instance. Simultaneously, the bonds they were
forging with Australia's Asian neighbours, especially with India and
Indonesia, reflected historical foresight and moral courage of a high
order.

It was the beginning of a policy consciously leading Australia into
South East Asia. The Chifley government had broken new ground in
showing that it was possible for Australia to take diplomatic iniatives
in association with its traditional friends, Britain and America, as
well as with its 'new' neighbours in the region, whose 'newness' consisted in their regained sovereignties.

THE CONSERVATIVE RESURGENCE IN AUSTRALIA

Australian conservatives did not share the assumptions on which
Labour foreign policy rested - let alone the policy itself. Their
priorities were stated clearly in the Liberal Party's 1946 policy
speech by Mr Menzies:

We support the ideal expressed in the United Nations and will be
prompt in Australia's obligations under the Charter. But at the same
time we are of the opinion that the first practical contribution which
can be made to the Australian security and world peace is to be
found in (a) a cohesive British Empire in which there also are . . .
permanent machinery for joint political, military and and economic
consultation and (b) a close friendship between the British Empire
countries and the United States of America, such friendship to include the making of mutually advantageous financial and economic
arrangement; (c) a real provision in Australia for a real Defence Force
of all arms.

Menzies was an outstanding proponent and practitioner of the
ideology which Dalley had first used to support his arguments in
the Sudan affair:

It is a basic error for Australia to act as if she were not only in
legal theory but in hard political fact a detached and independent
power like Norway or Sweden or Portugal or the Argentine. It is a
calamity for Australia to seek her special associations or even a
position of leadership among these small and smaller powers when
it should be clear that both British world authority and Australian
influence will be best served by the strengthening of the British
Empire association. [83]

Support for the British Commonwealth, or, later, the Commonwealth was never in dispute between the parties. It was common policy to all political parties in Australia. Curtin had worked towards a Commonwealth Secretariat, as had Menzies. Chifley and Evatt had sought Commonwealth agreement over matters of common concern in international affairs. Yet, when the Commonwealth Secretariat was established in 1965, Menzies' affection for the Commonwealth had visibly cooled. At any event, he had the honesty to admit his preference for the 'old Commonwealth' rather than the much larger 'multiracial' Commonwealth, as he made very clear especially after the departure of South Africa, when he laid himself open to serious misrepresentation.

The Chifley government was defeated in the general election of 10 December 1949. This defeat had its prelude in the resounding failure of the 1948 Referendum, held to enable the Commonwealth Parliament to legislate on prices, rents and charges. The government considered this a necessary prophylactic against inflation in a full-employment society which they were pledged to preserve. Until that time, price control and other economic measures had been covered by the Defence power, the validity of which was now of uncertain duration, being at any time subject to judicial review. Continuation of these policies therefore required a regular constitutional basis. Australia had been kept free of inflation and unemployment throughout the years of a total war effort and during the post-war re-adjustment of the economy with its huge re-employment of man-power.

The very success of Labour's reconstruction policies militated against its re-election. The well-dressed young couples who came to vote *NO* in 1948, and *Liberal* in 1949, reflected the success of a policy which they proceeded to defeat: it was a headlong flight into privacy and illusions of affluence which would be built on an enormous expansion of consumer credit; on a neglect of developing Australia's infrastructure of essential services; and on the proclaimed need for a new dependence - on great and powerful friends.

When the conservative coalition returned to office, with Mr Menzies as Prime Minister, in 1949, few would have believed that they would remain in power for twenty-three years.

INSERT ON
WHITE SHE

Part Five: 1950–1972
The Search for a New Dependence

The return to power of the Menzies-Fadden coalition, at the end of 1949, had aspects of the restoration of an old *régime*. It was not only the return of old faces: it was a return of old habits, old concepts and old methods.

In international affairs, the Menzies era began with the search for a new dependence. As far as Menzies was concerned, there was a strong residue of Empire loyalty; but there were also growing doubts. The independent Asian states - India, Pakistan and Ceylon - had also become full members of the Commonwealth. The Commonwealth was changing and British policy was turning the very term 'Empire' into an anachronism.

Britain and India had recognized the People's Republic of China in December 1949, just before the Australian election. Chifley has said[1] that his government would have done the same but for the impending election in which foreign affairs were an issue, the opposition making strenuous efforts to bracket the Labour Party with Communists in any conceivable way. In such circumstances, an offer of recognition would have been as imprudent from a diplomatic as from a domestic point of view.

Enquiries for suitable embassy premises in Peking, begun before the election, were continued under the coalition government until the outbreak of the Korean war. From that point onwards, the conservative search for a new dependence met with considerable success, leading, by way of the Japanese Peace Treaty, to the *ANZUS* Treaty Alliance. Recognition of the People's Republic of China did not fit into that pattern.

One of the undebated assumptions of Australian post-war foreign policy had been the oft-repeated necessity for a 'tough' peace settlement with Japan; in particular, Japanese disarmament of an industrial as well as of a military kind. Linked with this was the concept of an Asian-Pacific security system involving the United States.

Once the Australian conservatives had overcome their shock at Curtin's invitation to the United States in 1941, they not only saw merits in the American connection; they made themselves its advocates, especially after the massive victory of the British Labour Party in 1945. Not only were they now advocating a strong American connection, they were beginning to assert that it would be unobtainable by a Labour government: the implication was obvious.

Nonetheless, the United States were no more responsive to Spender's urgings than they had been to Evatt's - until the Korean conflict convinced American statesmen of the urgent necessity of a so-called 'soft' peace with Japan; a peace allowing Japan to re-arm. In connection with this proposed peace, a series of separate American defence agreements came into existence: with the Philippines, with Australia and New Zealand, and with Japan. With Japan, to regularize the continued presence of U.S. forces and their installations; with the other states, as a re-insurance for the 'soft' peace treaty. This, in brief, is the genesis of the *ANZUS* Security Treaty. On 18 April 1951, President Truman announced:

The Governments of Australia and New Zealand, in connection with the re-establishment of peace with Japan, have suggested an arrangement between them and the United States, pursuant to Articles 51 and 52 of the United Nations Charter which would make clear that in the event of an armed attack upon any one of them in the Pacific, each of the three would act to meet the common danger in accordance with its constitutional processes; and which would establish consultation to strengthen security on the basis of continuous and effective self-help and mutual aid.[2]

The price of this treaty was not only the 'soft' peace with Japan, but the exclusion of Great Britain from *ANZUS*. Although the Labour Party had reservations about this treaty which was submitted to Parliament at the same time as the Peace Treaty with Japan, they voted for the former but not for the latter.

These debates must be seen against the domestic political scene in Australia. I have referred to the restoration of an old *régime*; to the return of old thought habits and old political concepts of power. In a restoration, these include the concept of the purge. Conditions were not ripe for that and the oldest of political strategies was now employed, on a very large scale: to reduce the opposition to a point of impotence by means of the smear, the slander, now prefixed by the adjective 'Communist', and larded with terms such as 'traitor' - the self-evident proposition being that the conservatives had a monopoly not only of respectability and good sense but of loyalty and patriotism. A re-reading of the parliamentary debates for that period is a sobering though hardly an elevating experience.

It was in this atmosphere of tension and bitterness that these measures - the Peace with Japan and the American alliance - were debated. It might be tempting to quote some of the more outrageous. outbursts but that is not one of the functions of this study. Of the two debates, that of the Treaty of Peace (Japan) Bill 1952, seems the more interesting.

Since the government parties were on the defensive over a major foreign affairs measure, which was more divisive for them than for the A.L.P., that debate was less marred by abuse and vilification, then becoming a regular parliamentary spectacle - though it was not free of it. It was also remarkable for the silence of the Prime Minister who contributed not a word to its transactions though he was apparently in the House: at any rate, twenty minutes after the adjournment of Casey's second reading speech, the Prime Minister announced to the House the tragic news of the death of George VI.[3]

In restrospect, the debate reads like a period piece: it reflects a certain resentful and circumscribed nationalism that found itself unable to affect the course of events, while experiencing fears in the face of the role which, it was assumed, a re-armed Japan would adopt. It could be said, as the government did - echoing American policy - that Japan would fill a vacuum as a bulwark against communism, whether from the U.S.S.R., China or other parts of Asia. On the other hand, doubts remained on both sides of the House about other consequences of a renewal of Japanese armed strength. With the advantage of historical hindsight, we know of the third possibility, to which little attention was devoted at the time but which became reality: that Japan would not re-arm, would nonetheless become a major economic power, and would attempt not to be drawn into the conflicts of the principal world powers.

The Bill to approve the Treaty of Peace with Japan was introduced by Mr (later Lord) Casey of Berwick, who had succeeded Spender in

March 1951, when the latter went to Washington as Australian Ambassador. In Casey's words, the government was by no means satisfied with this treaty:

But then, the same can be said of every one of the forty-seven other Allied governments that have signed it. All of us are aware of its shortcomings: all of us have misgivings about it in one way or another. The governments of some countries believe that the treaty is too harsh; others of us feel that it is too soft. We in Australia — and this applies to the Government as well as to honorable members of the Opposition and, I think, the great majority of the Australian people — cannot avoid some doubts at the prospect of Japan being restored to the family of nations without certain controls over its conduct in the future. We are not convinced that democracy has taken firm root in Japan; we are not sure that the Japanese can be fully trusted to steer a course in the future away from the aggressive military and economic policies that have threatened our very existence in the past.[4]

However, in Casey's view, the real danger came, in one form or another, from Communist aggression. So far, Communists in Asia had suffered from a lack of the modern industrial facilities and techniques that were the contemporary basis of power. Japan must therefore appear as a tempting prize especially to the Chinese Communists:

It does not require much imagination to consider the threat they could mount to South East Asia, to Australia, and to the other democracies bordering on the Pacific and Indian Oceans if they had at their disposal the industrial resources of Japan.[5]

It had not been easy, Casey continued, to steer a middle course between the two dangers of an aggressive and fully-armed Japan which could threaten Australia as before and that of a defenceless and economically prostrate Japan, falling an easy prey to Communism and possibly becoming an important part of the general Communist threat to world peace. Common prudence demanded giving first thought to the immediate threat.

Casey went to the core of the matter - the most important provision of the treaty, article 5(c), under which the Allied powers in fact restored to Japan the right, without restriction, to re-establish its army, navy and air force:

The Australian Government has not been happy at the fact that Japan's right to rearm is to be restored without any limitations. We tried, without success, to have specific limitations written into the treaty, particularly limitations on naval rearmament and long-range military and naval aircraft. But, of the countries principally concerned with negotiating the treaty,

Australia and New Zealand were virtually alone in pressing for these restrictions; most of the principal Allies were, for one reason or another, not in favour of them.[6]

Casey stressed that, while the government had favoured some limitation of Japanese re-armament, they were not, in principle, opposed to some re-establishment of Japan's defence forces. They had fully agreed that the Japanese must bear the main responsibility for the defence of their own country. The Japanese could not expect to be protected indefinitely by the United States and others of their former enemies. As it was, Japan was virtually defenceless but for the presence of United States troops, and, Mr Casey added, they 'have not so far shown much eagerness to assume responsibility for their own self-defence'. No one, in that debate, was to develop or analyse this theme.

Once again, Casey stated his reservations. The ten years preceding Japan's entry into the war had shown how quickly and intensively the Japanese could prepare, given the necessary stimulus. Since the days before the war, the situation had, however, changed substantially and in considering the possibility of a revival of aggressive militarism in Japan, its loss of all but the home islands and adjacent minor islands had to be taken into account. It had further lost its former access to raw materials on the Asian mainland. The United States would maintain forces and military bases in Japan for an indeterminate period. Moreover, Australia now had its American alliance:

We for our part, can now contemplate our future as a Pacific nation more happily from the added security of our relationship with the United States and New Zealand in the Tripartite Pacific Security Pact signed last September.[7]

The provisions inserted wholly or mainly at Australia's initiative included payment of compensation to prisoners of war from the proceeds of Japanese assets in neutral or ex-enemy countries; the strengthening of provisions pertaining to the renunciation of territories, particularly in relation to possible Japanese claims in Antarctica, and the references in the preamble and in article 5 to Japan's acceptance of the obligations set forth in articles 2, 55 and 56 of the United Nations Charter. Forty-eight of the fifty-one countries attending the Peace Conference at San Francisco had signed the Treaty. The U.S.S.R., Poland and Czecho-Slovakia had refused to sign. Casey expressed his regret at India's and Burma's refusal to attend and he stressed that among India's reasons was her objection that the Treaty was too harsh. But there was another significant absentee:

The only other [*sic*] absentee was China, whose participation, of course, presented special difficulties. It can be assumed that, having regard to existing international differences about which is the true government of China – the People's Government at Peking or the Nationalist Government at Formosa – a substantial number of countries would have stayed away from the conference had either Chinese government been invited to attend. In the end it was decided that the only way to overcome the problem was to invite neither government, but to make provision in the treaty itself for Japan to conclude a separate bilateral treaty in the same or substantially the same terms within the next three years with the government of any other State that had been at war with Japan. I understand that the Japanese Government has now indicated that it proposes to sign a separate peace treaty with the Chinese Nationalist Government.[8]

After dealing with the ineffectual Soviet stance at the Conference, Casey outlined the ratification provisions and then concluded with the remark that, from the point of view of the security of Australia and the stability of Asia and the Pacific, the security of Japan was of even greater concern than the security against Japan.

In his reply, Dr Evatt* paid a handsome tribute to Casey for his approach to the problem. He noted Casey's frank scepticism which helped the discussion of the subject. It was necessary to safeguard Australia against possible aggression not only by Russia and China but by Japan which he termed a 'convicted aggressor'. He referred to the rise of democratic movements in Japan. There had been progress in the last thirty or forty years towards the democratic idea that people had civil rights:

But, because of the enormous power of the militarist-economic group called the *Zaibatsu*, which control not only armaments but heavy industry generally in Japan, those movements, as they have arisen from time to time, have been crushed, on some occasions in the most merciless and uncivilized manner.[9]

Those responsible were powerful again and, to Evatt, there was no doubt that there was a danger of a war of revenge. He made one important point about the preparation of this Treaty, from Australia's point of view:

. . . the situation has not been improved by the fact that when Mr Dulles came to Australia to talk over the terms of the treaty with the then Minister for External Affairs, Mr Spender, not one Australian expert on far eastern affairs was brought into consultation. We have a profound interest in the

*Chifley died on 13 June 1951. He was succeeded by Dr Evatt as leader of the Opposition.

peace settlement with Japan, and the matter had been worked on for years after the 1945 surrender. Nevertheless, no one from the Department of External Affairs or from outside of it was called into consultation. I do not think that any one possessing a knowledge of far eastern affairs would have advised the acceptance of the conditions embodied in the draft treaty without insisting upon the most resolute and determined attempt to modify or alter them.[10]

Evatt dealt exhaustively with the agreements and peace plans, beginning with the ultimatum from the Big Three which secured the Japanese surrender and, at great length, with the Far Eastern Commission. He referred to the British Commonwealth Conference held at Canberra in 1947, at which every Commonwealth country was represented which had, with minor exceptions, accepted the surrender settlement and the terms decided by the Far Eastern Commission. Then Russia demanded the right to veto those decisions. Of that Russian demand, Evatt said:

Russia had taken part in the fighting in the Pacific war for only six or seven days, whereas Australia, Britain, New Zealand, the United States of America, Holland and other countries had been engaged in it for years. We publicly denounced that claim as monstrous, but we did our utmost to get the definitive conference to arrange those matters as soon as possible because the uncertainty existing at that time was mischievous.[11]

At that time, there had been agreement with the Americans about the need to suppress the monopolist industrial groups and to exclude the fascist military elements from office. Evatt stated that the American view expressed by Dulles was of quite recent origin. The danger he foresaw was that the tragedies of the past would be re-enacted. He referred at length to the growing strength of the groups identified with *Zaibatsu* and the militarists. But he also emphasized that there was opposition to re-armament among the people of Japan.

Dr Evatt pointed to the fact that the Social Democratic Party of Japan was strongly opposed to re-armament, and its members included people who had waged a life-long struggle against the militarist groups, the *Zaibatsu* and the like. The Social Democratic Party was opposed to Communism and Fascism alike and Dr Evatt quoted their recent statement on this issue:

We adhere to the terms of the present Japanese Constitution which provide against re-armament and the terms of which were approved of by the Allied governments, including the U.S.A. and sponsored by General MacArthur when he was Supreme Commander in Japan.[12]

They were not a powerful group in the Japanese parliament although they had considerable voting support. They were irrevocably opposed to the militaristic policy that Japan had followed for so many years. And, we may add, between the reluctance to re-arm, mentioned by Casey, and popular opposition to it, mentioned by Evatt, there has been no revival of Japanese militarism to the time of writing.

The most thoughtful speech from the back benches was that made by Beazley, Labour member for Fremantle - Curtin's old seat. He displayed the kind of analytic approach to benefit a debate such as this. In a discussion of the likely future foreign policy of Japan, Beazley felt that one should analyse certain factors and re-cognize that, at best, one was dealing with probabilities. The govern-ment had adopted the view that war between Russia and the western democracies was probable and that Japan would be our ally. That proposition required analysis because any rational case for ratification rested on this assumption. For a very long time, the government had displayed a completely blind and uncritical attitude towards American foreign policy: 'But it will occur to anyone who takes the trouble to examine that policy that it has been far from being infallible in relation to Asia during the last seven years'.[13]

To begin with, there was the Yalta policy. At that stage, the United States did what they could to strengthen Russia in the Far East, handing to it Port Arthur and Darien, control over the Manchurian railways, of Sakhalin and special fishery rights which carried with them definite naval implications in the Pacific. Next, they attempted to fuse the Chinese Communists into a composite government with Chiang Kai-shek, a policy which greatly strengthened the Communists. Then, suddenly and sharply, American policy set about undoing what the United States of America itself had done. They supported Chiang Kai-shek at a time when his chances were almost hopeless, supplying millions of dollars worth of American arms to his forces, great numbers of which immediately deserted to the Communists who, as a result, obtained a large proportion of those arms. Another aspect of this reversal of policy became clear during the Korean campaign, the object of which was to prevent a spread of Russian influence in a sphere in which the United States had handed over to Russia the vital points of Port Arthur and Darien. Beazley said that he had mentioned those examples to show that 'we should not be hypnotized by American foreign policy'.

Now, Beazley turned to Japanese foreign policy:

Japan has always had a dual foreign policy, and it arises from the geographical position of that country, which is unchanged by any treaty. Japan must choose between a policy of continental expansion and a policy of oceanic expansion, and it is by no means impossible to conceive that Japanese statesmen will conclude that their mistake in 1941 was that they fell between two stools. They tried to continue a policy of continental conquest in China and locked up great armies in conflict with that country. They added to that venture the burden of carrying out a policy of oceanic expansion southwards.[14]

Since 1890, Japan had not faced a united China. In spite of that division and confusion, Japan had been unable to carry out a successful policy of conquest in China. Yet, one was asked to believe that Japanese statesmen would now turn round and say that they had not been able to conquer a China torn by civil war and confusion, but could now defeat a united China, backed by all the resources of Russian foreign policy.[15]

In a war between the western powers and the Soviet *bloc*, Japan would have to face the whole Asiatic littoral of China and Asiatic Russia. Even if Japan attacked that mainland with all the atomic bombs the United States could present it, it would make no dint on the Russian war potential or anything essential to that country. But if Japan were to be atom-bombed from Siberia, it would be struck a mortal blow - a subject on which Beazley then enlarged. He asked:

Can any sane person believe that Japan, choosing between the alternate policies, would throw itself at the whole continent of Asia, to be struck a mortal blow? Or will Japan seek an agreement in order to secure its continental rear if it resumes a policy of naval expansion southwards? Those are the probabilities that we can weigh.[16]

In Beazley's view, it should be anticipated that Japanese statesmen would prefer to embark on a policy of oceanic expansion and that they would seek to secure their continental rear. He felt that Stalin was anticipating that this is what the Japanese would do from overtures already being made in broadcasts showing that he considered it by no means impossible that an independent Japan would enter, however indirectly, the Russian *bloc*. Beazley added: 'Japan has always had that as a second policy'.[17]

He pointed to the fact that Japan's first alliance had been with Great Britain, first to eliminate Czarist Russia from Asia and, then, to eliminate Germany from the Pacific and from China: 'The moment Japan abandoned that policy, the moment it was prepared to take on the East and the West, the moment it was prepared to have oceanic enemies at the same time as it had continental enemies, it failed'.[18] Japan was the only power in Asia with a naval tradition and, in his view, Japan had every reason as well as the internal qualities, to turn back once more to a policy of naval expansion.

As for his criticism of American foreign policy, Beazley spoke very much more in sorrow than in anger:

The United States of America is inevitably and desirably the leader of all Western thought to-day. That is a new position for that country, and it is not one that it has so far shown it has sufficient wisdom to occupy. It has not the maturity of a power such as Great Britain which, in foreign policy, will usually commit itself only on something that matters fundamentally to Great Britain. There is a strain of rashness in American foreign policy; the United States of America commits itself to all sorts of actions in areas that do not matter much to it.[19]

Australia should refuse ratification as a friendly rebuke to the United States who alone would determine what was going to be done with Japan and who had been extremely foolish from their own point of view. The conference at which the treaty was signed had been the first conference at which nobody conferred. Everybody had been summoned to consider a treaty, incapable of amendment. There had been no basis for discussion. Beazley concluded:

If the United States of America is to exercize most effectively its rightful moral leadership of the Western powers, it must drop its cavalier attitude towards its associates. One way of persuading it to do so would be for Australia to refuse to ratify the Japanese peace treaty.[20]

The rest of the debate did not reach this level of analysis or approach. This was a sensitive topic and emotional language, often of an inferior sort, tended to predominate. The opposition was traduced with the usual Communist label and, on both sides of the House, fears about Japan predominated in the speeches. Occasionally, a Labour member would refer to the fact that the Japanese trade unions and the Social Democratic Party were anti-Communist bodies, opposing Japanese re-armament because the only way to save Japan from Communism was to improve people's living standards;[21] and a militant man of the Right who had been a prisoner of war of the Japanese, like Kent-Hughes, would say something noble about reconciliation.[22] It reflects something of

the atmosphere of the House that even a man of Casey's stature
would, in his reply, use language such as this:

Our survival as a free British country is at stake. I am talking in terms not of a
generation to come but of the immediate future. Even if the worst were to
happen and if there were a tremendous revival of militarism in Japan, that
country could not be a menace to us for a considerable period of years. The
menace is on our doorstep now.[23]

Menzies' non-participation in this debate has already been noted.
The Treaty of Peace Bill completed its parliamentary journey
together with the Bill ratifying the *ANZUS* Security Pact on 6 March
1952. The latter passed with Labour support, whatever their reservations; the Japanese Peace Treaty was ratified, following a vote
on party lines.

Evatt had sought multi-lateral regional arrangements including the
United States even before the end of the second world war. But
he had never considered any arrangement excluding Britain. Furthermore, Chifley had made it clear on more than one occasion that
nothing of this kind was desirable and that nothing should be
attempted without India. On 7 March 1951, in his last speech on
international affairs, three months before his death, Chifley warned:

The western powers would be unwise, when formulating policies for Asia, to
go further at any time than the distance they can carry India with them . . .
Pandit Nehru has the most influential voice in Asia today.[24]

That condition had been met, up to a point, in the action of the
United Nations under American leadership, to stop Communist
aggression in Korea, to which India had agreed. However, there was
now a great conceptual divergence between the Australian and the
Indian approach. To India, the Korean war was primarily an Asian
question, whereas the Australian government approached Korea
principally as a strategic arena, relevant to Australian security and to
commitments to the United States, the Commonwealth of Nations
and the United Nations.[25] India's chief aim was to strengthen its
independence in international affairs; Australia's was to use this
conflict to strengthen its defence links with the United States. It is
arguable that, had the earlier Australian policy towards Asia
continued, and relations with India been given the importance which
Chifley and Evatt had accorded to them, the frustrations and futility
of neutralism might, at least, have been lessened. The increasing
desire for identification with American policy tended to lessen

Australian flexibility and responsiveness towards the needs and interests of its Asian neighbours.

The deterioration in Australian relations with India was one, largely, of neglect rather than of positive policy though Pakistan's membership of *SEATO* played a part. Australian conservatives tended to look on Asia as an arena for action, rather than on Asians as actors. This is not a matter of a monolithic policy but, rather, one of tendencies of approach, of shifting emphases and pre-occupations. The change in Australian policy towards India in its war with China was symptomatic, and like much else, it fitted the view that foreign policy was primarily an instrument of domestic politics.

THE RECOGNITION OF CHINA

After the outbreak of the Korean war, the policies which led to the peace with Japan and the *ANZUS* alliance brought success to the conservative search for a new dependence.

The firm policy of the United States neither to recognize the People's Republic of China, nor to admit its credentials in the United Nations had, as J.G. Starke has shown in his study of the *ANZUS Treaty Alliance*, 'had a decisive bearing on the attitudes adopted by Australia and New Zealand'.[26] In this matter, Watt, more cautiously, has expressed a similar view.[27]

In direct relation to the *ANZUS* framework, Starke has pointed to the decisions of the second meeting of the *ANZUS* Council, held in Washington on 9 and 10 September 1953, not to entertain any question of the recognition of the People's Republic of China, or of its admission to the United Nations. These decisions were re-affirmed at the 13th Council meeting of *ANZUS* in Washington on 17 and 18 July 1964.[28]

Australian non-recognition of China must not be seen as reluctant submission to unwelcome American pressure but, rather, as an aspect of dependence fitting into the coalition government's political pattern. It is, therefore, irrelevant whether the United States made non-recognition a pre-condition for the alliance: non-recognition was welcome to the government at a time when they were engaged in a critical debate on the dangers of Communism.

The Labour Party continued to advocate the recognition of the People's Republic of China while they were in opposition and they carried out their policy within weeks of returning to office in 1972.[29]

The conservative concepts, often couched in exaggerated language fostering fears of imminent threats of grave danger to the region and to Australia, and the consequent need for protection by great and powerful friends, seem rather like the continuation of old attitudes and old policies.

Watt rightly points to the fact that Australia did, on certain issues go its own way. It opposed General MacArthur's suggestions for bombing targets beyond the Yalu river, i.e. in Chinese territory, or to use Kuomintang forces in Korea. So did the British and so did President Truman who dismissed MacArthur. Watt also refers to Albinski's account of Spender's active support, as ambassador in Washington, in 1953, of Burmese demands for the withdrawal of Kuomintang units from Burma.[30] They, unfortunately, are still there. Finally, and most significantly, there was the question of trade.

Large quantities of wool and wheat were sold to the People's Republic of China despite, writes Watt, 'strong American objections to such trade'. Smaller quantities of metals, machinery and other items also entered into it.[31]

It is my view that the very existence of this trade serves to buttress the hypothesis that the foreign policies of the conservative coalition tended to be subsidiary to, and in support of, their domestic strategy. The major part of this trade - wool and wheat - unquestionably took place for the benefit of important economic forces represented in both of the government parties. They had the active support of the forceful leader of the Country Party, Mr John McEwan, who was Deputy Prime Minister as well as Minister for Trade. He was not only a very powerful leader of the junior coalition party; he had built himself an important base by effective leadership of the Department of Trade and its active promotion of Australian exports. His base was much wider than the Country Party. Within Cabinet, his position was far stronger than that of any Minister for External Affairs, except when the Prime Minister held that portfolio.

Moreover, it appears that Menzies came to two important conclusions in the period between his loss of office in 1941, and regaining it in 1949. One was to ensure his supremacy within his own party, if need be by appointing colleagues, whose stature might threaten his position, to high office outside Parliament. The other was the principle of avoiding serious conflict with the Country Party, that is, any touching a substantial interest of that party or of its major supporters. This principle was a necessary condition for the survival of the coalition and Menzies was, above all else, a survivor.

The huge wheat and wool sales to China represented an essential interest not only for the Country Party and the forces supporting it; these sales also affected substantial rural interests in the Liberal Party. Although they caused the government embarrassment in the debate, that would have been far outweighed by the embarrassment which might have been caused, had these powerful rural and exporting interests withdrawn their support from the government parties, or had the Country Party left the coalition.

Whether such considerations were put to the Americans, it is not possible to say. Nor is it certain whether it was necessary. Canada was engaging in this trade. Why should Australia deny itself what share it could gain in it? As Albinski has put it, it was a very successful exercize in *Realpolitik*,[32] although it is hard to see why wheat went to China while, during a famine, India was refused.

There is another aspect to this subject, contributing to the fact that, as far as relations with China were concerned, the debate was not as shrill as it tended to become in relation to South East Asian questions. The core of the debate concerned South East Asia. It concerned Indonesia, Malaysia and Singapore in particular. It concerned Indo-China first by extension because of the American involvement and, then, as the result of the commitment of Australian forces to Vietnam.

In this debate, China was involved for the most part in terms of assumptions, evaluations or, quite simply, assertions about what she might do; about her actual or potential influence on South East Asian problems, culminating in the oft-repeated phrase about the downward thrust of China.

In a sense, the same is true of Japan. Feeling about Japan remained strong for many years after the war and it was about the proposed settlement with Japan that the Australian Labour government and India could not agree. The Indians objected to the Commonwealth Occupation Force and the Indian judge on the International Military Tribunal Far East, Mr Justice Pal held that all accused should be acquitted, any other action being the application of retro-active justice. In Australia, a so-called tough peace with

Japan was not a subject of debate before 1950. It was considered axiomatic. After the ratification of the peace treaty, it soon ceased to play an important part in the debate.

·Other issues seemed more pressing: the course of the Korean war itself in which Australian forces were involved; problems concerning Malaysia, Indonesia and Singapore and, hauntingly since 1954, and ten years' later overwhelmingly, Vietnam.

There was, in terms of audibility, a subsidiary debate of increasing importance about the exploitation of Australian new materials, ~~raw/~~ especially minerals, by foreign companies, more particularly Japanese. This was essentially a debate about economic priorities - whether the immediate substantial foreign currency earnings were to be preferred to the long-term industrial development of Australia. This was not a debate about absolute preferences but, rather, about ·'more' or 'less'. It did not follow clear party lines, although the government tended to be more interested in immediate income to be derived from concessions while Labour was more concerned about the preservation of resources or their exploitation for development. This argument came to be linked with the question of Australian equities in foreign-owned companies in Australia. It would go beyond the bounds of this study to enter into these questions here.

THE TWO LEVELS OF DIPLOMACY

It is perhaps not surprising that in the long period of conservative government between 1949 and 1972, two levels of diplomacy can be distinguished, characterized by diverse pre-occupations, policies, aims and styles, for they derived from diverse sources.

On the one hand, there were the traditionalist conservative politicians to whom foreign affairs were primarily a function of domestic politics, including the aspect of playing a part on the international diplomatic stage. For them, international affairs had to provide a constant and imminent threat to Australia's security - preferably a Communist threat. This aspect re-emerged following the events of 11 November 1975, with the return to conservative government in Australia. The conservative response consisted in a close association, frequently amounting to identification, with the policies of the great ally. Until 1941, that role had been filled for them by Great Britain; it was now increasingly filled by the United

States - although occasional reliance on Great Britain did occur. Foreign affairs, especially tensions in Asia, were constantly kept in the focus of public attention and the argument of the great threat played an important role in domestic political warfare.

The policy that assumed primary importance was the pursuit of guarantees for Australia's security against aggression - mainly Communist aggression - from the Asian region. That search for guarantees took place within a sustained political atmosphere suggesting an imminent threat from that environment, so that, in the 1960's an average Australian student could make the axiomatic link: 'Australia is part of South East Asia and therefore is in constant danger of being attacked by Communist forces'.[33]

The search for guarantees found satisfaction in *ANZUS* and *SEATO*; it also led to the pledges of good faith for future protection, most significantly by the commitment of Australian troops to Vietnam. This policy level resulted from assumptions about a constant threat to Australia; a desire to gain a large defence commitment to the region from the United States and a marked tendency to merge foreign and defence policies. It constituted a renewed search for dependence.

On the secondary level, Australian governments from 1949 to 1972, continued to extend aid and diplomatic co-operation to an increasing number of countries in South East Asia. Through the Colombo Plan, O.E.C.D., *ECAFE* and other agencies, the scale of its activities grew along with the number of its partners, on the basis of pragmatic and practical activities designed to assist regional development and co-operation, and to enhance Australia's regional standing.

The focus of public attention rested on the primary level for three reasons: it was the one constantly stressed by the government; it was the target of opposition attacks; it absorbed the bulk of the funds. The programmes and policies constituting the secondary level were not themselves a subject of dispute between government and opposition, except insofar as the latter attached far more weight to it. The emergence of the primary level of Australian foreign policy at the expense of the secondary level was a gradual but decisive process, the remarkable aspect of which has been the tenacity of the secondary level in surviving.

Although Menzies showed his disdain for, and dis-interest in Asia, some of his Ministers of External Affairs displayed greater flexibility. This was especially true of Casey who held the portfolio from 1951 to 1960. Unlike the Prime Minister he was a frequent visitor in Asian capitals. After his first round, shortly after taking over this portfolio, he said in a parliamentary statement:

Although Australia was colonized and developed by people of European stock, and although our cultural past and our present connexions are such that our eyes turn most naturally towards Europe, our geographical situation is such that we must inevitably be brought into close touch with the peoples of Asia. If we make no effort to understand their problems we can scarcely expect them to make an effort to understand ours. Differences of race, religion, language and culture could easily lead to regrettable misunderstandings which might adversely affect our relations with them.[34]

It was not sufficient, in Casey's view, to be vaguely conscious of the existence of near neighbours to the North. In fact, it was essential that Australians should get to know them, establish personal contacts, exchange visits and study 'their problems as well as our own. By endeavouring, within the limits of our capacity, to help them to solve their own great problems, we can do much to create mutual understanding and develop close and friendly relationships with them for the future, which I believe is not less than essential for both them and ourselves'.

Casey realised the strength of Asian independence movements, if not the historical inevitability of their success. His most vivid impression on that trip had been the intensity of the political problems which existed in South East Asia. All of the countries of the area were pre-occupied with the difficult task of maintaining their independence, in most instances only recently achieved. Casey reminded his audience that India, Pakistan, Ceylon, Indonesia, Indo-China and the Philippines were controlled by European nations before the war, that Korea had been controlled by Japan. In many cases those countries were still trying to recover from the devastation and chaos caused by the war with Japan. The Japanese occupation and subsequent withdrawal had greatly increased the speed with which nationalist movements moved towards complete independence. Occupation by Japan had cut immediate ties with the past, while Japanese withdrawal had provided weapons for large numbers of people, many of whom, during the war, had become accustomed to guerilla warfare. There would have been much dislocation in the countries of South East Asia, Casey went on, even if no such thing as Communist imperialism existed. In fact, of course. the problems of reconstruction and of maintenance of political stability were made infinitely more difficult because international Communism saw a golden opportunity to take advantage of the distress, chaos and general unsettlement caused by the last war.[35]

Casey was one of the rare exceptions among Australian conservatives who distinguished between national independence movements in Asia, fused, in many cases, with a good deal of socialist radicalism, and Communism which tried to profit from these movements - in Casey's words by 'pretending to espouse the cause of nationalism, Communism hoped to break quickly the control of the old "colonial powers"'.[36]

In fact, one might add to Casey's analysis that in all independence struggles, Communist success depends on non-communist failure. The first source of this was extraordinarily strict repression during the colonial period; the second, its extension, the adamant resistance to an independence struggle. The first, excluded the ruled people from participation in government and, by its very methods, in generating underground movements, tended to favour Communists. So did its after-affects: the lack of trained personnel, of an indigenous public service and of the experience of democratic methods. The second - a bitter and bloody Imperial resistance during an independence struggle - perpetuated and aggravated these conditions as well as disrupting the economy.

Even so, Communist success in South East Asia as a whole, had, at that time, neither been monolithic nor spectacular, a fact saying much for the political resilience and sophistication of the non-Communist forces. Nehru who was ever at pains to distinguish between radical reform and Communist aims, was certainly right in his warning against the idea of stopping the spread of radicalism in Asia by guns, soldiers or ships which, he considered to be the greatest possible mistake.

Casey's best work as Minister for External Affairs was his determination in 1954, to support Eden against Dulles at the time of Dien Bien Phu. Here, he had shown a much deeper understanding of the inherent problem than his cabinet colleagues:

Do not let us fall into the error of believing that the present situation in Indo-China has come about in recent months, or even in recent years. The fact is that when I was first in Indo-China, in 1951, the situation was not greatly different from the situation that existed just before the armistice a few weeks ago.

In 1951, and, indeed, Casey explained, for some appreciable time before 1951, the Communist Viet Minh had been in varying degrees of control of a large proportion of Vietnam. The recent and rapid deterioration was only the final crumbling of an edifice that had already been very seriously undermined. It could be said now that in the recent negotiations, whereas the non-Communist side negotiated from a position of weakness, the Communists negotiated from a position of strength in that they had not only become dominant in the field but also had, over a period of years and by one means or another, undermined the political allegiance of a formidable proportion of the population of Vietnam. The French had never really re-established their control of the country after the end of World War II, and, although the three associated States - Vietnam, Laos and Cambodia - had been given independence within the French Union, it was very difficult for any one to say exactly what this independence meant. Consequently, large numbers of Vietnamese, and to a lesser extent Cambodians and Laotians, did not think that they could exercise effective independence through co-operation with the French authorities:

There is no doubt that the Viet Minh, though completely under Communist control, originally had a strong nationalist basis and continued to have nationalist elements in their ranks. On the other hand, the non-Communist regime did not have sufficient nationalist appeal of its own with the result that large numbers of non-Communists remained neutral in the struggle rather than offering active resistance to the Communists.

At the beginning of this year, the Communist Viet Minh were in positions of considerable strength in a great many areas throughout Vietnam. They were especially strong in the North, which, of course, was adjacent to Communist China, able to give them encouragement and supplies. Their military strength grew steadily. The French, despite all their efforts and despite great sacrifices of French life, never really succeeded in rallying the Vietnamese themselves to resist the Communist Viet Minh. It became obvious that, if a solution was to be achieved by military defeat of the Viet Minh, the French could not do it alone. It is hard to see what even outside military participation would have achieved in view of the attitude of a large portion of the Vietnamese population.[37]

The struggle for Vietnam had always possessed international dimensions in that it involved France; although, in the French view, it was a domestic affair. Unlike the French struggle in North Africa and the Dutch actions in Indonesia, the French struggle in Indo-

China acquired a strategic significance after 1950, because of its geopolitical implications. After the outbreak of the Korean war and the emergence of China as a formidable force in land conflicts in Asia, it became American policy to support and retain the French presence in Indo-China for reasons distinct from French imperial policy: to secure the approaches to South East Asia against the Chinese and to put down the Communist offensive in Vietnam which, in the American view, originated in China. Anthony Eden (Lord Avon) recalled these events in his famous account, discussed below.

SEATO, BANDUNG, AND THE AUSTRALIAN DEBATE

The conceptual origins of *SEATO* need to be sketched. Its genesis, on the international plane, seems to be found in a proposal made by the Americans to the British government in the first week of April 1954, suggesting 'a solemn declaration' of the readiness of the countries concerned to take concerted action under article 51 of the U.N. Charter against continued interference by China in the Indo-China war; that this warning would include a threat of naval and air action against the Chinese coast and of active intervention in Indo-China: 'This *ad hoc* coalition, comprising the United States, France, the United Kingdom, Australia, New Zealand, Thailand, the Philippines and the three Associated States of Indo-China, would simultaneously set about organizing the collective defence of South East Asia'.[38]

Dulles was quite clear about his choices. He raised the idea of collective South East Asian defence again on 11 April 1954, in London, that is, *before* the Geneva conference. According to his own account, Eden 'told Mr Dulles that we welcomed the idea of an organization for collective defence in South East Asia . . . I emphasized that on no account should India and the other Asian Commonwealth countries be deliberately excluded'.[39]

During their formal talks on the following days, difficulties appeared on the question of membership of the proposed South East Asian security system. Eden repeatedly stressed that, although India and other Asian states might choose to remain outside such an arrangement, they should be given every opportunity to participate and they should be kept fully informed: 'If they could not be with us, we must not put them against us'.[40] Dulles, on the other hand, hoped that any indication that India might be invited to join would be avoided. Otherwise the question of inviting Japan and Nationalist China might be raised. Eden disliked this balancing of India against Formosa: 'The two did not seem to me comparable'.[41]

Eden states that, within three days of the conclusion of the London talks, it appeared that Dulles had taken steps to settle the membership question of the proposed South East Asian defence organisation in advance and on his own terms. The British Ambassador, Sir Roger Makin, reported on 16 April 1954 from Washington that Dulles would be convening a meeting on the 20th in Washington, of the Ambassadors of the United Kingdom, Australia, New Zealand, France, the Philippines, Thailand and the three Associated States. Its object was to set up an informal working group to study the collective defence of South East Asia. The State Department had also repeated its warning that any attempt to include India would be countered by the inclusion of Formosa. That was an extremely serious matter. Quite apart from the timing of such a meeting, it was clear to Eden that it would attract wide publicity, and the countries invited would be regarded as already constituting the proposed organization. He could not possibly accept this. Not only had India been given no opportunity to express her views, but Burma too, was closely concerned and there had been no time for proper consultation with either the Indian or the Burmese governments. To hold a 'mass meeting' (Eden's term) at this stage would be insulting to them both and consequently harmful in its effects on the Geneva Conference.[42]

On the other hand, Eden's later proposal, at the Geneva Conference, that the International Control Commission for Vietnam should include the Five Colombo Powers - India, Indonesia, Burma, Ceylon and Pakistan - because they were both Asian, and neutral, was rejected by the Communists.

Nehru's attitude to *SEATO* was, in these circumstances, no more surprising than U Nu's rejection of it.

Britain had finally succeeded in obtaining American agreement to an approach to the Colombo Powers before the Manila conference, and Eden sent to the Prime Ministers of Burma, Ceylon, India, Indonesia and Pakistan a message in which he said:

Your participation would do much to determine the nature and policies of the projected organisation. I have always hoped to see the Asian powers play a leading role in the defence of South East Asia. The area is of such importance and its peace is as yet so insecure, that we feel it vital to safeguard its peaceful development and ensure its stability.

Even if you feel that you must stand aside, therefore, I am sure you will understand why we, for our part, shall feel it right to go ahead with such countries as are willing to join with us. Though we should still do our best to take account of your views, our task would be far more difficult without your participation, at least in some form.[43]

The time had passed when the Asian powers could have been interested in joining the organization. The moves to exclude them in the first place had had their effect; the tone of Eden's letter indicates that he realised this. Therefore, it is largely of historic interest in showing the type of collective security organization he had hoped for, its style and partners, and in conveying the lively regret he obviously felt for the way things had gone. Of the Colombo Powers, only Pakistan accepted the invitation.

The Geneva Conference had only concluded on 21 July 1954, with its Final Declaration on the problem of restoring peace in Indo-China. Barely seven weeks later, on 6 September 1954, a conference assembled in Manila, which was intended to guarantee the security of the region.

The Manila Treaty did not create special forces of the *NATO* type; it provided for regular consultation between military advisers and for military co-operation. The Thai government of Phibul Songgram was anxious to have permanent *SEATO* forces stationed in their country, but the United States' view, expressed by John Foster Dulles, was opposed to this. In his view all fronts against the Communist danger were interdependent and therefore the anti-Communist forces in South Korea, Japan and Formosa formed in effect, part of the defences of South East Asia. In a broadcast to the American people after his return from the Bangkok council meeting on 8 March 1955, Mr Dulles said that he had pointed out at Bangkok that,

for military purposes, the Chinese Communist front should be regarded as an entity because if the Chinese Communists engage in open armed aggression this would probably mean that they have decided on general war in Asia.[44]

Dulles at that time regarded Communist activities in Asia as manifestations of the Chinese Communist aggression. However, he was still reluctant to commit land forces to fixed bases in South East Asian countries and, in Washington, he asserted that the most effective defence against Chinese Communist aggression lay in a mobile strategic force of great sea and air power which could strike swiftly wherever the need arose. Dulles' aims in promoting *SEATO* may well have been immediate rather than long-term: to create a new confidence among certain Asian countries and to reverse the political tide flowing after Dien Bien Phu.

The most important statement, critical of that policy, came from Nehru, setting out the Indian case against joining the Manila Pact. In the course of a speech in the ~~Lok Sabha~~ the Indian Parliament (during a foreign affairs debate on 29 September 1954, he dealt with the specific reasons for which India could not join *SEATO*; and then moved on to a general consideration of the concepts informing that treaty. It will be seen to have a close affinity with the positions taken by the Australian Labor Party in this and related subjects.

Nehru began, giving the specific reasons for which India was unable to join *SEATO* without giving up its basic policy as a non-aligned power, which it was not going to do. I have designated Indian concepts of non-alignment elsewhere[45] as a form of neutrality exercised by medium and major powers in relation to the two principal world powers.

Moreover, Nehru pointed out that there was an immediately relevant reason which would cause Indian membership of *SEATO* to be in conflict with obligations recently undertaken at the Geneva conference: India had been chosen to preside over the three Commissions in Indo-China because it was thought to follow a certain policy. To change that policy, would be to reverse India's whole position. This would have been a very improper thing to do.

Nehru's conceptual objections went beyond India's participation in a partisan grouping of one of the principal world powers. Nehru expressed every understanding for the existence of fears in Asian countries and in Australia and New Zealand. This fact could not be denied but, in Nehru's view, far from creating a bulwark for peace and security, the treaty did not add to the strength of its members but it did definitely add to the tensions and fears of the region. He went on:

It would be unrealistic for me to suggest that a country in South East Asia or India should live in a sense of false security or tell themselves, 'Let us sing a song of peace and nothing will happen.' . . . Responsible governments . . . have to take precautions against any eventuality. But they should also, I suggest, fashion their policy in such a manner that they will go in the direction of peace.

Nehru also criticized the concept of a defence area which did not comprise merely the territories of the countries that were parties to that treaty but which went beyond it by those countries designating by declaration any given place to be also in their area. This, to him, appeared to be a dangerous extension of the idea of defence. Nehru said that he did not wish to challenge their motives; he presumed that they wanted a measure of security but he felt that they had 'set about it in the wrong way'. The concept of extension and the exclusion of the views of vital parts of the area, all this seemed wrong to him. The treaty might not have carried events very far but he felt that it was going along a very dangerous direction.

Nehru expressed the view that the seating of the People's Republic of China in the United Nations would give a far greater assurance of security than could be obtained through this treaty because you could then deal with China face to face and, moreover, China would assume certain responsibilities under the United Nations. He stressed the anomaly of the passing of U.N. resolutions and giving directions to China to which she could reply that, without recognizing us, how can you expect us to recognize your directions? The door was shut, irresponsible behaviour was increased, and then this was called security, with the result that the influence of the United Nations was lessened. Nehru did not want it to be lessened because it was one of he biggest hopes for peace in the world.

Nehru also referred in this speech to the problem of the overseas Chinese in South East Asia who, because of their numbers and their national status, created an embarrassing problem for those countries, whether they were Chinese nationals or held double nationality. Traditionally, the Chinese view had been that a Chinese subject could not divest himself of his Chinese nationality and, when foreigners made up nearly half the population of a country, this created difficulties. Nehru pointed to the fact that both Chou En-lai and Mao Tse-tung had recently said that these communities had to choose either to become nationals of their country of residence or to retain their Chinese nationality in which case they should not interfere in the internal affairs of their host country. In Nehru's view that was a helpful move. But he added that most countries were not afraid of the official activities of governments as much as by what they might do, in his phrase, *sub rosa* through the activities of Communist Parties in those countries. He considered the rise of international groups 'tied up with another nation' as one of the serious difficulties in international affairs. He was not concerned, he said, with the theory and practice of Communism. It was not the case of one party among others in a country but, because these parties were mentally and otherwise tied up with groups in other countries, those other countries might well utilize such a party for their own advantage: 'That is the fear that Burma and Thailand and other South East Asian countries have . . . And now, as a reaction, we have other forms of international interference in national affairs growing up in various countries, not in that ideological way, but in a practical, governmental *sub rosa* way. This kind of thing is thus growing in most countries, not on one side but on every side.'

It was, in Nehru's view, necessary to come to grips with this problem if one wanted peace in the world and that could not be done by threats and military alliances. There was no alternative to co-existence but 'war and mutual destruction'.[46]

Nehru's statecraft was far removed from Luther's ideology, proclaiming that those who are not for me are against me. He saw where the rigidities would lead. He did not underestimate the dangers of Communist aggressiveness, Communist '*sub rosa*' activities - or other people's.

The Australian ratification of the Manila treaty, the South East Asia Collective Defence Treaty Bill 1954, was introduced by Casey on 27 October 1954. Although the Labour Party accepted it in principle, it did so with reservations. The United States had signed the Manila treaty subject to an Understanding, appended to the clauses of the treaty, above the signatures, that 'its agreement . . . apply only to Communist aggression . . .'[47] Evatt pointed out that that was 'an obligation . . . limited, definite and frank', while Australia's obligation was general. He foresaw that this was the road to Australia's military involvement in Vietnam. He raised two points -

that Australia should ratify this treaty on the definite understanding

that the United States, the United Kingdom and New Zealand
had ratified it, or were ratifying it; and

that armed contributions under this Bill would not be made by
the executive government without the prior approval of Parliament.

In the Committee stage, he moved amendments to that effect which
were defeated on party lines.[48]

Evatt also proposed that the treaty organization should not merely
be a military organization: it should be a permanent organization
which would contribute to the prevention of fighting in this vast
area.

He further pointed to the fact that, in addition to the preamble
of the treaty which formed part of the Bill, the Bill itself had a
preamble. Evatt considered the preamble to the treaty to be 'definite,
objective and positive', while the latter - i.e. the preamble to the
Bill in his words, resembled 'a manifesto against Communism'.
Yet, being the preamble to the Bill, it was legally meaningless:

It is a little placard so that the Right Honorable gentleman can still sail under
the anti-Communist banner but the fact is that he has committed Australia
to obligations which are far wider than those of the United States.[49]

Casey replied to Evatt's points in Committee, giving his explanation for the American *caveat*, restricting U.S. obligations to
cases of Communist aggression:

It is only Communist aggression — not general aggression, but Communist
aggression — that would attract the interest of the United States to a treaty
of this kind, because the view is held by the United States Congress that
Communist aggression, particularly successful Communist aggression, in any
part of the world would be an accretion to the strength of international
communism, and so, in the long run, could be regarded as an added menace to
the security of the United States. If the United States Congress could not be
assured that the United States Government is participating in this treaty only
to combat Communist aggression, the treaty might very well not be accepted
by Congress.[50]

Casey then gave his reasons for the lack of general limitation
of this treaty to Communist aggression. Having explained that
American ratification might have been jeopardized if their obligations
had not been limited to Communist aggression, Casey explained
that some of the Asian signatories would not have ratified it, if
it had been limited in that way:

If this treaty had been directed specifically and solely against communism, it is probable that some of the Asian signatories would not have ratified it. As I stated in my second-reading speech, certainly the treaty would have attracted the animosity of some of the Asian countries that are not signatories to it if it had been directed pointedly against communism. There is a certain touchiness among some Asian nations by reason of ideas, current on the Asian mainland, about not attracting the animosity of Peking. Therefore, in order to have the best atmosphere for this treaty, it was signed by the participating nations other than the United States of America without a reservation.[51]

Furthermore, if Australia had followed the American example by limiting its obligation in the same way, 'we could not have had this treaty'.[52] The fragile character of this construction was clear.

It is relevant to add that the Australian political atmosphere at that time was explosive and, as in some other parts of the world, 'Communism' had become a device in Australian political warfare of many uses and few limitations. The debate on this treaty bill gave opportunities for this exercise and, regrettably, Casey did not resist these temptations. In his concluding remarks, Evatt said of the preamble which, in his view, was inspired by higher authority than the Minister:

I do not think that it was the Minister who was responsible for that preamble being put in the bill, because it is contrary to everything he said at Manila. I understand that at Manila the Minister insisted that there should not be a limitation on Australia, but other forces wanted it.

I have dealt with all the points. The preamble of the bill contradicts the treaty. The Minister signed the treaty, but it is not good enough for Australia. He wants to put a label and a tag on it that will appeal to the basest elements in the community, who do not wish to defeat communism but to sneak in under it for their own purposes. I object to the preamble because I think it should not be in a bill of this kind. It does not conform to the treaty and the Minister's obligations, as he understood them, at Manila. I accept his challenge about the United States. I repeat that it is the attitude of the Australian Labor Party, and always has been, that, in respect of the United States of America in the Pacific, there should be partnership, not subservience. Australia should never be a satellite of the United States. The Americans would not respect us if we were. They are a great and a generous people. They may tolerate McCarthyism for a little while, but then they will kick it to death. That is what is going to happen in this country, too. The right honorable gentleman must not try to smear his opponents with communism, when he knows that it is not right to do so. He has done that during the debate on this bill.[52]

The relentless abuse, especially the slur of being sympathetic to Communism, was beginning to take its toll on Dr Evatt. A statesman of his stature should have been proof against such taunts. Evatt's high seriousness was unsuited to repartee. He sought indignantly to repudiate by argument what could not be reached on those levels. In contrast, Menzies' adroit use of world affairs for domestic ends appeared all the more effective.

Dr Evatt resigned in 1958, on his elevation to the bench, as Chief Justice of the State of New South Wales. He was succeeded by Calwell as Leader of the Opposition. Evatt retired from the bench in ill-health in 1962. He died in 1965.

The Evatt amendments being lost, the Labour Party nevertheless voted for the Bill to ratify *SEATO* of which it became steadily more critical.

The reply to Manila was Bandung and it was Nehru who exerted himself to obtain Australian and New Zealand participation in that first Afro-Asian Conference. The Australian Labor Party which shared many of Nehru's views on international affairs, strongly favoured participation. The government did not.

For Menzies, refusal to participate in the Afro-Asian Conference was a matter of course, a matter of principle and, a matter of expediency. We have seen what had been his attitude to Indian independence; to the Indonesian struggle; to multi-lateral diplomacy in general and with Asian powers in particular. He regretted for the rest of his life the passing, as he saw it, of the 'old Commonwealth'. If Australia could no longer be a junior and dependent partner of the British Empire, if his concept of the unity of the Crown had become meaningless, then the framework for a similar dependence had to be supplied by the American alliance. Bandung did not fit into this scheme. These, for Menzies, were clear issues and matters of principle.

They were joined by a matter of expediency, arising from internal division in the Labour Party. The pitch of this dissension was reached by the events following the defection of Mr Petrov, a third secretary of the Soviet Embassy at Canberra, about the time of the fall of Dien Bien Phu. This led to a Royal Commission and the temporary rupture of relations between the Soviet Union and Australia. Menzies' great gift as a tactician found a field which he played as a master. The 'Communist' taunt against the Labour Party gained fresh life from these affairs and accelerated its division. The govern-

ment having come close to defeat in the 1954 elections, was made
safe in elections held in the following year, fought in this emotional
atmosphere. For many years to come, the consequences were felt
and every phase of polarisation of world affairs was put to domestic
purposes. Such was the background to Australia's refusal to consider
participation at Bandung. An official invitation was never issued,
the unofficial feelers having been rebuffed. But Nehru expressed
his regret in his final speech at Bandung:

I should like Australia and New Zealand to come nearer to Asia. I would
welcome them because I do not want what we say or do to be based on racial
prejudices. We have had enough of this racialism elsewhere.[53]

In the pursuit of the new dependence, the Chifley view of the
importance of India to Australian diplomacy had no place. Australian-
Indian relations declined, reaching their lowest point when Menzies
and Nehru publicly crossed swords in ~~sessions of~~ the General
Assembly, on 5 October 1960.

It will be remembered that in May of that year, a 'summit'
meeting of the heads of the British, French, Soviet and U.S. governments was to have taken place in Paris; and that it was called off by
Khrushchev, his given reason being the U-2 incident, in which an
American aircraft, engaged in a 'surveillance flight' over Soviet
territory, had been brought down.

In these conditions, many heads of governments were attending
the Session of the General Assembly of that year, but the Australian
delegation was initially led by Barwick who was then Attorney
General. Following the announcement that the Prime Minister of
New Zealand would lead his country's delegation, Calwell apparently
urged Menzies to follow suit, which he did.[54]

It was widely felt that the future of the United Nations was in
jeopardy. Khrushchev's unmeasured attack on Hammerskjold, the
Secretary General, linked to a proposal to supplant his office by a
tri-partite Secretariat, did nothing to improve the situation and the
Soviet leader's use of his shoe, to emphasize his points captured
popular imagination without aiding the debate.

When Menzies reached the East River on Friday, 30 September,
he received, with a copy of Sukarno's speech, the text of a draft-
resolution, later moved by Nehru on behalf of Ghana, India, Indonesia, the United Arab Republic and Yugoslavia, seeking a renewal
of contacts between the American President and the Soviet Prime

Minister.[55]

As a result, according to Menzies, he and Mr Harold Macmillan
the British Prime Minister, were invited to meet President Eisenhower
in Washington, on Sunday morning, 2 October. On Saturday
Macmillan and Menzies lunched with Lord Home, the British Foreign
Secretary, and then flew to Washington.[56]

At this point, it should be said that Khrushchev's conditions for
a *meeting* with President Eisenhower were hardly encouraging or
acceptable, if indeed Khrushchev wished to meet an outgoing
President one month before the election. His demand for an apology
from President Eisenhower for the American flights over Soviet
territory had already been refused, and it was not making a meeting
very likely. In any case, the five-power draft-resolution spoke of the
renewal of contacts, not a meeting or a conference. As far as the
British government was concerned, it could not be expected to
rejoice at the proposal that the renewal of contact was envisaged as
a bi-lateral affair, at the expense of British and French participation.
For different reasons, then, the American and the British governments sought the defeat of the five-power proposal, without
however, wishing to meet it head-on. In the course of the Washington
meetings that Sunday, Menzies produced an amendment urging
meeting between the heads of the four governments that were to
have met in Paris, in May. His suggestion was adopted in Washington
but, when put to the vote in the General Assembly, it only received
five votes - those of Australia, Canada, France, Great Britain and of
the United States. Forty-five states voted against it, basically the
non-aligned group, and forty-three abstained, including the U.S.S.R.
and its allies, and Japan. Of the *SEATO* members, Pakistan voted
against it, while Thailand and the Philippines abstained.[57]

Thereupon, Argentina sought to have the words 'the President of
[the United States] and 'the Chairman of the Council of Ministers
of' [the Soviet Union] removed from the draft-resolution, and the
Chairman of the General Assembly ruled that the Argentine proposal
should be voted on separately and before the draft-resolution
was put to the vote.[58]

Menon and Nehru objected strongly that, if that proposal were
adopted, the remaining text of the draft-resolution would imply that
diplomatic relations between the two principal powers had been
severed which they had not, and that, consequently the draft

resolution would, by way of the Argentine proposal, be reduced to an absurdity.[59]

Nonetheless, the Argentine proposal was adopted and, though Menzies appeared to be scornful of the Argentine move when he reported to his Parliament, he nevertheless cast Australia's vote in its favour. After its adoption, Nehru, on behalf of the five sponsoring governments, withdrew the amputated draft-resolution.[60] The Argentine manoeuvre had succeeded where Menzies had failed. He had spoken twice that day[61] and been answered by Nehru with some heat, if not without logic.[62]

In the context of the Australian debate, the significance of the Menzies diplomacy in this case was two-fold. For one thing, before the matter had reached the floor of the General Assembly, Menzies had concentrated all his efforts on meetings with 'the two greatest powers in the free world and our most powerful and devoted friends', to use his own words. At that stage, he saw neither Nehru nor any other Asian statesman, nor did he seek a way out of the *impasse* by way of negotiation which, had he attempted it, even if it had failed, would have strengthened his hand as well as his stature.

Secondly, his diplomacy evoked a very negative response in Australia, even in the conservative press on whose support he and his party could, as a rule, count. On his return, Menzies defended his actions in a long parliamentary statement. It was a classic example of his political cosmology and, as such, it is reprinted in the Appendix.*

The government's pre-occupation with making dependence dependable continued to over-shadow all other diplomatic concerns. Significantly, Australia moved closer to India with the coming of the Sino-Indian conflict. That was a very different relationship to that established between Nehru and Chifley.

What had been the causes for the phase of division and decline in the Australian Labor Party in this period?

As a result of events during and after the first world war - the conscription referendums and the subsequent split in the party; the losses at the front, the foundation of a Communist Party under the exciting impact of the Russian revolution and the consequent

* Document No. ~~12~~ 11.

loss of many intellectuals and political activists - the A.L.P. had lost much of its pre-war vigour. What strength remained was further sapped by the imposition on the Labour Party, as on social democratic parties in other countries, of two-front political warfare not to mention further crippling divisions within its ranks and organisation, for instance the populist movement in New South Wales of Premier Lang - 'the man who was greater than Lenin'. All of this was compounded by the traumatic experience of the Scullin government and its shabby defeat. In these conditions, the impressive thing was the intellectual creativeness of some of its leaders - we have seen some of it in the case of Curtin - and the resurgence of the party *after* its return to power in 1941.

The A.L.P. depends for its finance on the trade unions and for its work on the individual members in the branches. As I wrote in 1951, in the Introduction to the Chifley speeches,[63] between the early 1920's and the late 1940's, there was little independent socialist thinking in Australia. Like all social-democratic parties, the A.L.P. is faced with difficulties of opposition from extremists at both ends of the political spectrum. It faces them in a specifically Australian form. Except for the short period of the Nazi-Soviet Pact when, according to the Communist Party, the war was purely an imperialist war, it was relatively easy for a movement that had never been too fond of theories to let intellectuals and militants play with the Communist theories of the day. However, a change occurred in the late 1930's and early 1940's - it is impossible to give precise dates for historical shifts of this sort - when the Communists began to infiltrate the Labour Party and the trade unions with some success. Then, the intellectual vacuum made itself felt.

Now, the only group that seemed able and willing to resist this movement with a definite doctrine and the means of organization was Catholic Action, and they did this in the simplest possible way, by creating within the Labour movement - the party as well as the unions - their own organization to fight the Communists. They carried on this fight with vigour, inspired by *their* ideals.

However, there was another important fact. A new generation had grown up in an atmosphere of full employment, without the experience of the bitter economic struggle of the past. It was a generation that knew the Labour movement as strong and successful. It had not had to tread the hard road that had led to the achievements and successes by which alone they knew the Labour movement-and which they took, it is now clear, too much for granted. Hence they saw the struggle too simply in terms of rivalry for organizational control and ideological monopoly. They were less aware of the social aims and idealism that had inspired earlier struggles. That preoccupation with power and indifference to idealism may be posited in this form. By their methods and aims these 'new men' in the Labour movement were apt to drive away, or at least to weary Socialists who would normally, as in Britain, have been leaders of the struggle against Communists - without forgetting their constructive tasks or their conservative opponents. Catholic Action tended to monopolize, or appear to monopolize, the struggle against the Communists and to gain a disproportionate influence in the Labour movement. Finally, there was the danger of militants of the left in the A.L.P. breaking away from it and, in doing so, seriously sapping its strength. Chifley, who agreed with this analysis when I put it to him in 1951, was aware of the grave danger of division and he was probably the greatest single influence against it. His death was felt by many Australians as a catastrophe.

The Labour leadership rallied, late, to stop this development and it was the right-wing militants who left to form their own party, at first known as the Australian Labor Party (Anti-Communist) and later, as the Australian Democratic Labor Party or simply, as the D.L.P. In my view, the time for Evatt to act was the week after the defeat of the Referendum held in 1952, as a result of the High Court judgement declaring the Communist Party Dissolution Act unconstitutional. The proposed measure had been the greatest single threat democracy had faced in Australia and its defeat was Evatt's greatest triumph. In that Referendum campaign, some of the 'new men' had openly worked against their party, even using their parliamentary facilities for this purpose. At that point, a select few might have been expelled with little loss to the party's unity.

Instead, Evatt attempted compromise; the organizational power of the 'groups', as they were called, grew and, when they went, the damage they were able to inflict on the Labour Party in electoral and organizational terms was serious and its effect prolonged, especially in two States - Queensland and Victoria - and, consequently in the Commonwealth Parliament. Although the D.L.P. never succeeded in winning a single seat in the House of Representatives, the Australian system of preferential voting allows a small, disciplined minority to use its second preferences to help to defeat a majority of votes in the first count. The policy of this group was to prevent the election of a Labour government and in this they were successful until 1972. In the Australian political spectrum, they stood on the far right of the conservative parties and, at times, beyond these.

The deaths of two Victorian parliamentary leaders, Cain and Shepherd, followed by that of a very able federal secretary, the Queenslander Schmella, facilitated the emergence of a new group of left militants, especially in Victoria, which further complicated the situation after the split. In many ways, these men resembled the right militants whom they had replaced. They, too, saw the struggle inside the movement too simply in terms of rivalry for organizational control and ideological monopoly and, like the militants on the right, they concentrated on these struggles at the expense of parliamentary success. Like them, they were at one and the same time, symptoms of and participants in the process of polarization of public debate. Useful to the conservatives in keeping them in office, they were fostered by newspapers and their television networks; for, argument between proponents of extreme positions appeared more dramatic on the screen than a reasoned debate between people who, whatever their point of departure, were prepared to assume that they might have some common ground.

Once again, intervention came late but, whatever its shortcomings, it was not without success. The federal officers of the A.L.P. intervened in the affairs of the Victorian branch of the party in 1970 and the resultant improvement undoubtedly helped in the return of a Labour government in 1972.

Though Casey had supported Eden at Geneva, in the long run, Australia adhered ever more closely to the rigid, polarizing American policies of the Dulles era. Casey's views, based on a more realistic and a more sympathetic knowledge of the countries of South and South East Asia, appeared less often to prevail. Initiative in foreign policy was increasingly exercized by Menzies who, on Casey's retirement from External Affairs in 1960, combined the offices of Prime Minister and that portfolio.

Casey accepted a life peerage on his retirement and his career was crowned in 1965, as the first Australian to be nominatec Governor General of Australia by a conservative government. He died in 1976. He had not been the only Liberal to be appointed away from Cabinet. Spender had become Ambassador at Washington, after eighteen months at External Affairs and, in 1958 a Judge of the International Court whose President he became in 1964. The jurist, Sir Garfield Barwick who succeeded Menzies at External Affairs in 1961, also held this portfolio for two years and was then appointed Chief Justice of the High Court of Australia. The consequences of this thinning out of the Liberal leadership became, with the passage of time, very noticeable indeed.

As Minister for External Affairs, Barwick went to some pains to obtain room to move in his relations with Asian governments. He was hardly one to care for *simpliste* solutions or unsubtle analyses, as the following summing up of Australia's situation, at the end of a ministerial statement, on 11 March 1964, revealed:

Australia is a middle power in more senses than one. It is clearly one in the general sense in which the expression is used. But also it has common interests with both the advanced and the under-developed countries; it stands in point of realized wealth between the haves and the have-nots. It is at the one time a granary and a highly industrialized country. It has a European background and is set in intimate geographical propinquity to Asia.

This ambivalence brings some strength and offers promise of a future of which Australia can be confident, a future of increasing influence. But it poses continuing problems in identifying peculiarly Australian objectives and in finding balance in the policies designed to attain them. As well, it emphasizes the need to seek and to accept collective security, with all the compromises which such a course so often entails. It involves support for the United Nations and participation in its activities, conscious that indispensable and useful as that organizaton is, it cannot provide the assured means of deterring or suppressing aggressive activity.[64]

This was, indeed, a new approach and Barwick was as good as his word. He was a frequent visitor to Asian capitals and, as far as he could, he used his office to lessen existing tensions and to forestall avoidable difficulties. He was especially active in preventing a breach with Indonesia in the very complex situation which he had inherited and in which his opportunities were very limited.

Not long after Barwick left External Affairs, Australian foreign policy was to be trapped by the Vietnam commitment and, as a result, ~~the debate became enmeshed in this issue.~~ This situation

this issue began to dominate the debate.

was compounded by the polarization in domestic affairs of which the split in the Labour Party and its long years in opposition were one symptom.

The debates about foreign policy from the *ANZUS* alliance until, but excluding the commitment of Australian troops to Vietnam, have one thing in common: an increasing level of ambiguity in the nature and extent of the Australian commitment, with the result that the Labour Party tended to ~~agree~~ with ~~increasing~~ unease to agreements which it compared to their disadvantage with preceding ones. From *SEATO* they looked back to *ANZUS*; from the engagements to Malaysia - when Menzies was pressed at last to reveal something about these - they looked back to *SEATO*. By 1965, with the commitment of forces to Vietnam, they finally said *No*. In those debates, the issue was not so much Australia's Asian policies as the nature and method of the government's proceedings. These were domestic issues in two senses: equivocation about the nature of the commitments; and their use for party warfare.

In his 1946 policy speech, Menzies had expressed his preoccupation with power politics, characteristic of Australian conservatives from the middle of the nineteenth century to this day. It is founded upon the desire to rely on a great ally and to follow him - not least in order to act like a great power by an association bordering on identification with him. There is a circular quality about this thinking: Australia is too weak to defend itself. Therefore, Australia needs a powerful ally to protect it. To ensure this continued protection, Australia must support and assist the great ally in all possible disputes. For a limited outlay, therefore, that policy aims to retain the protection of a great power and, through it, access to the world stage. But, on this stage, Australia's representatives are, under this scheme, restricted to reflected glory, for they cannot exercise any initiative of their own in the conduct of policy. They consider this self-denial a part of the price of protection.

While an effective British presence East of Suez continued, a measure of flexibility remained within the conservative assumptions of the primacy of power politics. Australia participated in the Commonwealth Strategic Reserve in Malaya, and later Malaysia, during and after the Emergency, and during the Confrontation by Indonesia. As we have seen, Australia, through Casey in particular, supported the British position before and during the Geneva Conference in 1954, when Casey made a very realistic assessment of the situation in Vietnam. Menzies supported Britain in 1956, during the Suez crisis when Casey showed his customary caution.

INDONESIA AND WEST NEW GUINEA

The Menzies government inherited from its predecessor a general atmosphere of good relations with Indonesia. ~~This~~ the new Minister for External Affairs, Mr, later Sir Percy, Spender took some pains ~~to foster, as well as~~ to allay the unfortunate effects of the fierce anti-Indonesian campaign which he and his colleagues had conducted for the four preceding years from the opposition benches. In his first ministerial statement, on 9 March 1950, Spender had this to say about Indonesia:

. . . in Indonesia, a new government has just assumed the responsibilities of sovereignty and is trying to mould a new nation out of Indonesia's seventy million people. I spent several days in Jakarta . . . and had the opportunity of meeting President Sukarno and most of his cabinet. I formed the conclusion that they were able men with moderate views and a sober realisation of the immensity of the tasks before them.[65]

There was in Spender's view, no question of their distaste for Communism and their determination to resist it, whatever form it might take. Their immediate worry arose not, however, from Communists but from other more powerful groups who were using nationalism and ~~the Moslem religion~~ to rally support against the government. The interim government was confident that it could suppress these groups and in due course deal with the Communists, many of whom were constantly infiltrating from Malaya to Sumatra and thence to Java, and who seemed then to be biding their time. But the situation was by no means free from danger and the government would need encouragement and active help from outside if it was to maintain order and at the same time give its attention to the urgent economic problems that had grown up during and since the war.

The old sense of insecurity came, however, to the fore in Spender's reference to West New Guinea which, though claimed by Indonesia, being a residency of the former Netherland's East Indies, had remained in Dutch hands. On this question, Spender said that Australia had a duty of ensuring by every means that in the island areas immediately adjacent to her, in whatever direction they lie, nothing took place that could in any way offer a threat to Australian security, either in the short or the long term. These islands were, as experience had shown, 'our last ring of defence against aggression, and Australia must be vitally concerned with whatever changes take place in them'. It could not be assumed by anyone that, should fundamental changes take place in any of these areas, Australia would take a purely passive role. Spender was thinking 'particularly, but not exclusively', of New Guinea, which was 'an absolutely essential link in the chain of Australian defence'. The Australian people were deeply interested in what happened anywhere in New Guinea. He concluded:.

An unofficial spokesman in Indonesia had recently declared that Australian New Guinea should be incorporated in Indonesia. I thought it desirable to make an immediate rebuttal of such a claim, and I am pleased to see that the Indonesian government lost no time in disclaiming that it enjoyed any official support.[66]

Coming from Spender, this statement showed considerable moderation, however questionable the diplomatic wisdom of making much of unofficial comment.

The basic policy of the Australian government was, as Spender had indicated, that on grounds of security they wished the Dutch to stay in West New Guinea. The official Australian view was that West New Guinea was under Dutch sovereignty and, therefore, a matter of Dutch domestic jurisdiction. Hence, it was beyond the competence of international debate which could do no more than inflame the atmosphere. This position was stated also by Casey, on 24 September 1954, in opposition to a recommendation from the General Assembly that an item on Netherlands New Guinea, submitted by the Indonesian government, should be included in the agreed Agenda of the United Nations General Assembly:

Most representatives will be aware of the seriousness with which the Australian government regards this matter . . . The Netherlands government . . . has no intention of abandoning its sovereignty over its territory in New. Guinea . . . it has no obligation to do so in law or by reason of any earlier event.

These then are the bare facts of the situation in West New Guinea. The Dutch have it and have no intention of abandoning their responsibilities; the Indonesians want it, - and we, who are neighbours to the Dutch in New Guinea, do not recognise any real claims on the part of the Republic of Indonesia. We support the Netherlands in their continued administration of Netherlands New Guinea.[67]

This position remained Australian policy on the Indonesian demand for West New Guinea. It was static and it excluded the exploration of alternatives, whether that of a Melanesian federation, or of a plebiscite, because it depended on the legal insistence that West New Guinea was under Dutch sovereignty and hence any alteration or even discussion of its status was precluded.

The Australian government had supported a European colonial power in the belief that it was in the best interests of Australia's security, and that it could rely on great and powerful allies - especially the United States. The calculation turned out to be wrong, and Australia was unprepared for a change in sovereignty in West New Guinea, resulting from a combination of circumstances that had been well within the realm of political imagination.

Sukarno had divested himself of the 'encumbrance' of parliamentary democracy. Foundation statesmen, like the Socialist leader Sutan Sjahrir and the Moslem democrat Hatta, were detained. The President developed a style of grandezza, ideological drift, adventurous diplomacy and economic neglect that brought him into closer relations with the Communist powers, and with the P.K.I. - and yet left him holding out the hope that he was the only barrier to a Communist take-over in Indonesia.

In these circumstances, Sukarno announced in a series of dramatic moves that, if necessary, West New Guinea would be liberated by Indonesian arms, and a 'confrontation' of the Netherlands was begun.[68] For a variety of reasons, the United States government advised the Dutch to agree to a face-saving formula. Accordingly, the Dutch handed over control to a United Nations team which, after a period of six months, was to transfer the territory to the Indonesian government. The Republic of Indonesia undertook to conduct a referendum before the end of 1969: 'an act of self-determination' in which the Papuans would express 'an act of free choice' with the assistance of a United Nations representative. The territory passed under Indonesian control on 1 May 1963. The Act of Free Choice went largely according to plan.

The lessons that might have been learned from the combination of circumstances which led to Australia's isolation in the New Guinea dispute were neglected.

The rigidity of the conservative frame of reference went very deep. It pervaded the conduct of Australia's foreign relations and of its domestic politics. Its permeation to apparently minor aspects may be judged by that ~~Australian~~ government's attitude to its own Papuan citizens, and to liaison with West New Guinea after the departure of the Dutch.

A week after Indonesian assumption of control, Sir Garfield Barwick was asked in the House by one of his supporters whether Australian-born Papuans had been victimized 'since the Australian liaison mission was withdrawn from Kota Baru'. The Minister replied, following a denial of any evidence that there had been any maltreatment 'of Papuan people who were born in East New Guinea and who are now in West New Guinea':

I think I should take this opportunity of saying that it is wrong to suggest that the liaison office was withdrawn, placing emphasis on the word 'withdrawn'. We had a liaison office in West New Guinea under an agreement between the Netherlands and Australia. We were minded to remove the liaison office at the time the Dutch left New Guinea and the United Nations temporary authority came in. However, at the request of the U.N. Temporary Executive Authority we allowed the officer to remain for liaison purposes with the temporary authority. Once the recent change-over was effected there was no basis upon which the liaison mission could be maintained.

I would like to say that the liaison officer would have had no function whatsoever connected with the treatment, or protection, for that matter, of East New Guinea Papuans in West New Guinea, and it is wrong to suggest that the closing of the office has had anything to do with either the treatment or protection of these people. [*sic*] Lastly, I would say that if people born in East New Guinea are in West New Guinea they are, of course, quite free to return to East New Guinea.[69]

There was, then, no attempt to continue a liaison office or establish a consulate in West New Guinea either to co-operate with the Indonesians or to protect Australian Papuans. British policy has always been to protect British subjects, including those from British colonies, as well as British Protected Persons, in foreign countries. Here, the Minister had no more to offer than the right to return to East New Guinea. A small point; but one denoting a characteristic approach.

Within a few months of his success in West New Guinea, now known under its Indonesian name of Irian Barat, Sukarno began the diplomatic and military confrontation of the new Federation of Malaysia.[70] The facts of this second and wider confrontation heightened the sense of insecurity in Australia, and Sir Garfield

Barwick was stating a political fact when he wrote in a learned paper, in January 1964: 'I am sure it came as a tremendous psychological shock to many people in Australia when a land border with Indonesia developed'.[71]

CONFRONTATION OF MALAYSIA

Sukarno's confrontation of Malaysia, may be seen in retrospect to have been a limited, intra-regional conflict, but the dangers it implied at its height should not be over-looked now by a process of reading history backwards. Confrontation was part of a policy that took Indonesia further away from the mainstream of international life than any other member state of the United Nations had ever gone. Sukarno took his guided democracy out of the United Nations and attempted unsuccessfully to establish a competitive organisation. Other newly independent states, the Communist countries, even Nasser's United Arab Republic, all remained in the world organisation however critical they may have been of its workings.

Australian-military support of Malaya had been by arrangement with Great Britain. However, the position and purpose of the Australian land and air forces in Malaya had never been very clear. On 1 April 1955, Menzies had announced that Australian troops were to be stationed in Malaya and, when this matter came before the House on 20 April 1955,[72] this decision was opposed by the Labour Party because it infringed the principle of not committing Australian forces overseas in peace time. In Menzies' view, Australia with its vast territory and small population could not survive a surging Communist challenge without the co-operation of the United Kingdom and the United States and that Australia could not accept this co-operation in a comprehensive defence against Communism unless Australia was prepared to take her share of the responsibilities.

At times, the forces, belonging to the Commonwealth Strategic Reserve in Malaya, were said to be relevant to *SEATO* purposes and, at other times, this was denied. Likewise, statements about their relation to the Malayan Emergency varied. It was stressed and, then, it was played down.

Following a great deal of prodding from the Labour Party, Sir Robert Menzies tabled a number of papers and made a ministerial statement, entitled *Malaysia Defence*, on 25 September 1963.

On this occasion, he denied that Australian forces were primarily in Malaysia for internal security. He defended the lack of formal agreement as the golden rule of mutual obligation, applied in the spirit of mutual confidence. He then made this declaration:

But for the benefit of all concerned, honorable members would not wish me to create or permit any ambiguity about Australia's position in relation to Malaysia. I therefore, after close deliberation by the Cabinet, and on its behalf, inform the House that we are resolved, and have so informed the Government of Malaysia, and the Governments of the United Kingdom and New Zealand and others concerned, that if, in the circumstances that now exist, and which may continue for a long time, there occurs, in relation to Malaysia or any of its constituent States, armed invasion or subversive activity - supported or directed or inspired from outside Malaysia - we shall to the best of our powers and by such means as shall be agreed upon with the Government of Malaysia, add our military assistance to the efforts of Malaysia and the United Kingdom in the defence of Malaysia's territorial integrity and political independence.[73]

In his reply to the Prime Minister, Mr Calwell began by saying that the Labour Party supported the concept of Malaysia and welcomed its creation. He stressed that Britain had attempted to leave former colonies in a condition giving them some prospect of economic and political viability: 'Those who welcome the end of colonialism, should welcome the beginning of this latest independent State'.[74] He referred to the United Nations mission which had been appointed by the Secretary General, U Thant, at the request of the Philippines and Indonesia. The fact that, after a full and fair investigation, the mission believed that a majority of the people of Sarawak and North Borneo were willing to join Malaysia, weighed heavily with the Labour Party in supporting Malaysia. The Party felt that it had been proper to conduct the survey and it was proper to stand by the verdict: as the United Nations had a direct responsibility for the creation of Malaysia, it now had a direct responsibility for its security. The proper forum for possible future disputes about Malaysia was the United Nations.

However, the question which Australians were asking and to which Calwell demanded an answer in Parliament was:

What is the extent of our direct commitment to the new State and how is it to be regulated? The Government's attitude has been marked all along by a peculiar procrastination - by a reluctance to give facts, and a refusal to face facts. Until this afternoon very little information was vouchsafed to the Parliament and I propose to show how unsatisfactory even that little really is.[75]

Calwell went on to examine the series of contradictory ministerial statements. Summarizing these dealings, Calwell said:

The Australian Labor Party maintains that this indecision, this ambiguity - disturbing in the eyes of our allies, confusing to our neighbours - must not be allowed to continue in our relations with Malaysia.

We regarded the arrangement with Malaya as completely unsatisfactory. If nothing more formal than the same arrangement is to continue with Malaysia, we will regard that as equally unsatisfactory.[76]

The A.L.P. Federal Conference had, in August 1963, adopted a policy which superseded the demand for the recall of Australian troops from Malaya. This policy stated:

Labor does not believe that Australian forces should be committed overseas except subject to a clear and public Treaty which accords with the principles of the declaration [of policy] which gives Australia an effective voice in the common decision of the Treaty Powers.[77]

In Calwell's view, the formation of Malaysia demanded a new approach to Australia's possible commitments in the area and there was a need for open, honest diplomacy, expressed in public treaties based on mutual obligations. These had been reasons for the change in A.L.P. policy and Calwell clearly relished quoting the basically conservative daily press in his party's support. There was, as he put it, a clear interest and duty to dispel the hostility and suspicion which had surrounded the birth of Malaysia. Vague military arrangements, unratified by Parliament would have the reverse effect:

Surely the Government has learnt its lesson in West New Guinea. Surely we do not contemplate a repetition of that shameful episode. In that case, we misled the Netherlands and confused Indonesia. Both had cause to be doubtful of our attitude, and in the end both grew contemptuous of our ambiguity. I have said that we owe it to our neighbours to clarify our intentions by means of open treaty. Let it not be forgotten that we owe it also to our allies - the allies with which we have mutual commitments by virtue of the very type of treaty which we on this side of the House advocate.[78]

The Labour Party opposed Indonesian confrontation of Malaysia but it continued to demand 'clear and public international agreements'.[79]

Although Australian forces came to be engaged at Indonesia's farther border - as seen from Australia - on Borneo (Kalimantan), the earlier Australian stance on Indonesian independence and the realization on both sides of a permanent neighbourhood, kept channels of communications open throughout this period. In this context, the secondary level of Australia's diplomacy very quietly assumed a primary importance, for a time.

In the months preceding *Gestapu*, the abortive *coup d'état* and the counter-coup in Indonesia on 30 September and 1 October 1965, there had been a considerable escalation in Sukarno's confrontation programme. At the same time, there was rising military pressure in Vietnam. The United States was increasing its commitments on a large scale.

Having ardently pursued 'great and powerful friends' for its own security, the Australian government now found itself called upon by both powers simultaneously, the United States as well as Great Britain, to support separate military efforts. Neither operation was covered by a 'clear and public treaty': Malaysia would not be involved with any *SEATO* arrangements and Vietnam did not come under it, either. By April 1965, Australia had one hundred military instructors in Vietnam and six Caribou aircraft.

On 29 April 1965, the Prime Minister announced the government's decision, he claimed, 'in response to a request from the government of South Vietnam and after close consultation with the United States government', to provide one battalion of 800 men for service in South Vietnam. Sir Robert assured the House that close attention had been given to defence priorities:

We have commitments in Malaysia which we are meeting. We have to bear in mind, and make preparations against, the possibility of other developments in the region which could make demands on our Australian defence capacity.[80]

Sir Robert Menzies claimed that, in this assessment, to commit one battalion in Vietnam represented the most useful additional contribution to the defence of the region at that time. The takeover of South Vietnam would be a direct military threat to Australia and all the countries of South and South East Asia: 'It must be seen as part of a thrust by Communist China between the Indian and Pacific Oceans'.[81]

Calwell's reply to the Prime Minister's statement was a major contribution to the debate about Australia's Asian policies. He left no doubt where his party stood on this issue or what he saw as the implications of this decision for Australia's relations with the

untries of Asia: '. . . on behalf of all my colleagues of Her Majesty's
pposition,' he said, 'we oppose the government's decision to
nd 800 men to fight in Vietnam. We oppose it firmly and
mpletely'.

Calwell saw in it a misinterpretation of Chinese policy:

. . we believe that it mistakes entirely the nature of [Chinese] power, and
at it materially assists China in her subversive aims. Indeed we cannot
nceive a decision by this government more likely to promote the long-term
terests of China in Asia and the Pacific.

Furthermore, the government 'grotesquely oversimplified' the
tuation by stating that it was a straightforward case of North
ietnamese aggression:

he government then takes this theory a little further by cleverly pointing
the undoubted fact that just as Communist North Vietnam lies North of
outh Vietnam, so Communist China lies North of North Vietnam. Thus
ccording to this simplified, not to say simple, theory, everything fell into
lace and the whole operation becomes, in the Prime Minister's words
part of the downward thrust by Communist China between the Indian
nd Pacific Oceans'. And by this reasoning, the very map of Asia became a
ind of conspiracy against Australia.

Calwell also pointed out that these 800 constituted one-quarter
f 'our pitifully small effective military strength'. He anticipated
hat re-inforcements and a probable increase in the commitment
vould have to be met from conscripts and that the decision in
act reversed government policy on the first priority of Australian
defence - Malaysia:

A short time ago, the government informed the United Kingdom and Malaysian
governments that it was not possible to spare another battalion from our
already strained resources. Now we have found a battalion for service in
South Vietnam. Thus, our troops are involved on several fronts. We are the
only country in the world fighting on two fronts in South East Asia.[82]

Calwell disputed the claim that the request for these troops
had come from the free and independent government and people of
South Vietnam; and that increased support from North Vietnam
was a new factor in the situation. Even if this view were accepted,
it could not lend any credence to the belief that the Vietcong would
collapse if this new, increased aid from the North were cut off.
Aggression from the North was not the major problem.

In fact, Australian troops would be fighting the largely indigenous
Vietcong in their home territory, in the midst of a largely indifferent,

if not resentful, and frightened population. They would be fightin at the request of, in support, and presumably, under the directio of an unstable, inefficient and partially corrupt military *régim* lacking even the semblance of being, or becoming, democraticall based. But, it would be said, even if this were true, that there wer far larger considerations - that China had to be stopped and th United States not be humiliated in Asia. He agreed wholeheartedl with both those propositions - except that the present policies wer playing right into China's hands and, if not changed, would lea surely and inexorably to American humiliation in Asia.

China's aim to increase her power and influence would not b advanced by military means because her military machine was nc adapted to that purpose now, or, possibly, within the next ten years Therefore, China chose other means:

Yet we have preferred to look at China mainly in terms of a military threa and thus have neglected to use other, far more effective weapons at our disposa or, because of our pre-occupation with the military threat, we have use those weapons badly and clumsily.[83]

Australia had been pre-occupied, Calwell argued, with the ide of monolithic imperialist Communism, with the military threat o Chinese communism, with the fear of Communist revolution with so-called Western interests and with the universality of it Christian beliefs. Australia had supported military reactionary *régimes*, loudest in their professions of anti-Communism; and hac relied on the support of those who would prevent any sort o revolution, even when inevitable or needful; it had never supportec nationalism, except when it supported the West, although nationalism was a mighty force against Communism, nor tried to understanc the power of the other great world religions against Communism:

Each of those pre-occupations had worked for our defeat in Vietnam and were working for our defeat in Asia. This failure was contributing to the spirit of defeatism and impotence in the face of Communism: that is the greatest enemy we have to fear.

If Australia believed in its own professions and principles, the threat of Chinese subversion could be fought and beaten. But tc exhaust resources in the bottomless pit of jungle warfare, in a war of which not even the purpose was honestly defined, in which it was not explained what would be considered victory, were the very height of folly and the very depth of despair.

Humiliation of America, he predicted, could come in one of two
ays: by outright defeat which was unlikely, or by her becoming
terminably bogged down in the awful morass of this war, as
rance had been for ten years. That situation in turn could lead
) one of two things: withdrawal through despair, or all-out war,
irough despair. Either would be equally disastrous. The only possible
bjective of this war could be the destruction of the North Viet-
amese *régime*, which would create a vacuum. Although America
ould destroy that *régime*, it could neither conquer nor hold North
'ietnam and, into that vacuum, China would undoubtedly move.
i that case, one would have displaced a nationalistic Communist
gime in a country with a thousand years' history of hostility
wards China. One could then either accept that disaster or face
ie even greater disaster of all out war with China.

The British and Canadian Prime Ministers, he went on, the Pope,
he Secretary General of the United Nations all realized that this
'as the terrible prospect which they tried to avert. They were all
ue friends of the United States who did not want the United
tates to be humiliated. That is why they had called for negotiations
/hile the United States remained in a position of comparative
trength. And this was the time when Australia had said that there
iust be no pause for reflection, no pause for reconsideration.
'y its decision, the Australian government had withdrawn unilaterally
rom the ranks of the negotiators, if indeed it had ever been concerned
bout them. The Australian contribution would be militarily
iegligible, but it would reduce Australia to diplomatic impotence.
ts aim should have been to extend the principle of negotiation.
t had now lost all power to help end it, by being committed to
he proposition that Communism could be defeated by military
neans alone and that it was the function of European troops to
mpose the will of the West on Asia.

Calwell argued that Australia had set its face against the correct
neans of opposing Communism and had declared against the social,
olitical and economic revolution which alone could effectively
ombat Communism. The key to the future of Indo-China was the
Mekong River delta and valley. The Communists understood
his well: 'But imagine the thundering reply we could have given
o Communism if, under the auspices of the United Nations, we
vere to join in a vastly increased programme for the reclamation

and development of the Mekong. The work has started . . . how much
more could be done if we were really determined to turn our
resources from war to peace. This surely is the key to the door of
hope of which President Johnson spoke . . . But this government
has closed the door and thrown the key away'.

Calwell added that he could not refrain from making an observation
about Australia's trade with China. The government's decision
and especially the grounds upon which it had been justified, raised
in a particularly acute form the moral issue of that trade. The
government had justified its action on the ground of Chinese
expansionist aggression and this same government was willing
to expand its trade in strategic materials with China. It was
a position which was logically and morally indefensible.

In conclusion, Calwell spoke, beyond the House, to the fighting
men and to the men and women of the Labour movement:

I cannot close without addressing a word directly to our fighting men who
are now by this decision, committed to the chances of war: Our hearts and
prayers are with you. Our minds and reason cannot support those who have
made the decision to send you to this war, and we shall do our best to have that
decision reversed. But we shall do our duty to the utmost in supporting you
to do your duty. In terms of everything that an army in the field requires
we shall never deny you the aid and support that it is your right to expect
in the service of your country. To the members of the Government, I say
only this: If, by the process of misrepresentation of our motives, in which you
are so expert, you try to further divide this nation for political purposes, yours
will be a dreadful responsibility, and you will have taken a course which
you will live to regret.
And may I, through you, Mr Speaker, address this message to the members
of my own Party - my colleagues here in this Parliament, and that vast band
of Labour men and women outside: The course we have agreed to take today
is fraught with difficulty . . . When the drums beat and the trumpets sound,
the voice of reason and right can be heard in the land only with difficulty.
But if we are to have the courage of our convictions, then we must do our
best to make that voice heard. I offer you the probability that you will be
traduced, that your motives will be misrepresented, that your patriotism will
be impugned, that your courage will be called into question. But I also offer
you the sure and certain knowledge that we will be vindicated; that generations
to come will record with gratitude that when a reckless Government wilfully
endangered the security of this nation, the voice of the Australian Labor
Party was heard, strong and clear, on the side of sanity and in the cause of
humanity, and in the interests of Australia's security.
Let me sum up. We believe that America must not be humiliated and must
not be forced to withdraw . . . But we believe that the military involvement

in the present form decided on by the Australian Government represents a threat to Australia's standing in Asia, to our power for good in Asia and above all to the security of this nation.[84]

As Calwell had foreseen, the Australian commitment in Vietnam was subsequently increased by conscript forces. Holt, who succeeded Menzies in January 1966, announced on 8 March 1966 that the Australian contingent in Vietnam would be increased to 4,500 men, including national servicemen, that is, conscripts.[85] This decision led to a shift in the debate. The central argument now was the use of conscripts in Vietnam. It led to increased acrimony with the result that the proponents of extreme positions were also those most audible. In October of that year, President Johnson visited Australia shortly before a general election, due to be held on 26 November 1966. Mr Holt's campaign slogan was *All the way with LBJ*. Once again, the coalition won with a handsome majority. Mr Calwell announced his retirement from the leadership of the Labour Party and he was succeeded by Mr Whitlam. Following that general election, the then Prime Minister of South Vietnam visited Australia in January 1967.

That year ended with the tragic disappearance of the Prime Minister, Mr Holt, in the surf off the Victorian coast. Mr McEwan became interim Prime Minister until the Liberals could choose a new leader. The choice was an unusual one: the incumbent, Senator Gorton, had to resign from the Senate and be elected to the House of Representatives into the seat left vacant by the late Prime Minister. There was no substantive shift either in policy or in the debate.

DÉNOUEMENT

On 26 March 1968, the Minister for External Affairs opened a debate on international affairs with a statement strongly opposing 'talk of negotiations' and equally strongly defending the need for the bombing of North Vietnam: '. . . we believe that the bombing of targets in the North serves important military objectives. It is important for interdiction and for its cumulative effects.'[86] The Minister of Defence likewise objected to 'yet another limitation in the form of the cessation of the bombing, which is the only thing that prevents the whole of North Vietnam being added to the demilitarized zone, Laos and Cambodia as complete sanctuaries for North Vietnamese aggressors'.[87]

On 31 March 1968, which, by Australian time was, appropriately, the First of April, President Johnson made his famous speech, announcing a substantial halt in the bombing in order to create conditions for negotiations; as well as his determination neither to seek nor to accept nomination in the forthcoming election.[88]

Gorton made a statement to the House on the following day on the President's speech. He referred to —

decisions lately taken concerning the war in Vietnam. Those decisions were, firstly, to build up the South Vietnamese forces to . . . 800,000 men . . .; secondly to maintain the United States Forces at the level of approximately 525,000 men . . .; thirdly, to renew a resolve to continue the military struggle in South Vietnam until . . . a just and lasting peace could be worked out in that country; and fourthly, to cease or halt aerial bombardment over a major part of North Vietnam in the hope that such cessation might lead to the beginning of talks designed to secure such a just peace.

Mr Gorton then read a statement he had previously made outside the House, whereby he associated himself with President Johnson, though he had not been consulted:

. . . the United States is firmly resolved to continue the military struggle to the point where it becomes recognised that talks designed to secure a just and lasting peace must take place . . . the United States is prepared now, as it has been prepared in the past, to enter into such talks at once, and is prepared to make concessions in an effort to bring about such talks. The Australian government has repeatedly indicated that it would support peace negotiations provided they held promise of leading to a just and lasting peace which effectively safeguards the security and freedom of choice of the people of South Vietnam.

The Australian government regarded this initiative by the American President as a further significant exhibition of willingness to engage in talks aimed at this end. Halting the bombing over most of North Vietnam, without insisting on an indication from Hanoi of willingness to negotiate or of a reciprocal cessation of military build-up by North Vietnam, would test the willingness of Hanoi to enter into discussion aimed at a peaceful settlement of a genuine kind. It was to be hoped that this response by Hanoi would be forthcoming quickly. At the same time the continuation of bombing in the area to the North of the battlefields would continue to hamper the flow of troops and war material from North to South and would not leave allied troops at too great a military disadvantage.

Gorton said that the President's decision had 'naturally attracted world attention because of recent suggestions made in many quarters, and supported, I understand [*sic*], by U Thant' that a halt in the bombing would find the North Vietnamese prepared to enter into peace talks. This gesture by the United States was the most significant and generous gesture, giving up as it does a military advantage, yet made in the hope of starting negotiations.

The Prime Minister emphasized however that not all the bombing had stopped:

In those areas contiguous to the battlefields in North [*sic*] and South Vietnam, those areas where North Vietnamese troops and munitions of war gather and flow towards the South, the continuation of the bombing to hamper, hinder and reduce this flow will continue . . . we believe that there is military advantage in the bombing of controlled and selected targets of military significance in North Vietnam. We have as consistently made it clear that we supported the halting [of] such bombing when the North Vietnamese were prepared to enter into peace talks, subject to the military build-up in the South by the North Vietnamese not continuing because of the bombing halt.[89]

Gorton said nothing about Australia asking to be consulted, much less to participate in any talks. He only added that 'we for our part are ready to stand with our allies, as we have in the war's prosecution. We are ready to support our allies as we have in actions designed to seek talks to secure a true peace'.

~~Whitlam began his reply by saying:~~   *In reply, Whitlam said:*

On the notice paper there is listed for resumption a debate on a ministerial statement made last Tuesday - a week ago - by the Minister for External Affairs. The government's policy, as enunciated by the Minister for External Affairs, is in ruins . . .

He quoted the relevant parts of the preceding week's ministerial speeches and continued:

No Australian Minister was consulted by the United States before the change of policy was announced. The Prime Minister was told by an Embassy official on Sunday afternoon . . . The Prime Minister's statement showed his reluctance to follow the American change of policy and his disappointment that there had been a change of policy. Grabbing at straws, he justified the continued bombing of the area just North of the demilitarised zone where troops accumulated and where supplies are stored.

It was also left to Whitlam to stress the great significance of President Johnson's decision. In his view the American decision had a meaning and significance of its own quite apart from any response which might come from Hanoi. This was a definite and profound change of strategy. It was not merely an incident in the war. It took the war into an entirely new phase. The Prime Minister had not referred to the crowning part of the President's speech - that he would not seek nomination by the Democratic Party; that he would not stand for the Presidency of his country again: there had been some great abdications in history - Diocletian and Charles V - but never in such dramatic circumstances as this. It might well be 'the turning point in the history of the world, particularly in our region. But', Whitlam added, 'the future of our region will remain insecure unless one of the great developed countries in this area . . . Australia, supports more actively efforts for peace in this area . . .' In his view, the Australian government should not just be a camp-follower. It had a prime part to play in this part of the world. 'Our wealth, our gross national product, is as great as that of all the nations which lie between us and India and China and Japan'.

In Whitlam's view, it was clear that Australia should take a lead in this area. The United States had increased their aid to Indonesia in a year in which it was spending less on total overseas aid than in any year for the past twenty years. The Australian government had been grudging and sluggish in making a proportionate increase in its commitment to Indonesia. If Australia, the most developed country in this part of the world, was not prepared to take the lead, how could other countries be expected 'to pitch in if we do not? We have this responsibility. Listening to the Prime Minister . . . we realize the little Australianism of his attitude. How disappointing and inadequate in our region is Australia's role to be?'[90]

What these events had shown, was the inadequacy of the primary level of Australian foreign policy, as it had been conceived and practised by successive conservative governments. The risks involved in this policy had always been there, though they had not been so apparent. It had needed the watershed of President Johnson's speech of 31 March 1968, to give them such emphasis that they could be ignored no longer. President Johnson's decision resulted in a disorientation of Australian conservative policy, slow in becoming apparent, partly because of the game about the shape of the table in Paris - the table at which the Australian government neither had nor claimed a seat.

Once it made itself felt, this disorientation had profound consequences for the conservative coalition and, then, for Australia. The first symptom on the surface of the coalition took three years to mature and it then provided Australia with that rare spectacle in its politics, a palace revolution, leading to a change in the conservative leadership. In March 1971, Gorton used his casting vote against himself in a vote of no confidence in the party room and resigned. He was succeeded by McMahon as Prime Minister and leader of the Liberal Party.

The growing realization of this disorientation provided one interlude in which it played a curious part: the Australian government's policy in the Bangladesh crisis.

BANGLADESH

The South Asian crisis of 1971, which resulted in the establishment of Bangladesh, was the one occasion since 1956, on which a conservative government departed from U.S. policy clearly and completely. American policy not only displayed some of the old indophobe attitudes of the Dulles era; now, it was also particularly concerned to avoid any action that might prejudice the planned presidential visit to Peking. Australian-Indian relations had improved since 1961. It was also clear that British policy and public opinion were far from hostile to India or to Bangladesh.

On 7 December 1971, following the outbreak of hostilities between India and Pakistan, Mr Bowen, then Minister for Foreign Affairs, made a statement in Parliament beginning with an account of Australian attempts at mediation and defining Australia's position which, 'as a friend of both Pakistan and India, will continue to be that of a neutral'. In accordance with established policy, no arms or warlike stores had been supplied to either country. This would continue to be the government's policy. Humanitarian and economic aid to both countries would be maintained 'subject to certain practical restrictions, including those imposed by security'.

The new element introduced by India's recognition 'of the Bangla Desh organization as the Government of an independent state' did not at that time change the Australian position which was that Pakistan was recognized as the legal government of both East and

West Pakistan. 'The question of Australian recognition of a new state of Bangla Desh does not arise at this time. Australia is particularly disappointed that there has so far been no successful outcome from the debates of the Security Council'. Although the government recognized the General Assembly's limitations in taking positive action, they would 'explore energetically any initiatives that may be made in the United Nations context to achieve some useful result'.[91]

Replying for the opposition, Whitlam, who agreed with the government's policy on this subject, presented his analysis of the implications of the changed world situation. He began by tracing the setting of this conflict:

The actions of the Pakistan Army in East Pakistan have created more refugees in six months than the escalation of the war in Vietnam caused in six years, and possibly as many deaths . . . It has taken massive culpability on the part of the world community to allow so massive a human tragedy to become possible. None of us is without blame; our sins vary from the niggardliness of the smaller but wealthy nations including Australia to the tardiness of the great powers. It is too late, however, for recrimination and too soon to apportion blame between the principal parties, Pakistan and India. The immediate objective is, of course, to stop the fighting. But beyond the indescribable sufferings facing millions of people in the subcontinent, it is essential that the great powers, particularly the Soviet Union, the People's Republic of China and the United States, do not become further and directly involved.

Whitlam argued that the catastrophe on the subcontinent had heralded fundamental changes in the uneasy power arrangements and accommodations 'which had maintained some semblance of peace in some of the world's potential flashpoints'. The world had become used to taking for granted that if the United States and the Soviet Union were determined to prevent or confine a war, their will would prevail. Now there was no such guarantee. Equally significant about the new period and relationships was the fact that the first time China had acted in the Security Council, she had aligned herself with the United States and Japan, in opposition to the Soviet Union. Nor was it without significance that the two old imperial powers, Britain and France, had abstained on this occasion.

To Whitlam, the world was entering a period of unparalleled complexity in international relations. Even so it was possible to discern one fundamental factor which provided a key to this struggle and to the region: it was that nationalism was still the most powerful force in the region. In the final analysis, nationalism would transcend religion as was happening in East Pakistan. It transcended ideology, as sooner or later would happen in Vietnam. Communism's only real success in the third world had occurred when it had been successfully grafted onto nationalism, and the West's greatest failures had occurred in allowing Communism to assume a monopoly of nationalism.

Whitlam stressed the impossibility of ignoring 'East Pakistan's national aspirations indefinitely' as Pakistan had done and had 'tried genocide to silence them'. He was not proposing the recognition of Bangladesh 'at this time . . . because Pakistan would choose total extinction before total separation'. But, the fact could not be evaded that, whether by war or international settlement a new independent state would be created in East Bengal: 'The task for the community of nations is to try to see that it comes into being through an internationally guaranteed settlement rather than by prolonged war'.[92]

The war, though brief, did not lead to an 'internationally guaranteed settlement'. However, the Australian government was among the first governments to recognize Bangladesh, on 31 January 1972. A month later, on 29 February 1972, the Prime Minister, Mr McMahon, announced in Parliament that, in addition to A\$2 million emergency relief to Bangladesh, a further A\$4 million would be provided for special rehabilitation, as 'the first stage of Australia's long-term assistance . . . Our aim is to help Bangladesh to take her place as a stable and developing economy which will make a constructive contribution to the South Asian region'.[93]

The policy of the conservative coalition in this crisis stood out as a statesman-like act in the long years in which it held power. On behalf of the Australian Labor Party, Whitlam applauded both the recognition of, and the commencement of direct aid to Bangladesh. He had the grace to acknowledge that in waiting a few weeks, it had become possible to synchronize recognition with many other countries 'particularly those from our region'. Whitlam referred to the fact that Indonesia and Malaysia had done so. 'Australia was playing a proper role politically and economically in rehabilitating this new nation.' He decided to forgo his right to move the adjournment of the debate and, instead, took this 'early . . . opportunity to assure the nations in our region and above all . . . Bangladesh, that on all sides of the Australian Parliament we wish that new nation well and we will collaborate . . . in our region to help her to have a peaceful and one would hope, a prosperous future.[94]

That was an unusual and remarkable event. It is difficult, and possibly too early, to determine whether the disorientation resulting from President Johnson's great decision and the China policy of his successor, made the Australian conservatives receptive, on this occasion, to the very precise and prompt policy decisions of the Foreign and Commonwealth Office. It is also possible that, here, the second level of Australian foreign policy seized the opportunity to assert itself in support of Indian and of British policy, and, in clear contradistinction to that of the U.S. government.

If the latter hypothesis is correct, it may be that Chinese opposition would have assisted support for the Indian and British policies, for Chinese aggression had been the cause for the Australian *rapprochement* with India, ten years before. Most likely, it was a combination of factors which resulted in a hard-pressed government taking a series of decisions in the Bangladesh crisis, bound to find wide approval in a community deeply divided, not so much by the Vietnam war as by the domestic implications of the government's continued intervention in it.

DISORIENTATION

The changes in the relations among the major powers contributed to the discomfiture of a coalition that had, for twenty years, treated concepts such as the threat of international communism and the down-ward thrust of China, as articles of faith on which they had been arguing their policies of dependence and intervention.

Nonetheless, the government showed great tenacity in holding on to positions, the hollowness of which had been revealed by the changed policies of the United States government. It continued its rigid pursuit of intervention in Vietnam and conscription remained a major issue of domestic conflict, heightened by the prosecution and imprisonment, under the National Service Act, of young men who refused to serve.

The resultant tensions were ~~almost~~ unique in a time of peace and considerable affluence. The government launched a fierce attack on Whitlam's visit to China, nine months before that of the American President. ~~That latter visit~~ caused the coalition even greater embarrassment and revealed further aspects of their disorientation and confusion.

In 1970, this disorientation was reflected in the government's approval of the allied intervention in Cambodia without, however, committing Australian forces in Vietnam to a similar course of action. The Cambodian affair is the more remarkable in view of the government's recognition and respect of the territorial integrity of the kingdom, expressed in January 1968, at a time when the United States were not prepared to do the same.

Disorientation - a gap between irrelevant habits of thought and an unpalatable, undigested reality - found expression in the Prime Minister's policy speech on 14 November 1972. Mr McMahon described the difference in the defence and foreign affairs policies of his government and the Australian Labor Party in these words:

We live in a region of turbulence and change. This makes it imperative that we should have effective and mobile defence forces to defend ourselves, and that we should have reliable allies. For these reasons we must strengthen our close links with the United States, Britain and New Zealand.

Labor's attitude to foreign policy and defence is different. Labor would draw the teeth of the *ANZUS* Treaty as a defence pact, abandon *SEATO*, withdraw from Malaysia and Singapore and would reduce the army dangerously below strength by the abolition of national service.

We will honour all those treaties and arrangements. Under the Liberal and Country Party policy, Australian defence capability is designed to protect our interests wherever they might be. Our strength is not limited to continental defence.

Labor would turn Australia into a friendless and isolated country and leave the seas and islands around us defenceless. Labor would take risks that are unnecessary and entirely unacceptable to us.

During the past year, I have been to the United States and Britain, to Indonesia, Singapore and Malaysia and have had frank and friendly talks with the leaders of those countries. They value our goodwill and friendship. They trust us.

My [sic] Minister for Foreign Affairs has recently visited India and Japan. Our relations with these countries, too, are on a sound basis. We will not put any of those relationships at risk. In dealing with Soviet Russia and the People's Republic of China, ideological differences have not been and will not be allowed to deter us from seeking to develop in every sensible and practical way those areas where common interests exist. But we will proceed at all times with care and prudence, bearing in mind that Australia's long-term interests are paramount.

We believe our policies and attitudes are understood and respected in both these countries.[95]

In the altered international situation of the time, McMahon's words reflected much of the fear, and the appeal to fear, which had informed conservative arguments in this debate for more than a century. In the Australian context, the desire for dependence on reliable allies had always been regarded as a logical remedy, as the *Realpolitik* of the weak. But Australia was no longer so weak or so under-developed; and these policies had lost whatever basis in reality they had once possessed. In his policy speech, Whitlam pointed to these facts and challenged the conservative conclusions.* Three weeks later, he became Prime Minister. An analysis of that Labour government's Asian policies and the debates about them will have to be left to other hands.

see Appendix, Document 12.

Conclusion

THERE IS a sense in which the debate reflected a dialogue between world historical events and the events in Australia.

Even in the earliest period of settlement, fear rippled with the sighting of every foreign vessel. The growth of the colonies into more viable societies coincided with the ascendancy of European imperialism in Asia, and Australians began to notice Asia in that setting, as an arena of conflict between Great Britain and other imperialist powers. The Asian environment re-inforced the fears of Australians about their own security, the assessment of which was an issue in the domestic political debate shaping the attitudes to Asia and to Asians.

Among the considerations affecting those attitudes, Australian concepts of Asia played a major part, as did a sense of pride in the expansion of the British Empire and, conversely, magnified fear of possible threats to Imperial positions. By contrast, there was some awareness, especially among radicals, of the imperialist causes of Asian misery, giving rise to sympathy and understanding for exploited Asians.

Expressions of fear multiplied after the Japanese victory over the Russian Empire in 1905, followed in Australia by a veritable avalanche of tendentious publications. One might be permitted to wonder whether a Russian victory over Japan - England's ally - would not have produced a similar torrent about the Russian menace.

As it was, the visit of the American fleet in the wake of these events, reflected the first, barely conscious questioning of Australian traditional wisdom on world events. It coincided with the period leading to the introduction of military conscription for home service and, following a long debate with the British government, the establishment of the Royal Australian Navy which, however, passed under Imperial command during the first world war.

Australian volunteer forces had been sent, before federation, i
support of British colonial wars, to the Sudan, to South Afric
and to China. They were the forerunners of the Australian Imperi
Force of the Great War. Its unquestioned achievements and staggerin
losses in the field, as much as the bitter debate about re-inforc
ments by conscription, resulted in lasting effects for Australia
society.

When the Australian government intervened in support of Imperi
interests in China, by making the *Brisbane* available to the Chin
Station of the Royal Navy, it acted with elaborate secrecy. Tha
was a period of government by conservatives whose major interest
were closely linked with British commerce. It was also a period o
conscious refusal to develop an Australian foreign policy, mad
possible by the Balfour declaration and freely offered by th
British government.

Lyons faced that paradox by his decision to establish Australia
legations in Washington and Tokyo. Although Menzies had oppose
that proposition, he made it his own on becoming Prime Minist
after Lyons' death in 1939, and he announced it in recognition o
Australia's primary responsibilities in East Asia and the Pacific
Paradoxically, he carefully avoided an Australian declaration of wa
on Germany because, in his view, a British declaration of wa
included Australia. His government then raised the Second Australia
Imperial Force and despatched it to the Middle East.

That further contradiction was resolved by Curtin and Evat
in 1941-2. They decided on separate Australian declarations of wa
on direct military dealings with the United States, on the ratifica
tion of the operative sections of the Statute of Westminster, an
on the repatriation for the defence of Australia of troops from th
Middle East. The disasters Curtin had considered five years befor
as possible contingencies, assumed a magnitude that made his policie
almost inevitable.

The strategic assumptions underlying Australian dependence o
British power were not questioned until 1936, when Curtin analyse
the feasibility of reliance on the Royal Navy and on the Singapor
base for the defence of Australia in a Pacific war, while Britai
was engaged in Europe.

It was significant that the basic concepts of dependence o
Great Britain were questioned by a statesman who had never playe

the game of using fears of foreign dangers in the domestic political debate. In office, his government then faced the real dangers and they faced them effectively: first, by Curtin's appeal to Roosevelt and close co-operation with the Americans, balanced by the nomination of the King's brother, the Duke of Gloucester, as Governor General; and then, by doing their utmost to obtain all possible Australian participation in the decision-making during the war and for the peace.

The coming of the Pacific war and the events symbolized by the fall of Singapore, brought up short a debate that had hitherto reflected world events taking place elsewhere. Now, Australia was a 'party principal', as Curtin and Evatt insisted.

After the war, Australia faced two alternatives. It could conduct a foreign policy based on multilateral relations, with Great Britain and the Commonwealth, with the United States, with sovereign Asian powers and with European states, taking account of Asian interests in Asian affairs. It could, if possible, strengthen this system by multilateral security arrangements.

Or, Australia could revert to its pre-war role, with the possible addition of making forces available to fight in Asia for the restoration of the *status quo ante bellum*. That was conservative policy, advocated in the first instance in the Dutch-Indonesian conflict. However, at that time the conservatives were in opposition and the Labour government co-operated with India in support of Indonesian independence, in conscious acceptance of Australia's role in an Asia that would be more than an arena for imperial gladiators.

However: where might the conservative alternative have led? Would military support for the Dutch attempt at colonial restoration in Indonesia have had a chance of success, or, would it have led to an unwinnable war, unimaginable in its proportions and incalculable in its consequences? Would it have been fused with the emergency in Malaya? The Vietnam war presents sobering analogies.

The degree and speed of the diminution of Britain's role in the Far East may not have been foreseen at that time, but, before the Korean war, the lack of American interest in the Asian-Pacific region was very plain. Moreover, when the United States agreed to enter security agreements in conjunction with the Japanese peace treaty, they were bi-lateral treaties or, in the case of Australia and New Zealand, tri-lateral. American policy towards India was negative, and the *ANZUS* alliance was not open to Great Britain.

Whereas the first alternative had been chosen by the Labour government, until its fall in 1949, the second was followed by the conservative coalition from that time until its defeat in 1972. Its limitations and its rigidity became evident with the failure of its policy on West New Guinea. It was finally exposed by the events of the Vietnam war.

Those same events have shown that it can no longer be assumed that a foreign policy of dependence on a principal world power will either afford Australia the kind of security which it requires, or enable it to adapt its diplomacy in changing conditions.

Appendix

DOCUMENT NO. 1

Plan proposed for importing Chinese mechanics and laborers from Singapore to New South Wales by G.F. Davidson.
Source: *Chinese Repository*, Canton, October 1837, VI (6), pp. 299 - 300, [Reprinted from an advertisement in the *Sydney Herald*, 19 June 1837, p. 4, col. 1]

The plan proposed by the undersigned for the importation of Chinese laborers and mechanics, having met with very considerable success, he is now induced to publish it in full, for the information of those distant settlers, who may not have had an opportunity of perusing it at either of the Sydney banks. My plan is to write to Singapore, in the early part of August, for four or five hundred Chinese, to be hired from the annual supply by the junks from various ports in China, which arrive there in December and January in large numbers, and may be hired for this or any other country with very little trouble. With my order to hire the men, I mean to send a ship from hence to bring them to Sydney; or, if a vessel cannot be had here on fair terms, my agent in Singapore shall have the necessary orders on that subject. From each subscriber I will require an advance of £5 for every Chinaman to be brought to him. This sum is to be expended in paying ten dollars (that being the amount due to the junk by each emigrant on board) for passage money from China, in food and clothing for the voyage to this port, and other contingent charges at Singapore. On the arrival of the men in Sydney, I would deliver each subscriber his number, and require from him immediate payment of whatever balance might be due me over and above the advance of £5 per man already mentioned. For the satisfaction of subscribers, I would, on the arrival of the vessel in Sydney, make out an account of the whole expenses of the undertaking, such account to be deposited in some public office for the perusal of those concerned.

From a calculation I have made, I feel convinced I can land the men in Sydney at £10 a head, say £11, and add £1 for commission to my Singapore agent; for this the men would serve twelve months after their arrival in the colony, getting fed of course, and they would serve a second year for £1 per month and rations; after the second year they would expect wages something nearly equal to what free Europeans get here. I would not begin with fewer than four hundred men, as it would require that number to fill a ship, and make it worth while. As many more as I can get subscribers for, will be obtained, and I have no objections to contract for an annual supply. From my long experience amongst Chinese, I have no hesitation in recommending strongly to the settlers of New South Wales, the importation of them into this country; as carpenters, cabinet-makers, wheel-wrights, millers, blacksmiths, bricklayers and brickmakers, gardeners, cooks, growers of maize, sugar, and tobacco, and general laborers, I can with perfect safety recommend them. As shepherds, I doubt whether they would answer.

For several years past, I have not seen less than six or eight thousand Chinese brought to Singapore in the months of December and January, and have invariably seen them willing to go anywhere with those who paid their debt to the junk they came in; they leave their country so very poor, that a fair prospect of plenty to eat, will induce them to go anywhere. From what I have seen on board the junks, I should say that 20 per cent. of the men brought here will be mechanics, perhaps more, but I cannot bind myself on that head. It will, of course, be my duty to bring the number of each trade required, as near as I can, and in the event of a deficiency in any particular trade, I would recommend the drawing of lots for a priority of choice. As to the distribution of the laborers, I must let them go in parties; were I to allow drawing of lots for them, a son might be separated from a father, a brother from a brother, and so on, which would tend very much to render the men discontented. Supposing 20 per cent. of the men prove to be mechanics, a subscriber for ten will have a claim for two tradesmen, for five one tradesman, and so on, any number under five will not give a claim to a tradesman, unless more than twenty in the hundred should prove such. In case of loss by shipwreck, I propose taking out a policy of insurance, to cover the sum advanced by the subscribers, previous to my dispatches leaving this. Any subscriber failing to make the necessary advance will, of course, forfeit his men.

Rice being the principal article of a Chinaman's food, I would recommend the importation of fifteen hundred or two thousand bags in the ship, the men came in; it might be landed here at three halfpence per pound, and would go as far as flour in rationing the men.

It seems to be a prevailing opinion that the Chinese will not remain with their masters after their arrival here, of this I have very little fear. After the expiration of two or three years, numbers of them will, no doubt, wish to return to China, which I consider will tend to induce many more to come here the following year, particularly if those who go carry accounts of good treatment, &c., with them. Chinese emigrants never bring their wives and families from their native country; but this does not prevent their remaining many years in those countries where they find constant and profitable employment. If they get £15 a year and rations, it will be double what they earn in and about Singapore, and, in my opinion, will be sufficient to keep up a constant supply of Chinese laborers in this market. On the subject of ill-treatment, I would caution the settlers of New South Wales; a Chinese will not put up with it, and will spread such reports about it, as will tend to prevent future supplies reaching this part of the world.

(Signed) G.F. DAVIDSON

Sydney, June 15th, 1837.

[*Note.* The foregoing appears as an advertisement in the *Sydney Herald* of June 19th, 1837. In a postscript, Mr Davidson gives a list of the subscribers which he had already obtained, amounting to fifty-seven, requiring 335 Chinese. Mr Davidson says, the advance of £5 per annum, is to be paid in to the commercial bank, Sydney, on or before the first of August next *1837), in order to give time for the men to be there by March, 1838.]

The *Note* forms part of the Document.

DOCUMENT NO. 2

Petition from Members of the Ipswich School of Arts (Mechanics Institute) against Coolie Immigration, in 1862; transmitted by Sir G.F. Bowen, Governor of Queensland, with Despatch No. 38 of 18 July 1862, to the Duke of Newcastle, Secretary of State for the Colonies.
Source: Public Records Office (C. O. 243/6)

To the Queen's Most Excellent Majesty
in Council

May it please Your Majesty

The humble Petition of your Majesty's dutiful and loyal subjects Inhabitants of the Town and District of Ipswich in the Colony of Queensland

Respectfully Sheweth

That in the opinion of Your Majesty's Petitioners, it would have been better, in a matter of such importance to the future material interests and moral well-being of this portion of Your Majesty's dominions as the introduction of a Helot class of Laborers into this Colony, had the Act recently passed by the Legislature of Queensland intituled *An Act to give the force of Law to regulations for the introduction and protection of Laborers from British India* been reserved for Your Majesty's gracious pleasure thereon, rather than have been immediately assented to by His Excellency the Governor of Queensland, pursuant, as he deems, to instructions received from His Grace the Duke of Newcastle, relative thereto.

That inasmuch as the regulations intended by the Government were not submitted to the Queensland Parliament, nor any Act passed by the said Parliament similar to the Ordinance dated October 20th 1858 enacted by the Governor of Mauritius with the advice and consent of the Council of Government thereof your Petitioners are of the opinion that constitutional Government has been virtually violated and set in abeyance.

That the majority of the Colonists of Queensland are decidedly opposed to the introduction, in the manner proposed, of Hindoo laborers and residents, as foreign to our customs and policy and adverse to our best interests as a nascent country.

That their introduction to Queensland would be but the prelude to enormous and unbearable Social evils and to frightful and devastating diseases, which would decimate our population, as proved by their prevalence in the Mauritius consequent upon the introduction of Coolie labour:

That the special plea for the importation of Coolies, viz., that the tropical parts of Australia are unfitted for European industry, if true, must necessarily hinder the settlement there of Immigrants from the mother country; and if not true, as proved by house-building, road-making, and other laborious out-door pursuits being carried on in Summer as well as Winter in those very parts, the fallacious ground of this contemplated experiment in Cotton growing is at once rendered apparent. And your Majesty's attention is specially drawn to the fact, that 200 bales of Cotton, all raised by European labour, without the assistance of Coolies, will be sent this year from Queensland to Great Britain. Moreover, the Cotton-picking season, is not in the hottest period of the year, but in the Autumn and Winter, or cool portion of the year, so that no European need complain of excessive heat; and Cotton-picking will be found on experience to be far healthier than the usual occupations in Cotton-Mills and Cotton Factories. And it may be further stated as a matter of fact that children between ten and fifteen years of age have found it a light and agreeable occupation to pick Cotton.

That if Coolie labour were dearer than British, no thought of its employment would be for a moment entertained, it is therefore evident that the idea of cheapness is one that is dominant in the minds of those wishful to inundate the Colony with this undesirable species of labour; but this idea is exceedingly erroneous, arrived at by merely counting the prima facie costs of such labour, without reckoning for its commitments, such as special and appropriate education for Coolie children, increased Police for the suppression of fearfully augmented vice, enlarged and fresh Hospitals for the cure of diseases, some of which are fortunately unknown amongst us at present, - all which when duly met, will show Coolie labour to be doubly expensive as compared with British; and it is no exaggeration to say that the presence of Coolies amongst us in great numbers would entail woes which no money can compensate:

That the promoters of Coolie immigration to Queensland are either ignorant of the evils inevitably connected with their establishment here, or callously defiant of the consequences, and in either case totally disqualified to be entrusted with the destinies of thousands who foresee and desire to arrest those evils[.]

That your Petitioners are further of the opinion, that in the present state of distress experienced in certain districts of Great Britain, it would have been far wiser as a measure of policy and far more acceptable to the Colonists of Queensland, had a large immigration of the sturdy races from the British Isles been introduced even by considerable assistance from the local and Imperial Governments.

Your Petitioners therefore pray, that on these grounds added to the distinct avowal of His Grace the Duke of Newcastle in his Despatch bearing [the] date April 26th 1861 that the Bill just sanctioned by His Excellency the Governor of Queensland, is simply *provisional* and not final, Your Majesty will be pleased to discourage any further attempts at Coolie immigration and to issue instructions to the Government and Parliament of Queensland to rescind the regulations about to be issued and to abolish this provisional measure.

AND your Petitioners as in duty
bound will ever pray etc., etc., etc.

Signed by Two Hundred
an[d] thirty two persons

DOCUMENT NO. 3

.oyal Commission on Federal Union; First Report.
ource: Victoria, *Papers printed for Parliament,* 1870, Second Session, vol. II.

To His Excellency the Right Honorable JOHN
HENRY THOMAS VISCOUNT CANTERBURY,
K.C.B., *Governor and Commander-in-Chief of
the Colony of Victoria.*

We, the undersigned Commissioners, appointed under Letters
Patent from the Crown, bearing date the 31st day of August
1870, to consider and report upon the necessity of a Federal
Union of the Australian Colonies for Legislative Purposes,
and the best means of accomplishing such a union, beg to
submit to Your Excellency this our First Report:—

1. The two questions referred to the Commission have been care-
ully and separately considered.

I. – ADVANTAGES OF A FEDERAL UNION

2. On the primary question of a Federal Union of the Australian
olonies, apart from all considerations of the time and method of
ringing such a union about, there was a unanimity of opinion.
he indispensable condition of success for men or nations is that
hey should clearly understand what they want, and to what goal
hey are travelling, that life may not be wasted in doing and un-
oing; and as we are persuaded that the prosperity and security
f these Colonies would be effectually promoted by enabling them
o act together as one people under the authority of a Federal
ompact, they cannot, we believe, too soon come to an under-
tanding upon this fundamental point.

3. The difference in strength and *prestige* between isolated
ommunities having separate interests and a national confederation,
vith a national policy, has been illustrated in the history of almost
very great State in the world, and conspicuously in the history of
tates of which we share the blood and traditions. The effects of
uch a confederation, when it is voluntary and equal, are felt

throughout all the complicated relations of a nation's life, adding immensely to its material and moral strength. By its concentrated power it exercises an increased gravitation in attracting population and commerce. It multiplies the national wealth by putting an end to jealous and wasteful competitions, and substituting the wise economy of power which teaches each district to apply itself to the industries in which it can attain the greatest success. It enlarges the home market, which is the nursing mother of native manufactures. It forms larger designs, engages in larger enterprises, and by its increased resources and authority causes them to be more speedily accomplished. It obtains additional security for peace by increasing its means of defence; and, by creating a nation, it creates along with it the sentiment of nationality — a sentiment which has been one of the strongest and most beneficent motive-powers in human affairs. The method, indeed, by which States have grown great, is almost uniform in history: they gathered population and territory, and on these wings rose to material power; and with the sense of a common citizenship there speedily came, like a soul to the inert body, that public spirit by whose inspiration dangers are willingly faced and privations cheerfully borne in the sacred name of country.

4. We cannot doubt that it is the destiny of the Australian Colonies to pursue a similar career, and their duty to prepare for it. They possess resources and territory which fit them to become in the end a great empire; they are occupied by a population already larger than the population of many Sovereign States; and they yield a revenue greater than the revenue of six of the kingdoms of Europe, and we believe they share the sentiment, which may be noted as among the most subtle and pervading influences of our century, the desire to perfect the union and autonomy of peoples of the same origin.

II. – BEST MEANS OF EFFECTING A UNION

5. The form which a Federal Union ought to assume, and the time at which it ought to be brought into operation, are subjects which must be reserved for a Conference of Colonial delegates accredited by the respective Governments and Legislatures concerned.

6. In approaching the second question referred to us, however — the best means of effecting a union — it is necessary to point out that a Federal Compact for legislative purposes may represent widely

different ideas and measures of power. The Canadian Dominion
furnishes the most perfect example of Federated Colonies. Canada,
Nova Scotia, New Brunswick, and Prince Edward's Island, enjoyed
constitutions substantially the same as ours, and were consequently
under the control of Governments responsible only to the Local
Legislatures. For the purpose of attaining the increased vigor and
authority which result from union, these Colonies agreed to abandon
some of the powers enjoyed by the Local Legislatures in favor of a
General Parliament and Government authorized to act on behalf of
all the Confederated Colonies. A constitution was framed accordingly,
under which each Colony retains a Local Legislature, possessing
complete control over purely local interests, and over the public lands
of the Colony, while the Parliament and the Executive of the
Dominion are charged with what may be distinguished as national
interests. We have printed in an Appendix the principal clauses of
the Act of the Imperial Parliament creating the Dominion of
Canada*, from which the functions of the Local and General
Legislatures respectively may be seen in detail. On the other hand,
there have been examples of a Federal Council having authority only
on a few specified subjects, and on such other subjects as were
afterwards from time to time referred to it by the Local Legislatures.
And there have been intermediate methods of more or less perfectly
organized union. Opinion in the Colonies seems to be divided
between these methods; and a decision can only be arrived at after
much debate and negotiation.

7. But there is preliminary work to be done upon which there
would probably be little difference of opinion. To effect a union
of any kind, binding alike upon all, an Imperial Act is necessary.
Such an Act might be a permissive one, and might authorize the
Queen, by proclamation, to call into existence a Federal Union of
any two or more of the Australian Colonies as soon as they had
passed Acts in their respective Legislatures providing, in identical
terms, for the powers and functions to be exercised by the General
Legislature, and the distribution of seats; and for the adjustment
of the Colonial debts in case the nature of the union should render
an adjustment necessary. The bases of these identical Acts would of
course be determined by conference between the Colonies.

8. The Permissive Act ought to provide for the admission of
Colonies not joining the union in the first instance, and might also

* *not reproduced*

provide a mode of withdrawal upon certain notice for any Colony
dissatisfied.

9. We are distinctly of opinion that 'the best means of accomplishing a union' is to remove, by such an Act, all legal impediments to it without delay, and leave the Colonies to determine, by negotiation among themselves, how far, and how soon, they will avail themselves of the power thus conferred on them.

10. The Commission are disposed to regard it as part of the duty committed to them to prepare a Bill for transmission to the Imperial Parliament of the nature which they have indicated, and to ascertain by communication with the leading public men in the other Colonies whether they are disposed to co-operate in securing the sanction of the Imperial Parliament for it. While all questions of intercolonial relations must be reserved for a Colonial Conference, it seems plain that, unless those who make a proposal of this nature give it practical shape and take means to ascertain how far it will be acceptable, it may prove as barren of results as many proposals on the same subject which have preceded it. They intend therefore to print such a Bill with their second Report.

III.– THE NEUTRALITY OF THE COLONIES IN WAR

11. A cognate question has been brought under the consideration of the Commission, as belonging to its general object, the existing relation of the Colonies to each other and to the Mother Country.

12. The British Colonies from which Imperial troops have been wholly withdrawn present the unprecedented phenomenon of responsibility without either corresponding authority or adequate protection. They are as liable to all the hazards of war as the United Kingdom; but they can influence the commencement or continuance of war no more than they can control the movements of the solar system; and they have no certain assurance of that aid against an enemy upon which integral portions of the United Kingdom can confidently reckon. This is a relation so wanting in mutuality that it cannot safely be regarded as a lasting one, and it becomes necessary to consider how it may be so modified as to afford a greater security for permanence.

13. It has been proposed to establish a Council of the Empire, whose advice must be taken before war was declared. But this measure is so foreign to the genius and traditions of the British Constitution,

and pre-supposes so large an abandonment of its functions by the House of Commons, that we dismiss it from consideration. There remains however, we think, more than one method by which the anomaly of the present system may be cured.

14. It is a maxim of International Law that a Sovereign State cannot be involved in war without its own consent, and that where two or more States are subject to the same Crown, and allies in peace, they are not, therefore, necessarily associates in war if the one is not dependent on the other.

15. The sovereignty of a State does not arise from its extent, or power, or population, or form of Government. More than a century ago, Vattel formulated the principle now universally accepted, that a small community may be a Sovereign State, no less than the most powerful kingdom or empire, and that all Sovereign States inherit the same rights and obligations.

16. 'Two Sovereign States' (says Vattel) 'may be subject to the same prince without any dependence on each other, and each may retain its rights as a free and Sovereign State. The King of Prussia is Sovereign Prince of Neufchatel in Switzerland, without the principality being in any manner united to his other dominions; so that the people of Neufchatel, in virtue of their franchises, may serve a foreign power at war with the King of Prussia, provided that the war be not on account of that principality.'

17. Wheaton and other modern public jurists have illustrated the same principle by the case of Hanover and England, which, though they were allied by personal union under the same Crown, were not necessarily associates in war or responsible for each other. And the latest writers on International Law cite the more modern and analogous case of the Ionian Islands, a State garrisoned by British troops, and having as Chief Magistrate a Lord High Commissioner appointed by the Queen; and which was, notwithstanding, adjudged before the British Court of Admiralty (on a private question arising) to constitute a Sovereign State not associated with the United Kingdom in the Crimean war. The last Chief Magistrate but one of this Sovereign State was since promoted to the Governorship of the Colony of New South Wales, and thence to the Governorship of the Dominion of Canada. The last Lord High Commissioner was transferred to the Governorship of the dependency of Jamaica.

18. Without overlooking the distinction between Colonies consisting

of men of the same origin, as the population of the United Kingdom, and States inherited by the Crown, like Hanover, or obtained by treaty, like the Ionian Islands, it is suggested for consideration whether the rule of International Law under which they are declared neutrals in war would not become applicable to Colonies enjoying self-government by a single addition to their present power.

19. The Colony of Victoria, for example, possesses a separate Parliament, Government, and distinguishing flag; a separate naval and military establishment. All the public appointments are made by the Local Government. The only officer commissioned from England who exercises authority within its limits is the Queen's Representative; and in the Ionian Islands, while they were admittedly a Sovereign State, the Queen's Representative was appointed in the same manner. The single function of a Sovereign State, as understood in International Law, which the Colony does not exercise or possess, is the power of contracting obligations with other States. The want of this power alone distinguishes her position from that of States undoubtedly sovereign.

20. If the Queen were authorized by the Imperial Parliament to concede to the greater Colonies the right to make treaties, it is contended that they would fulfil the conditions constituting a Sovereign State in as full and perfect a sense as any of the smaller States cited by public jurists to illustrate this rule of limited responsibility. And the notable concession to the interest of peace and humanity made in our own day by the Great Powers with respect to privateers and to merchant shipping renders it probable that they would not, on any inadequate grounds, refuse to recognize such States as falling under the rule.

21. It must not be forgotten that this is a subject in which the interests of the Colonies and of the Mother Country are identical. British statesmen have long aimed not only to limit more and more the expenditure incurred for the defence of distant Colonies, but to withdraw more and more from all ostensible responsibility for their defence; and they would probably see any honorable method of adjusting the present anomalous relations with no less satisfaction than we should.

22. Nor would the recognition of the neutrality of the self-governed Colonies deprive them of the power of aiding the Mother Country in any just and necessary war. On the contrary, it would

enable them to aid her with more dignity and effect; as a Sovereign State could, of its own free will, and at whatever period it thought proper, elect to become a party to the war.

23. We are of opinion that this subject ought to be brougnt unaer the notice of the Imperial Government. If the proposal should receive their sanction, they can ascertain the wishes of the American and African Colonies with respect to it, and finally take the necessary measures to obtain its recognition as part of the public law of the civilized world.

check

Town Hall, Melbourne,
   October 3rd 1870.

(L.S.)	C. GAVAN DUFFY, Chairman.
(L.S.)	FRANCIS MURPHY,
(L.S.)	THO. HOWARD FELLOWS,
	(As to Parts I. & II.)
(L.S.)	C. MAC MAHON,
(L.S.)	JOHN MACGREGOR,
(L.S.)	J.F. SULLIVAN,
(L.S.)	EDWARD LANGTON,
	(Except as to Part III.)
(L.S.)	J.J. CASEY,
(L.S.)	G.B. KERFERD,
(L.S.)	GRAHAM BERRY,
(L.S.)	JAS. GRAHAM.

DOCUMENT NO. 4

Speech by Sir Thomas McIlwraith, Premier of Queensland.
Source: *The Sugar Planter*, Maryborough, Queensland, vol. 2, No. 18 [1883], pp. 93-4

THE PREMIER AT ROMA : ON THE SUGAR INDUSTRY

The banquet was the most numerously attended and successful gathering ever held in Roma.

The chairman rose to propose the toast of the evening. 'The health of our guest, Sir Thomas McIlwraith'.

The toast was enthusiastically drunk with the usual musical honours and three cheers, with 'one more' for Lady McIlwraith.

Sir Thomas McIlwraith (who on rising to respond was received with tremendous applause, which continued for some time) said he could not but feel grateful for the way in which he had been met that night. He did not think there was a more appropriate place in the colony for him to appear on an occasion of this kind than in Roma. He remembered very well when about ten years ago he sought the suffrages of this community, and he remembered also that he was not very much believed in on that occasion. He fought a hard battle, and he won it. He told them plainly that he believed he deserved to win it, and he was satisfied now, from the way in which this town and district had treated him since, that they were of the same opinion. (Applause.) Being the leader of what is called the Conservative party in Queensland, he had at the same time made that party the progressive party in the colony —(applause)— and the party having acquired that character he believed they would maintain it under the present Ministry and the men who worked with it. It was a difficult matter to fill the position of Premier of this colony. It required a man of iron frame and of some determination. He had done his utmost to properly fill that position, and he had some trials to go through. The first point on which the leader of the Opposition had said the Government had not stood to their principles was in connection with the coolie question. He would speak at length on this question, because he considered it one of the most important subjects before the constituencies at the present time. He wished to point out that the Government had gone steadily forward in one path with regard to this question, and had not receded in the least. In 1876, when the sugar industry had not spread to anything like its present large proportions, and the matter of kanaka immigration was brought periodically before Parliament, he took up very strong ground in reference to it. In 1875, in 1876, and in 1877, the last Government brought in bills to deal with the kanaka question. They were evidently brought forward for the purpose of shelving, and not of settling the question, and merely to raise a popular cry in favour of the Ministry of the day. His experience had then extended only to the squatting districts, and he did not believe in black labour. He saw that little capital had been put into the sugar industry, but he saw it was a matter of vital importance that they should deal in good faith with the men who were about to put capital into it, and say definitely whether we would have black labour on the sugar plantations then being formed or not. He therefore challenged the Ministry to put an amendment in the bill they brought forward to the effect that at the end of three years the employment of black labour within the colony should cease. By this means a fair warning would have been given to those making use of this kind of labour, and the thing would have been put on an equitable footing. What was the result? The Ministry shirked the responsibility, and left the question as it was. The Liberal party then in power distinctly refused his challenge to put a determination to this class of labour, and by so refusing what amounted to a distinct invitation to the sugar-growers to go on cultivating sugar, and to depend on the support of the Liberal party in getting black labour for the future. These men were actually invited to cultivate sugar because they were satisfied the Liberal party would never prevent their getting black labour. Since then he had given a good deal of time to the consideration and examination of the whole of the coast districts, and he found there was a class of labour wanted on the sugar plantations that would never be supplied by Europeans. (Applause.) He had had the most intimate relations with the working men engaged in different industries in the colony, and he found that from top to bottom they rejected the proposition that they should work at certain kinds of labour in our sugar-fields. They say they would do nothing of the sort. The question was — Are we to flood the market with cheap labour from Great Britain and the Continent of Europe, until the labour introduced became so low that it would be low enough to suit the planters at the present time. That is a proposition the present Government would never sanction. We had invited the community generally to select the sugar lands all along our coast. They had done so on the faith of being placed in a position to provide themselves with labour for their plantations. If we broke faith with them we should prevent the colony from having the advantage of this industry, which would be an infinite advantage not only to the country people, but to the whole of the towns of the colony. You wipe out the sugar industry, or let it be understood that it could only be conducted by the labour that is in the colony, or to be imported from England, Scotland, and Ireland, and there would come a period of depression such as had not yet been seen in Queensland. (Applause.) He had occupied the position of Colonial Secretary for a short time and he gave his assurance that the most laborious part of his duties had been to investigate charges connected with the kanaka trade. He could say there was not one of the abuses that had been stated in the Press, where details and data had been given, but what had always previously been inquired into, the proper persons punished if necessary, and where possible, and a remedy applied. Sensational stories were often heard from missionaries, but he could say that every case that had been substantiated had been investigated by him before it had been brought forward in the public Press. He had by this means been led to the belief that many of the stories circulated had been greatly exaggerated. At the same time he did not lose sight of the fact that there must be some foundation for them. There was a great demand for labour, and in the anxiety to get it some abuses were perpetrated which he could not possibly reach. He had done all he could to prevent any kanaka being brought away from the islands against his free will, and he thought there were very few cases within the reach of justice where the islanders were brought away against their will. At the same time, the trade was open to that objection, and we had to consider the opinion entertained of us by the public of England. He was satisfied no grosser injustice had ever been done to any community than had been done to us in connection with this trade. He had been filled with infinite disgust at the stories he had heard from Exeter Hall about this matter. He was an intense believer in this colony being a white man's colony, influenced by white men, and owned by white men. He referred to the efforts made during the last few generations to improve the condition of the working classes, and said that, on the other hand, upon the east coast of Asia there were millions who had been brought up under a perfectly different regime, the working man being there forced into as low a position as it was possible to place him. We found that Chinamen had done work more cheaply than our own men, and it would be an injustice to say to the white man, 'If you cannot do it as cheaply you must be wiped out.' He said that in all the ordinary avocations of life we must look to the Europeans to maintain the colony; but in other directions, where the white man says he cannot do the work, let us bring in another race who can, and let us keep them separate from the white population. That was what he had been working for all along. He thought he had attained his object in what he had been working for all along. He thought he had attained his object in what he had done to bring coolies from India for the plantations in this colony. It [If] they had shirked this question - that they tried all they could to keep it back, and prevent Parliament from putting out the present Government upon it. What prevented the Government from putting the regulations on the subject before Parliament last year was simply that they had not been matured. He insisted that regulations should be made by which it could be ensured that the men who employ the coolies for sugar plantations should confine them to those plantations. (Applause.) That he believed he had done. It was only within the last week or two that he had received intimation that the Indian Government had assented to regulations under which coolies could be brought here, could be confined to the sugar plantations, and under which it would be certain they would be returned at the end of their engagements, and not allowed to contaminate the white population outside of those plantations.

DOCUMENT NO. 5

Part of a speech by Mr T.C. O'Mara, dealing with the Sudan expedition, in the New South Wales Legislative Assembly, on 15 September 1885, in the debate on the Address-in-Reply.
Source: *N. S. W. Parliamentary Debates*, First Series, vol XVII, Second Session, 1885.

I am not in the habit, as is well known to my friends, of defending Sir Henry Parkes, but for the Governor or any one else to describe him as speaking in the colony without authority or influence is not only to say that which is not true but that which is childish. I remember that some years ago a man of high position was speaking in terms of contempt of Sir Henry Parkes in the presence of a gentle-man who had been long associated with Sir Henry Parkes, and who had no reason to remember that association with pleasure or with gratitude, and the answer which that gentleman gave then I will give now: He said: 'Sir Henry Parkes is a power and you must deal with him as such, and do not talk of him in the way in which you are talking.' As to the rest of us who are insignificant in person and in influence, if we are personally insignificant we are members of Parliament, and in that light we have a right to be spoken of with respect, even by his Excellency. I shall run over some of the names of those of whom the Governor thought proper to speak so contemptuously, and upon whom he invoked the contempt of the Imperial Secretary of State. Two are the names of ex-ministers of the Crown, one has been his Excellency's principal law adviser. Another, the hon. member for The Hunter, has been two or three times a minister of the Crown. The hon. member for The Hastings and Manning is a gentleman of whom his Excellency should not have spoken in language of that kind, for hon. members on both sides of the House will admit that he has always taken a most intelligent part in the debates in Parliament. My friend, the hon. member for Eden, is as well-informed on political matters as nine-tenths of hon. members of this House, and he commands as much weight. That hon. gentleman moved an amendment on the address last session. I say that he is too respectable and too much respected a man to be spoken of in the terms which have been applied to him. Of myself I will say nothing except this: that I think that I understand, at least as well as his Excellency, questions of the kind which I then discussed. Whatever education I possess was not acquired in the atmosphere in which he lived for so many years; not in St Petersburg or Vienna. I do protest against this document of his Excellency, and I think we are not outstepping the proper bounds when we as members of Parliament complain that an indignity has been put upon us by no less a person than the Governor. There is one other point to which I wish to refer as illustrating the development of this contingent business. It is the history of the opinion of the newspapers. We know that when the idea of sending the contingent was first started, two newspapers, the *Daily Telegraph* and the *Evening News*, spoke in the most laudatory terms of the undertaking, as a happy idea, and as a thing that would be useful to the empire, and that might help to preserve it in its then undoubted perils. After the contingent had been for some time in the Soudan, one of these papers being disappointed with its performance there, said if this kind of thing was to go on and not to improve we must look upon this campaign as the 'nannygoat campaign'. The campaign did not improve to the end; it must therefore have continued to be a 'nannygoat campaign'. The *Telegraph* spoke of the contingent business as a miserable 'fizzle'. This shows how events have been on our side, and that which was regarded as an emergency has in its latest development taken in the opinion of one newspaper the form of a 'nannygoat campaign', and in the opinion of the other has turned out a 'fizzle'. The hon. member for Argyle the other night unintentionally did an injustice to us who formed the insignificant and contemptible minority when the question was formerly before the House. He said that we did now draw attention to the new character of this expenditure on the contingent. I, however, pointed out at the time that this was an entirely new departure. I said:

All the positions which I take up are granted by the other side of the House. In the first place there has been a totally new departure in our politics; in the next place, by that new departure we have for the first time in our lives dignified ourselves with the possession of a foreign policy; we might be further said to have established quite a new department of government - I might say that we have added a new minister to our Cabinet in the shape of a minister of war. All these things are admitted by hon. members opposite, and they must also admit that these things have been done − first, by a violation of the Constitution; second, by suspending the fundamental rights of Parliament, and by a usurpation on the part of a minister of those rights.

That is the case to-day still more emphatically than it was then; and when at that time we were discussing the action of the ministry, and contending that it was unconstitutional, we conceded to them as much as we could. We refused to discuss the merits of the war. We assumed, for the purpose of argument, that it was a just war. We did not insist upon what was the fact, that it was a war in the interests of the Egyptian bond-holders. We granted, for the sake of their position, that it was a war in the interest of civilisation, though it was no such thing. Let us now discuss the nature of the war in which we were engaged. I have a condemnation of the war from a source as authentic as any from which information can be obtained on the subject. Many have heard of the grand young fellow named Power, who was for a long time at Khartoum, and who was a companion of Gordon. He had the privilege of being addressed in the most familiar terms by General Gordon, and I submit that he never would have enjoyed that privilege had it not been in virtue of a good, truthful, and chivalrous character. What did this young fellow write concerning his daily experience, not for any political purpose, not with any idea of publication, but writing to his mother for her confidence? Telling the truth out of his heart, what does he say?

The Soudani and the Arabs are splendid fellows; ground down and robbed by every ruffian who has money enough (ill-gotten) to buy himself a position of Pasha, or free license to rob. They are quite right to rebel and hurl the nest of robbers to the other side of Siout. For years it has been *kourbash, kourbash, et toujours kourbash*. This gets monotonous, and the poor devils rebel. I will, indeed, forgive the fellow who puts his lance into me, if that is to be my fate, because I will feel that he is right as long as I am of the same colour as the scoundrels who have robbed him and his for so many years. How is the government of the country carried on? It is only the plains along the banks of the Nile which are cultivated. Every Arab must pay a tax — for himself, children and wife or wives. This he has to pay three times over — once for the Kedowi, once for the tax-collector or local Beys, and once for the Governor-General. The last two are illegal, but still scrupulously collected to the piastre. To pay this he must grow some corn, and for the privilege of growing corn he must pay £3 per annum. To grow corn the desert earth must have water; the means of irrigation is a 'sakeh', a wheel like a mill-wheel with buckets on it, which raise the water into a trough, and then it flows in little streams over the land. A sakeh is turned by two oxen. Every man who uses a sakeh must pay £7; if he doesn't use it he must go into prison for life, and have his hut burned. Every one must pay for the right of working to earn money; every one must pay if they are idle; in any case every one must pay to make the officials rich. If you have a merkeb, or trading-boat, you are fined £4 if you don't continually fly the Egyptian flag, and you must pay £4 for the privilege of flying it. It is this system, and not the Mahdi, that has brought about this rebellion. The rebels are in the right, and God and chance seem to be fighting for them, and, as long as I live to see you once more, I hope they will hunt every Egyptian neck and crop out of the Soudan. Better a thousand times the barbarities of slavery than the detestable barbarities and crimes of the Egyptian rulers.

It is these detestable cruelties and barbarities of the Egyptian rulers that you have done your best to perpetuate. This is the kind of war in which you are engaged — a war of which England herself has grown ashamed — a war from which England herself has withdrawn, sickened and disgusted with the whole thing — a war, no matter what its issue, which will add nothing of prowess to her arms, nor one atom of prestige to her policy. It is, I say, a war of which England herself has grown ashamed; and it is in this war that ministers drew the maiden sword of this colony. We, on this side of the House, ought to be thankful that we had no hand, and took no part in that war, except to protest against it. We ought to be thankful for that as long as we live, and I think that on the strength of that we may not fear to go before the country at the next general election. My attention has just been called to a contradiction made by the Colonial Treasurer of certain utterances attributed to him. During the debate on the Soudan expedition he said:

> I am prepared to admit — and perhaps I should disarm a certain amount of criticism when I say so — that when I became acquainted with the offer made by the Cabinet during my temporary absence from Sydney I was taken a great deal by surprise. It was calculated to take away the breath of a man of much larger dimensions than I possess.

I do not think that the breath of the hon. gentleman is at any time taken away without some cause. What was it took away his breath? Will he tell us that? What is the use of the hon. member saying that he did not condemn it in the first instance? More than that, I say that other ministers condemned it. I am certain Sir Alexander Stuart never approved of it.

DOCUMENT NO. 6

Article by 'Cintra' in *The Worker*, Sydney, 10 July 1909, p. 5.

INDIA'S TROUBLES

What's the matter with India? The blessings of British rule don't seem to agree with her.

The country is spoken of as in a state of unrest. 'It is seething with sedition,' say the leading papers.

Well, there must be a cause for it. The Hindu is not a restless person by nature; he doesn't seethe under ordinary circumstances to any great extent. He is quiet, contemplative, stoical under suffering, patient under wrong.

The man who will squat on his haunches for hours, and never move; who will slowly starve to death and reach out no hand of violence against those who overfeed, is not a seething person by any means.

Yet cable news comes of a prominent official of the India Office in London being assassinated by a Hindu student in a highly dramatic manner. And the crime is admittedly of a political character.

What's the matter with India? — with dreamy, romantic, quiescent, almost somnolent India?

The matter is that our Eastern Empire is being governed on lines that were well enough, perhaps, a hundred years ago, but to-day have become impossible.

Millions of these people perished of famine, while the British sahibs-battened upon the wealth that India produced. And scarcely a groan was heard from their lips, though the land was a charnel-house that the Union Jack waved arrogantly over, and the British sahibs feasted riotously amidst scenes of hunger and horror.

Scarcely a word of complaint did they utter, though those whom famine spared were weighed down under the burden of an intolerable oppression, condemned to unremitting toil for the merest pittance, denied all hope of constitutional redress.

The beasts in the jungle are better off than the Indian ryot, whose very name is a byword for the lowest condition of human wretchedness.

Remember, now, that the Hindus are also a proud people, and you'll begin to understand the situation in India.

There is reason for that pride. They are an ancient race, of honourable history. When we were barbarians their civilisation was a world's wonder. Art, poetry, and science flourished there, when Europe was sunk in ignorance. They have a moral code as exalted as our own, a philosophy as profound. And they were thousands of years in front of us.

India had fallen from her former glory, and degenerated, when the British trader came, and turned a profitable market into an Empire of Greed.

But suffering and sorrow have awakened the spirit that made India great in the old days, and we are witnessing to-day the reincarnation of a people.

India is demanding control of her own destiny. India is tired of being the slave of a useless aristocracy trampling her under the feet of an alien contempt.

India is demanding what even Persia and Turkey have had to

be granted, what no nation now with an atom of self-respect will willingly forego — the right of self-government, the right to direct its own affairs, and mould its own future, according to its own will and its own genius.

This right, this guarantee of national development, which America conceded to the Filipinos as soon as the Star-spangled banner was unfurled above them, Great Britain has withheld from India for one hundred and fifty years.

She has treated the Hindus worse than the negroes of the United States, who have at least been given a voice in the government of the country.

That is what's the matter with India.

It is regrettable that a high official should have been assassinated, for he was only the creature of a system.

But it is infinitely more regrettable that a nation should be decimated by rapacity and misrule, that it should be held in subjection by the sword, and its reasonable appeals for the franchise, to a country boasting its love of liberty, be answered by the methods of the Tsar.

DOCUMENT NO. 7 6

Article in *The Australian Worker*, 14 May 1914, p. 17; in a regular feature - *Outlook, A Survey of World Progress*, conducted by H.E. Boote.

THE YELLOW PERIL

China is to be the happy hunting ground of Western Capitalism. That is, of course, if the big 'captains of industry' succeed in their designs.

The Young China patriots may be strong enough to defeat this foreign-devil conspiracy, but on the present look of things it does not seem that they will.

Western Capitalism has already got a strong grip upon the Celestial Republic, and behind it are the guns of the Great Powers, breathing the menace of 'partition'.

It would suit the 'captains of industry' fine to have the docile millions of China at their disposal. They are clever and tireless workers; day and night they will toil without complaint, and meekly put up with wages and conditions which in the West would make the poorest worms spit fire.

The factories established by foreign enterprise in China are about the most hellish holes on earth to-day.

Here Capitalism reigns as supreme as in England a hundred years ago. The law imposes no restrictions worth speaking of, and the seven devils of greed run riot, devouring whom they please.

A THROW-BACK

The favourite victims of the old-time English factory lords were the women and children. To read of the barbarities inflicted upon them makes the blood turn cold with horror, and then turn hot with rage, even a century after.

We say to ourselves that such things could not be at the present day. We lay the flattering unction to our souls that there has been such a growth of humanitarian sentiment that the greediest of our profitmongers would not be guilty of the cruelties perpetrated by their class in the ages gone by.

But it seems, with the example of China staring us in the face, that the lust of wealth can be intimidated, but not educated. Given the opportunity, it will indulge its passion with all the unbridled ferocity of the past.

In the factories established in China by Western capitalists, women and children are again being exploited with murderous effects. In the cotton mills of Shanghai there are 15,000 female and juvenile workers, and only 500 men.

These wretched victims of the modern Moloch toil from 74 to 88 hours a week, under frightfully insanitary conditions, and the pay for women ranges from 5d. to 10d. a day.

Needless to say, enormous dividends are made by the firms that run these factories. The Ewo mill, which is owned by Jardine, Matheson and Co., an English combine, makes a profit of 57½ per cent. on the capital employed. The International Spinning Company, which is American, has realised 50 per cent. on its invested capital.

Such profits are from eight to ten times greater than those of the cotton industry in Lancashire, and six to eight times those of the American mills.

There is consequently a scramble to get a footing on Chinese soil. The great Boot and Shoe Trust, which controls 96 per cent. of the production in America, and 98 per cent. in England, has put up an experimental factory at Shanghai, and here first-class shoes have been turned out at a labor-cost of 2½d. a pair!

The Tobacco Trust has also started operations in China. In a very short time, by the exercise of the most unscrupulous and shameless methods, it has stamped out all native competitors, and to-day its Chinese profits are equal to 35 per cent. on the capital at stake.

A LOOMING DANGER

This attempt of European and American capitalists to capture the patient, industrious, much-enduring, rice-eating millions of China, and turn them into wage slaves who will count themselves passing rich on a shilling a day, is the real Yellow Peril.

The workers of Europe and America are discontented. They are enlightened and comparatively high-spirited.

Their demands for higher wages and better conditions are becoming more and more insistent. Not even with bludgeons and bayonets can they be beaten into a state of passive servitude.

But if the capitalists of the West can transfer their works to the East, and obtain control of the cheap and servile labor there, the Western workers will be confronted with a danger greater than any which has yet beset their path.

DOCUMENT NO. 8 7

Article by John Curtin in the Melbourne *Labor Call*, 22 October 1914.

BACK TO THE ABYSS
The Mailed Fist of Moloch in our Teeth

'Everywhere do I perceive a conspiracy of rich men seeking their own advantage in the name and pretence of the Commonwealth.' Sir Thomas More.

'We are going to suffer terribly in this war; whether we are in it, or whether we stand aside. Foreign trade is going to stop, not because the trade routes are closed, but because there is no trade at the other end'. Sir Edward Grey.

'There shall they rot. — Ambition's honored fools!
Yes, Honor decks the turf that wraps their clay!
Vain sophistry! in these behold the tools,
The broken tools that tyrants cast away.
By myriads, when they dare to pave their way.
With human hearts. To what? A dream alone.
Can despots compass aught that hails their sway?
Or can with truth one span of earth their own,
Save that wherein at last they crumble bone by bone?'

Byron.

THE EVIDENCE

Five profound aspects of social phenomena mark the later development of Capitalism. They are Industrial Monopoly, Militarism, the Problem of the Increased Cost of Living, the Universality of Social Unrest, and the remarkable progress in the Economic and Political Organisation of the Wage-workers. For the whole of the last decade, world-politics has been dominated by the driving force of economic chaos. Everywhere production has outgrown the assimilative capacity of the market. Each influential business interest has — in pursuance thereof — steadily sought to find for its surplus productions a dumping-ground outside the limits·of the exhausted area. Germany, France, Britain and America have relentlessly pursued a definitely planned policy of colonisation — not in order to meet any pressure of population at home, but to ease the increasingly urgent economic problem begotten of the inherent contradictions in the laws governing capitalist economy.

IMPERIALISM

The fact that America is not actually participating in the European blood-letting, is due to the venue being other than south of the equator. It further happens that while Britain, Germany, France, and, to a lesser extent, Belgium, have developed important and rival interests in Africa, they have been practically compelled to leave Southern America an open economic door to the United States. In more recent years the activity of the great powers in Asia tended to make the Pacific a potential centre of international disturbance, and was the outstanding influence hastening the entry of Australia into the maelstrom of militarism.

MONOPOLY AND MARKETS

Thus the mad fever for armaments has been derived from and nourished by the competition for oversea markets, made necessary by the advent of monopoly at home. In proportion as success attended the efforts of particular groups in this connection influence was brought to bear on the national, foreign, and colonial policy of each country, so that support and protection would be assured against hostile trade competitors, and, further − and equally important − facilities given to enable difficulties in the new area being effectively met. That is why America fought Spain, Britain the Transvaal Republics, Belgium despoiled the Congo, and the Australian Parliament enacted native labor ordinances in Papua. That is why the professions of universal peace, made by every responsible statesman in the world, were confirmed by the most staggering, aggressive preparations the wit of man could devise.

FINANCIAL DESPOTISM

The inexorable procession from cause to effect, has thrown an ever-increasing power into the hands of the men who operate the machinery of capitalist industry. To the extent that large scale manufacture rose . up from the ruins of the multitude of small shops, civilisation has evolved an economic despotism more absolute than is to be found in all the records of the race. In every field of industrial enterprise, the joint-stock corporation has gradually separated capital 'from the presence and direct control of its owners, and placed it at the disposal of big business men'. (J.A. Hobson)

These Napoleons of finance have thus gathered under their control the entire available investments of society. They decide where and when new industries shall commence, when dislocation or cessation shall occur. They bull, bear and hammer on Stock Exchanges, give advances and foreclose, gamble in futures, corner wool and wheat, determine the success or failure of national loans, and, in short, sit enthroned monarchs of the world, ruling with an icy sceptre, and decreeing disaster and death to all who say them nay.

WORKERS OF THE WORLD

It is this class of monetary experts who have controlled the cabinets of Europe. Another decade of uninterrupted working-class progress would have witnessed their political annihilation. Capitalism was drifting towards the rapids of revolution. In each country the social democracy was building from the base up the foundations of a new society. Strike on strike, agitation on agitation, and growth in the number of powerfully compacted industrial organisations was surely and persistently making the multitude a determined force. In Germany and France the Socialist parties were the largest separate political party in the Parliament. In Great Britain, Home Rule – the last of the issues left to an expiring Liberalism – was disappearing. The whole future was to be given to the discussion and determination of social problems.

WAR AND PROGRESS

Thus 'twas the beginning of the end. Only a vast human fratricide could meet the emergency and drive the populace back to its hole. Let the workers of the world slash and rend each other, revive the old national enmities, resurrect from the grave the racial hatreds, the beastly hunger for murder, the intoxication of blood, and the frightful horror of the shambles. 'Twill put back the clock of international solidarity, which alone the Capitalists fear. So humanity retires toward the chasm, out from which it climbed with bleeding feet and staggering steps. The day turns back to the night, even as our eyes are fixed on the noontide sun. But we will learn our lesson, and will not forget. Governments that know no method but that of musketry, must find in us uncompromising opponents. The political state has been the instrument of the great financiers. They have used it to our discomfiture and their own gain. It remains for the Social Democracy to realise definitely and decisively that the indispensible condition to the orderly progress of economic organisation and industrial solidarity is the conquest of the coercive authority of the law.

THE IMMEDIATE PROSPECT

Meanwhile, all the countries outside the actual theatre of battle will experience the economic paralysis inevitably due to the stoppage of commercial exchange. Australian wheat, wool and minerals are not sold to Europe for money — they are exchanged for machinery, textiles, metals, apparel of all descriptions, paper, timber, etc. Immediately Europe ceases exporting exchangeable products — more particularly the products constituting the raw materials of Australian manufacturers — our trade and our industry pulls up with a full stop. Even now unemployment is assuming appalling proportions. Thousands of men are out of work absolutely, and huge numbers are on partial time. To maintain the wage-standard in these circumstances is going to be a task of supreme difficulty. War is not only the assassin's trade, it is the exploiter's auxiliary. The condition of Europe after the Napoleonic wars was horrible. Following on the Franco-Prussian conflict ensued an epoch of working-class disaster, marked by penal legislation and unrestrained social tyranny. More recently the aftermath of the South African upheaval was but a confirmation of the retrograde influence war has on the social condition.

POVERTY AND THE POPULACE

So we are face to face with a period of dire distress. Wages will go down in proportion as work becomes scarce. All the characteristic associations of social impoverishment will become accentuated. Soon the streets will echo to the tramp of the hungry men, while wives and children weep in silence and sorrow. Private enterprise is about to add to the innumerable demonstrations it has given of its incapacity to serve popular needs.

Yet there are alternatives. Even in the midst of the worst that will occur, there will be food and homes and clothing, provided there is insistence that the organised State shall be responsible for their production. The states have complete control over domestic requirements. They can start sawmills — for there are plants in existence in forest areas, and merely waiting to do the work.

They can produce coal in abundance, for there are mines un-developed and men ready, they can take over the boot factories, the flour-mills, the bakeries and slaughter yards, and use the equip-ment private enterprise is unable to employ, in order that starvation and want may be effectually prevented. If it is a sound principle that the State shall be responsible for feeding, clothing and equipping the soldiers defending the nation, it is an equally valid proposition that it shall be responsible for the organisation with which communi-ties combat destitution and death within the gates. But they will not do it unless there is compulsion; for the State is the handmaiden of Moloch and will not interpose between the mailed fist and its victims, unless we prove greater even than Moloch. So all is not yet lost. There still remains the power of a united and alert democracy to save itself with courage and resource. There are not two ways. We have to choose finally, once and for all, between a bold and determined policy, negativing the interests of Capitalism, or continu-ing to hold to the timid ways monopoly would have us travel in its service.

DOCUMENT NO. 9 8

Article by Professor Chiang K'ang-hu [Kiang Kang Hu], National Secretary of the Socialist Party in China.
Source: *The Australian Worker*, 4 July 1918, p. 17.

Chiang K'ang-hu, born in 1883 (not, as sometimes stated, in 1885), was the founder of the Chinese Socialist Party which flourished in the short libertarian phase between 1911 and its brutal repression in the summer of 1913. At its peak, it probably had around 300,000 members in more than 200 branches within a radius of 300 km around Shanghai, as well as in places as far afield as Szechwan and Kwangtung.

Though, as the present document shows, his ideas in socialist theory were not highly developed, he held strong views on the equality of women, based on his reading of August Bebel's germinal *Die Frau und der Sozialismus* (Woman and Socialism), and he was an opponent of racism. His party had links with the Socialist International which insisted on the inclusion of the article, 'All organs of production should be publicly owned' in its programme. He was clearly a pioneering propagandist for socialist and egalitarian ideas. The Chinese Communist Party does not claim him as a predecessor.

He lived in the United States from 1913 to 1920, hence the spelling of his name used in the *Worker*. In 1921, he visited Russia. His later life included the bizarre attempt to convert the deposed Manchu emperor to socialism, as a result of which Chiang was accused of favouring a Manchu restoration. He became increasingly conservative and, by 1940, he held office in the Japanese-sponsored government of Wang Ching-wei. His literary and philosophic studies led him to find merit in the Greater East Asia Co-prosperity ideas. That does not detract from his earlier achievements.[1]

The text of this article, like much else in the earlier Australian working-class press, was obtained, it would seem, through regular contact with sympathetic·overseas publications.

CHINA AND THE SOCIAL REVOLUTION

China, too, has its Socialist Party. The following article by Kiang Kang Hu, National Secretary of the Socialist Party in China, is a timely reminder that even in that country the workers are waking up.

The idea of collectivism or Socialism is very old in China. It can be traced back to the very beginning of Chinese civilisation, over 4000 years ago.

When, about a decade ago, modern Socialist thought began to be propagated in China, it met with two sets of critics, each holding opposite views, yet each equally severe in their criticism of the new doctrine. One set said: 'Socialism – why, that is nothing new. We have had that for ages.' The other set said: 'Socialism is an importation. It is foreign to our soil. It may fit European conditions, but it certainly does not fit Chinese conditions.'

Both of these critics were partially correct, and yet, because of their narrow view, both were wrong. True, the traces of communistic thought are to be found in Chinese life and history for centuries. But their ideas are distinctly Utopian in their character and cannot be identified with modern scientific Socialism. True, likewise, was it at that time (a decade ago) that scientific or Marxian Socialism was an imported plant which could not flourish in Chinese soil. But China is changing. Machine production is rapidly displacing handicraft. Where yesterday stood the little cobbler shop, to-day the great shoe factory rears its ugly form. Where yesterday the coolie porter trotted with his burden, the automobile truck rushes on its way. Railroads have come, and power looms. This is the soil in which scientific Socialism will grow. Nothing can stop it.

The Chinese, like the whole human race, have natural collectivist leanings. If we mine into the mountain of Chinese philosophy, we will soon find a rich vein of collectivism running throughout, persisting throughout its entire length and breadth. Material enough is at hand to fill a bulky volume.

Greatest of all Chinese philosophers is Confucius. Says this sage: 'All mankind is a brotherhood. More than that, they are even as the parts of one body, of which you cannot injure the slightest without giving pain to the whole.' Again, he says: 'Equality is the ideal of society.' And again: 'The well-being and stability of a nation lie not in its wealth, but in the equal distribution of that wealth among its people.'

THE BEGINNING OF SOCIALISM IN CHINA

In the last decade, here and there, were to be found individuals and small groups scattered throughout the empire of China who studied and advocated humanitarianism, communism and Socialism. But these groups had no connection with one another, and their ideas, for the most part, were vague and misty.

Kiang Kang Hu, a professor at the University of Peking, was publishing a radical newspaper which had for its aim the introduction of new ideas into China. This paper translated and published portions of the works of Balzac, of Victor Hugo, Byron and Shelley, Goethe and Heine, and towards the end of its career some of the works of Peter Kropotkin, Karl Marx and August Bebel.

Kiang Kang Hu, thus coming into contact with Socialism, became interested and, finally, was converted to the new doctrine. He began an agitation for the freedom of woman immediately, and went on many lecture tours in the interest of Socialism.

In Shanghai, on July 10, 1911, at the Chang Shu Ho Gardens Kiang Kang Hu organised a Socialist Club, and on the same day the first Socialist paper in China, 'The Socialist Star', made its first appearance.

The Shih Hui Tong [Chung Kuo she-hui Tang], or Socialist Party, was the first political party as such in China. The Socialist Party, although not being composed of clear-cut Marxians, was nevertheless earnest and enthusiastic in its desire for the establishment of a Socialist republic. On November 5, 1911, the Socialist Party of China met in its first annual convention at Shanghai and adopted a preamble and a platform.

AN EIGHT PLANK PLATFORM

In considering the platform of the Socialist Party of China, we must remember the particular historic and economic conditions of that country. China is still partly submerged in the handicraft stage of economic development. Only portions of China have emerged into the machine process of production, or Capitalism. And this further fact must be borne in mind: China has an immense agricultural population, among whom there are a great many tenants and absentee landlords. Historically, China had just awakened from an age-long lethargic sleep, and was more or less bewildered by the white light of dawning day.

The eight planks of the platform were as follows:

(1) The establishment of a republican form of government.

(2) The wiping out of all racial differences.

(3) The abolition of all the remaining forms of feudal slavery and the establishment of the principle of equality before the law.

(4) The abolition of all hereditary estates.

(5) Free and universal school system, on co-educational lines, together with free text books and the feeding of school children.

(6) The abolition of all titles and castes.

(7) To levy taxes in the main upon land and to do away with all personal taxes.

(8) The abolition of the army and navy.

REVOLUTIONS DISASTROUS TO SOCIALISTS

The subsequent revolutions in China played havoc with the Socialists. The Secretary of the Party, Chen Ye Long, was beheaded on August 8. The Party headquarters at Peking were raided by the Government authorities and a decree of dissolution was issued against the Socialist Party. A similar decree was issued later.

After these decrees had been issued, the Socialist Party branches everywhere were forcibly dissolved. Many of the comrades were thrown in jail and a number were executed. The Party, as a unit, ceased to exist, although individuals secretly kept up a sporadic agitation.

But the Socialist movement in China will re-assemble its forces, and will fall in step with the great Red International and march with it to victory.

DOCUMENT NO. ~~10~~ 9

Letter from the Rt Hon W.M. Hughes, Prime Minister of Australia, to the Rt Hon David Lloyd George, British Prime Minister, dated 4 November 1919; and the second Draft Reply of the Foreign Office.
Source: Public Records Office (F. O. 371/3236, folios 402-14)

COMMONWEALTH OF AUSTRALIA

Prime Minister,
Australia House,
MOST SECRET   Strand, London, W.C.2.

4th November 1918.

My dear Prime Minister,
I desire to call your attention to the forecast of Japanese policy contained in extracts from an article (published in the *Times* 30th October) entitled *Peace Problems and the future of the Japanese Empire* by the Marquis Okuma who was Prime Minister of Japan at the outbreak of war.

I feel that in view of the cordial reception accorded to Prince Yorihito of Fushimi it is necessary to remind you of Australia's deeply rooted mistrust of Japan, and to enter an emphatic protest on behalf of the Commonwealth against Japan's right or even claim to the islands mentioned by Marquis Okuma, viz, the Marshalls, Caroline and Ladrones.

In order that you may understand more readily that Japan has neither right nor just claim to these islands, and what menace to the trade and national safety of Australia and the Empire is involved in the Marquis Okuma's claim I am setting out the following facts for your consideration:-

The extract from the *Times* referred to above, and enclosed herewith, contains the following:-

The Marshall, Caroline, and Ladrone Islands, which the Japanese occupy, are valueless to Japan but dangerous in the hands of Germany. As there is no reason why they should be given to a third Power, Japan must continue in possession of them.

The disposition of these islands is of great, and perhaps vital importance to Australia, and I therefore call attention to the subject in some detail.

Shortly after the outbreak of war, the Imperial authorities asked that an Australian Expeditionary Force should be despatched for the purpose of dealing with German possessions in the Pacific. The Force despatched in accordance with this request compelled the surrender of German New Guinea. This took place on the 17th September, and the first term of capitulation made to the Commandant of the Australian Force was:-

The name of German New Guinea includes the *whole of the German possessions in the Pacific Ocean lately administered from Rabaul.*

That definition includes all the German possessions in the Pacific except Samoa, which is the seat of a separate administration. There is, therefore, no doubt that the surrender to Australia comprised the Pelew, Caroline, Marianne, and Marshall groups as well as the German section of the New Guinea proper and the Bismarck Archipelago.

A London message of 13th October stated that in the course of a cruise in the Pacific in search of the German squadron the Japanese squadron discovered that Yap Wireless station had been repaired and used by the Germans, although it had since been destroyed again:

They (the Japanese) have temporarily occupied it, *but they are ready to hand it over to an Australian force.* On account of strategical importance island must be occupied by some force. Your Ministers will remember that it was originally intended that they should send force to occupy Yap, and they will no doubt agree that it is desirable to relieve Japanese as quickly as possible of the task of holding the island. *Japanese Government have therefore been informed it is intention of your Government to occupy Yap* and I am communicating with Admiralty as to provision of transport.

An Expeditionary Force was accordingly prepared in Australia, but on the 24th November and 3rd December, this instruction was countermanded, the cable from London stating:-

We consider it most convenient for strategic reasons to allow Japan to remain in occupation for the present, leaving the whole question of future to be settled at the end of the war.

In accordance with the terms of surrender of the German possessions, Australia has established a military administration in the islands occupied by Australian Forces. Japan followed the same course, at least until July 1918.

On the 6th July, however, the following paragraph appeared in the *Times*.

TOKYO. July 7th. It has been decided to institute civil administration in the South Pacific Islands in Japanese occupation. Reuter.

It is not known whether any steps have been taken in pursuance of this announcement.

The foregoing facts demonstrate:-

(a) That the actual surrender of the German Islands north of the Equator was made to Australian forces
(b) That the present occupation of these islands by Japan is purely provisional
(c) That such occupation does not in any way conclude the question of the ultimate destiny of the islands.

The statement of the Marquis Okuma is that the islands mentioned are 'valueless to Japan'. If this is actually the case there can be no objection on the part of Japan to give them up to Great Britain for administration by Australia.

The Marquis goes on to say that the islands are 'dangerous in the hands of Germany'. The Marquis reaches his conclusion that Japan must continue in possession of them by stating that 'there is no reason why they should be given to a third power'.

I submit the following additional reasons which commend themselves to me as being very weighty in support of the proposition that these islands should be entrusted to Great Britain for administration by Australia.

The islands are most important to Australia from the point of view both of defence and of possible offence.

They contain many harbours, several of which are capable of holding very large fleets.

In British hands the islands could be provided with wireless stations, and would serve as advance bases for aeroplane and seaplane patrol.

Seaplanes could be based on vessels which could be withdrawn from an approaching enemy. Seaplanes and aeroplanes could be used not only for purposes of observation, but also for bombing craft. The situation of the islands in relation to Australia appears on the enclosed map. Truk, in the centre of the Carolines, is about

1,700 miles from Townsville, Queensland. It is 1,920 miles from Yokohama.

An air patrol based on these islands would enable Australia to obtain the following information in the event of an attack from the north:-

(a)   Direction of attack - whether to the East or West of Australia.
(b)   Probable date of arrival of hostile forces off Australia.
(c)   Strength of enemy forces.

This information would be of the highest value and importance, as it would enable Australia to make suitable dispositions of naval and, if necessary, military forces to the East or West of Torres Straits, as required; would give time to establish a patrol of the Straits, and to guard the openings between the islands to the north with cruisers, seaplanes, and aeroplanes.

If, on the other hand, these islands were in foreign hands, Australia might lose all the advantages I have mentioned. The islands could serve as possible enemy bases and as points for the secret concentration of large naval and military forces, and all the consequential advantages would accrue to the armed forces so using them.

In the event of offensive action by Australia becoming necessary, the islands would afford to the enemy all the advantages already mentioned of advance observation posts.

The possession of the islands by an enemy would probably halve the number of days available to Australia for mobilisation, and would make it necessary to maintain much stronger naval and military forces, in order to secure adequate protection at alternative threatened points. The annual increase in cost to Australia might well involve many millions of pounds.

America has a keen interest in the decision reached upon this subject. The Pelew islands, it will be observed upon reference to the map, are very close to the Philippines, lying due East of Mindanao. In the Pelew islands there is a harbour at Babeldoab which can shelter an immense fleet. These islands would form an admirable advance base for operations either against the Phillippines, Dutch East Indies, or the North West Coast of Australia.

I am aware of course that certain communications relating to these islands have passed between the British and Commonwealth Governments, and certain conversations took place between the representatives of Japan and the British Government in 1916 at some of which I myself was present. But since then, much water has run under the bridges, and I need not remind you what Japan's attitude towards the Empire in this war has been.

I am sure you quite realise that had the German offensive of March 21st been successful, we could hardly have looked for much help, to put the case at its best, from Japan. As to her present attitude I need only refer you to the Foreign Office No. 199, Nov. 1st cable, which shows quite clearly what Japan's purpose in Siberia really is.

It only remains to remind you once more that Australia profoundly distrusts Japan, that its national welfare and its trade are alike seriously menaced by Japan. The recognition of Japan's claims to these islands will enable her to pursue much more effectively her policy which is directed towards securing for herself the trade which Britain and Australia have built up.

I have only to express the hope that you will make it clear to Japan that the recognition of her claim to the islands mentioned by the Marquis Okuma may be raised at the Peace Conference, but meanwhile cannot be raised.

Yours sincerely,

(sgnd) W. M. HUGHES

The Rt Hon The Prime Minister,
10 Downing Street,
London.

DRAFT

PRIME MINISTER TO MR HUGHES

[Marked:] *Cancelled but keep for reference P.R.*

[Endorsed:] *Copy private and secret to Mr Long. Perhaps it would be better to ask the Prime Ministers Private Sec. to send Mr Hughes letter and this proposed reply to Mr Long.*

November 1918.

MOST SECRET

I have given my careful consideration to your most secret letter of the 4th instant calling my attention to the forecast of Japanese policy contained in extracts from an article by Marquis Okuma entitled *Peace Problems and the future of the Japanese Empire*, and published in the *Times* of October 30th last.

2. I am of course aware of the distrust of Japan which prevails in Australia, but, in view of the official assurance given to the Japanese Govt by H.M.G. on the 14th of February 1917 after consultation with, and with the consent of the Govts of the Commonwealth and New Zealand, in circumstances with which you are acquainted, I had hardly anticipated that you would come forward at this juncture with a protest on behalf of the Commonwealth against Japan's right or even claim to the former German possessions in the Marshall, Caroline and Ladrone Islands.

3. The destruction of the enemy bases and ships in the Pacific was carried out by the close cooperation of the Allied forces. Although the German Governor of New Guinea included all the German possessions in the Pacific in the terms of his surrender to the Australian force in October 1914, the Japanese Govt contended that the actual surrender of the islands North of the Equator had been obtained by the Japanese naval forces, and it at once became evident that the Japanese Govt and public had no intention of evacuating them. In Feb and March 1915 copies of correspondence on the subject of the Japanese claims were communicated to the Commonwealth and New Zealand Govts by Mr Harcourt with an assurance that up to that time no other verbal or written communications had passed of a nature to commit H.M.G.

4. Baron Ishii, when on his way to Tokyo in Aug 1915 to assume the portfolio of Foreign Affairs, urged the claims of Japan to the

islands in their occupation but was informed by Sir E. Grey that
H.M.G. were bound by agreement to enter no such engagement
and that occupations of territory would have to be regarded
as provisional until the end of the war.

5. I need not remind you that in your conversations with Lord
Grey and the Japanese Ambassador in March and May 1916
on the question of the preliminary conditions for Australia's
adhesion to the Anglo-Japanese Commercial Treaty, you made
a point of Japan being excluded from Australian coast-wise trade
and accepting the Commonwealth definition thereof as including
all islands in the Pacific which are now or may hereafter be
British possessions', and that you acquiesced in Japan claiming
a similar definition of her coastwise trade with the islands in her
occupation. It would seem therefore that you at that time contemplated the eventual retention by Japan of the German islands
North of the Equator.

6. In Feb 1916, at the urgent request of the Admiralty, the
Japanese Govt were invited to lend their naval assistance in
the Mediterranean as well as in the Indian Ocean and Malacca
Straits. It was granted in April for the Indian Ocean and Malacca
Straits. In December the Admiralty asked that Japanese cruisers
be sent to the Cape to operate against enemy raiders in the
South Atlantic and Indian Oceans and renewed the request for
Japanese destroyers for the Mediterranean asking that the Japanese
Govt be strongly pressed to acquiesce. These requests were complied
with early in Feb 1917.

7. The Japanese Govt, however, before acceding to our applications
for naval assistance, and pretexting the necessity of strengthening
their hands against Japanese opposition to such a course, approached
H.M.G. in January 1917 with a view to obtaining an assurance
of their willingness to support Japan's claims at a future Peace
Conference to the disposal of Germany's rights in Shantung and
possessions in the Pacific Islands North of the Equator. To meet
the previous objection made by Sir E. Grey, they referred to the
recent publication of the Allies' assent to the occupation   of
Constantinople by Russia and the signature of a special agreement
in connection with the entry of Italy into the war, and stated
that they proposed to approach the French and Russian Govts
with a similar request.

8. Mr Long communicated this demand by Tel on Feb 1st and
2nd to the Govts of the Commonwealth and New Zealand, and
explained that H.M.G. were very unwilling to give any pledge
to Japan before peace negotiations and doubted whether they
were justified in so doing without obtaining the consent of their
Allies, but that the Admiralty were very anxious to obtain immediate
Japanese naval assistance in the South Atlantic and Mediterranean.
H.M.G. therefore desired to be in a position to give some undertaking showing willingness to meet the wishes of Japan as regards
the German islands North of the Equator. It would be practically
impossible to induce Japan to surrender them and we should be
giving up nothing of our own by recognizing her claim. The
assent of the Dominion Govts was therefore asked in the event of
H.M.G. being unable to avoid giving some such pledge to Japan
before the Peace Conference. In any case no assurance would be
given without obtaining a corresponding assurance from Japan
as to our retention of the German Pacific colonies South of the
Equator. Mr Massey saw and approved the terms of this Tel before
despatch.

9. In communicating to the Commonwealth and New Zealand
Govts on Feb 5th the reply of the Japanese Govt acceding to our
requests for naval assistance and again referring to their wish for
an assurance, Mr Long added the following considerations to those
previously submitted to the two Govts. As well as useful assistance
to our Admiralty the Japanese Govt had rendered great service
to ourselves and the Russians in supplying guns and munitions of
war. We attached importance to the continuance of this help and
it was also necessary to frustrate the efforts that Germany had
been and was still making to detach Japan from the Allies. Any
answer which could be interpreted as unfavourable to the aspirations
of Japan would inevitably react on the general attitude of Japan
and adversely affect the general course of the war.

10. The New Zealand Govt replied on Feb 5th concurring with
the view expressed by Mr Massey.

11. The Commonwealth Govt replied on Feb 7th to Mr Long's
Tels of the 1st and 5th, stating that you had had several conversations
in England with the Secs of State for the Colonies and Foreign
Affairs and with the Japanese Ambassador on the subject the
delicacy and importance of which was fully realized by the

Commonwealth Govt. As explained by you in London Australia would not object to Japan's occupancy of the Pacific Islands North of the Equator, except one or two small ones on or near the line such as Nauru and Ocean Island. The Commonwealth Govt would carefully abstain from saying or doing anything likely to strain the relations of H.M.G. with Japan either in regard to the future partition of the Pacific or in regard to trade. In the event of your attending the War Conference you would represent the views of the Commonwealth.

12. Mr Long replied on the 8th of Feb asking whether, if H.M.G. found it impossible to defer the question until the Conference, he could take it that the Commonwealth Govt agreed to some such pledge as was referred to in his Tel of Feb 1st being given to Japan, and asking to what islands north of the Equator you referred to as being exceptions to the general rule. Your reply telegraphed on Feb 10th was to the effect that there was no objection to some such pledge being given and that you did not know the names of any Islands slightly North of the Equator, Nauru and Ocean Islands being South of it.

13. Mr Balfour accordingly informed the Japanese Ambassador on February 14th that H.M. Ambassador at Tokyo had been instructed to make the following statement to the Japanese Govt:-

His Majesty's Govt accede with pleasure to the request of the Japanese Govt for an assurance that they will support Japan's claims in regard to the disposal of Germany's rights in Shantung and in possessions in islands North of the Equator, on the occasion of a Peace Conference, it being understood that the Japanese Govt will, in the eventual peace settlement, treat in the same spirit Great Britian's claims to the German islands South of the Equator.

14. The Japanese Govt declared in their official acknowledgement of this assurance that they would have no hesitation in supporting the claims of H.M. Govt with regard to the German islands South of the Equator.

15. The French, Russian, Italian and United States Govts were informed that this assurance had been given to Japan.

16. * I think it is clear from the above that H.M. Govt are committed to support Japan's claims at the Peace Conference to the Pacific Islands North of the Equator, and that they cannot now or at the Conference go back on their official assurance without incurring the charge of committing a gross breach of faith, with all the consequences to Anglo-Japanese relations.

17. If objections were raised by any other Power at the Conference to the Japanese remaining in possession of the German islands North of the Equator, it would probably be on a general plea of 'no annexations' and would equally apply to our retention of the German possessions South of the Equator.

* In the first F.O. draft reply to Hughes, this section includes the autograph amendment by Balfour, who had succeeded Grey as Foreign Secretary, printed in the left-hand column and the part crossed out by him, as shown in the right-hand column:

It is clear that H.M. Govt ~~cannot~~ neither now, nor at the Peace Conference, go back on this official assurance without committing a breach of faith ~~with -serious- prejudice -to- their good- name -in -the East-and-to-Anglo-Japanese-relations. -You -will- doubtless agree -with- me -in- the -view -that -it -is essential-that the British Empire should preserve -a- united- front- at -the- Peace Conference; - and - I - think - that- any action-of- the nature-suggested- by you would play into-the hands of those who may- seek -at -the- Conference -to-create dissentions - within- the - Empire. - - -~~ If successful objection were made from a foreign quarter to the Japanese retaining possession of the German Pacific Islands North of the Equator, it would probably be on the plea of 'no annexations' and would equally apply to our retention of the islands South of the Equator.

[of which no Australian Govt would wish them to be guilty. I am confident that you will not assist the enemies of the Empire by exposing before the nations in council a difference of opinion at a point with regard to which Britain has obviously no selfish interest, and the honour of the two great Australasian Dominions is not less pledged than that of the Mother Country.

[Let me further point out that if]

18. I do not think that either the Japanese Govt or the Japanese public would endorse Marquis Okuma's statement that the islands North of the Equator are of no value to Japan. The claims of the Japanese Govt above referred to and the attitude of the Japanese Press quite dispose of that suggestion. It would be a mistake to attach too much importance to Marquis Okuma's statements, though he is one of the Elder Statesmen and was Prime Minister at the outbreak of war. He is known for his indiscretions in speeches and newspaper articles.

19. It is important that we should approach the Conference with a united front and that we should refrain from any action, such as you suggest, which would be playing into the hands of those who may seek to create dissensions within the Empire, and might result in depriving the Commonwealth and New Zealand of the German possessions South of the Equator, as well as further embittering their relations with Japan. To encourage the claims of Australia to the Islands in Japanese occupation would, in my opinion, be simply preparing a gratuitous disappointment for Australia and creating unnecessary friction with Japan, which latter the Commonwealth Govt under-took to avoid.

DOCUMENT NO. 11 | D

Pronouncement by the Hon. John Curtin, Prime Minister of Australia, on 27 December 1941.
Source: *Digest of Decisions and Announcements and important speeches by the Prime Minister*, No. 13, pp. 11 - 13.

STATE OF THE WAR

FACING 1942

That reddish veil which o'er the face
of night-hag East is drawn . . .
Flames new disaster for the race?
Or can it be the dawn?

So wrote Bernard O'Dowd. I see 1942 as a year in which we shall know the answer. I would, however, that we provide the answer. We can and we will. Therefore I see 1942 a year of immense change in Australian life.

The Australian Government's policy has been grounded on two facts. One is that the war with Japan is not a phase of the struggle with the Axis Powers, but is a new war. The second is that Australia must go on to a war footing. Those two facts involve two lines of action — one in the direction of external policy as to our dealings with Britain, the United States, Russia, the Netherlands East Indies and China in the higher direction of war in the Pacific; the second is the re-shaping, in fact, the revolutionizing, of the Australian way of life until a war footing is attained, quickly, efficiently and without question.

As the Australian Government enters 1942, it has behind it a record of realism in respect of foreign affairs. I point to the forthright declaration in respect of Finland, Hungary and Rumania which was followed, with little delay, by a declaration of war against those countries by the democracies. We felt that there could be no half-measures in our dealings with the Soviet when that nation was being assailed by the three countries mentioned. Similarly, we put forward that a reciprocal agreement between Russia and Britain should be negotiated to meet an event of aggression by Japan. Our suggestion was then regarded, wrongly as time has proved, to be premature.

Now, with equal realism, we take the view that while the determination of military policy is the Soviet's business, we should be able to look forward with reason to aid from Russia against Japan. We look for a solid and impregnable barrier of democracies against the three Axis Powers and we refuse to accept the dictum that the Pacific struggle must be treated as a subordinate segment of the general conflict. By that is not meant that any one of the other theatres of war is of less importance than the Pacific, but that Australia asks for a concerted plan evoking the greatest strength at the democracies' disposal determined upon hurling Japan back.

The Australian Government, therefore, regards the Pacific struggle as primarily one in which the United States and Australia must have the fullest say in the direction of the democracies' fighting plan. Without any inhibitions of any kind, I make it quite clear that Australia looks to America, free of any pangs as to our traditional links or kinship with the United Kingdom. We know the problems that the United Kingdom faces. We know the constant threat of invasion. We know the dangers of dispersal of strength. But we know, too, that Australia can go and Britain can still hold on. We are, therefore, determined that Australia shall not go and shall exert all our energies towards the shaping of a plan, with the United States as its keystone, which will give to our country some confidence of being able to hold out until the tide of battle swings against the enemy. Summed up, Australian external policy will be shaped towards obtaining Russian aid and working out, with the United States as the major factor, a plan of Pacific strategy along with British, Chinese and Dutch forces.

Australian internal policy has undergone striking changes in the past few weeks. These, and those that will inevitably come before 1942 is far advanced, have been prompted by several reasons. In the first place, the Commonwealth Government found it exceedingly difficult to bring the Australian people to a realization of what, after two years of war, our position had become. Even the entry of Japan bringing a direct threat in our own waters was met with a subconscious view that the Americans would deal with the short-sighted, under-fed and fanatical Japanese.

The announcement that no further appeals would be made to the Australian people and the decisions that followed were motivated by psychological factors. They had an arresting effect. They awakened in the somewhat lackadaisical Australian mind the attitude that was imperative if we were, to save ourselves, to enter an all-in effort in the only possible manner. That experiment of psychology was eminently successful and we commence 1942 with a better realization by a greater number of Australians of what the war means than in the whole preceding two years.

The decisions were prompted by other reasons, all related to the necessity of getting on to a war footing, and the results so far achieved have been most heartening — especially in respect of production and conservation of stocks. I make it clear that the experiment undertaken was never intended as one to awaken Australian patriotism or sense of duty. Those qualities have been ever present; but the response to leadership and direction had never been requested of the people and desirable talents and untapped resources had lain dormant.

Our task for 1942 is stern. The Government is under no illusions as to 'something cropping up' in the future. The nadir of our fortunes in this struggle, as compared with 1914-1918, has yet to be reached. Let there be no mistake about that. The position Australia faces internally far exceeds in potential and sweeping dangers anything that confronted us in 1914-1918.

The year 1942 will impose supreme tests. These range from resistance to invasion to deprivation of more and more amenities — not only amenities of peace-time but those enjoyed in two years of war. Australians must realize that to place the nation on a war footing every citizen must place himself, his private and business affairs, his entire mode of living on a war footing. The civilian way of life cannot be any less rigorous; can contribute no less than that which the fighting men have to follow.

I demand that Australians everywhere realize that Australia is now inside the fighting lines. Australian governmental policy will be directed strictly on those lines. We have to regard our country and its 7,000,000 people as though we were a nation, and a people with the enemy hammering at our frontier. Australians must be perpetually on guard — on guard against the possibility of any hour, without warning, of raid or invasion; on guard against spending money or doing anything that cannot be justified; on guard against hampering by disputation or idle, irresponsible chatter, the decisions of the Government taken for welfare of all.

All Australia is the stake in this war. All Australia must stand

together to hold that stake. We face a powerful, ably-led and unbe-
lievably courageous foe. We must match the enemy accordingly. We
shall match him accordingly.

DOCUMENT NO. 12 11

Parliamentary Statement, on 20 October 1960, by the Rt Hon R.G. Menzies, Prime Minister of Australia and Minister for External Affairs, on his return from the 15th General Assembly of the United Nations.
Source: *Commonwealth Parliamentary Debates* [of Australia], HR 20:2264-74

I arrived at the United Nations General Assembly on the afternoon of Friday, 30th September. The general debate was on. President Soekarno spoke for two hours. He circulated a copy of his speech. The speech consisted of 66 pages of foolscap. There was an added slip circulated. It was marked 'Vital', and was to be inserted at page 65. This sheet contained the terms of the proposed five-power resolution, of which I became aware for the first time, the five powers being Ghana, India, the United Arab Republic, Yugoslavia and Indonesia. The terms of the proposed resolution were these —

The General Assembly
Deeply concerned with the recent deterioration in international relations which threatens the world with grave consequences
Aware of the great expectancy of the world that this Assembly will assist in helping to prepare the way for the easing of world tension
Conscious of the grave and urgent responsibility that rests on the United Nations to initiate helpful efforts
Requests, as a first urgent step, the President of the United States of America and the Chairman of the Council of Ministers of the Union of Soviet Socialist Republics to renew their contacts interrupted recently so that their declared willingness to find solutions of the outstanding problems by negotiation may be progressively implemented.

For some reason my distinguished friend, the Prime Minister of India, rose at the end of President Soekarno's speech and formally moved the resolution. I was, I confess, greatly concerned about the terms of the resolution, not because of its opening paragraphs, with which everybody would agree, but because of the operative clause, that operative clause being the request that the President of the United States of America - named as such - and the Chairman of the Council of Ministers of the Union of Soviet Socialist Republics should renew their contacts.
That was a very, very important proposal. First of all, it had

defects and it had dangers. 'To renew their contacts, interrupted recently' was a clear reference, if to anything, back to the Paris conference when there was to be a summit conference, when the four people were to meet. That was the only period of interruption, and the contacts which were interrupted were interrupted at Paris when those four great men were to meet. Yet, Sir, the resolution moved by Mr Nehru did not call for a summit meeting of the four; it called for something quite different. It did not call on the four great men, the four responsible men, the four men who led atomic powers, to meet again; it called on two people out of the four. That seemed to me to lend colour to what I believe to be the false but not uncommon propaganda that the real world issue is between the Soviet Union and the United States of America.

The first real step was to get the four atomic powers, the four powers which have, beyond all understanding, the great powers of peace and war in their hands, to meet. I would have thought that that was the first thing — to get those four people to come together, not because of some oddities about Great Britain or the United States or France - not at all - but because they happened to be the people who had atomic weapons and who, therefore, had enormous powers of life and death for all the rest of us in the world. Something could come, from my point of view, of a meeting between the four; nothing could come of a resolution which said that two out of the four ought to meet together.

That resolution was moved, and then the distinguished Prime Minister of Great Britain, the Right Honorable Harold Macmillan, and I - he very naturally, and I by some chance - were invited to come to Washington to see the President of the United States early on Sunday morning, 2nd October. Very naturally we agreed. We said we would go.

On Saturday, 1st October, I had lunch with Mr Macmillan and with Lord Home. We had a little talk and we then flew to Washington. I dined with them at the Australian Embassy, with our Ambassador, Mr Howard Beale. We dined, and we talked about these matters. Like me, they were troubled about the resolution — and they were troubled about it for very obvious reasons. Straight-out support of the resolution would be travelling, we all thought, in the wrong direction. Here was a resolution which said, 'Let two people get together and then everything may be arranged'. But, on the other hand, straight-out opposition – if we all voted 'No' – would be misinterpreted. People would look at the first three or four recitals in the resolution, all in favour of peace, and then, if we voted 'No', we would be told that we did not want peace. Therefore, straight-out opposition would be misinterpreted.

That was a very difficult problem, Sir. I suggested on the Saturday night that an amendment in positive terms might be put, and my distinguished friends, Mr Macmillan and Lord Home, having heard what I had to say about this matter, said that they would like to think it over. On the next morning at 9.30 – a rather intolerable hour on Sunday morning – we went to the White House. My former colleague, our distinguished Ambassador, Mr Beale, was there, and we had a close discussion – President Eisenhower; Mr Herter, the Secretary of State; Mr Macmillan, the distinguished Prime Minister of Great Britain; Lord Home, the Foreign Secretary, and myself.

I think, Sir, that I might be allowed to say that that morning, and under those circumstances, the Americans were worried about the position that had been created by the five-power motion. The President himself had received letters from the five powers – India, Indonesia, Ghana, Yugoslavia and the United Arab Republic – enclosing the resolution. The President had been working on a draft reply setting out reasons why a personal and special meeting with Khrushchev was not, in the then atmosphere, acceptable. I would not wish honorable members to believe that this was a rather dour attitude on the part of the United States of America. All who have witnessed these things know that Khrushchev had made it just about as difficult as anybody could make it for a meeting to occur.

In the course of the talks on the Sunday morning, I said – and let me say at once that I take full responsibility for this – that I thought it quite useless to be coming down in favour of a resolution which, on the face of it, did some wrong things, as I understood them, or to be coming down flat-footed against the resolution, in which case a lot of people would misinterpret the vote and misinterpret the views. Therefore, for better or for worse, and I still think for better, I said, 'This kind of resolution is not one that you can flat-footedly oppose or flat-footedly support. Why do we not have an amendment of this resolution which will bring the whole of the United Nations back to the realities of the position?'

I say this, because I understand that there are some people who think that I was a sort of 'fall guy' — I think that is the term. On the contrary. I have great pride in being the Prime Minister of this country and in having views of my own on behalf of my country. Therefore, I said, 'Well, why not have an amendment? Why meet this thing full face? Let us have an amendment which in positive terms will say what we believe to be the truth?' We had a discussion about that. I do not want anybody to believe that they all agreed at once with what I had to say, but at least I said it.

I want honorable members to understand that the United States of America was itself deeply concerned about this matter. It knew that to have a resolution passed which put the whole onus on the President of the United States was wrong. The Americans knew that this was putting the whole situation out of balance. They knew, as I believe, that this idea that the whole conflict in the world is between the United States and the Soviet Union is a false idea, a wicked idea; something that has been devised and promulgated by people for no good purpose. Therefore, they were deeply concerned. So, Sir, after an hour and a half of discussion that morning, I said that I thought we ought to have an amendment. I did not care very much who moved it, but we ought to have an amendment. There we were — the President of the United States of America; Mr Herter, the Secretary of State; Mr Macmillan, the Prime Minister of the United Kingdom; Lord Home, the United Kingdom Foreign Minister; and myself. We were all discussing this matter to and fro.

In the meantime, President Eisenhower had received a letter from the five powers, signed by Dr Nkrumah of Ghana, and containing the resolution, about which I will say something later. The President himself had been, for the previous 24 hours, discussing with his advisers the problem of how this letter ought to be answered. For better or for worse, for richer or for poorer, I came in with idea that you could not deal with a problem of this kind by saying 'Yes' or 'No'; that you might deal with it by saying, 'Here is a positive proposal'. And the positive proposal that I had to make was that there ought to be a renewed effort to get a Summit meeting of the Four — not some theoretical meeting of the Two, but a positive Summit meeting of the Four.

We debated that and they said, 'Well, do you have an amendment in mind?' I said, 'Yes'. They said, 'What is it?' I indicated it in a rather vague way, and said, 'All right, I will go away and draft it.'

This is very interesting. We finished at 11 o'clock on Sunday morning. I went off, having promised to draft an amendment and to send it to the Secretary of State, Mr Herter, at lunch-time, and to Mr Macmillan and Lord Home. They got it by lunch-time. There it was. With some small amendment, that was the amendment that I moved in the United Nations General Assembly. They received it at lunch-time, and after lunch we met at the British Embassy — the British Prime Minister, Lord Home, Mr Herter and I. They had the terms of this proposed amendment. By the time we had talked it out on the Sunday, I understood — I have no reason to believe now that I had been wrong — that they approved of it.

I think it is proper, Sir, to tell this House in my own country what the proposal was. In the early part of the five-power resolution there had been three paragraphs with which nobody could quarrel. My amendment was designed, not to omit the earlier paragraphs, which were quite good, but to omit the last paragraph. The amendment was in these terms —

Omit the last paragraph of the draft resolution submitted by Ghana, India, Indonesia, the United Arab Republic and Yugoslavia (A/4522), and substitute therefor the following:

I must ask honorable members to forgive me for this strange form of words used in the United Nations —

RECALLING that a Conference between the President of the United States of America, the Chairman of the Council of Ministers of the Union of Soviet Socialist Republics, the President of the French Republic and the Prime Minister of the United Kingdom of Great Britain and Northern Ireland was arranged to take place in Paris on 17 May 1960, in order that these four leaders should examine matters of particular and major concern for their four nations,

I think that is something that every honorable member would agree with: Recalling the fact that the four great leaders had met, not to discuss all the problems of the world, but to discuss matters on which they, as the leaders of the four great atomic powers, might have something to say. The amendment continued —

RECALLING FURTHER that the Conference did not actually begin its work,
NOTING that the President of the United States of America, the President of the French Republic and the Prime Minister of the United Kingdom of Great Britain and Northern Ireland thereupon made a public statement

n the terms following:

I quote the words of three out of the four —

'They regret that these discussions, so important for world peace, could not take place. For their part, they remain unshaken in their conviction that all outstanding international questions should be settled not by the use or threat of force, but by peaceful means through negotiation. They themselves remain ready to take part in such negotiations at any suitable time in the future.'

I think it is not a bad idea to recall the minds of honorable members to the fact that three out of the four leaders of the powers at Paris used those words, and meant them. I went on from that to say in my amendment —

Believing that much benefit for the world could arise from a co-operative meeting of the Heads of Government of these four nations in relation to those problems which particularly concern them, —

Obviously, those problems were, for the atomic powers, Berlin and all those things which are flash-points of international affairs —

BELIEVING FURTHER that progress towards the solution of those problems would be a material contribution to the general work for peace of the United Nations,

URGES that such a meeting should be held at the earliest practicable date.

I would have expected, Sir, speaking in my own Parliament and among my own people, that nothing would be said against that view. Here it was. Here was a call to the four great powers to sit down together and try to make the world more safe for ordinary people.

I put in my amendment. That was on a Monday. At that moment, it was well known that Khrushchev was not going to meet Eisenhower — unless, of course, Eisenhower went through the remarkable performance of apologizing about the U2 incident and withdrawing all his claims about the RB47 incident — and that the President himself had said that he was not going to meet Khrushchev on those terms. Therefore, the position was that the current President of the United States, and the current — if that is the right word — head of the Soviet Union were not willing to meet personally without conditions which mutually were completely unacceptable. On top of all that — and let us be sensible about this matter — at the very time at which we were having this debate, a new President of the United States was about to be elected, and what he would do or say, who would know?

I want to pause here, Sir, to make a few observations, because I have been told by my friends — nobody is so frank as a friend — that some complaints have been voiced in Australia. I have tried to understand them, because I am really a tolerably broad-minded fellow. I understand that the first complaint is that I was being used by the United States and the United Kingdom, which happen to be the two greatest powers in the free world and our most powerful and devoted friends. I hope I have answered that complaint. For better or for worse, the proposal for an amendment was mine, not theirs. I thought, in my new-found innocence, that Australia was entitled to a mind of its own. Indeed, I have been told by some of my friends opposite in the past that their great complaint is that we do not have a mind of our own. As I have said, I thought we were entitled to a mind of our own. Believing that a certain course was right, I advocated it. I need not add any words to that.

In the second place, I gather from the critics that, in the interests of Australia, I should have preferred pleasing the five nations which I have named by supporting something with which I strongly disagreed — and with which I utterly disagree at this moment — to acting in concert with our most powerful and most unambiguous friends. If that is the price of admiralty, then I resign from admiralty. I have learnt, perhaps, very little in my life, but I have learnt to know who are our friends.

Contrary to my expectation, it was ruled that the five-power resolution and my amendment should be discussed separately from the general debate, on Wednesday morning, 5th October. My major speech — which appears to have missed fire here, for some reason or other — had been listed for the afternoon. Therefore, unlike anybody else at the United Nations, I had to make two separate speeches instead of one. Therefore, on Wednesday morning — knowing that on Wednesday afternoon I had to make my most considerable speech — I moved my amendment.

At question time this morning, when I was treated so kindly, my distinguished friend, the Deputy Leader of the Opposition (Mr Whitlam) said to me, 'I would like to know what you said on your amendment'. I want to say at once that I have arranged that the full text of what I said will be made available to members, because, unhappily, it does not appear to have been rather widely reported. I will permit myself the luxury of quoting a few of the things that I said that morning to the cold and unresponsive audience of the United Nations General Assembly. I think I should do so. A motion had been put down in the name of five powers, and I was moving an amendment. Among other things, I said —

Let me say at once, that nobody can more warmly appreciate the high motives of the sponsors of the resolution than I do. They feel, no doubt, that it would be a bad thing if all the Heads of State and Heads of Government departed from this Assembly without leaving behind some visible evidence in the shape of a decision. They believed, no doubt, that the people of the world would be disappointed and perhaps disillusioned if we all departed and nothing at all emerged. They therefore introduced this resolution and part of its purpose, as it has been explained to me, was to try to take advantage of the presence in North America at the same time of President Eisenhower and Mr Khrushchev. But if I believe, as I do, that the effect of the resolution, if carried, would be undesirable, then I am bound to say so.

I hope that honorable members will realize that that was an authentic Australian voice upon this matter. I went on to talk about the conference in Paris — the conference which did not occur, the conference which broke down because of Khrushchev's attitude. I said —

Many of us had thought that the discussions about nuclear tests could have been brought within reach of finality.

I still believe that. I continued —

After all, the great nuclear powers were not so widely separated on this issue that some effective lead could not have been given. But the Paris conference failed even to begin, because the leader of the Soviet Union would not participate. I have my own view about his stated reasons, but at this moment I would not desire to debate them.

This was said in the morning.

The material and relevant fact was that the leaders of the United States, the United Kingdom and France, promptly made a statement in which they said:-

I trust that this will be remembered for years, but not, I hope, with tears —

'They regret that these discussions, so important for world peace, could not take place. For their part, they remain unshaken in their conviction that all outstanding international questions should be settled not by the use or threat of force, but by peaceful means through negotiation. They themselves remain ready to take part in such negotiations at any suitable time in the future.'

My speech continued —

This, it will be agreed, was a fair enough proposition, good-tempered an tenacious in the cause of peace. Should it be rejected now? If we have nov reached a point in our discussions when we feel that talks of this kind shoul proceed, why should we not say so? Why should we, by carrying the five nation resolution, dismiss the United Kingdom and France from the first act?

Then I went on to say this, and it is worth remembering —

Mr Nehru himself has frankly stated that there are serious limits to th usefulness of bilateral talks; but what I would wish to know is whether an valid reason can be advanced for supposing that in some way the Presiden of the United States was the stumbling block, and that therefore in an renewed discussions he should be the one leader of what we call the Wester World to be brought under persuasion or pressure.

My own view is that we should encourage the resumption of these summi talks. No doubt, a meeting at the Summit cannot be arranged quickly or withou preparation. We shall have to feel our way forward, and a way may be found But it will not be found in the next few days, and I doubt whether it car be found by trying to rush at it. The Australian amendment reflects what I believe is the view of the majority here, that we should try to recapture th hope that was offered to us in the early part of this year when we were moving towards a Summit meeting.

I concluded this excerpt by saying —

There may indeed be other amendments. I should like to say for myself that I am much less concerned about the details of draftsmanship than I am to avoid the perpetuation of the notion that the world conflict is between the United States and the Soviet Union.

Well, Sir, before the morning session ended, in the course of which I regret to say that my distinguished friend, Mr Nehru, made a somewhat remarkable commentary upon my amendment and my speech, the President indicated that two further amendments were being circulated and that the matter would be concluded at the night session. This was on the Wednesday. I will by-pass, for the moment, the afternoon session. At the night session Cambodia, which after all is an Asian country, indicated that it would have supported my amendment as a separate resolution. This was a merely technical objection to its form. For some reason or other, and I still do not understand it, because in these United Nations affairs I am a new boy, the foreshadowed further amendments that had been referred to by the President in the morning were not submitted.

So, the first thing that happened after Cambodia had said this was that we voted on the Australian amendment. Of course, the result has given immense pleasure to a few people. I do not know why they should be so pleased that an Australian amendment should be defeated. Still, one lives and learns. So the Assembly voted on my amendment. It was supported, on the vote, by France, by the United Kingdom, by the United States of America, by Canada and by ourselves – not a bad voting group, I think. There were 45 people who voted 'No' and 43 who abstained. Very interestingly, among the people who abstained and so said neither 'Yes' nor 'No' were the Soviet Union, the entire Soviet bloc, Japan, Laos, the Philippines, Thailand, and Cambodia – for the reason I have referred to. It was then proposed that separate votes should be taken – this is a highly technical but fascinating problem for us who are parliamentarians – on the inclusion in the five-power resolution of the words 'the President of'. See what I mean? The President of the United States of America – and then 'the Chairman of the Council of Ministers of'. This, of course, is something which we in our innocence in this Parliament know nothing about. Anyway, it was proposed that separate votes should be taken, and my distinguished friend, the Prime Minister of India, Mr Nehru, objected, I thought, with great force, that if these words were omitted the five-power resolution would be meaningless because, of course, diplomatic relations had not been cut off between the United States of America and the Soviet Union. They had never been interrupted.

I might say I thought he had a great deal of force in that but, as I did not like the five-power resolution, I remained relatively unmoved, except intellectually, by this argument. Sir, what happened? Separate votes were put to the vote of the Assembly. I want to mention this to honorable members because some people rather foolishly have tried to make it appear that I, representing you in this Parliament, had done something foolish and had been left out on a limb. But when the separate votes were put to the vote those in favour of separate votes – in other words those who must be regarded as being not in favour of the five-power resolution as a whole – were 37, and against them were 36, with 22 abstentions. It is lovely, you know. Some of you have been there, but I had not been there before. Somebody says 'abstention' in English and somebody, being brought up in the French language, says 'abstention' in French, but it amounts to the same thing. There we were, 37 in favour of separate votes, 36 against and 22 abstentions. Those in favour of separate votes — and I mention this because some silly fellow who tried to pretend that I am becoming bad friends with the Asian countries suggested the contrary — included Pakistan, China, Japan, the Philippines and Thailand.

And if I may permit myself to say so, I do not mind finding myself standing, as to three of these countries, alongside our colleagues in the South-East Asian Treaty. When the separate votes were taken, because it had been decided there ought to be separate votes, those in favour of retaining what I will call the 'separate phrases' — the President of the United States of America, the Chairman of the Council of Ministers of the Soviet Union — numbered 41 with 37 against and 17 abstentions. The President ruled that there should be a two-thirds majority. There was not a two-thirds majority, and the President's ruling was upheld. All this was going on in the one day when oddities of all kinds — Heaven help me! — were being published in my own country. Those who voted against the retention of these personal phrases, in other words those who voted against the idea that we should be telling President Eisenhower and Chairman Khrushchev to get together, included all of the South-East Asian countries. That, I think, is something worth noting.

After all this argy-bargy — I think that is the expression — Mr Nehru, the very distinguished leader of India, stood up and said that, having regard to the voting, the five-power resolution would be withdrawn. So at one o'clock in the morning of the same sitting day the five-power resolution had gone. You may ask what had happened to my amendment submitted on behalf of Australia. Many people have been eager beavers to say that my amendment was just ridiculous and that I had made a fool of my country. When I make a fool of this country I hope that you will expel me.

The fact was that by one o'clock in the morning the resolution to which my amendment had been an unsuccessful alternative had been withdrawn — withdrawn because other amendments had been moved or other procedures adopted which persuaded its sponsors to withdraw it.

I want to stress to honorable members that this is not a party political matter. All of us are Australians and we want to feel that our country counts. The fact is that by the end of that day two remarkable things had occurred. First, the proposal sponsored primarily by Yugoslavia, the United Arab Republic, Indonesia and others had gone. It had been withdrawn. In the meantime, in the meantime, in the course of the voting, four atomic powers – the only four atomic powers – had been called to the ballot. You may think that I am rather foolish, but at any rate I called them to the ballot. Four [sic] of them, Great Britain, France and the United States, had voted unhesitatingly for a convening of the Summit conference as contained in my amendment, and the Soviet Union had not voted 'No', but had abstained from voting.

Four days later, under circumstances which vex the honorable member for East Sydney (Mr Ward), I had a talk with the head of the Soviet Union, Mr Khrushchev, in which he made it abundantly clear that he wanted a Summit conference. That was why he had not voted against my amendment. He wanted a Summit conference and by one o'clock – after midnight that day – I went back feeling in my simple vanity that at any rate we had now got to a state of affairs in which there would be, after the American presidential election, a Summit conference. It is very difficult, even for such an old hand as myself, to understand why this achievement – because it was something of an achievement – should be regarded as in some way discreditable to our country, to which most of us were born.

To sum up, Sir, my amendment was lost, but the resolution was withdrawn. Three atomic powers had voted for a Summit meeting and the Soviet Union had abstained. Not one of the four atomic powers was opposed to a Summit meeting.

I pass on from that. I made a speech that afternoon. In my simplicity I thought that that was the major speech, and my distinguished colleague, the Treasurer, who was present probably – God bless him – thought likewise, because the speech in the morning was on this technical problem. As I have said, I made a speech in the afternoon. It lasted for about 40 minutes. It is very interesting for an Australian to go abroad and make a speech on the great United Nations platform. This was the only occasion in my life when the American press swept a speech of mine into its columns. But that did not happen here in Australia. A pity! It is a pity that we should have this inferiority complex because after all, Mr Speaker, in my speech in the afternoon I had made up my mind that if Mr Khrushchev were to come and bully people – taunt people, and beat things on the table, including his shoes – it was really high time that somebody speaking for 10,000,000 people — that is all — should make it quite clear to him that we are not frightened. Therefore I let myself go, as you might say. But of course, what happened in the United Nations Assembly, apart from all the beating on the table and the wearing out of boot leather which was all very funny from our point of view? I think that Mr Khrushchev wanted to persuade or terrify new nations into coming into his camp. We know nothing about that. We are not easily persuaded, and we certainly are not easily terrified into somebody else's camp. But that seemed to be his idea. He had his heelers with him. There were with him about half a dozen representatives from his satellite nations who would not dare to applaud without first looking round to see whether he gave the high sign. Wonderful! I wish that I could organize that sort of thing some day! Mr Khrushchev talked about colonialism. He tried to read into the minds of some of the delegates a bitterness about their old status. He was talking for the most part to people who represented countries in Africa which, by wise providence on the part of the United Kingdom, had ceased to be colonies and had become independent nations. I thought that was a monstrosity. Anyhow he did it. Therefore, I thought on your behalf — if you do not agree with what I did you will say so — that I ought to use a few words mildly about this situation. Let me quote one or two of the words that I used, because apparently there has been some difficulty in reporting them in Australia. I said —

I beg of all these distinguished representatives —

I was referring to the representatives of the new countries, primarily in Africa —

to put bitterness out of their minds. So far as they are concerned, the past has gone. The dead past should bury its dead. It is the present and future that matter. Most of them know that political independence can be won more swiftly than economic independence.

I pause here to repeat the last sentence because some rather silly fellow has said that I was not on the same wave-length as the new countries. I leave it to the House to decide. I said —

Most of them know that political independence can be won more swiftly than economic independence. And yet both are essential to true nationhood. Under these circumstances, nations which are older in self-government should

1ot be looking at new nations as people whose support should be canvassed,)ut as people who need objective assistance with no strings if the material >rosperity of their people is to be improved.

It is one of the significant things in contemporary history that the 1dvanced industrial nations are, because of their scientific and technological 1dvantages, improving their standards at a phenomenal rate; while less 1dvanced countries, lacking the same techniques on the same scale, are advancing 1t a slower rate.

This is not one of the facts of life, which one may observe and, having >bserved, forget. Its significance is that the gap between the advanced and the 'elatively unadvanced tends, unless we do something about it, to grow wider >very year. It is not a state of affairs which civilized and humane thinking :an indefinitely tolerate.

[said this on Australia's behalf, and I am sure that no honorable nember will disagree with it.

If in this Assembly and in the nations here represented we will constantly 'emember that our trust is for humanity and that, indeed, the United Nations tself has no other reason for existence, we will more and more concentrate our >fforts on providing economic and technical help for new nations to the very imit of our capacity; not because we want, to put it crudely, to buy them nto our own ideas of things, not only because we really and passionately >elieve in independence and freedom, but also because we believe that our ellow human beings everywhere are entitled to decent conditions of life, and 1ave enough sense to know that independence and freedom are mere words inless the ordinary people of free countries have a chance of a better life to-mor- ow.

This point of view seemed to me to underlie the temperate and persuasive >peech of Mr Macmillan and other speeches made by democratic leaders.

But there are others who have so far misunderstood the spirit of the Jnited Nations as to resort to open or veiled threats, blatant and in some nstances lying propaganda, a clearly expressed desire to divide and conquer. They should learn that 'threatened men live long', and that free nations, 1owever small, are not susceptible to bullying.

am still quoting myself, which is an ill business. I continued –

I will permit myself the luxury of developing this theme, though quite >riefly, in the particular and in the general.

hope honorable members will not think me boring but this was a >hase of my speech which, I believe, had an immense impact >n the Assembly. I said –

In his opening speech, Mr Khrushchev made his usual great play about 'colonialism'. As Mr Macmillan reminded us, the answer to much of his story s to be found in the presence in this Assembly of many new nations, once colonies and now independent.

Mr Khrushchev said among other things: 'Nations who oppress other nation cannot themselves be free. Every free nation should help the peoples sti oppressed to win freedom and independence.' This was, in one sense, a mos encouraging observation. It made me wonder whether we were perhaps abou to see a beginning of an era in which the nations of Europe, which were once ir dependent and are now under Soviet Communist control, are going to receiv the blessings of freedom and independence. What a glorious vista of freedor would be opened up by such a policy! How much it would do to relieve th causes of tension, and promote peace!

I venture to say that it is an act of complete hypocrisy for a Communis leader to denounce colonialism as if it were an evil characteristic of the Wester Powers, when the facts are that the greatest colonial power now existing i the Soviet Union itself.

This brings me now to the point. I said —

Further, in the course of this Assembly, Mr Khrushchev was good enougl to make some references to my own country and its position in relation to th territories of Papua and New Guinea. He calls upon Australia to give immediate full independence and self-government to New Guinea and Papua. As a piece o rhetoric this no doubt has its points. But it exhibits a disturbing want o knowledge of these territories and of the present stage of their development Nobody who knows anything about these territories and their indigenous peopl could doubt for a moment that for us in Australia to abandon our responsibilitie would be an almost criminal act.

I am quoting this part of my speech because, subject to correction, I feel that these words impressed themselves upon our friend I said —

Here is a country which not so long ago was to a real extent in a state o savagery. It passed through the most gruesome experiences during the las war. It came out of it without organized administration and, in a sense without hope.

It is not a nation in the accepted term. Its people have no real structure of association except through our administration. Its groups are isolated among mountains, forests, rivers and swamps. It is estimated that there are more than 200 different languages.

Probably my distinguished colleague, the Minister for Territories (Mr Hasluck) would tell me that I underestimated the number. I continued—

The work to be done to create and foster a sense and organism of community is therefore enormous.

But, with a high sense of responsibility, Australia has attacked its human task in this almost unique area.

Since the war some form of civilised order has been established over many
thousands of square miles which were previously unexplored.
We have built up an extensive administration service . . .

Really, I do not need to trouble honorable members about this. I
told them the simple, dramatic and moving story of what has been
done in Papua and New Guinea, and I ended by saying —

I could go on like this almost indefinitely.
The achievement has not been without cost. We have put many more
millions into Papua and New Guinea than have ever come out.
We have established many local government councils, democratically elected
on an adult franchise, and we have set up a Legislative Council on which
there is a growing number of indigenous members.
Mr Khrushchev includes us in his diatribe against 'foreign administrators
who despise and loot the local population'. I have shown how exactly opposite
to the truth this is in our case. His further extravaganza about 'the overseer's
lash' and the 'executioner's axe' must relate to areas with which he is more
familiar than he is with New Guinea and Papua.
We do not need to be lectured on such matters by a man who has no
record whatever of having brought colonial people into freedom and self-
government. We indeed are proud to be in the British tradition of the 20th
century — a tradition which has by sensible degrees and enlightened administration brought the blessings of self-government and a seat in the councils
of the world to many former colonies.

also spoke about neutralism, and I inflict this on honorable
members —

Neutralism is, of course, one of those rather rotund words which does not
readily admit of definition. If, when we say that a nation is neutral, we mean
that it will not under any circumstances take arms in any conflict which does
not concern the protection of its own immediate boundaries, it seems to be a
notion hard to reconcile with the Charter of the United Nations   which
contemplates under certain circumstances the use of combined force in terms
of the Charter itself.
Mr Nehru, the distinguished leader of India, has not, I think, used the word
neutral' in this sense. He and his government maintain large defences in their
own country, and are active supporters of the Charter. What he has consistently
made clear is that he stands for non-alignment, in the sense that he will not
engage in any special military or quasi-military alliance.
My own country does not subscribe to this view, since we are party, for
example, to the South-East Asian Treaty with the military associations which
are either expressed or implied in it. But we do not quarrel with each other
about these matters. I would think it impossible to believe that some of
the greatest leaders of so-called 'neutral' countries would regard themselves as
being neutral in the great conflict of ideas.

Sir, having said all that at, I am afraid, too great length, I now turn, quite briefly I hope, to some general observations about this rather historic General Assembly meeting. First of all, a determined attack was made by the Communist powers upon new nations to encourage what I have already described as 'retrospective bitterness'. I do not think that on this matter the table-thumping succeeded.

In the second place, attempts were made to defeat or to undermine the Secretary-General. In particular, a very remarkable proposal was put forward that there should be three secretaries-general instead of one; and for some very odd reason, one ought to be from what we would call the Communist group but what Mr Khrushchev — I apologize to my friends opposite — calls the socialist group, a second from the neutralist group and a third from the capitalist group of which, no doubt, I was one of the representatives. There ought to be three secretaries-general, and everybody would have a veto on everybody else, and therefore, of course, nothing would happen, and therefore the United Nations would come to an end. He did not get very much success with that remarkable proposal.

But there are some aspects of his general campaign about which I think I should report to this Parliament. First of all, I believe that what he has been saying and what he has been doing are designed to divide the United Nations into the disunited nations. After all, if there is one thing about the United Nations that matters, it is that it possesses a sort of universality. As I said in my own speech, he wants to produce a result like ancient Gaul — according to our late respected friend, Julius Caesar, all Gaul was divided into three parts. This man wants to divide the United Nations into three parts and therefore into the disunited nations.

One of the groups that he wants to produce in this disunited body is what he keeps on describing as the neutralist group. What is a neutralist group? Sir, one of the things that I beg all honorable members on both sides of the House to avoid is this fallacy of easy classification. So-and-so is an African, therefore he must think like all other Africans! If one African is neutralist, therefore he must be neutralist! This is an insult to people. Does anybody suppose that because people were born west of the Soviet boundary in Europe, whether they are Germans, Frenchmen, Englishmen or Italians, they are the same kind of men with the same kind of ideas? This, of course, is utter nonsense. You may go over the whole zone of Africa and tell me that so-and-so, so-and-so, and so-and-so must think the same way because they are all Africans and they are all African leaders. Sir, I tell you that the greatest speech made at this General Assembly was made by the Prime Minister of Nigeria. He is a most remarkable man, and his speech made an unforgettable impact on the minds of all of us. It would insult this great man — the head of the Government of the greatest single nation in the whole African continent, a nation of 40,000,000 people — to be told that his country must be classified, along with other countries, in a group or a bloc. No one could have been more explicit than he was about the need for every nation to live its own life, to face its own future, to accept its own responsibilities. The people who want to denigrate the whole of modern independence, and to treat new nations as if they were merely groups to be bought like bunches of bananas, make a very great blunder. That was perhaps the greatest blunder that Khrushchev made.

Let us consider the ways in which Mr Khrushchev failed. He failed to undermine the Secretary-General. He failed to destroy the work that has been done with regard to the Congo. He failed on occasion after occasion, and I will not take up the time of the House in recounting them all, because I have already taken up too much of its time. He had some success, no doubt. He may have frightened somebody and he may have weakened a little the position of the Secretary-General; I do not know. You and I in this House are fortunate to have grown up in such an atmosphere that we can laugh at nonsense and not be frightened by it, so how am I to know to what extent Mr Khrushchev succeeded in frightening people? He tried to disunite the United Nations. He tried to introduce some strange dogma about neutralist groups.

He had some point, I suppose. He said that when the United Nations was established it had 50 member nations, that now it has nearly 100, and that therefore there ought to be some reconstruction of the structure of the organization. I do not object to that suggestion, so long as it is understood that one of the dangers that have grown up in the modern world is that the General Assembly, which has relatively little power, has become tremendously important because the heads of government attend it, whereas the chief executive body — I am not using the word 'executive' in a technical sense — the Security Council, has been put rather on one side. The

Security Council, Sir, must continue to include in its membership people who represent the great powers, which themselves are the backbone of the United Nations and which themselves carry the major responsibility for peace. But, subject to that proviso, I do not object to the suggestion that a reconstruction of the United Nations should be considered.

I want to say only one or two things more. I had the very valuable opportunity of seeing, on your behalf, a number of world leaders. I would not wish any member of this Parliament, on either side, to believe that I was being exclusive, talking to this side and not to that side. In the course of rather less than three weeks I had the closest discussions with President Eisenhower, with the American Secretary of State, Mr Herter, with Mr Macmillan and Lord Home and with Mr Nehru. I had a long interview with Mr Khrushchev. I sought the interview, and I tell you quite frankly that the main reason why I sought it was that I thought that if I came back here and my friends, or friendly opponents who sit opposite, asked me whether I saw Khrushchev and I replied that I had not, they might think it rather odd. So I sought an interview with Mr Khrushchev.

I had already expressed myself, as honorable members will have gathered from what I have already said, with a certain degree of clarity. Nevertheless, I had 70 minutes with Mr Khrushchev. I want to say to the House that I came away from the interview quite satisfied that he would like a Summit conference. Being more interested, as I am, in substance than in form, and as what I was trying for from the day I arrived at the United Nations was the substance of a Summit conference, I am very pleased to say that three of the atomic powers voted for a Summit conference on my amendment, and that the fourth, through Mr Khrushchev, has indicated to me in the clearest possible terms that a Summit conference is considered a good idea.

I saw, of course, the Prime Minister of Ethiopia, who is an old friend of mine. I had a talk with President Tito. I spoke to Mr Luns, the Foreign Minister of the Netherlands. Dr Subandrio, of Indonesia, was a guest of mine, and I had a long talk with him. Indeed, one would be surprised at the number of people who concern us in this world with whom, in the course of a fortnight or three weeks, one can have useful talks.

I have occupied the time of the House long enough. Having said that I believe that Mr Khrushchev wants Summit talks, and that I think something might come of them, I would like to conclude by saying that I have by no means been disposed to defend myself on the matters about which I have spoken. I believe in my heart and my mind that I pursued the right course at New York, and that I spoke and acted in the best interests of my country.

DOCUMENT NO. 13 *12*

Section of the A.L.P. Policy Speech, dealing with International Relations and Defence, by the Hon. E.G. Whitlam, on 13 November 1972

Source: *Labor Party Policy Speech*, 1972; Canberra, A.L.P. Secretariat; pp. 41–44

INTERNATIONAL AFFAIRS AND DEFENCE

Let us never forget this: Australia's real test as far as the rest of the world, and particularly our region, is concerned is the role we create for our own aborigines. In this sense, and it is a very real sense, the aborigines are our true link with our region. More than any foreign aid program, more than any international obligation which we meet or forfeit, more than any part we may play in any treaty or agreement or alliance, Australia's treatment of her aboriginal people will be the thing upon which the rest of the world will judge Australia and Australians — not just now, but in the greater perspective of history. The world will little note, not long remember, Australia's part in the Vietnam intervention. Even the people of the United States will not recall nor care how four successive Australian Prime Ministers from Menzies to McMahon sought to keep their forces bogged down on the mainland of Asia, no matter what the cost of American blood, treasure, no matter how it weakened America abroad, and even more at home. The aborigines are a responsibility we cannot escape, cannot share, cannot shuffle off; the world will not let us forget that.

VIETNAM

We now enter a new and more hopeful era in our region. Let us not foul it up this time. Australia has been given a second chance. The settlement agreed upon by Washington and Hanoi is the settlement easily obtainable in 1954. The settlement now in reach — the settlement that 30,000 Australian troops were sent to prevent, the settlement which Mr McMahon described in November 1967 as treachery — was obtainable on a dozen occasions since 1954. Behind it all, behind those eighteen years of bombing, butchering and global blundering, was the Dulles policy of containing China.

CHINA

Until barely a year ago, to oppose this policy, even to question it, was being described by Mr McMahon — and even some other people — as treason. If President Nixon had not gone to China nine months after I did, Mr McMahon would still be denouncing me, just as he was on the very eve of President Nixon's announcement that he would go to Peking. This is the man, this is the party, which expects you to trust them with the conduct of your nation's international affairs for another three years. *A Labor Government will transfer Australia's China Embassy from Taipei to Peking.*

NEUTRALISATION

The two Asian mainland nations with which Australia has been most closely associated in defence agreements — Malaysia and Thailand — have both declared for neutralisation of the South East Asian region. *Australia under Labor will support the efforts of those nations and encourage the United States to support them.* The Government of Malaysia has noted that 'as neutralisation is phased in, the Five Power arrangements must be phased out'. The Government of Thailand has noted that neutralisation means the effective end of *SEATO*.

FIVE-POWER ARRANGEMENTS

The Australian Labor Party supports these propositions. Pending neutralisation, *we will honor the full terms of the Five-Power Arrangements* under which Australia agrees to provide Malaysia and Singapore with personnel, facilities and courses for training their forces and assistance in operational and technical matters and the supply of equipment. *We will be willing to make similar arrangements with Indonesia, Papua New Guinea, New Zealand and Fiji.* The Five-Power Arrangements do not require an Australian garrison in Singapore; *the battalion and battery there will not be replaced when they complete their tour of duty.*

A nation's foreign policy depends on striking a wise, proper and prudent balance between commitment and power. Labor will have four commitments commensurate to our power and resources:

Firstly - to our own national security;

Secondly - to a secure, united and friendly Papua New Guinea;

Thirdly - to achieve closer relations with our nearest and largest neighbour, Indonesia;

Fourthly - to promote the peace and prosperity of our neighbourhood.

SOUTH PACIFIC

Our relations with our neighbours in the Pacific and across the Pacific are crucial in achieving each of these objectives. We should be the natural leaders of the South Pacific. A Labor Government will give that leadership on two immediate questions.

NUCLEAR TESTS

We will take the question of French nuclear tests to the International Court of Justice to get an injunction against further tests. We shall act in this matter on the same high legal advice which Mr McMahon has received — but failed to act upon. *We will ratify the Treaty on the Non-Proliferation of Nuclear Weapons.*

SPORTING TEAMS

We will give no visas to or through Australia to racially selected sporting teams.

ANZUS

Australia's basic relationship in the Pacific and the Indian Oceans rest upon two great associations — *ANZUS* and the Commonwealth of Nations. The majority membership of the Commonwealth nations are around the shores of these oceans. Both associations are too valuable to be permitted to die through indifference.

The Australian Labor Party will foster close and continuing co-operation with the people of the United States and our Commonwealth partners to make these associations instruments for justice and peace and for the political, social and economic advancement of our region.

We now have a new opportunity for sane relations with China, the opportunity for a settlement of the war in Vietnam, the opportunity to institute an era of peace and progress in our region. The time is short. Nothing worthwhile can be done unless we have a government that is willing to break out from and beyond its own path, its own inhibitions, its own failures. Above all, it is a time for a government which will base its foreign policy on Australia's

true national interests and on Australia's true international obligations, not on the shifts and deceptions of domestic political need.

The nation's security requires balanced, mobile, highly professional
and highly flexible armed forces. Labor will maintain such forces,
and back them with strong defence industries in Australia. Conscription is an impediment to achieving needs. It is an alibi for
failing to give proper conditions to regular soldiers. *We will abolish
conscription forthwith.* By abolishing it, Australia will achieve a
better army, a better paid army — and a better, united society.

Sources

Full bibliographic details to all printed sources are given at first citation, as well as to a number of works on related major questions. In this way, the bibliography has been incorporated in the Sources.

The following abbreviations are used:

Adm Serial prefix for Admiralty files at the Public Record Office

AFAR *Australian Foreign Affairs Record*, Department of Foreign Affairs, Canberra; until December 1972, *Current Notes on International Affairs* (see *C.N.*)

CAB Serial prefix for Cabinet papers at the Public Record Office

C.I.D. Committee of Imperial Defence

C.N. *Current Notes on International Affairs* (from January 1973, *AFAR*), Canberra, Department of Foreign Affairs

C.O. Colonial Office; serial prefix for C.O. files at the Public Record Office

C.P.D. Commonwealth of Australia. *Parliamentary Debates;* vols. 1 to 221, to 27 March 1953, include debates of both houses; from 8 September 1953, separate series were published of the debates of the Senate and the House of Representatives, beginning with *C.P.D.* : S1 and *C.P.D.* : HR1, respectively.

C.P.P. Commonwealth of Australia. *Parliamentary Papers*

Digest *Digest of Decisions and Announcements and Important Speeches of the Prime Minister*; Canberra, 1941 - 9, Prime Minister's Department

F.O. Foreign Office; serial prefix for F.O. files at the Public Record Office

F.O.C.P.	*Foreign Office Confidential Print*
Hansard	Great Britain. *Hansard's Parliamentary Debates*
HC	House of Commons
HL	House of Lords
HR	House of Representatives; see *C.P.D.*
L.A.	Legislative Assembly
L.C.	Legislative Council
L.G.	*London Gazette*
N.S.W.	New South Wales
N.S.W. P.D.	*N.S.W. Parliamentary Debates*
P.C.	Serial prefix for Privy Council papers at the Public Record Office
P.P.	*Parliamentary Papers*
P.R.O.	Public Record Office, London
PRO	Serial prefix for certain classes of papers at the P.R.O.
Q.P.D.	Queensland. *Parliamentary Debates*
V. & P.	*Votes & Proceedings*
V.P.D.	Victoria. *Parliamentary Debates*
W.O.	War Office; serial prefix for War Office files at the P.R.O.
see, Appendix	Refers to the Appendix of the present work
D.O.	Dominion Office; serial prefix for D.O. files at the Public Record Office.

MOTTO

Giambattista Vico, *Prinçipij di sçienza nuova*, 3a impressione; Naples, 1744 Stamperia Muziana, a spese di Gaetano e Steffano Elia; the original quotation reads: *'L'ordine dèlle idee* dee procedere secondo *l'ordine delle cose.'*

PROLEGOMENA

Darling to Goderich, 13 October 1827; C.O. 201/183, *folios* 13–16. Stirling to Hay, 30 July 1828; C.O. 18/1, *folios* 61–64, *but, compare with*:
Stirling to Darling, Official Report, 18 April 1827; C.O. 18/1, *folios* 5ff.

PART I

1 Gipps to the Marquis of Nomanby, No. 111, 31 July 1839; C.O. 201/286 folios 415-7.

2 *ibid.*

3 Orders of the King-in-Council, for creating a Court of Justice at Canton, 9 December 1833; P.C. 2/214, pp. 362-4; *also*, Papers relative to the Establishment of a Court of Judicature in China [etc.], 1838; *P.P.* 1837-8 [128] XLI.

4 Roger Pelissier, *The Awaking of China, 1793 - 1949*, ed. and trans. M. Kieffer; London, 1963, Secker & Warburg; p. 66; *see also*, G.W. Overdijking, *Lin Tse-hsü : een biographische Schets;* Leiden, 1938, Brill (Sinica Leidensia ed. Institum Sinologicum [etc.] vol. IV); *and* Gideon Chen, *Lin Tse-hsü : pioneer promoter of the adoption of Western means of maritime defense in China;* Peking, 1934, Dept. of Economics, Yenching University.

5 Arthur Waley, *The Opium War through Chinese Eyes;* London, 1958, Allen & Unwin; p. 39.

6 *ibid;* p. 42.

7 Gipps was appointed to Lord Gosford's Royal Commission on Canada, 19 June 1835, *L.G.*, 1835, I, p. 1170; knighted, 8 July 1835, *L.G.*, 1835, II, p. 1331, promoted Major by Brevet, 10 January 1837, *L.G.*, 1837, I, p. 689; appointed *Governor of New South Wales and Van Diemen's Land and their respective dependencies*, 27 July 1837, *L.G.*, 1837, II, p. 1910.

8 C.O. 201/290, *folio 323.*

9 *ibid., folio* 149.

10 C.O. 201/302, *folio 39 verso.* Bremer also signed - *Given under my hand... Commandant of the Settlement of Victoria* [the Port Essington area].

11 *see,* Captain Stirling's Report, New Settlement on the North Coast of Australia, 20 June 1827, with Darling to Lord Goderich, C.O. 201/83 folios 297 - 303; Copies or Extracts of any Correspondence relative to the Establishment of a Settlement at Port Essington, *P.P.*, 1843 (141) vol. XXXIII for the *Estimates of the sum required in aid of . . . the settlement at Port Essington*, 1841 - 52; *also, General Index to Accounts and Papers* [etc.], *1801 - 1852*, p. 733.

12 H.M.S. *Pelorus* sailed from Sydney at 4 p.m. on 28 July 1839, and arrived at Port Essington on 23 August, staying till 1840, Adm. 51/3360; H.M.S. *Alligator* arrived at Sydney on 9 July 1839, staying until 15 September, when she sailed for Norfolk and Phillips Islands, but returned to Sydney for shelter; she left for Phillips Island on 25 September, and returned to Sydney on 14 October, sailing on 14 November 1839, by way of King Island, Cape

Leeuwen, Cocos Island, Acheen, Sumatra; she ran aground at Pula Penang on 2 January 1840, but left on the following day, reaching Madras on 17 January 1840, Adm. 51/3049 and 3551, *also* Adm. 37/8646; H.M.S. *Herald* left Sydney on 30 July 1839, sailing as far as Java Head, returning to Sydney on New Year's Eve, Adm. 51/3217.

13 *see*, Adm. 1/1587.

14 *Hansard*, Third Series (HC) LVII : 1491.

15 *see*, Lord Ellenborough's account, 1 August 1839, *Hansard*, (HL) XLIX : 1052 ff.; *for the government's evasiveness* : 20 February 1840, (HC) LII : 424; 21 April 1840 (stalled question), *ibid.*. cols. 433-4; 6 March 1840, (HL) LII : 978; 19 March 1840, LII : 1220-3

16 *Hansard*, 7 April 1840, (HC) LIII : 669-748; 8 April, *ibid.*, cols. 749-836; 9 April, cols. 845-950; division lists : cols. 950-55

17 Gipps to Lord John Russel[1]. No. 163. C.O. 201/299, *folios* 435 ff.

18 FitzRoy to the Earl Grey, No. 100, *.* 201/381, *folio* 283 *verso.*

19 Same to same, No. 227, W.O. 1/521, *folio* 58.

20 *ibid., folios* 58 *verso, and* 59.

21 Earl. Grey to FitzRoy, No. 39, 21 June 1850, W.O. 1/521, *folios* 67-75, *esp.* 72-3.

22 Lt.-Col. Edward Macarthur, Deputy Adjutant General, *Australian Fencibles or Militia,* 31 January 1854, *in* Special Bundle, *Defence Reports etc. brought together for Sir W. Denison;* Archives Office of N.S.W., 4/1155.2.

23 *loc. cit.*

24 *ibid.*

25 *ibid.*

26 *ibid.*

27 Lord Stanley to Denison, No. 6, 11 March 1858; C.O. 202/66, *folios* 447-454.

28 The Duke of Newcastle to Young, 26 December 1861 (circular), N.S.W. L.A., *V. & P. 1862*, p. 1078.

29 same to same, 22 January 1862 (circular), *ibid.*

30 *Hansard* (Third Series), 4 March 1862, (HC). CLXV : 1060.

31 *loc. cit.*, 26 April 1870 (HC) CC : 1884.

32 Lord Edmund Fitzmaurice, *The Life of Granville George Leveson Gower, Second Earl of Granville, KG, 1815 - 1895;* London, 1906, Longmans; vol. II, p. 21.

33 T.R. Reese, *The History of the Royal Commonwealth Society, 1868 - 1968;* London, 1968, O.U.P.; p. 16.

34 Earl of Granville to Belmore, 25 March 1869; N.S.W. L.A., *V. & P. 1869*, vol. 1, pp. 217-8.

35 G.E. Marindin (ed.), *Letters of Frederic* [*Rogers*], *Lord Blachford;* London, 1896, John Murray, p. 279; *see also*, Reese, *op. cit.*, pp. 31-38.

36 *Hansard*, Third Series, 8 May 1868, (HL) CXCI : 1963 - 2001.

37 E.E. Morris, *A Memoir of George Higinbotham : an Australian politician and Chief Justice of Victoria;* Melbourne, 1895, Macmillan; p. 285.

38 *V.P.D.*, IX : 2123.

39 *ibid.*, p. 2657.

40 Melbourne *Argus*, 3 February 1859; *in*, Morris, *op. cit.*, p. 57.

41 *see*, R. Koebner and H.D. Schmidt, *Imperialism : the story and significance of a political word, 1840 - 1960;* Cambridge, 1964, C.U.P,; e.g., p. 37.

42 *V.P.D.*, IX : 2659-61.

43 *ibid.*

44 Edgar Bonjour, *Geschichte der Schweizerischen Neutralität : vier Jahrhunderte eidgenössischer Aussenpolitik;* fifth, revised ed., 6 vols.; Basel, 1970, Helbig & Lichtenhahn; *e.g.*, vol. I, p. 22: *Zwischen Freiheit in ihrer schweizerischen Ausprägung und Neutralität besteht eben eine geheime-Anziehungskraft.* Elsewhere, Bonjour speaks of the secret alliance between federalism, neutrality and freedom.

45 *V.P.D.*, X : 867-8.

46 *ibid.*, p. 880.

47 *ibid.*, p. 883.

48 Earl of Carnarvon to Robinson, Nos. 68 and 69; *Carnarvon Papers*, PRO 30/6/25, 201 ff.

49 Parkes to Robinson, *loc. cit.*, 212-17.

50 N.S.W. L.A., *V. & P. 1889*, vol. II, pp. 347-8.

51 C.D. Cowan, *Nineteenth Century Malaya : the origins of British political control;* London, 1966, O.U.P. (London Oriental Series, vol. II); *for* Jervois as Governor of the Straits Settlements, *esp.* chps. 6 to 8.

52 The Earl of Carnarvon's delight at the Australian request for Jervois' services was reflected in the first comment on the file, by his Private Secretary, M.F. Ommaney : *This disposes of the question of employment for Sir W. Jervois.* However, the initial move of the C.O. was to suggest Scratchley who later accompanied Jervois to Australia, *see* C.O. 201/581, *folios* 416 ff.

53 Sir William Jervois, *Preliminary Report on Defences, New South Wales;* N.S.W. L.A., *V. & P. 1876 - 77*, vol. 3, pp. 85 ff.

54 *ibid.*

55 Clarke to Lord Carnarvon, cable No. 80, secret, 10 February 1875; C.O. 437/45, *folio* 86.

56 Same to same, confidential, 11 February 1875; C.O. 537/79, *folios* 157-162.

57 Same to same, No. 346, 21 December 1874, enclosure; C.O. 537/76, *folios* 533-6.

58 Royal Commission (Military Defences Enquiry Commission), N.S.W. L.A., *V. & P. 1881*, voL 4, pp. 619 ff.

59 *ibid.*, p. 658.

60 Denison to Labouchere, No. 61, 10 April 1858; C.O. 201/502, *folios* 448-452.

61 Sydney *Empire*, 25 March 1858, p. 2.

62 *ibid.*, 9 April 1858, p. 2; *Sydney Morning Herald*, 9 April 1858, pp. 4-5.

PART II

1 *see*, Myra Willard, *History of the White Australia Policy;* Melbourne, 1923 and 1967, M.U.P.; Persia Crawford Campbell, *Chinese Coolie Immigration to the Countries within the British Empire*; London, 1923, King; *and* A.T. Yarwood, *Asian Immigration to Australia*; Melbourne, 1964, M.U.P.

2 Bowen to the Duke of Newcastle, No. 38, enclosure, 18 July 1862; C.O. 243/6, *folios* 414-424; *see also*, O.W. Parnaby, *Britain and the Labor Trade in the Southwest Pacific;* Durham, N.C., 1964, Duke U.P.

3 Bowen to Newcastle, *loc. cit., folios* 406-12; Bowen quoted J.S. Mill in support of his case.

4 Newcastle to Bowen [by Rogers], No. 37, 20 November 1862; C.O. 243/6 *folios* 425-6.

5 *Q.P.D.*, 6th Session of the 8th Parliament, 28 June 1883, p. 7, coL 3 (Mr Kellett).

6 *The Australian Sugar Planter*, Maryborough, voL II, No. 18, June 1883, pp. 93-4.

7 *Q.P.D.*, 6th Session of the 8th Parliament, No. 1, 27 June 1883, p. 5, coL 2.

8 *see*, P. Knaplund, Sir Arthur Gordon and the New Guinea Question, 1883; *Historical Studies Australia and New Zealand* [*Hist St ANZ*], voL VII, No. 27, pp. 329 ff.; *also*, P. Knaplund, Gladstone-Gordon Correspondence, *Transactions of the American Philosophical Society*, voL 51, pt. 4, 1961; pp. 88-90.

9 *ibid.*

10 Service to Stuart, 13 June 1883; N.S.W. L.A., *V. & P. 1883-4*, vol. 9, p. 53, No. 12.

11 Stuart to Samuel, 8 June 1883; *ibid.*, No. 11.

12 Service to Stuart, 8 June 1883, *ibid.*, No. 9.

13 *Hansard*, (Third Series), 2 July 1883, (HL) CCLXXXI : 6.

14 *ibid.*, cols. 10-11.

15 *ibid.*, cols. 14-15.

16 *ibid.*, col. 15.

17 *ibid.*

18 *ibid.*, col. 18.

19 *ibid.*

20 Earl of Derby to Palmer, 11 July 1883, N.S.W. L.A., *V. & P. 1883-4*, vol. 9, pp. 91-92.

21 *V.P.D.* XLIII : 41.

22 *ibid.*, p. 137.

23 *ibid.*, pp. 137-8.

24 *ibid.*, p. 138.

25 *ibid.*, pp. 144-5.

26 *ibid.*, p. 145.

27 Melbourne *Argus*, 19 April 1883, p. 7.

28 *V.P.D.*, XLII : 298 *(The Prorogation,* 19 April 1883*).*

29 Melbourne *Argus*, 20 April 1883, p. 5.

30 *N.S.W. P.D.*, 1st Series, XV : 410.

31 Sydney *Bulletin*, vol. 1, No. 9 (New Series), 14 July 1883, p. 1.

32 *Q.P.D., loc. cit.*

33 *ibid.*, No. 6, 5 July 1883, p. 1, cols. 1-2.

34 *Hansard* (Third Series), 2 June 1883, (HC) CCLXXXI : 55-6.

35 *Q.P.D., loc. cit.*, p. 1, col. 2.

36 *ibid.*, cols. 2-3.

37 *ibid.*, col. 3.

38 The Agents General [for N.S.W., N.Z., Qld., and Victoria] to Lord Derby, 21 July 1883; N.S.W. L.A., *V. & P., loc. cit.*, pp. 70ff.

39 C.O. [Bramston] to the Agents General [*see*, n. 38], 31. August 1883, *loc. cit.*, pp. 76-77.

40 Stuart to Samuel, 8 September 1883; *ibid.*, No. 36, p. 59.

41 *in* Agents General to Lord Derby, *ibid.*, p. 72.

42 Gordon to Gladstone, 8 October 1883, Knaplund, *Hist St ANZ*, pp. 332-3.

43 Minister of Foreign Affairs [of Hawaii], by Hawaiian Consul at Hobart, to Chief Secretary, Tasmania, 23 August 1883 (covering note, 11 November 1883), N.S.W. L.A., *V. & P., loc. cit.*, pp. 33-4.

44 *ibid.*, pp. 139-40.

45 Marjorie Jacobs, The Colonial Office and New Guinea, 1874 - 1884; *Hist St ANZ*, vol. V., No. 18, p. 108.

46 Lord Ampthill to Lord Granville, 15 March 1884; *Granville Papers, 1884;* Private Germany; from Berlin, January 1882 to September 1884; PRO 30/29/178.

47 Stuart to Lord Augustus Loftus, 1 August 1883; N.S.W. L.A. *V. & P. Loc. cit.*, p. 55.

48 Theophile Gautier fils, une visite au Comte de Bismarck, Versailles: octobre 1870; *Revue de Paris*, August 1903; p. 786; the full passage reads:
   Enfin l'on proposait à l'Allemagne [sic] *la cession de la Cochinchine: c'était une possession très prospère qui, sous la sage administration de la Marine, couvrait ses dépenses et même donnait des excédents à la métropole.*
   A ce nom de Cochinchine, le comte qui m'avait jusqu'alors écouté sans m'interrompre, eut un mouvement d'épaules et, mu par le vieil instinct de parcimonie prussienne, que n'avait pas encore remplacé la mégalomanie impériale allemande, me dit, avec une nuance d'humilité:
   - Oh! oh! la Cochinchine! C'est un bien gros morceau pour nous; nous ne sommes pas assez riches pour nous offrir le luxe de colonies!
   see also, H.U. Wehler, *Bismarck und der Imperialismus;* Kiepenheuer & Wiesch, Cologne and Berlin, 1969, p. 203.

49 Lord Odo Russell to Lord Granville, 11 February 1873; *Granville Papers, 11 February 1873 PRO 30/29/93 (Private. Prussia, from Berlin, 1873 and 1874).*

50 Wehler, *op. cit., esp.* Part 6.

51 Bismarck's notation on Münster to Bismarck, No. 85, 7 July 1884, J. Lepsius, A. Mendelsohn-Bartholdy *and* F. Timme (eds. *for* German Foreign Office), *Die Grosse Politik der Europäischen Kabinette, 1871 - 1914;* 13 vols. Berlin, 1922, Deutsche Gesellschaft für Politik und Geschichte; vol. 4, pp. 63-4.

52 Bismarck to Münster, No. 756, 6 December 1884; *ibid.*, p. 93.

53 Hatzfeld to Herbert v. Bismarck, No. 802, 20 October 1886; *ibid.*, p. 155; Prince Bismarck's notation, p. 156.

54 Lord Derby to Gordon, 4 December 1883; Stanmore Papers, 49201; *in* Knaplund, *Hist St ANZ*, p. 293.

55 *Grosse Politik*, vol. 4; p. 103.

56 Herbert v. Nostitz, *Bismarcks unbotmässiger Botschafter : Fürst Münster von Derneburg (1820 - 1902);* Göttingen, 1968, Vandenhock & Ruprecht; p. 103 (my translation).

57 *AFAR*, vol. 46, No. 9, pp. 483 - 503.

58 *C.P.D.*, IV : 4811.

59 *see*, A.C. Palfreeman, *The Administration of the White Australia Policy,* Melbourne, 1967, M.U.P.; *also*, Willard, *op. cit.* and Yarwood, *op. cit.*

60 *Minute*, Acting Colonial Secretary [Dalley] to Cabinet, 27 April 1885, N.S.W. L.A., *V. & P. 1885*, vol. II, pp. 623-4.

61 Dalley to Samuel, cable, 23 April 1885; *loc. cit.*

62 Dalley to Richardson, cable, 23 April 1885; *ibid.*

63 Richardson to Dalley; *ibid.*

64 Samuel to Dalley, 24 April 1885; *ibid.*

65 Same to same, 12 May 1885; *ibid.*

66 *N.S.W. P.D.*, XVI : 22ff.

67 *N.S.W. P.D.*, XVII : 92ff.

68 *ibid.*, pp. 130 ff.

69 *ibid.*, pp. 150 ff.

70 *ibid.*, 15 September 1885, pp. 202-3.

71 *ibid.*, 23 September 1885, pp. 407-8.

72 A resolution by Lyne (based on Chamberlain's cables), to equip and despatch a military force for service with the Imperial army in South Africa, led to informed opposition by Arthur Griffith, Holman and Hughes in the debate; *see*, *N.S.W. P.D.*, 100 : 1373-96, 1428-70 *and* 1495-1585; there was no opposition in the L.C. debate, pp. 1473-8.

73 Sir Robert Randolph Garran, *Prosper the Commonwealth*, Sydney, 1958, Angus & Robertson, p. 89.

74 N.S.W. L.A., *V. & P. 1889*, Second Session, vol. I, pp. 167-72; Bevan Edwards on railways, pp. 170 and 172.

75 *Official Record of the Debates of the Australasian Constitutional Convention* Third Session, Melbourne, 1898, vol. I, p. 30; Barton had indicated that the omission of the words *and treaties* was to protect the exclusive treaty-making power of the Imperial government.

PART III

1 *C.P.D.*, LXXXIX : 12175.

2 *C.P.D.*, 159 : 193.

3 Alfred Manes, *Ins Land der Sozialen Wunder* (a study tour of Japan, the South Seas, Australia and New Zealand); Berlin, 1911, Mittler; p. 153 (my translation).

4 Trench to the Earl of Kimberley, 26 December 1894; Further Correspondence respecting the Revision of the Treaty between Great Britain and Japan, *F.O.C.P.* 6735, p. 9.

5 F.O. to C.O., 27 April 1895, *ibid.*, p. 26.

6 Lord Hardinge to the King, 28 March 1908, *Hardinge Papers*, vol. 14, folio 77; same to Lord Bryce (in similar terms), 27 March 1908, *ibid.*, folios 28-9.

7 F.O. 371/564; *folio* 13 *verso* (seen by Grey).

8 *ibid.*

9 *ibid., folio* 108.

10 Lord Bryce to Grey, 15 March 1908, telegram, *ibid, folio* 39.

11 *C.P.D.*, XLVII : 16.

12 Sydney *Worker*, 31 December 1908, p. 20.

13 *ibid.*, 10 July 1909, p. 5.

14 *ibid.*, 14 May 1914, p. 17.

15 Field Marshall Viscount Kitchener of Khartoum, Defence of Australia, *C.P.P., 1910*, vol. 2, pp. 87 ff.

16 Keith Robbins, *Sir Edward Grey : a biography of Lord Grey of Fallodon;* London, 1971, Cassell; p. 236; Professor Robbins has kindly supplied me with the context for the excerpt, *Grey to Albert, Earl Grey*, 27 January 1911, (from the original in the Grey of Howick Papers, Department of Palaeography and Diplomatic, University of Durham):

> *It would be better that we should not discuss the Japanese Alliance with the Premiers unless we can do so privately when the Dominion Premiers are over here this year.*
>
> *Laurier, I have no doubt, understands the different aspects of it. But one or two others, and certainly the Australians, require a great deal of education.*
>
> *They must realize that, if we denounce the Japanese Alliance, we can no longer rely on the assistance of the Japanese Fleet, and we must prepare for the possibility that Japan may enter into arrangements which may bring her into hostility with us. This would mean maintaining on the China Station a Fleet superior not only to the Japanese Fleet, but also to any possible combination of the Japanese Fleet with any other Fleet in those waters. This would, of course, be in addition to maintaining the two-Power standard in European waters, both in home waters and in the Mediterranean. The logical conclusion of denouncing the Japanese Alliance would be that Australia and New Zealand should undertake the burden of naval supremacy in Chinese seas. This they are neither willing nor able to do.*
>
> *I do not believe that there is the least danger that Japan will ever attempt forcible measures on the American side of the Pacific. Such action is no part of her policy, and it is not within her power. But I agree with you that we ought not to treat her in the spirit of an attorney in Manchuria or other regions in which she is naturally interested.*
>
> *I will work with Knox for the maintenance of the open door wherever it is guaranteed by treaty rights. But the principle of the open door must not be harshly interpreted. For instance, we cannot construe it as entitling us to support China in making railways in Manchuria that would ruin the South Manchuria Railway . . .*

17 C.I.D. *Minutes*, 111th Meeting, 26 May 1911, CAB 38/18 No. 40, p. 23.

18 *Hansard*, Fifth Series, (HC) LIX : 1931-8.

19 Melbourne *Age*, 19 March 1914, p. 9.

21 Melbourne *Labor Call*, 2 April 1914, p. 4.

22 *Sydney Morning Herald,* 3 August 1914, p. 10.

23 *ibid.,* 4 August 1914, p. 9.

24 *ibid.,* 8 August 1914, p. 14.

25 *Albury Daily News*, 6 August 1914; cited in Parliament by Senator Gardiner, 13 June 1918; *C.P.D.,* LXXXV : 5940.

26 *The Australian Worker,* 6 August 1914, p. 21.

27 P. Walker (ed.), *Caucus Minutes, 1901-1949: minutes of the meetings of the Federal Parliamentary Labor Party,* vol. I, 1901-1917; Melbourne, 1975, M.U.P.; pp. 438ff. 484-8 and 494ff.

28 *C.P.D.,* LXXXII : 58; *see,* E.L. Piesse, Australia and Japan, *Foreign Affairs,* vol. IV, No. 3 (New York, April 1926), p. 482. This article by an accomplished Australian diplomat and Japanologist is very revealing.

29 *ibid.,* IX : 7423.

30 *ibid.,* p. 7424.

31 *ibid.,* p. 7415,. where Fisher praised McIlwraith's *forsight and judgment.*

32 *Labor Call,* 22 October 1914; *see,* Appendix, Document No. 8.

33 C.D. Rowley, *The Australians in German New Guinea;* Melbourne, 1958, M.U.P.; p. 2.

34 e.g., Peter Lowe, *Great Britain and Japan, 1911-15 : a study in British Far Eastern policy;* London, 1969, Macmillan; W.R. Louis, *Great Britain and Germany's Lost Colonies, 1914-19;* Oxford, 1967, Clarendon Press; I.H. Nish, *The Anglo-Japanese Alliance : the diplomacy of two island empires;* London, 1966, Athlone Press (University of London) [Nish, I]; *Alliance in Decline : a study in Anglo-Japanese relations, 1908-1923;* London, 1972, Athlone Press [Nish II].

35 F.O. 371/2016, *folios* 329ff.

36 F.O. 371/2017, *folio* 91 (margin).

37 F.O. 371/3236, *folio* 414 *verso, see* Appendix, Document No. 10, p. 326.

38 Nish, II, p. 173.

39 *ibid.,* p. 206.

40 *ibid.,* pp. 151-2, 162-3 *and* 233-4.

41 Balfour to Greene, Tel. No. 83, 14 February 1917, F.O. 371/2950, *folio* 205.

42 F.O. 371/3236; *folios* 402-14; *see* Appendix, pp. 322-3.

43 *C.P.D.,* LXXVIII : 5564.

44 *C.P.D.,* LXXVI : 2366.

45 *C.P.D.,* LXXX : 9710.

46 *C.P.D.,* LXXXII : 60.

47 *C.P.D.* LXXXII : 912.

48 Millen's amendment of Bakhap's motion, *C.P.D.*, LXXXII : 915; the motion is at p. 911.

49 Senator Ferricks, *C.P.D.*, LXXXII : 918-9.

50 *C.P.D.*, LXXXV : 5729.

51 *C.P.D.*, LXXXV : 5729-30.

52 Melbourne *Argus*, 1 June 1918, quoted by Finlayson; *C.P.D.*, LXXXV : 5730.

53 *C.P.D.*, LXXXIX : 12174 ff.; *see also*, L.F. Fitzhardinge, W.M. Hughes and the Treaty of Versailles, 1919; *Journal of Commonwealth Political Studies;* vol. V, No. 2 (July 1967), pp. 130 ff.

54 *C.P.D.*, *loc. cit.*

55 *C.P.D.*, LXXXIX : 12393.

56 *ibid.*, p. 12419.

57 *ibid.*, p. 12425.

58 *ibid.*, p. 12423.

59 *ibid.*, p. 12435.

60 *ibid.*, p. 12175.

61 *ibid.*, pp. 12597-8.

62 *ibid.*

63 A.L.P., Annual Conference, 1924, *Report*, pp. 50-51; Blackburn had also written a fine obituary on Karl Liebknecht; *Australian Worker*, 23 January 1919, p. 7.

64 *C.P.D.*, XCVII : 11735.

65 *see*, Jean Chesneaux, *The Chinese Labor Movement, 1919-1927.* (trs. H.M. Wright); Stanford, Calif. 1968, Stanford U.P.

66 *C.P.D.*, 110:419.

67 *ibid.*,

68 *ibid.*, pp. 463-4.

69 *C.P.D.*, 115:21.

70 *ibid.*, p. 151.

71 J.R. Poynter, The Yo-Yo Variations : initiative and dependence in Australia's external relations, 1918 - 1923, *Hist St ANZ*, vol. XIV, No. 54, pp. 231-49.

72 *C.P.D.*, 104:1735 ff; Charlton criticized the building of the Singapore base, p. 1737; so did Dr Maloney, on 17 March 1927, quoting Japanese press claims that a British fleet could reach it no more than the Russian fleet could reach Vladivostok in the Russo-Japanese war; he, too, favoured air and submarine defences; *C.P.D.*, 115:624.

73 J.H. Scullin, *Labor Policy for the Commonwealth*, Policy Speech, 4 October 1928; Melbourne, 1928.

74 *C.P.D.*, 144:327-38.

75 *ibid.*, p. 337.

76 The exception was the abortive Lyons proposal for a Pacific Pact, raised at the Imperial Conference, 1937, and leading to the decision to establish diplomatic relations with some countries in the Pacific region; *see* J.G. Starke, *The ANZUS Alliance;* Melbourne, 1965, M.U.P.; pp. 4ff. Australia. Department of Foreign Affairs, *Documents on Australian Foreign Policy, 1937-49;* vols. I (1937-38) *and* II (1939), R.G. Neale (ed.); Canberra, 1975 *and* 1976, Australian Government Publishing Service; vol. I, and Subject List of Contents: *Pacific Pact,* p. XXIII.

77 *C.P.D.,* 148 : 1972.

78 *C.P.D.,* 152 : 1547.

79 *ibid.,* p. 1549.

80 *ibid.,* p. 1553.

81 *ibid.,* p. 1554.

82 the decision was conveyed in Lyons to Inskip, cablegram No. 34, 30 March 1939, *Australian Documents,* vol II, pp. 88-90; for its genesis, see *Australian Documents,* vol I, Nos. 2, 7-10, 93 *and esp.* 328, 33, *and* Appendix II. For Menzies' opposition, *see,* vol. II, 5, *cited below,* p. 171. When Menzies became Prime Minister on 26 April 1939, he announced it as his decision. The British view was expressed to Australia by cable the full text of which is at D.O. 35/663 *folios* 12 ff. (K 123/11). Craigie having cabled his reservations from Tokyo (that the Japanese government wanted an Australian legation in Tokyo in the hope of weakening and dividing British opposition to their China policies), the cable went out of its way to add that the Foreign Secretary, *Lord Halifax finds himself in agreement with Sir Robert Craigie's observations.* Craigie (and the F.O.) also felt that the prior establishment of a *legation in Washington would be more of a compliment to the United States.* The F.O. was very put out by Menzies' unilateral announcement about which neither the King nor the foreign governments concerned had been advised, much less consulted: *Not the least unfortunate aspect of Mr. Menzies' announcement is the possible restrictive effect of the Commonwealth freedom of action . . . Now that the cat is out of the bag, it may be difficult for the Commonwealth Government to postpone action in Japan, however much they may be impressed by Sir R. Craigie's arguments.* (Dunbar, 28 April 1939). The final comment on the file was *And the Commonwealth Government's consultations with us seem to have been rather pointless.* In the event, the Australian Legation in Washington was opened before that in Tokyo. Menzies, it seems, had difficulty in finding a suitable appointee, having apparently tried Sir David Rivett and Sir Ernest Fisk. He wanted to send Bruce but the British government were anxious for him to remain in London; *see* British High Commissioner, Canberra to Dominion Office, 21 August 1939 *at* F.O. 372/3319, *folio* 347, *and* Menzies to Chamberlain, 14 November 1939, *ibid., folio* 315; It appears that he had considered Pearce, whose views on Asians we know, as Minister to China; *ibid., folio* 340-41.

83 *C.P.D.* 159:236.

84 *Commonwealth of Australia Gazette,* No. 63, 1939, Canberra, Sunday, 3 September 1939.

85 *C.P.D.,* 161 : 28-9.

86 *ibid.,* p. 36.

87 *ibid.*

88 *ibid.*, p. 37.

89 A.L.P. Special Commonwealth Conference, 1940, *Report*, pp. 12 *passim.*

90 *ibid.*

91 John Curtin, *National Unity: Where Labor Stands*; Federal Parliamentary Labor Party, Melbourn, n.d. [1940] ; p. 3. Menzies had made that request in his interview with Curtin on 22 June 1940.

92 *ibid.*

93 *ibid.*, pp. 3-4.

94 *ibid.*, p. 4.

95 *ibid.*, p. 6.

PART IV

1 Australia. Department of External Affairs. *List of Consular Representatives in Australia;* Canberra, 1939, Commonwealth Government Printer.

2 W. MacMahon Ball (1946-7), succeeded by two Australian career diplomats, P. Shaw (1947-9) and Col. W. R. Hodgson (1949-52).

3 Lt. Gen. Sir John Northcott who, on becoming Governor of N.S.W. in 1946, was succeeded by another Australian, Lt. Gen. Sir Horace Robertson.

4 Sir William Webb.

5 Menzies to Lyons, 5 January 1939, *Australian Documents*, vol. II, p. 5.

6 *ibid.*

7 The Governor General sent for Curtin in the evening of 3 October 1941. Curtin met Parliament as Prime Minister on 7 October.

8 *see above*, p. 124.

9 *Digest*, No. 13, pp. 11-13; *see* Appendix, Document No. 11.

10 H.V. Evatt, *Australia in World Affairs*; Sydney, 1946, Angus & Robertson; pp. 7-8.

11 Douglas MacArthur, *Reminiscences*; London, 1964, Heinemann; pp. 152-3.

12 *ibid.*, pp. 158, *passim; C.P.D.* 152 : 1547.

13 Curtin to Bruce, 3 December 1941, *C.P.P. 1940-41-42-43*, vol. II, p. 351.

14 *ibid.*, p. 352.

15 *ibid.*, p. 353.

16 Garran, *op. cit., (see,* Part II, n. 73), p. 333.

17 *C.P.D.* 169 : 722.

18 A.L.P., Special Federal Conference, 16 November 1942 and following days, and 4 January 1943 and following days, *Report*; Melbourne, 1943, Industrial Print; p. 32.

19 *ibid.*

20 Reply by Mr J.M. Fraser, then Minister for the Army, on the front-line use of conscripts in Vietnam because of their short - two-year - period of service : *C.P.D.*, HR54 : 901-2.

21 A.L.P., *loc. cit.*, p. 33.

22 *ibid.*, pp. 39-41.

23 *ibid.*, p. 42.

24 *C.P.D.*, 173 : 168.

25 *C.P.D.*, 177 : 14.

26 *C.P.D.*, 177 : 71-9; the *ANZAC* agreement is at pp. 79-83.

27 *Hansard*, Fifth series (HC) 413 : 667-8. Attlee's comment on Dr Evatt's work at San Fransisco stands in remarkable contrast to the strange silence observed on that subject in the *Australian Documents*. In Appendix II, "The Organisation of Australia's External Relations" (vol. I, p. 549), we read:

Australia [sic] sent a delegation of 47, including consultants, to the United Nations Conference at San Fransisco from April to June 1945; it included six members of the Department [of External Affairs] Dr J.W. Burton, Mr W.D. Forsyth, Mr P.M.C. Hasluck, Mr A.S. Watt, Mr J.K. Waller, and Mr M. A. Greene.

No mention of the delegation's official leader, Mr F.M. Forde, then Deputy Prime Minister, or of the intellectual origins of the decision to participate on such a scale; for Evatt's, far from uncritical, views on the U.N. in his Oliver Wendell Holmes at the Harvard Law School in 1947, see H.V. Evatt, *The United Nations*, London and Melbourne, 1948, O.U.P.

28 Colonel J.K. Murray, In Retrospect, 1945-52 : Papua-New Guinea and the Territory of Papua and New Guinea; in *The History of Melanesia*; papers delivered at a seminar . . . at Port Movesby from 30 May to 5 June 1968; Canberra, Research School of Pacific Studies, A.N.U.; p. 178.

29 Golo Mann, *The History of Germany since 1789* (trs. M. Jackson); London, 1968, Chatto and Windus; p. 3; *for the following section, see*: R.P. Kangle, *The Kauṭilīya Arthaśāstra*, 3 vols., Bombay, 1963, University of Bombay; H.G. Creel, *The Origins of Statecraft in China, vol I, the Western Chou Empire;* Chicago, 1970, University of Chicago Press; D. Bodde, *China's first Unifier : a study of the Ch'in dynasty as seen in the life of Li Ssu, 280? - 208 B.C.;* Leiden, 1938, Brill (Sinica Leidensia ed. [etc.], vol III); Janice Stargardt, Government and Irrigation in Burma – a comparative survey, *Asian Studies*, University of the Philippines, vol. VI, No. 3, 1968; Social and Religious Aspects of Royal Power in Medieval Burma : from inscriptions in Kyansittha's reign, 1084-1112; *Journal of the Economic and Social History of the Orient (JESHO);* vol. XIII, No. 3, 1970; Burma's Economic and Diplomatic Relations with India and China; from medieval sources; *JESHO*; vol. XIV, No. 1, 1971; Southern Thai Waterways: new archaeological evidence on agriculture, shipping and trade; *Man, Journal of the Royal Anthropological Institute*; vol. VIII, No. 1, 1973; The Extent and Limitations of Indian Influence on the Protohistoric Civilizations of the Malay Peninsula, *in* N. Hammond (ed.), foreword by Sir Mortimer Wheeler, *South Asian Archaeology;* London, 1973, Duckworth; Man's Impact on the

Ancient Environment of the Satingpra Peninsula, South Thailand, through Agriculture and Hydraulic Works : an archaeological study; Part I, The Natural Environment and Natural Change; *Journal of Biogeography*, Oxford, vol. III, No. 3; Part II, The Impact of Ancient Agriculture; *ibid.*, vol. IV, No. 1; The Archaeology of Burma : research since 1959 and its interpretation, *in*, J. Stargardt (ed.), *Asia Antiqua : the archaeology of East and South East Asia*; London, 1977, Duckworth; L'isthme de la peninsule malaise, l'ancien dialogue entre l'homme et son environment : techniques agricoles et hydrauliques; paper presented to the *75e anniversaire de l'Ecole francaise d'extreme orient*, Paris, June 1976; in *Actes du colloque* [etc.]; Wang Yitung, *Official Relations between China and Japan, 1358-1549;* Cambridge, Mass., 1953, Harvard U.P.; P. Wheatley, *The Golden Khersonese : studies in the historical geography of the Malay peninsula before A.D. 1500;* Kuala Lumpur, 1961, University of Malaya Press; B. Schrieke, *Indonesian Sociological Studies*, 2 vols., The Hague, 1966, van Hoeve *for* the Royal [Netherlands] Tropical Institute, Amsterdam; J.C. van Leur, *Indonesian Trade and Society : essays in Asian social and economic history;* The Hague, 1967, van Hoeve; *and* B.H.M. Vlekke, *Nusantara : a history of Indonesia,* The Hague, 1965, van Hoeve.

30 Maung Maung (ed.), *Aung Sang of Burma*; The Hague, 1962, Marinus Nijhoff, *for* Yale University Southeast Asian Studies; pp. 4-5 (from, Aung Sang, *Life Sketch of the Author, Burma's Challenge*, July 1946).

31 J. Bingham, *U Thant, the search for peace;* London, 1966, Gollancz; p. 148.

32 Even at the end of the colonial period, Burma had an abnormally high crime rate : a gauge of the economic and social dislocation of that time; *see*, J.R. Andrus, *Burmese Economic Life;* Stanford, 1947, Stanford U.P.

33 Sutan Sjahrir, *Out of Exile* (M. Duchateau-Sjahrir, ed., C. Wolf, jnr. trs. and Intro.); New York, 1949, Day; p. 211, and pp. 211-12.

34 *ibid.*, pp. 144-5; *see also*, Sutan Sjahrir, *Our Struggle* (B.R. O'Anderson, trs, and Intro.); Translation Series, Modern Indonesia Project, Cornell University, 1968, Ithaca, N.Y.; *and* H.Feith and L. Castles, *Indonesian Political Thinking; 1945-65*; Ithaca, 1970, Cornell U.P.

35 At the Imperial Conference, Tokyo, 5 November 1941 (at which the decision for war with the United States and Great Britain was made), the Minister for Finance, Kaya Okinori offered this prognosis of the probable effects of a Japanese occupation of South East Asia:

The areas in the South that are to become the object of military operations have been importing materials of all kinds in large quantities. If these areas are occupied by our forces, their imports will cease. Accordingly, to make their economies run smoothly, we will have to supply them with materials. However, since our country does not have sufficient surpluses for that purpose, it will not be possible for some time for us to give much consideration to the living conditions of the people in these areas, and for a while we will have to pursue a so-called policy of exploitation. Hence even though we might issue military scrip and other items that have the character of currency in order to obtain materials and labor in these areas, it would be difficult to maintain the value of such currency. Therefore, we must adopt a policy of self-sufficiency in the South, keep the shipment of materials from

Japan to that area to the minimum amount necessary to maintain order and to utilize labor forces there, ignore for the time being the decline in the value of currency and the economic dislocations that will ensue from this, and in this way push forward. Of course it is to be recognized that the maintenance of the people's livelihood there is easy compared to the same task in China because the culture of the inhabitants is low, and because the area is rich in natural products.

Nobutaka Ike (trs., ed. and Intro.), *Japan's Decision for War : records of the 1941 Policy Conferences;* Stanford, California, 1967, Stanford U.P.; pp. 223-4.

36 *see* J.B. Crowley, A New Asian Order : some notes on pre-war Japanese Nationalism; Kuala Lumpur, 1968, *International Conference on Asian History; Paper No. 73.*

37 Lionel Wigmore, *The Japanese Thrust;* Canberra, 1957, Australian War Memorial; pp. 588 passim.

38 Lim Chong Yah, Malaya, *in* Cranley Onslow (ed.), *Asian Economic Development;* London, 1965, Weidenfeld and Nicholson; p. 96, n. 1.

39 Wigmore, *op. cit.,* p. 589, n. 2.

40 U Nu, *Burma under the Japanese : pictures and portraits* (J.S. Furnivall, ed., trs. and Intro.); London, 1954, Macmillan; p. 36.

41 Maung Maung, *op. cit.,* p. 105.

42 The official name of the present Kingdom of Thailand was Siam until 1939, and from 1946 to 1949; *see,* D.A. Wilson, Thailand, *in* George McT. Kahin (ed.), *Government and Politics of Southeast Asia*; second ed., Ithaca, N.Y., 1965, Cornell U.P., pp. 3-4, n. 1.

43 *see,* W. Stargardt, Neutrality and Neutralization in South East Asia, *in* B. Dahm *and* W. Draguhn (eds.) *Politics, Society and Economy in the ASEAN States;* Wiesbaden, 1975, Harrassowitz, *for* Institute of Asian Affairs, Hamburg.

44 E.T. Flood, The 1940 Franco-Thai Border Dispute and Phibuun Songkraam's Commitment to Japan, *Journal of Southeast Asian History,* vol. X, No. 2 (Singapore, September 1969), p. 316.

45 F.C. Jones, *Japan's New Order in East Asia, 1937 - 1945;* London, 1954, O.U.P.; p. 233.

46 Flood, *op. cit.,* p. 324.

47 Jones, *op. cit.,* pp. 344-5.

48 Direck Jayanama, *Thailand im Zweiten Weltkrieg;* Tubingen and Basel, 1970, Horst Erdmann Verlag, *for* Institute of Asian Affairs, Hamburg, *esp.* chps. IV and V.

49 *ibid.,* p. 51 *and* chp. V.

50 Jones, *op. cit.,* p. 321.

51 *ibid.*

52 *ibid.,* p. 322.

53 Jayanama, *op. cit.,* pp. 80 ff.

54 *L.G.* (Supplement), 6 February 1942; *C.N.,* 1942, No. 4, pp. 110-111; *see*

also, Ike, *op. cit.,* p. 281; A. Peterson, Siam and Britain, the latest phase, *Pacific Affairs,* 1946, pp. 364 ff.; T.H. Silcock, *Thailand : social and economic studies;* Canberra, 1967, A.N.U. Press; pp. 6-7.

55 *see,* Koichi Kishi, Recent Japanese Sources for Indonesian Historiography, *in,* Soedjatmoko *et al., An Introduction to Indonesian Historiography;* Ithaca, 1965, Cornell U.P.; pp. 206-210, *for* Nanpo Senryochi Gyosei Jisshi Yoryo (General Principles for the Administration of the Southern Occupied Territories) Liaison conference between Headquarters and government, 20 November 1941, and Senryochi Gunsei Jisshi ni Kansuru Riku Kaigun Chuo Kyotei (Basic agreement between the Army and Navy concerning Military Administration of the Occupied Territories), 26 November 1941.

56 Abdul Haris Nasution, *Principles of Guerilla Warfare;* London, 1965, Pall Mall Press; pp. 15 *and* 28-9.

57 Osamu Shudan, *Java no Kizoku ni Kansuru Iken (Osamu* Command, Proposal concerning the future of Java) *in,* Kishi, *loc. cit.* p. 208.

58 *ibid.,* pp. 208-9.

59 *C.P.D.,* 190 : 854.

60 Menzies called Sukarno *The Quisling of Java,* in Parliament on 25 September 1945; *C.P.D.* 185:5819. On Sukarno's relations with the Japanese, *see* J.D. Legge, *Sukarno:* a political biography; London, 1972, Allen Lane, The Penquin Press; *and* Bernhard Dahm, *Sukarno and the struggle for Indonesian Independence,* trs. M.F.S. Heidhues; Ithaca, 1969, Cornell U.P.

61 P.S. Gerbrandy, *Indonesia;* London, 1950, Hutchinson; Part II, chp. II, *and* pp. 192-4.

62 The term *colon* is used advisedly; for an excellent, concise description of the significance of Indonesia for the Netherlands, and the extent and nature of Dutch settlement in Indonesia, *see* Herbert Feith, The Decline of Constitutional Democracy in Indonesia; Ithaca, N.Y., 1962, Cornell U.P. (under the auspices of the Modern Indonesia Project); pp. 2-3.

63 Sjahrir, *Out of Exile;* for a description of the Communists at Boven Digul, *see* p. 74 *and* pp. 101-2, for the colonial government's practice of calling *anyone a communist if they fear or cannot tolerate him from a political point of view.* Bruce Grant, *Indonesia;* Melbourne, 1964, M.U.P.; p. 154 mentions *six hundred political evacuees . . . including a number of communists under Sardjono, former chairman of the PKI who took up wartime propaganda work in Brisbane.* On Boven Digul, see also I.F.M. Salim,*Vijftienjaar Boven Digul: Concentratiecamp in Nieuw Guinea* [etc.]; Amsterdam, 1973, Uitgeverij Contact.

64 *C.P.D.* 182:1901.

65 The demands were: Payment of a bonus of [A]£110, being savings money at £1.25 a month from 1 June 1942 to August 1945, paid in Australia; Refund in Australia of monthly dependants' allowance deducted from the seamen's wages every month but not paid during the occupation period; and the fixation of a minimum monthly wage and a maximum working week; Brisbane *Courier-Mail,* 25 September 1945, p. 3.

66 *ibid.*

67 *ibid.*

68 Grant, *op. cit.*, p . 154.

69 *C.P.D.*, 187 : 2097.

70 J.A.C. Mackie, Indonesia, *in* G. Greenwood and N.D. Harper, *Australia in World Affairs*, 1956-60; Melbourne, 1963, Cheshire for A.I.I.A.; p. 278.

71 *Digest*, No..128, pp. 32-3.

72 *ibid.*

73 *ibid.*

74 *C.P.D.*, 193 : 179.

75 Herbert Feith, Indonesia, *in* George McT. Kahin (ed.), *op. cit.*, p. 201.

76 *C.P.D.*, 199 : 2636.

77 *Digest*, No. 141, p. 52.

78 New Dehli Conference on Indonesia; statement by . . . Dr H.V. Evatt, *C.N.*, vol. 20, No. 1, pp. 111-113; Australian acceptance of invitation to that Conference, *ibid.*, p. 283; *for* the Conference Resolutions, pp. 283-5.

79 *Jawaharlal Nehru's Speeches;* Delhi, 1959, Publications Division, Ministry of Information and Broadcasting, Government of India; vol. I, 1946-49, p. 327.

80 *C.P.D.*, 201 : 400.

81 on 27 February 1962 : *C.P.D.*, HR34 : 257.

82 A.L.P. 1948 Commonwealth Conference, *Report*, p. 25.

83 R.G. Menzies. *Policy Speech*, 1946 General Election; Melbourne, 1946.

PART V

1 *C.P.D.*, 212 : 85.

2 *The Public Papers of the Presidents of the United States : Harry S. Truman; January 1 to December 31, 1951;* Washington, 1965, U.S. Government Printing Office; pp. 234-5; *see also*, R.N. Rosecrance, *Australian Diplomacy and Japan, 1945-1951;* Melbourne, 1962, M.U.P.; *and* T.R. Reese, *Australia New Zealand and United States : survey of international relations;* London, 1969, O.U.P. (under auspices of the Royal Institute of International Affairs).

3 *C.P.D.*, 216 : 18.

4 *ibid.*, pp. 19-20.

5 *ibid.*

6 *ibid.*

7 *ibid.*, p. 21.

8 *ibid.*, p. 23.

9 *ibid.*, p. 229.

10 *ibid.*

11 *ibid.*

12 *ibid.*, p. 235.

13 *ibid.*, pp. 349-50.

14 *ibid.*, pp. 350-51.

15 *ibid.*, p. 351.

16 *ibid.*

17 *ibid.*

18 *ibid.*, p. 352.

19 *ibid.*

20 *ibid.*, p. 353.

21 *ibid.*, p. 365.

22 *ibid.*, p. 240.

23 *ibid.*, p. 485.

24 *C.P.D.*, 212 : 81.

25 R.G. Neale, India, in, G. Greenwood and N.D. Harper, *Australia in World Affairs, 1950-55*; Melbourne, 1957, Cheshire; *esp.* pp. 250 ff.

26 J.G. Starke, *The ANZUS Treaty Alliance;* Melbourne, 1965, M.U.P.; p. 240.

27 Watt states: *That Australia continually took into account, both before and after ANZUS, the attitude of the United States towards recognition of Communist China was both natural and inevitable. But any suggestion that Australian policy towards China, even after ANZUS was ratified, was completely rigid and merely echoed American policy is a gross over-simplification.* A. Watt, *The Evolution of Australian Foreign Policy, 1938-1965;* Cambridge, 1967, C.U.P.; p. 243.

28 Starke, *op. cit.,* p. 241.

29 *C.N.,* vol. 43, p. 631; the exchange of letters between Whitlam and Chou En-lai of 5 and 10 December 1972, respectively, is at p. 632.

30 Watt, *loc. cit.*

31 Australia.*Overseas Trade,* Annual Bulletin, Commonwealth Bureau of Census and Statistics, Canberra.

32 H.S. Albinski, Australia and the Chinese Strategic Embargo, *Australian Outlook,* vol. XIV, No. 2, pp. 127-8, *quoted in* Watt, *op. cit.,* p. 244. In his Roy Milne Memorial Lecture on 5 July 1965, on *Australia's Overseas Economic Relationships,* McEwen did not refer to trade with China with a single word; Rt. Hon. John McEwen, M.P., Acting Prime Minister, Minister for Trade and Industry, Leader of the Australian Country Party, *op. cit.;* Melbourne, 1965, Australian Institute of International Affairs.

33 the quotation is authentic.

34 *C.P.D.*, 214 : 152.

35 *ibid.*

36 *ibid.*

37 *C.P.D.*, HR4 : 96.

38 *ibid.*, HR4 : 96-7.

39 Anthony Eden [Lord Avon], *The Memoirs of the Rt Hon Sir Anthony Eden, K.G., P.C., M.C.; Full Circle;* London, 1960, Cassell; pp. 92-3.

40 *ibid.*, p. 96.

41 *ibid.*, p. 97.

42 *ibid.*, p. 98.

43 *ibid.*, p. 143-4.

44 *N.Y. Times*, 9 March 1955, *in* Marshal of the R.A.F. Sir John Slessor, G.C.E., D.S.O., *et. al., Collective Defence in South East Asia : the Manila treaty its implications;* a report by a Chatham House group; London and New York, 1956, Royal Institute of International Affairs; pp. 121-2.

45 A.W. Stargardt, Neutrality within the Asian System of Powers, *in* Lauk Teik Soon (ed.), *New Directions in the International Relations of Southeast Asia : the great powers and Southeast Asia* [confernece proceedings]; Singapore 1973, Singapore U.P. *for* Institute of Southeast Asian Studies; pp. 108-9.

46 *Jawaharlal Nehru's Speeches;* Delhi, 1959, *op. cit.*, vol. III, pp. 264-73.

47 Australia.*Treaty Series, 1955, No. 3*, p. 5.

48 *C.P.D.*, HR5 : 2694.

49 *ibid.*, p. 2581.

50 *ibid.*, p. 2695

51 *ibid.*

52 *ibid.*, p. 2699.

53 *Jawaharlal Nehru's Speeches, op.cit.*, vol. III, p. 291.

54 Calwell's account, *C.P.D.*, HR20 : 2275.

55 Menzies' account, *ibid.*, pp. 2264 ff.; the full *Statement* is in the Appendix, Document No. 12.

56 *ibid.*

57 United Nations, *Official Records of the General Assembly,* Fifteenth Session (Part I), Plenary Meetings, vol. 1, 20 September - 17 October 1960, New York, p. 459.

58 *ibid.*, p. 460.

59 *ibid.*

60 *ibid.*, p. 469.

61 *ibid.*, pp. 421-3 *and* 434-7.

62 *ibid.*, pp. 427-9.

63 Chifley shared these views; *see*, A.W. Stargardt (ed. and Intro.), *Things Worth Fighting For : speeches by Joseph Benedict Chifley;* Melbourne, 1952, M.U.P., pp. 5-8.

64 *C.P.D.*, HR41 : 486.

65 *C.P.D.*, 206 : 628.

66 *ibid.*, p. 633.

67 United Nations, *loc. cit.*, Ninth Session, 24 September 1954, p. 46.

68 *see*, Feith, Indonesia, *in* Kahin, *op. cit.*, pp. 268-9

69 *C.P.D.*, HR38 : 1105-6.

70 *see*, J.A.C. Mackie, *Konfrontasi : the Indonesia-Malaysia dispute, 1963-1966;* Kuala Lumpur, 1974, O.U.P. *for* Australian Institute of International Affairs; I. Anak Agung Gde Agung, *Twenty years Indonesian Foreign Policy, 1945-1965;* The Hague and Paris, 1973; Mouton, pp. 444-506; *and* B. Dahm, *History of Indonesia in. the Twentieth Century* (trs. P.S. Falla); London, 1971, Pall Mall Press; pp. 211-4.

71 Sir Garfield Barwick, Australia's Foreign Relations, *in*, J. Wilkes (ed.), *Australia's Defence and Foreign Policy* [Proceedings, 30th Summer School, Australian Institute of Political Science] ; Sydney, 1964,, Angus and Robertson; p.6.

72 *C.N.*, vol. 26, pp. 278-9.

73 *C.P.D.*, HR40 : 1338-9.

74 *ibid.*, p. 1365.

75 *ibid.*

76 *ibid.*, p. 1367.

77 *ibid.*

78 *ibid.*, p. 1369.

79 *ibid.*

80 *C.P.D.*, HR45 : 1061.

81 *ibid.*

82 *C.P.D.*, HR46 : 1107.

83 *ibid.*, p. 1105.

84 *ibid.*, p. 1107.

85 *C.P.D.*, HR50 : 27 *passim.*

86 *C.P.D.*, HR58 : 451.

87 *ibid.*, p. 591.

88 The President's Address to the Nation Announcing Steps to Limit the War in Vietnam and Reporting his Decision Not to Seek Reelection, March 31, 1968; *No. 170*, in, *The Public Papers of the Presidents of the United States : Lyndon B. Johnson, 1968-69;* Book I; Washington, 1970, U.S. Government Printing Office; pp. 469-76.

89 *C.P.D.*, HR58 : 641-3.

90 *ibid.*, pp. 643-5.

91 *C.P.D.*, HR75 : 4160.

92 *ibid.*, p. 4161.

93 *C.P.D.*, HR76 : 347-8.

94 *ibid.*, p. 348.

95 Rt Hon William McMahon, *Federal Election 1972, Policy Speech;* Canberra, 1972, Federal Secretariat, Liberal Party of Australia.

APPENDIX

1 Martin Bernal, Chinese Socialism before 1913, *in* J. Gray, Modern China's Search for a Political Form; London, 1969, under the auspices of R.I.I.A; pp. 89-95; *see also*, "Chiang K'ang-hu" *in*, H.L. Boorman (ed.) and R.C. Howard, Biographical Dictionary of Republican China; New York and London, 1967, Columbia U.P.; vol. I, AI - CH'U, pp. 338-44.

Index

d refers to documents in the Appendix

Index 403

Thakin Soe, 194

Tocsin, Melbourne,
see also Labor Call, 99
Trade Diversion Policy, 154
Curtin warns on consequences of, 159-60
Truman, President H.S.
ANZUS, on, 218
dismisses MacArthur, 229
Tudor, F.G., 141, 144-5
U Ba Swe, 194
U Kyaw Nyein, 194
U Ne Win, 194
United Australia Party (U.A.P.)
formation of, 153
foreign policy of, 154-5, 156
defence policy of, 156
Menzies leader of, 161
loss of office by, 167
see also Conservatism in Australia, Liberal
Party of Australia and National Party
United Nations
Conference on International Organiza-
tion, Attlee on, 182-3
Relief and Rehabilitation Administration (UNRRA), 210
General Assembly, 1960 Session, 245-7
Menzies on, 247, d, 336-355
withdrawal of Indonesia from, 257
mission to Sarawak and North Borneo,
258
Indo-Pakistan War, 1971, and, 269-70
United States of America, 38, 104, 120, 135,
143
seen as threat to Australia, 8, 23, 43, 45,
103
threat discounted, 46-7
Hawaii and, 78, 113
Philippines and, 113
invitation of fleet to Australia, 113-7;
to Japan, 115-6
115-6
visit by Hughes to, 132; speech in New
York, 139-40
attitude to disposal of German possessions
possessions, 138
Millen on, 138-9
propose internationalization of, in
Pacific, 142
Australian trade discrimination against,
154
opposed by Curtin, 159, 160
diplomatic relations with, 156, 161, 171
Curtin's appeal to, 172-3
wartime co-operation with Australia,
173-4

without political consequences, 174-5,
219
Peace with Japan and, 218-27
ANZUS, 218-27, 273, d
foreign policy of, Beazley's view, 224-5
involvement in Vietnam, dangers for, Calwell's view, 263
President Johnson speech of 31 March
1969, Australian debate on, 266-9
Indo-Pakistan war, 1971, and; Whitlam's
view, 270-71
U Nu, 194, 237
U.S.S.R.
refuses to sign San Francisco Peace
treaty with Japan, 221
rupture of relations between Australia
and, 244
U.N. General Assembly 1960, and, 245-7
Menzies Statement on, 247, d, 336-355
Indo-Pakistan war, 1971, and (Whitlam's
view), 270-71
McMahon on relations with, 273
see also Russia
U Thant
on Burma under Japanese occupation,
187-8
appoints mission to Malaysia, 258
Vietnam war and, 263, 267
Vattel, E. de, d, 297
Versailles, treaty of, 87
Australian debate on, 140-46
Curtin on, 1939, 164
Vietnam, 187, 190, 230, 251, 252
Casey view of war in, 234-5
Australian intervention in, 260-69, 272-
273
Prime Minister of Republic of, visits
Australia, 265
see also Indo-China
Ward, E.J.
policy on New Guinea of, 182-3
Watt, Sir Alan, 229
Webb, Sir William, F., J., 171
Werthern, Georg v., - Bleichlingen, 86-7
Waterside Workers, 205-6
Watson, J.C., 132-3
'White Australia', see coolies and indentured
labourers and immigration
Whitlam, E.G.
Leader of the Opposition, 265
President Johnson's speech of 31 March,
1969, on, 267-8
Indo-Pakistan war, on, 1971, 270-71
Bangladesh, on, 271-2
visits China, 273

Printed in Great Britain by Colour Artisans, Beccles, Suffolk